MICROSOFT® QUICKC®
PROGRAMMER'S TOOLBOX

MICROSOFT® QUICKC®
PROGRAMMER'S TOOLBOX

An essential collection of more than 200 programs, functions, and utilities for supercharging QuickC programs

JOHN CLARK CRAIG

PUBLISHED BY
Microsoft Press
A Division of Microsoft Corporation
One Microsoft Way
Redmond, WA 98052-6399

Library of Congress Cataloging in Publication Data
Craig, John Clark. 1952–
    Microsoft QuickC programmer's toolbox.
  1. C (Computer program language)   2. Microsoft QuickC (Computer program)
I. Title.
QA76.73.C15C73   1990   005.13'3   89-12192
ISBN 1-55615-207-8

Printed and bound in the United States of America.

1 2 3 4 5 6 7 8 9   MLML   3 2 1 0 0

Distributed to the book trade in Canada by General Publishing Company, Ltd.

Distributed to the book trade outside the United States and Canada by Penguin Books Ltd.

Penguin Books Ltd., Harmondsworth, Middlesex, England
Penguin Books Australia Ltd., Ringwood, Victoria, Australia
Penguin Books N.Z. Ltd., 182–190 Wairau Road, Auckland 10, New Zealand

British Cataloging in Publication Data available

PostScript is a registered trademark of Adobe Systems, Inc. IBM®, PC/AT®, and PS/2®
are registered trademarks of International Business Machines Corporation.
Microsoft®, MS-DOS®, and QuickC® are registered trademarks of Microsoft Corporation.

Acquisitions Editor: Dean Holmes
Project Editor: Eric Stroo
Principal Proofreaders: Cynthia Riskin and Ward Webber
Principal Word Processors: Debbie Kem and Cathy Thompson

CONTENTS

Acknowledgments   *vii*

PART I: GETTING STARTED

A Few Mechanics   3

TOOLBOX1: A Sample Module   6

ADDUP: A Sample Utility   12

PART II: TOOLBOX MODULES

BIOSCALL   *ROM BIOS interrupt calls*   17

BITS   *Bit manipulations*   40

BOX   *Text area manipulations*   48

CALENDAR   *Date calculations*   68

CLOCK   *Time calculations and clock display*   90

COMPLEX   *Complex number math*   106

DOSCALL   *MS-DOS system calls*   124

EDIT   *Text-editing functions*   137

FRACTION   *Fraction math*   156

GAME   *Common game functions*   168

GEOMETRY   *Two- and three-dimensional calculations*   179

GETKEY   *Keyboard input functions*   209

GRAPHICS   *Enhanced graphics functions*   219

MENU   *Drop-down menus*   240

MONEY   *Monetary calculations*   271

MOUSEFUN   *Mouse driver interface*   278

PROBSTAT   *Probability and statistics*   330

RANDOMS   *Random number generators*   340

SOUND   *Sound effects*   357

STRINGS   *Enhanced string functions*   370

PART III: UTILITIES

About the Utilities 391

BASE *Converts a value to equivalents in other bases* 393

BINTOHEX *Converts a binary file to hexadecimal characters* 396

CALC *Performs calculations using reverse Polish notation* 399

CAT *Generates a directory list* 408

CHKSUM *Computes binary checksum for any file* 411

CIPHER *Enciphers and deciphers files* 413

COLORS *Displays any of the 262,144 VGA colors* 419

DETAB *Replaces tabs with spaces in a given file* 426

FREQ *Tabulates occurrences of bytes in a file* 430

HEXTOBIN *Converts a file of hexadecimal characters to binary* 433

LOG *Logs date, time, and message in a log file* 436

LOOK *Lets you view files* 439

MOUSGCRS *Lets you edit a graphics mode mouse icon* 447

MOVE *Moves files to another subdirectory* 463

OBJECT *Lets you edit graphics icons* 467

OUT *Sends any bytes to standard output* 481

PI *Precisely calculates pi* 485

PS *Filters text for PostScript printer output* 493

REFRESH *Updates a file's time stamp* 498

SEE *Displays text embedded in a binary file* 501

SETVIDEO *Sets any video mode* 504

TIMEDATE *Displays the time and date* 507

WORDS *Counts the words in a file* 509

PART IV: APPENDIXES

Appendix A: Function-to-Module Cross-Reference 513

Appendix B: Line-drawing Characters 525

ACKNOWLEDGMENTS

I want to thank all the people at Microsoft Press for the tremendous help, support, and patience they've provided along the way. Eric Stroo and Dean Holmes deserve special mention for their professional guidance and expertise. Rex Jaeschke's thorough review of the book resulted in a number of useful revisions and improvements to the style.

Other friends have provided indirect help. Thank you Dave A. and Merle B. for never being sheepish with your support. Thank you Jeanie, Jennifer, and Adam for your patience and love. Thank you Jeff B. for the enlightening "computer talk" and for being a good friend. Thank you Greg N. for helping me get the "big picture." And thank you, whoever you are, for buying this book. I hope you enjoy working with QuickC as much as I have.

SPECIAL OFFER
Companion Disk Set for
MICROSOFT QUICKC PROGRAMMER'S TOOLBOX

Microsoft Press has created a Companion Disk Set for MICROSOFT QUICKC PROGRAM-MER'S TOOLBOX, available in either 5.25-inch (two disk set) or 3.5-inch (one disk) format. The companion disks contain all the toolbox modules, demonstration programs, and utilities listed in the book. In addition, the disks contain make files for all the programs that require them. Altogether, you get more than 13,000 lines of code! You'll find that these disks spare you the drudgery of typing the listings (and also save the valuable time you'd spend to find and correct typing errors). With the companion disks, you can begin to use these powerful QuickC toolbox routines immediately. Order your Companion Disk Set today!

Domestic Ordering Information:

To order, use the special reply card bound in the back of the book. If the card has already been used, please send $21.95, plus sales tax if applicable (CA residents 5% plus local option tax, CT 8%, FL 6%, IL 5%, KY 5%, MA 5%, MN 6%, MO 4.425%, NJ 6%, NY 4% plus local option tax, SC 5%, TX 6% plus local option tax, WA state 7.8%), and $2.50 per disk set for domestic postage and handling charges. Mail your order to: Microsoft Press, Attn: Companion Disk Offer, 21919 20th Ave SE, Box 3011, Bothell, WA 98041-3011. Specify 5.25-inch or 3.5-inch format. Payment must be in U.S. funds. You may pay by check or money order (payable to Microsoft Press) or by American Express, VISA, or MasterCard; please include both your credit card number and the expiration date. Allow 23 weeks for delivery.

Foreign Ordering Information (except within the U.K., see below):

Follow procedures for domestic ordering and add $6.00 per disk set for foreign postage and handling.

U.K. Ordering Information:

Send your order in writing along with £19.95 (includes VAT) to: Microsoft Press, 27 Wrights Lane, London W8 5TZ. You may pay by check or money order (payable to Microsoft Press) or by American Express, VISA, MasterCard, or Diners Club; please include both your credit card number and the expiration date. Specify 5.25-inch or 3.5-inch format.

Microsoft Press Companion Disk Guarantee

If a disk is defective, send the defective disk along with your packing slip (or copy) to: Microsoft Press, Consumer Sales, One Microsoft Way, Redmond, WA 98052-6399.

Send your questions or comments about the files on the disks to
QuickC Toolbox Editor,
Microsoft Press, One Microsoft Way, Redmond, WA 98052-6399.
The Companion Disk Set for MICROSOFT QUICKC PROGRAMMER'S TOOLBOX
is available only from Microsoft Press.

PART I

GETTING STARTED

A FEW MECHANICS

Most computer books that deal with a specific programming language take a tutorial approach to their subject. They provide a second source for much of the information presented in the language documentation, and they often deal with particular topics in greater detail than does the documentation. Tutorial books of that type are valuable for reinforcing and enhancing your knowledge of the language.

Microsoft QuickC Programmer's Toolbox takes a slightly different approach. The goal of this book is to provide a useful collection of QuickC "toolbox modules" and utilities that you can put to immediate use; at the same time, the modules and utilities provide tested, functional code examples that you can study to expand your knowledge of C programming.

The source code in this book covers a variety of common programming tasks. Of course, you can always find several ways to accomplish a programming task, especially given the flexibility of the C language. The toolbox modules present one approach to each task—collections of functions organized in a coherent, useful manner for QuickC software development. After you use a few of the toolbox modules, you'll probably have numerous ideas of your own: routines to add or customize, functions to implement as macros, or entire toolbox modules to develop. Organizing your software development efforts in this structured way is a powerful way to increase productivity.

Advantages of QuickC

During the last few years, C has become the programming language of choice for everything from operating systems to commercial applications. C provides the low-level power necessary for efficient and fast hardware interaction, yet it also provides the modern structure, data types, and portability that you associate with a high-level language.

Until recently, C competed poorly with other programming languages, many of which could boast a faster learning curve and higher productivity. BASIC, for example, has generally been considered a good language for beginners, whereas C has been reserved for professionals. QuickC is changing that perception rapidly.

3

Microsoft QuickC provides a nice balance between programming power and ease of use. The integrated development environment is a breeze to use, and the on-line hypertext help facility makes learning the C language immensely more enjoyable. After you use QuickC for a few days, you'll find it hard to go back to anything else. And if you're new to the C language, your decision to start with QuickC will prove to be a good decision indeed. You'll become proficient with C much faster than your Quickless predecessors, and you'll have more fun getting there!

QuickC has several powerful features that deserve immediate mention. As already noted, the integrated development environment reduces development time and improves the learning curve. If you've programmed in BASIC, you'll also be pleasantly surprised at the execution speed of C. The extensive library of graphics functions provides advanced features, such as animation and a variety of character fonts. Probably the most important new feature of QuickC is its ability to process the in-line assembly language code. It's now possible to optimize critical sections of code "by hand" without having to buy or use a separate assembler. By using in-line assembly code, you can accomplish many programming tasks far more simply and effectively than you can with BASIC. For example, most of the mouse programming functions presented in this book were simplified and optimized by using short blocks of in-line assembly code. (Take a quick look at MOUSEFUN.C, beginning on page 278, to see an example of in-line assembly coding.)

Modules and Libraries

There are several ways to organize, group, and use functions you write in QuickC. The collection of toolbox modules presented in Part II of this book shows an approach that's convenient for developing and debugging the functions presented. Depending on the type of software project you've undertaken, you might find that a different approach to working with the functions makes your programs a little smaller or makes the inclusion of the toolbox modules a little simpler.

One option is to collect all or some of the modules into a single library. To use any of the functions in a program, you can simply add the name of this library file to the program list. You must also include at the beginning of your program the appropriate header files for the functions you use, but you could conceivably combine all the header files into one file that declares all the functions in the library.

An advantage of the library-building approach is the time it saves during easy, fast program development: All the toolbox functions you want to call are already compiled and available in a single library. A drawback to this approach, however, is its effect on the size of your program. If your program calls one function from a toolbox module, QuickC links all the functions in that module to your program. For example, the use of one or two mouse functions provided in the MOUSEFUN.C module causes all the mouse functions (over two dozen of them!) to be linked into your program.

The library of toolbox modules is an example of a library with low "granularity." The smallest linkable unit from the library is the size of the individual toolboxes.

If program size is a major concern, consider building a more "granular" library. This approach takes a little more work up front and results in a larger library, but programs you create with it will be smaller and will contain less unnecessary code. For maximum granularity, separate the functions in the toolboxes into individual files. Compile each of these files to create a set of OBJ files. Then use the LIB program to combine these object code files into a single library. When you add this library file to a program list, QuickC links only the functions your program calls to form the executable file.

High-granularity library files can be created for each toolbox module or for multiple modules. For example, I conducted one test in which I split the MOUSEFUN.C file into about two dozen small source code files, each containing one of the mouse functions. Then I compiled these files and combined them to create a library file named NEWMOUSE.LIB. When I rebuilt the OBJECT utility program using this library in place of the MOUSEFUN.C toolbox module, the resulting OBJECT.EXE program file was about 3 KB smaller; only the handful of mouse functions actually called by OBJECT were linked into the program, instead of the entire MOUSEFUN toolbox.

The ability to trade off between size and ease of development is one of the flexible features of QuickC that makes it an ideal program development system. Generally, until you're ready to squeeze a program to a minimum size, the use of toolbox modules helps you organize your efforts and reduce development time. For more information about building and maintaining libraries, see *Microsoft QuickC Tool Kit,* which came with your QuickC package.

TOOLBOX1:
A SAMPLE MODULE

Part II of this book presents the toolbox modules. The overall construction of each module is the same.

Each toolbox module is composed of two related files. The main collection of functions occupies a program source file (with the extension C). A second file (with the same filename but with the extension H) contains prototypes for the functions implemented in the source file and defines any constants or data structures that the functions use.

To demonstrate each toolbox module, an accompanying source file tests the functions and illustrates the technique for calling them. The name of the demonstration file is similar to that of the toolbox module, except that the filename concludes with *TEST.C*.

QuickC creates a program list file when you select the various files necessary for running a demonstration program. The program list file is more appropriately called the "make" file, and its name is similar to the name of the toolbox module except that it ends with *TEST.MAK*. (The contents of make files are not included in this book. For convenience, the files *are* included on the companion disk.)

To better understand the toolbox files and how they work together, let's walk through the procedure for building a small demonstration program and the toolbox module that supports it. The following listings illustrate the way in which the toolbox modules in Part II are presented. The first file, TOOLTEST.C, is the demonstration program. It illustrates the usefulness of the functions in the module and shows you how to call them. In this case, the functions are two simple routines that perform integer addition and subtraction. Function prototypes for these two functions are provided in the next file, TOOLBOX1.H. The routines themselves are implemented in the last file, TOOLBOX1.C. As you will see, the make file, TOOLTEST.MAK, is created from within the QuickC environment.

To begin, start QuickC, choose File from the menu bar at the top of the screen, and then choose the Open command. Type the name of the file you want to create and press Enter. If the file doesn't already exist on

your disk, QuickC responds with the prompt *File doesn't exist. Create?*
Select Yes to create the file. At this point, you have an empty window in
which to type your source code.

Type the lines of the file, as provided in the listings that follow. To
save the new file contents on disk, choose Save from the File menu.
Repeat this series of steps to create all three files.

```
/* ------------------------------------------------------------------

    Name:           TOOLTEST.C
    Type:           Demonstration program
    Language:       Microsoft QuickC
    Video:          (no special video requirements)

    Program list:   TOOLTEST.C
                    TOOLBOX1.C

    Variables:      a          First integer value
                    b          Second integer value
                    sum        Sum of the two values
                    dif        Difference of the two values

    Usage:          (no command line parameters)

    Description:    Demonstrates functions in TOOLBOX1 module
    ------------------------------------------------------------------
*/

#include <stdio.h>
#include "toolbox1.h"

main()
{
    int a, b, sum, dif;

    a = 3;
    b = 4;

    sum = add( a, b );
    dif = sub( a, b );

    printf( "\n\na = %d, b = %d\n\n", a, b );
    printf( "add( a, b ) = %d, sub( a, b ) = %d\n", sum, dif );
}
```

```
/* -----------------------------------------------------------------
  Name:          TOOLBOX1.H
  Type:          Include
  Language:      Microsoft QuickC
  Demonstrated:  TOOLBOX1.C  TOOLTEST.C  ADDUP.C
  Description:   Prototypes and definitions for the toolbox
  -----------------------------------------------------------------
*/

#ifndef TOOLBOX1_DEFINED

int add( int, int );
int sub( int, int );

#define TOOLBOX1_DEFINED
#endif
```

```
/* -----------------------------------------------------------------
  Name:          TOOLBOX1.C
  Type:          Toolbox module
  Language:      Microsoft QuickC
  Demonstrated:  TOOLTEST.C  ADDUP.C
  Model:         (no special model)
  Video:         (no special video requirements)
  -----------------------------------------------------------------
*/

#include "toolbox1.h"

/* - - - - - - - - - - - - - - - - - - - - - - - - - - - - - - - -
  Function:      add()
  Toolbox:       TOOLBOX1.C
  Demonstrated:  ADDUP.C

  Parameters:
    (input)        i            First integer value
    (input)        j            Second integer value

  Returned:      Integer sum of i and j

  Variables:     (none)
```

(continued)

TOOLBOX1.C *continued*

```
   Description:    Sums two integers and returns the result
   - - - - - - - - - - - - - - - - - - - - - - - - - - - - - - -
*/

int add( int i, int j )
{
    return ( i + j );
}


/* - - - - - - - - - - - - - - - - - - - - - - - - - - - - - - -
   Function:       sub()
   Toolbox:        TOOLBOX1.C
   Demonstrated:   ADDUP.C

   Parameters:
     (input)       i             First integer value
     (input)       j             Second integer value

   Returned:       Integer difference between i and j

   Variables:      (none)

   Description:    Subtracts two integers and returns the result
   - - - - - - - - - - - - - - - - - - - - - - - - - - - - - - -
*/

int sub( int i, int j )
{
    return ( i - j );
}
```

After you create the three source files, you need to take one more step before you can run the TOOLTEST program. To access TOOLBOX1.C from the demonstration program, you must add it to the program list for TOOLTEST.C. Within the QuickC environment, load TOOLTEST.C, and then choose Set Program List from the Make menu. The resulting dialog box prompts you for the name of a make file. Type *TOOLBOX1* and press Enter. A subsequent dialog box lets you confirm that you want to create the new file, TOOLBOX1.MAK.

To edit the program list, select files from the File List box. The file-names you choose appear in the Program List box immediately below. For our example, select the files TOOLTEST.C and TOOLBOX1.C so that your screen resembles the one shown below. Choose the Save command to finish editing the program list.

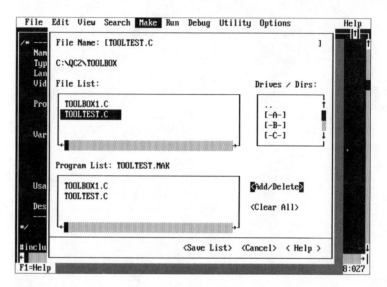

The TOOLTEST.C program is now ready to run. Press F5 (or choose Start from the Run menu) to compile, link, and execute the program. The displayed output shows the sum and difference for the integer variables *a* and *b*.

Notice that both TOOLBOX1.C and TOOLTEST.C use an *#include* statement to include the contents of TOOLBOX1.H. The declarations in the header file tell the QuickC compiler the data types that the *add()* and *subtract()* functions return and the types of the two parameters that each function requires.

To call toolbox functions from your own programs, simply add the appropriate *#include* statement at the start of your program and add the name of the toolbox module to the program list for your program. When QuickC compiles your calls to the toolbox functions, the include file enables it to check all parameters and verify the type of the return value. The program list guides the compiler and linker as they combine the necessary parts of your program.

You can replace some of the functions in the toolbox modules with macros. Define the macros in the header file for the module and include the header in your program. If your program uses only the macros (and none of the functions in the module), you need not add the module to the program list. The first toolbox module, BIOSCALL, shows a technique (in BIOSCALL.H) for implementing functions as macros and embedding the definitions in conditional directives.

ADDUP:
A SAMPLE UTILITY

Part III of this book presents a collection of utility programs written in QuickC. These utilities are stand-alone programs that are designed to be useful programs in themselves. In most cases, they call one or more functions in the toolbox modules presented in Part II.

As a short demonstration of the construction of these utility programs, the following program, ADDUP.C, sums integers entered on the command line. This ADDUP utility uses the *add()* function provided in the TOOLBOX1 module described previously.

Start up QuickC and choose Open from the File menu to open or create the file ADDUP.C. Type the program lines in the listing that follows and be sure to save the file on disk.

```
/* -----------------------------------------------------------------
    Name:          ADDUP.C
    Type:          Utility program
    Language:      Microsoft QuickC
    Video:         (no special video requirements)

    Program list:  ADDUP.C
                   TOOLBOX1.C

    Usage:         addup n1 [ n2 ... ]

    Description:   Demonstrates the use of a simple toolbox in a
                   utility program.  Sums integers entered on the
                   command line.
    -----------------------------------------------------------------
*/

#include <stdio.h>
#include <stdlib.h>
#include "toolbox1.h"
```

(continued)

ADDUP.C *continued*

```
main( int argc, char *argv[] )
{
    int i, sum = 0;

    for ( i = 0; i < argc; i++ )
        sum += atoi( argv[i] );

    printf( "\n\nSum = %d\n", sum );
}
```

To call functions in the TOOLBOX1 module from the ADDUP utility, you must create a program list that includes the file TOOLBOX1.C. Choose Set Program List from the Make menu, and enter *addup* as the name for the make file. Then select ADDUP.C and TOOLBOX1.C from the File List box so that they appear in the Program List box. Finally, save the program list (ADDUP.MAK) on disk.

The ADDUP utility is nearly ready to run. Because command line parameters are expected (although not necessary in this case), modify the command line contents before running the program. Choose the Run / Debug item from the Options menu, and type some numbers into the Command Line entry field. As a simple example, type *1 2 3* (separated by spaces) and press Enter.

Now the ADDUP program is ready to roll! Press F5 to compile, link, and run the program. The displayed output shows that the sum of 1, 2, and 3 is 6.

This sample program demonstrates how you can use toolbox routines in the development of your own programs. The utility programs in Part III provide similar examples of the use of toolbox functions. In addition, these utilities provide unique productivity tools that you can use from day to day.

13

PART II

TOOLBOX
MODULES

BIOSCALL

FUNCTION	DESCRIPTION
hardware_coprocessor()	Checks for coprocessor
hardware_start_videomode()	Gets initial video mode
hardware_floppies()	Gets number of floppy disk drives
hardware_serial_ports()	Gets number of serial ports
hardware_game_adapter()	Checks for game adapter
hardware_serial_printer()	Checks for serial printer
hardware_printers()	Gets number of printers
shift_right()	Determines right Shift key status
shift_left()	Determines left Shift key status
shift_ctrl()	Determines Ctrl key status
shift_alt()	Determines Alt key status
shift_scroll_lock()	Determines Scroll Lock status
shift_num_lock()	Determines Num Lock status
shift_caps_lock()	Determines Caps Lock status
shift_insert_state()	Determines Insert status
prntscrn()	Prints the screen
reboot()	Performs system reboot
scroll()	Scrolls area of screen

Your computer's ROM BIOS (Basic Input/Output Services stored in Read-Only Memory) makes available a number of useful routines and data tables. The BIOSCALL toolbox module provides a sampler of useful functions that return the information provided by the BIOS.

The functions implemented in the file BIOSCALL.C rely on many of the low-level functions in the QuickC run-time library that access BIOS services and data. Most of these QuickC library functions have the prefix _bios_. For example, the function _bios_equiplist() returns a bit pattern that is loaded with information about the number of disk drives, printers, and other equipment available to your program.

The toolbox routines in this book are uniformly presented as functions, with the result that all routines for a particular module are defined in the same file and accessed in the same manner. Most of the functions defined in BIOSCALL.C have a single executable instruction, however, and these functions can also be written as macros, as you'll see in BIOSCALL.H. When implemented as macros, the routines execute more rapidly because the compiler can dispense with the overhead that function calls require.

To invoke any of the BIOSCALL functions from your own program, add the #*include "BIOSCALL.H"* directive, and then add the name of the toolbox module, BIOSCALL.C, to the program list. To use the macro replacements for the BIOSCALL functions, enable the following line in BIOSCALL.H:

```
/* #define BIOSCALL_AS_MACROS */
```

by deleting the enclosing comment characters, /* and */. If you use the macro replacements, include the header file and omit BIOSCALL.C from the program list. (The *scroll()* function has no macro equivalent— to use it, you *will* need to compile with BIOSCALL.C.)

The demonstration program, BIOSTEST.C, calls each function in BIOSCALL.C and displays the result of each function in a straight-forward way. By examining BIOSTEST.C, you can see how the program calls each function and how it uses the returned data.

BIOSTEST first demonstrates the hardware functions provided in the module. The hardware functions let your application obtain infor-mation about the user's hardware configuration—how many serial ports are available, whether a coprocessor is installed, and so forth. BIOSTEST presents this information in a table.

The next demonstration shows how you can monitor the various keyboard states. As you press each shift key, the screen updates a simple representation of the keyboard states. Note that the Ins key is active only when Num Lock is not in effect.

Another useful BIOS service, which is provided as a video function, allows fast scrolling of the characters in a rectangular area of the screen. The *scroll()* function in the toolbox module provides an easy way to call this BIOS service. To demonstrate the function, BIOSTEST displays 21 lines of characters on the screen and then quickly scrolls blocks of letters.

The last two demonstrations are optional because they provide ser-vices you might want to bypass. The *prntscrn()* function sends a screen dump to your printer, duplicating the effect of pressing the PrtSc key. The advantage this function offers is that your application can control the screen dump without relying on the user to press the PrtSc key. To bypass this demonstration, press the Esc key.

The last demonstration calls the *reboot()* function. Press Esc if you prefer to bypass this demonstration. On some computers the *reboot()* function causes an incomplete reboot, as a result of which your computer "hangs" indefinitely. If this occurs, press the Ctrl-Alt-Del key combination or perform a full reboot by turning off your computer briefly and then turning it on again.

Each function in this toolbox module is described in the following pages. For more information on the available BIOS services, refer to the technical reference manual for your computer.

Demonstration Program: BIOSTEST.C

```
/* ------------------------------------------------------------------
   Name:          BIOSTEST.C
   Type:          Demonstration program
   Language:      Microsoft QuickC version 2
   Video:         (no special video requirements)

   Program list:  BIOSTEST.C
                  BIOSCALL.C

   Variables:     c          Character code from keyboard press
                  i          Looping counter
                  j          Looping counter

   Usage:         (no command line parameters)

   Description:   Demonstrates the BIOSCALL toolbox functions
   ------------------------------------------------------------------
*/

#include <stdio.h>
#include <conio.h>
#include <stdlib.h>
#include "bioscall.h"

#define NORMAL 7
#define INVERSE 112
#define ESC 27
```

(continued)

BIOSTEST.C *continued*

```
main()
{
    int c = 0, i, j;
    /* List hardware details */
    printf( "\n\n\nHardware...\n\n" );
    printf( "Coprocessor\t\t%5d\n", hardware_coprocessor() );
    printf( "Starting video mode\t%5d\n", hardware_start_videomode() );
    printf( "No. floppy drives\t%5d\n", hardware_floppies() );
    printf( "No. serial ports\t%5d\n", hardware_serial_ports() );
    printf( "Game adapter\t\t%5d\n", hardware_game_adapter() );
    printf( "Serial printer\t\t%5d\n", hardware_serial_printer() );
    printf( "No. printers\t\t%5d\n", hardware_printers() );

    /* Demonstrate the shift key states */
    printf( "\n\n\nShift keys and shift states...\n\n" );

    printf( "Try the shift keys, then press Esc to continue\n\n" );
    printf( "left  right            scroll num   caps  insert\n" );
    printf( "shift shift ctrl  alt   lock  lock  lock  state\n" );
    do
        {
        printf( "%3d%6d%6d%6d%6d%6d%6d%6d\r",
        shift_left(),
        shift_right(),
        shift_ctrl(),
        shift_alt(),
        shift_scroll_lock(),
        shift_num_lock(),
        shift_caps_lock(),
        shift_insert_state() );

        if ( kbhit() )
            c = getch();
        }
    while ( c != ESC );

    /* Demonstrate the scroll function */
    printf( "\n\n\nScroll test...\n\n" );
```

(continued)

BIOSTEST.C *continued*

```
    /* Fill the screen with a recognizable character pattern */
    for ( i = 0; i < 20; i++ )
        for ( j = 0; j < 80; j++ )
            putchar( i + 65 );

    /* Scroll or blank four rectangular areas */
    scroll( 7, 7, 17, 17, 0, NORMAL );
    scroll( 7, 27, 17, 37, 3, INVERSE );
    scroll( 7, 47, 17, 57, -4, INVERSE );
    scroll( 7, 67, 17, 77, 0, INVERSE );

    /* Demonstrate the screen-printing function */
    printf( "\n\nIF YOU WANT TO TEST prntscrn() PRESS BOTH SHIFT KEYS\n" );
    printf( "Press the Esc key to skip this test" );

    c = 0;
    while ( c != ESC )
        {
        if ( shift_left() && shift_right() )
            prntscrn();
        if ( kbhit() )
            c = getch();
        }

    /* Demonstrate the reboot function */
    printf( "\n\nIF YOU WANT TO TEST reboot() PRESS BOTH SHIFT KEYS\n" );
    printf( "Press the Esc key to end the program without rebooting" );

    c = 0;
    while ( c != ESC )
        {
        if ( shift_left() && shift_right() )
            reboot();
        if ( kbhit() )
            c = getch();
        }
}
```

Include File: BIOSCALL.H

```
/* ----------------------------------------------------------------
    Name:          BIOSCALL.H
    Type:          Include
    Language:      Microsoft QuickC version 2
    Demonstrated:  BIOSCALL.C  BIOSTEST.C
    Description:   Prototypes and definitions for BIOSCALL.C
   ----------------------------------------------------------------
*/

#ifndef BIOSCALL_DEFINED

#include <bios.h>

/* NOTE:  To replace all functions--except scroll()--with macros, */
/* enable the next line.          */
/* #define BIOSCALL_AS_MACROS */

#ifndef BIOSCALL_AS_MACROS

/* Function prototypes */
int hardware_coprocessor( void );
int hardware_start_videomode( void );
int hardware_floppies( void );
int hardware_serial_ports( void );
int hardware_game_adapter( void );
int hardware_serial_printer( void );
int hardware_printers( void );
int shift_right( void );
int shift_left( void );
int shift_ctrl( void );
int shift_alt( void );
int shift_scroll_lock( void );
int shift_num_lock( void );
int shift_caps_lock( void );
int shift_insert_state( void );
void prntscrn( void );
void reboot( void );

#else

/* Macro replacements for the BIOSCALL.C functions... */
#define hardware_coprocessor() (( _bios_equiplist() >> 1 ) & 1 )
```

(continued)

```
#define hardware_start_videomode() (( _bios_equiplist() >> 4 ) & 3 )
#define hardware_floppies() (( ( _bios_equiplist() >> 6 ) & 3 ) + 1 )
#define hardware_serial_ports() (( _bios_equiplist() >> 9 ) & 7 )
#define hardware_game_adapter() (( _bios_equiplist() >> 12 ) & 1 )
#define hardware_serial_printer() (( _bios_equiplist() >> 13 ) & 1 )
#define hardware_printers() (( _bios_equiplist() >> 14 ) & 3 )
#define shift_right() ( _bios_keybrd( _KEYBRD_SHIFTSTATUS ) & 1 )
#define shift_left() (( _bios_keybrd( _KEYBRD_SHIFTSTATUS ) >> 1 ) & 1 )
#define shift_ctrl() (( _bios_keybrd( _KEYBRD_SHIFTSTATUS ) >> 2 ) & 1 )
#define shift_alt() (( _bios_keybrd( _KEYBRD_SHIFTSTATUS ) >> 3 ) & 1 )
#define shift_scroll_lock() (( _bios_keybrd( _KEYBRD_SHIFTSTATUS ) >> 4 ) & 1 )
#define shift_num_lock() (( _bios_keybrd( _KEYBRD_SHIFTSTATUS ) >> 5 ) & 1 )
#define shift_caps_lock() (( _bios_keybrd( _KEYBRD_SHIFTSTATUS ) >> 6 ) & 1 )
#define shift_insert_state() (( _bios_keybrd( _KEYBRD_SHIFTSTATUS ) >> 7 ) & 1 )
#define prntscrn() _asm { int 5 }
#define reboot() _asm { int 0x19 }

#endif

void scroll( int, int, int, int, int, int );  /* No macro equivalent */

#define BIOSCALL_DEFINED
#endif
```

Toolbox Module: BIOSCALL.C

```
/* -------------------------------------------------------------------
   Name:           BIOSCALL.C
   Type:           Toolbox module
   Language:       Microsoft QuickC version 2
   Demonstrated:   BIOSTEST.C
   Video:          (no special video requirements)
   -------------------------------------------------------------------
*/

#include <stdlib.h>
#include <bios.h>
#include <dos.h>
#include "bioscall.h"

/*See BIOSCALL.H for instructions on replacing functions with macros */
#ifndef BIOSCALL_AS_MACROS
```

Function: *hardware_coprocessor()*

The *hardware_coprocessor()* function determines whether the hardware is equipped with a floating-point math coprocessor that is available for use. The function returns 1 if a coprocessor is present; it returns 0 if no coprocessor is available.

```
/* - - - - - - - - - - - - - - - - - - - - - - - - - - - - - - - - -

   Function:      hardware_coprocessor()
   Toolbox:       BIOSCALL.C
   Demonstrated:  BIOSTEST.C

   Parameters:    (none)

   Returned:      1 if coprocessor installed
                  0 if coprocessor not installed

   Variables:     (none)

   Description:   Checks for the existence of a math coprocessor
   - - - - - - - - - - - - - - - - - - - - - - - - - - - - - - - - -
*/

int hardware_coprocessor( void )
{
    return (( _bios_equiplist() >> 1 ) & 1 );
}
```

Function: *hardware_start_videomode()*

The *hardware_start_videomode()* function returns a number from 1 through 3, which indicates the video mode that is set by the system at bootup time. If the system has a monochrome display, the function returns 3. If a color card is installed, the function usually returns 2, which indicates 80-by-25 black-and-white text mode. If the return value is 1, the system wakes up in 40-by-25 black-and-white text mode.

```
/* - - - - - - - - - - - - - - - - - - - - - - - - - - - - - -
   Function:       hardware_start_videomode()
   Toolbox:        BIOSCALL.C
   Demonstrated:   BIOSTEST.C

   Parameters:     (none)

   Returned:       Initial video mode...
                   1 = 40 x 25 black-and-white text, color card
                   2 = 80 x 25 black-and-white text, color card
                   3 = 80 x 25 black-and-white text, monochrome

   Variables:      (none)

   Description:    Determines the initial video mode set by the
                   system when rebooted
   - - - - - - - - - - - - - - - - - - - - - - - - - - - - - -
*/

int hardware_start_videomode( void )
{
    return (( _bios_equiplist() >> 4 ) & 3 );
}
```

Function: *hardware_floppies()*

The *hardware_floppies()* function returns the number of floppy disk drives attached to the system. (Fixed disk drives are not included.) This function always returns a number from 1 through 4. It is assumed that at least one floppy disk drive is installed.

```
/* - - - - - - - - - - - - - - - - - - - - - - - - - - - - - -
   Function:       hardware_floppies()
   Toolbox:        BIOSCALL.C
   Demonstrated:   BIOSTEST.C

   Parameters:     (none)

   Returned:       Number of floppy drives

   Variables:      (none)
```

(continued)

BIOSCALL.C *continued*

```
   Description:    Returns the number of floppy disk drives
   - - - - - - - - - - - - - - - - - - - - - - - - - - - - - - - - -
*/

int hardware_floppies( void )
{
    return ((( _bios_equiplist() >> 6 ) & 3 ) + 1 );
}
```

Function: *hardware_serial_ports()*

The *hardware_serial_ports()* function returns the number of serial ports
available. The BIOS service that obtains this information returns the
number of serial ports in a 3-bit field, which limits the possible return
values to the range 0 through 7.

```
/* - - - - - - - - - - - - - - - - - - - - - - - - - - - - - - -
   Function:       hardware_serial_ports()
   Toolbox:        BIOSCALL.C
   Demonstrated:   BIOSTEST.C

   Parameters:     (none)

   Returned:       Number of serial ports

   Variables:      (none)

   Description:    Returns the number of serial ports
   - - - - - - - - - - - - - - - - - - - - - - - - - - - - - - - - -
*/

int hardware_serial_ports( void )
{
    return (( _bios_equiplist() >> 9 ) & 7 );
}
```

Function: *hardware_game_adapter()*

The *hardware_game_adapter()* function returns 1 if a game adapter is attached to the system. If none is available, the return value is 0.

```
/* - - - - - - - - - - - - - - - - - - - - - - - - - - - - - - - - -
    Function:       hardware_game_adapter()
    Toolbox:        BIOSCALL.C
    Demonstrated:   BIOSTEST.C

    Parameters:     (none)

    Returned:       1 = Game adapter is installed
                    0 = Game adapter is not installed

    Variables:      (none)

    Description:    Checks for existence of a game adapter
    - - - - - - - - - - - - - - - - - - - - - - - - - - - - - - - - -
*/

int hardware_game_adapter( void )
{
    return (( _bios_equiplist() >> 12 ) & 1 );
}
```

Function: *hardware_serial_printer()*

The *hardware_serial_printer()* function checks for the existence of a serial printer attached to the system. If a serial printer is available, the function returns 1; if no serial printer is available, the return value is 0.

```
/* - - - - - - - - - - - - - - - - - - - - - - - - - - - - - - - - -
    Function:       hardware_serial_printer()
    Toolbox:        BIOSCALL.C
    Demonstrated:   BIOSTEST.C

    Parameters:     (none)

    Returned:       1 = Serial printer is attached
                    0 = Serial printer is not attached

    Variables:      (none)
```

(continued)

BIOSCALL.C *continued*

```
    Description:    Checks for existence of a serial printer
    - - - - - - - - - - - - - - - - - - - - - - - - - - - - - - - -
*/

int hardware_serial_printer( void )
{
    return (( _bios_equiplist() >> 13 ) & 1 );
}
```

Function: *hardware_printers()*

The *hardware_printers()* function returns the number of printers attached to the system. The returned number always falls in the range 0 through 3.

```
/* - - - - - - - - - - - - - - - - - - - - - - - - - - - - - - - -
    Function:       hardware_printers()
    Toolbox:        BIOSCALL.C
    Demonstrated:   BIOSTEST.C

    Parameters:     (none)

    Returned:       Number of printers attached

    Variables:      (none)

    Description:    Returns the number of attached printers
    - - - - - - - - - - - - - - - - - - - - - - - - - - - - - - - -
*/

int hardware_printers( void )
{
    return (( _bios_equiplist() >> 14 ) & 3 );
}
```

Function: *shift_right()*

The *shift_right()* function returns 1 if the right Shift key is pressed at the moment the function is called. If the right Shift key is not pressed, the return value is 0.

```
/* - - - - - - - - - - - - - - - - - - - - - - - - - - - - - - - -
   Function:      shift_right()
   Toolbox:       BIOSCALL.C
   Demonstrated:  BIOSTEST.C

   Parameters:    (none)

   Returned:      1 = Right Shift key pressed
                  0 = Right Shift key not pressed

   Variables:     (none)

   Description:   Returns the status of the right Shift key
   - - - - - - - - - - - - - - - - - - - - - - - - - - - - - - - -
*/

int shift_right( void )
{
   return ( _bios_keybrd( _KEYBRD_SHIFTSTATUS ) & 1 );
}
```

Function: *shift_left()*

The *shift_left()* function returns 1 if the left Shift key is pressed at the moment the function is called. If the left Shift key is not pressed, the return value is 0.

```
/* - - - - - - - - - - - - - - - - - - - - - - - - - - - - - - - -
   Function:      shift_left()
   Toolbox:       BIOSCALL.C
   Demonstrated:  BIOSTEST.C

   Parameters:    (none)

   Returned:      1 = Left Shift key pressed
                  0 = Left Shift key not pressed
```

(continued)

BIOSCALL.C *continued*

```
    Variables:       (none)

    Description:     Returns the status of the left Shift key
    - - - - - - - - - - - - - - - - - - - - - - - - - - - - - -
*/

int shift_left( void )
{
    return (( _bios_keybrd( _KEYBRD_SHIFTSTATUS ) >> 1 ) & 1 );
}
```

Function: *shift_ctrl()*

The *shift_ctrl()* function returns 1 if the Ctrl key is pressed at the moment the function is called. If the Ctrl key is not pressed, the return value is 0.

```
/* - - - - - - - - - - - - - - - - - - - - - - - - - - - - - -
    Function:        shift_ctrl()
    Toolbox:         BIOSCALL.C
    Demonstrated:    BIOSTEST.C

    Parameters:      (none)

    Returned:        1 = Ctrl key pressed
                     0 = Ctrl key not pressed

    Variables:       (none)

    Description:     Returns the status of the Ctrl key
    - - - - - - - - - - - - - - - - - - - - - - - - - - - - - -
*/

int shift_ctrl( void )
{
    return (( _bios_keybrd( _KEYBRD_SHIFTSTATUS ) >> 2 ) & 1 );
}
```

Function: *shift_alt()*

The *shift_alt()* function returns 1 if the Alt key is pressed at the moment the function is called. If the Alt key is not pressed, the return value is 0.

```
/* - - - - - - - - - - - - - - - - - - - - - - - - - - - - - - -
   Function:       shift_alt()
   Toolbox:        BIOSCALL.C
   Demonstrated:   BIOSTEST.C

   Parameters:     (none)

   Returned:       1 = Alt key pressed
                   0 = Alt key not pressed

   Variables:      (none)

   Description:    Returns the status of the Alt key
   - - - - - - - - - - - - - - - - - - - - - - - - - - - - - - -
*/

int shift_alt( void )
{
   return (( _bios_keybrd( _KEYBRD_SHIFTSTATUS ) >> 3 ) & 1 );
}
```

Function: *shift_scroll_lock()*

The *shift_scroll_lock()* function returns 1 if the Scroll Lock state is active at the moment the function is called. If Scroll Lock is inactive, the return value is 0.

```
/* - - - - - - - - - - - - - - - - - - - - - - - - - - - - - - -
   Function:       shift_scroll_lock()
   Toolbox:        BIOSCALL.C
   Demonstrated:   BIOSTEST.C

   Parameters:     (none)

   Returned:       1 = Scroll Lock on
                   0 = Scroll Lock off

   Variables:      (none)
```

(continued)

BIOSCALL.C *continued*

```
    Description:    Returns the Scroll Lock state
- - - - - - - - - - - - - - - - - - - - - - - - - - - - - - - - - -
*/

int shift_scroll_lock( void )
{
    return (( _bios_keybrd( _KEYBRD_SHIFTSTATUS ) >> 4 ) & 1 );
}
```

Function: *shift_num_lock()*

The *shift_num_lock()* function returns 1 if the Num Lock state is active at the moment this function is called. If Num Lock is inactive, the return value is 0.

```
/* - - - - - - - - - - - - - - - - - - - - - - - - - - - - - - -
    Function:       shift_num_lock()
    Toolbox:        BIOSCALL.C
    Demonstrated:   BIOSTEST.C

    Parameters:     (none)

    Returned:       1 = Num Lock on
                    0 = Num Lock off

    Variables:      (none)

    Description:    Returns the Num Lock state
- - - - - - - - - - - - - - - - - - - - - - - - - - - - - - - - -
*/

int shift_num_lock( void )
{
    return (( _bios_keybrd( _KEYBRD_SHIFTSTATUS ) >> 5 ) & 1 );
}
```

Function: *shift_caps_lock()*

The *shift_caps_lock()* function returns 1 if the Caps Lock state is active at the moment the function is called. If Caps Lock is inactive, the return value is 0.

```
/* - - - - - - - - - - - - - - - - - - - - - - - - - - - - - - - - -
   Function:      shift_caps_lock()
   Toolbox:       BIOSCALL.C
   Demonstrated:  BIOSTEST.C

   Parameters:    (none)

   Returned:      1 = Caps Lock on
                  0 = Caps Lock off

   Variables:     (none)

   Description:   Returns the Caps Lock state
   - - - - - - - - - - - - - - - - - - - - - - - - - - - - - - - - -
*/

int shift_caps_lock( void )
{
   return (( _bios_keybrd( _KEYBRD_SHIFTSTATUS ) >> 6 ) & 1 );
}
```

Function: *shift_insert_state()*

The *shift_insert_state()* function returns 1 if the Insert state is active at the moment the function is called. If the Insert state is inactive, the return value is 0.

```
/* - - - - - - - - - - - - - - - - - - - - - - - - - - - - - - - - -
   Function:      shift_insert_state()
   Toolbox:       BIOSCALL.C
   Demonstrated:  BIOSTEST.C

   Parameters:    (none)

   Returned:      1 = Insert on
                  0 = Insert off
```

(continued)

BIOSCALL.C *continued*

```
    Variables:      (none)

    Description:    Returns the Insert state
    - - - - - - - - - - - - - - - - - - - - - - - - - - - - - -
*/

int shift_insert_state( void )
{
    return (( _bios_keybrd( _KEYBRD_SHIFTSTATUS ) >> 7 ) & 1 );
}
```

Function: *prntscrn()*

The *prntscrn()* function causes the screen contents to be dumped to the printer, exactly as though the user had pressed the PrtSc key.

Whenever you press the PrtSc key, the operating system performs an Int 05H to activate the BIOS-level code for performing the screen dump. With the *prntscrn()* function, you can program such a screen dump at any point in the operation of a running program without requiring user intervention.

Because the screen dump BIOS routine is interrupt driven, any changes to the screen dump code are automatically taken into account. For example, if your computer loads and patches in an improved version of the screen dump routine at bootup time, this subprogram simply activates the new routine. That's one of the nice features of the interrupt mechanism provided by the 8086 family of computers.

```
/* - - - - - - - - - - - - - - - - - - - - - - - - - - - - - -
    Function:       prntscrn()
    Toolbox:        BIOSCALL.C
    Demonstrated:   BIOSTEST.C

    Parameters:     (none)

    Returned:       (none)

    Variables:      (none)
```

(continued)

BIOSCALL.C *continued*

```
    Description:     Dumps screen to printer exactly as if the PrtSc
                     key were pressed
    - - - - - - - - - - - - - - - - - - - - - - - - - - - - - -
*/

void prntscrn( void )
{
    _asm { int 5 }
}
```

Function: *reboot()*

The *reboot()* function causes the system to reboot. The success of this function depends on the model of your computer and its specific configuration. If you plan to use the function regularly, test it carefully for your specific circumstances.

Perhaps the best and safest use for this function is as an escape route for unauthorized access to software: Rebooting can frustrate attempts to overcome copy protection schemes. For example, try rebooting the system if a user fails to enter a password correctly for the third time or if an unauthorized copy of a program is detected.

```
/* - - - - - - - - - - - - - - - - - - - - - - - - - - - - - -
    Function:        reboot()
    Toolbox:         BIOSCALL.C
    Demonstrated:    BIOSTEST.C

    Parameters:      (none)

    Returned:        (none)

    Variables:       (none)

    Description:     Causes the system to reboot
    - - - - - - - - - - - - - - - - - - - - - - - - - - - - - -
*/

void reboot( void )
{
    _asm { int 0x19 }
}
```

Function: *scroll()*

The *scroll()* function uses BIOS video Int 10H to provide quick scrolling of text lines in a rectangular area of the screen. You place the correct arguments in the processor registers, and the BIOS code does the rest.

The *scroll()* function requires six parameters. The first four of these values define the upper left and lower right corners of the area to be scrolled. These coordinates refer to text mode character locations, with the upper left corner of the screen defined as row 1, column 1. The lower right corner of the screen is defined as row 25, column 80 for 80-column text mode; row 25, column 40 for 40-column text mode.

The last two parameters provide the line count and the color attribute. If the line count is a positive number, the lines scroll up by the indicated number of rows, leaving blank lines at the bottom of the scrolled area. If the line count is negative, the lines scroll down. The region vacated by scrolling is filled with space characters. Their color is set by the attribute byte passed in the sixth parameter.

Usually this function is used to scroll text one line at a time, as occurs when you invoke the MS-DOS TYPE command to display the contents of a long file. A handy feature of the function is its ability to clear the screen or a region of the screen and to set the background color at the same time. To clear the screen, pass a line count of 0. The BIOS routine fills the specified rectangular area with spaces. The region clears much faster than it does if you use *printf()* to print the same number of space characters.

The *scroll()* function demonstrates the powerful in-line assembler that was included with version 2 of QuickC. The same function can be written without using the *_asm* keyword, but the resulting code is not as fast or as concise. For the sake of comparison, the following lines of source code implement the *scroll()* function without recourse to in-line assembly language code.

```
void scroll( int row_1, int col_1, int row_2,
             int col_2, int lines, int attribute )
{
    union REGS regs;

    if ( lines > 0 )
        regs.h.ah = 6;
    else
        regs.h.ah = 7;
```

(continued)

continued

```
            regs.h.al = abs( lines );
            regs.h.bh = attribute;
            regs.h.bl = 0;
            regs.h.ch = --row_1;
            regs.h.cl = --col_1;
            regs.h.dh = --row_2;
            regs.h.dl = --col_2;

            int86( 0x10, &regs, &regs );
        }
```

This implementation results in fast code, but in-line assembly code is even faster because it requires less overhead and compiles to object code that is closer to ideal, optimized assembly language.

```
#endif
/* The scroll() function has no macro equivalent... */


/* - - - - - - - - - - - - - - - - - - - - - - - - - - - - - - - - - - -
    Function:       scroll()
    Toolbox:        BIOSCALL.C
    Demonstrated:   BIOSTEST.C

    Parameters:
      (input)       row_1     Upper left corner, row number
      (input)       col_1     Upper left corner, column number
      (input)       row_2     Lower right corner, row number
      (input)       col_2     Lower right corner, column number

      (input)       lines     Number of lines to scroll up or down:
                              - If positive, lines scroll up
                              - If negative, lines scroll down
                              - If zero, area becomes blank
      (input)       attribute Color attribute for blank lines

    Returned:       (none)

    Variables:      (none)

    Description:    Scrolls a rectangular area of a text mode screen
   - - - - - - - - - - - - - - - - - - - - - - - - - - - - - - - - - - -
*/
```

(continued)

BIOSCALL.C *continued*

```
void scroll( int row_1, int col_1, int row_2,
             int col_2, int lines, int attribute )
{
    unsigned char reg_ah;

    /* Determine whether AH = 6 or 7 */
    if ( lines > 0 )
        reg_ah = 6;
    else
        reg_ah = 7;

    /* The sign of lines is no longer needed */
    lines = abs( lines );

    /* The rest can be done efficiently in assembler */
    _asm
        {

        /* Set BH = attribute, BL = 0  */
        mov   ax, attribute
        mov   bh, al
        xor   bl, bl

        /* Set CH = row_1 - 1 */
        mov   ax, row_1
        dec   ax
        mov   ch, al

        /* Set CL = col_1 - 1 */
        mov   ax, col_1
        dec   ax
        mov   cl, al

        /* Set DH = row_2 - 1 */
        mov   ax, row_2
        dec   ax
        mov   dh, al

        /* Set DL = col_2 - 1 */
        mov   ax, col_2
        dec   ax
        mov   dl, al
```

(continued)

BIOSCALL.C *continued*

```
        /* Set AL = lines */
        mov    ax, lines

        /* Set AH = 6 or 7 (reg_ah) */
        mov    ah, reg_ah

        /* Video interrupt */
        int    0x10
        }
}
```

BITS

FUNCTION	DESCRIPTION
bitset()	Sets bit in a buffer
bitclr()	Clears bit in a buffer
bittog()	Toggles bit in a buffer
bitget()	Gets bit from a buffer

The BITS toolbox module provides four bit-manipulation functions. These functions operate on bits stored in an array of unsigned characters. Each array element contains 8 bits, so a character array dimensioned 1000, for example, provides a storage area, or buffer, of 8000 bits. The functions let you set, clear, toggle (invert), or retrieve bit values.

BITS.C declares and initializes two arrays of mask bytes that let the functions isolate individual bits. Mask bytes provide faster selection of bits than would be possible using shifts or other calculations. Notice in the table below that each of the eight bytes in *mask_set[]* has one bit set; conversely, each byte in *mask_clr[]* has all but one bit set, as shown in the table on the following page.

The bit-manipulation functions would be useful for data acquisition and process control applications involving a large number of contact closures. For example, the state of a relay can be represented by one bit, for which a 0 value means the relay is open and a 1 value means the relay is closed.

ELEMENT	VALUE (Hex)	BINARY EQUIVALENT
mask_set[0]	\x01	00000001
mask_set[1]	\x02	00000010
mask_set[2]	\x04	00000100
mask_set[3]	\x08	00001000
mask_set[4]	\x10	00010000
mask_set[5]	\x20	00100000
mask_set[6]	\x40	01000000
mask_set[7]	\x80	10000000

(continued)

ELEMENT	VALUE (Hex)	BINARY EQUIVALENT
mask_clr[0]	\xFE	11111110
mask_clr[1]	\xFD	11111101
mask_clr[2]	\xFB	11111011
mask_clr[3]	\xF7	11110111
mask_clr[4]	\xEF	11101111
mask_clr[5]	\xDF	11011111
mask_clr[6]	\xBF	10111111
mask_clr[7]	\x7F	01111111

The demonstration program BITSTEST.C uses three of the functions— *bitclr()*, *bitset()*, and *bittog()*—to clear a buffer of bits, set bits to represent ASCII characters in the first two bytes, and then set all the bits in the buffer. In its final demonstration, BITSTEST.C uses *bitclr()* and *bitget()* to apply the famous sieve of Eratosthenes for finding prime numbers. The program keeps track of the bit values in a 125-element character buffer. By using the bit values to represent the integers 1 through 1000, BITSTEST.C finds and then displays the prime numbers in that range.

The functions in the BITS module are implemented as macros in BITS.H. See the BIOSCALL module if you are unsure how to use the macro definitions instead of the functions defined in BITS.C.

Demonstration Program: BITSTEST.C

```
/* -------------------------------------------------------------------
    Name:           BITSTEST.C
    Type:           Demonstration program
    Language:       Microsoft QuickC
    Video:          (no special video requirements)

    Program list:   BITSTEST.C
                    BITS.C

    Variables:      bit      Bit number
                    i        Looping index
                    j        Looping index
                    bitbuf   Buffer of 1000 bits
```

(continued)

BITSTEST.C *continued*

```
    Usage:          (no command line parameters)

    Description:    Demonstrates the BITS toolbox functions
    ----------------------------------------------------------------
*/

#include <stdio.h>
#include "bits.h"
main()
{
    int bit;
    int i, j;
    unsigned char bitbuf[125];

    /* Zero all the bits in the bit buffer */
    for ( bit = 0; bit < 1000; bit++ )
        bitclr( bitbuf, bit );

    /* Set bits in first byte to set 'A' */
    bitset( bitbuf, 0 );
    bitset( bitbuf, 6 );

    /* Toggle bits in second byte to set 'B' */
    bittog( bitbuf, 9 );
    bittog( bitbuf, 14 );

    /* Print "AB" (third byte is \0, terminating the string) */
    printf( "\nFirst two bytes of bitbuf = %s\n", bitbuf );

    /* Now set all the bits */
    for ( bit = 0; bit < 1000; bit++ )
        bitset( bitbuf, bit );

    /* Print decimal value of one of the bytes (should be 255) */
    printf( "bitbuf[97] = %d\n", bitbuf[97] );

    /* Sieve of Eratosthenes, creates table of primes */
    for ( i = 2; i < 500; i++ )
        if ( bitget( bitbuf, i ))
            for ( j = i + i; j < 1000; j += i )
                bitclr( bitbuf, j );

    /* Output all primes less than 1000 */
    printf( "\nPrimes less than 1000 ...\n" );
```

(continued)

BITSTEST.C *continued*

```
    for ( i = 1; i < 1000; i++ )
        if ( bitget( bitbuf, i ))
            printf( "%d\t", i );
}
```

Include File: BITS.H

```
/* ------------------------------------------------------------------
   Name:          BITS.H
   Type:          Include
   Language:      Microsoft QuickC
   Demonstrated:  BITS.C  BITSTEST.C
   Description:   Prototypes and definitions for BITS.C
   ------------------------------------------------------------------
*/

#ifndef BITS_DEFINED

/* NOTE: To replace all functions with macros, */
/* enable the next line. */
/* #define BITS_AS_MACROS */

#ifndef BITS_AS_MACROS

/* Function prototypes */
void bitset( unsigned char *, unsigned );
void bitclr( unsigned char *, unsigned );
void bittog( unsigned char *, unsigned );
int  bitget( unsigned char *, unsigned );

#else

/* Macro replacements for the BITS.C functions... */
#define bitset( buf, bit ) ( buf[(bit) >> 3] |= ( 1 << ( (bit) & 7 )))
#define bitclr( buf, bit ) ( buf[(bit) >> 3] &= ~( 1 << ( (bit) & 7 )))
#define bittog( buf, bit ) ( buf[(bit) >> 3] ^= ( 1 << ( (bit) & 7 )))
#define bitget( buf, bit ) ((( buf[(bit) >> 3] >> ( (bit) & 7 )) & 1 ))

#endif

#define BITS_DEFINED
#endif
```

Toolbox Module: BITS.C

```
/* - - - - - - - - - - - - - - - - - - - - - - - - - - - - - - - -
    Name:           BITS.C
    Type:           Toolbox module
    Language:       Microsoft QuickC version 2
    Demonstrated:   BITSTEST.C
    Video:          (no special video requirements)
    - - - - - - - - - - - - - - - - - - - - - - - - - - - - - -
*/

#include "bits.h"

/* See BITS.H for instructions on replacing functions with macros
/* #define BITS_AS_MACROS */

#ifndef BITS_AS_MACROS

unsigned char mask_set[] = { 0x01, 0x02, 0x04, 0x08, 0x10, 0x20, 0x40, 0x80 };
unsigned char mask_clr[] = { 0xfe, 0xfd, 0xfb, 0xf7, 0xef, 0xdf, 0xbf, 0x7f };
```

Function: *bitset()*

The *bitset()* function makes the value of a given bit equal to 1 (sets the bit). The bit must occupy a buffer that has been declared as an array of unsigned *char* values, each element of which holds 8 bits. For an array of n characters, bit positions are numbered from 0 through $8 * n - 1$.

The function does not verify that a specified bit is within the array. Unpredictable results can occur if the bit position is out of range.

```
/* - - - - - - - - - - - - - - - - - - - - - - - - - - - - - - - -
    Function:       bitset()
    Toolbox:        BITS.C
    Demonstrated:   BITSTEST.C
    Parameters:
      (input)       buf      Unsigned char buffer
      (input)       bit      Bit position in buffer

    Returned:       (function returns nothing)
```

(continued)

```
    Variables:      (none)

    Description:    Sets one bit in buffer
    - - - - - - - - - - - - - - - - - - - - - - - - - - - - - -
*/

void bitset( unsigned char buf[], unsigned bit )
{
    buf[bit >> 3] |= mask_set[bit & 7];
}
```

Function: *bitclr()*

The *bitclr()* function makes the value of a bit equal to 0 (clears the bit). The bit must occupy a buffer that has been declared as an array of unsigned *char* values, each element of which holds 8 bits. For an array of n characters, bit positions are numbered from 0 through $8 * n - 1$.

The function does not verify that a specified bit is within the array. Unpredictable results can occur if the bit position is out of range.

```
/* - - - - - - - - - - - - - - - - - - - - - - - - - - - - - -
    Function:       bitclr()
    Toolbox:        BITS.C
    Demonstrated:   BITSTEST.C

    Parameters:
      (input)       buf       Unsigned char buffer
      (input)       bit       Bit position in buffer

    Returned:       (function returns nothing)
    Variables:      (none)

    Description:    Clears (sets to 0) one bit in buffer
    - - - - - - - - - - - - - - - - - - - - - - - - - - - - -
*/

void bitclr( unsigned char buf[], unsigned bit )
{
    buf[bit >> 3] &= mask_clr[bit & 7];
}
```

Function: *bittog()*

The *bittog()* function inverts the value of a bit (toggles the bit). The bit must occupy a buffer that has been declared as an array of unsigned *char* values, each element of which holds 8 bits. For an array of *n* characters, bit positions are numbered from 0 to $8 * n - 1$.

The function does not verify that a specified bit is within the array. Unpredictable results can occur if the bit position is out of range.

```
/* - - - - - - - - - - - - - - - - - - - - - - - - - - - - - - - -
    Function:       bittog()
    Toolbox:        BITS.C
    Demonstrated:   BITSTEST.C

    Parameters:
      (input)       buf       Unsigned char buffer
      (input)       bit       Bit position in buffer

    Returned:       (function returns nothing) ·

    Variables:      (none)

    Description:    Toggles (inverts) one bit in buffer
    - - - - - - - - - - - - - - - - - - - - - - - - - - - - - - - -
*/

void bittog( unsigned char buf[], unsigned bit )
{
    buf[bit >> 3] ^= mask_set[bit & 7];
}
```

Function: *bitget()*

The *bitget()* function returns the value of a bit, either 0 or 1. The bit must occupy a buffer that has been declared as an array of unsigned *char* values.

```
/* - - - - - - - - - - - - - - - - - - - - - - - - - - - - - - - - - - - -
   Function:       bitget()
   Toolbox:        BITS.C
   Demonstrated:   BITSTEST.C

   Parameters:
     (input)       buf        Unsigned char buffer
     (input)       bit        Bit position in buffer

   Returned:       1 or 0, value of the bit

   Variables:      (none)

   Description:    Returns one bit from a buffer
   - - - - - - - - - - - - - - - - - - - - - - - - - - - - - - - - - - - -
*/

int bitget( unsigned char buf[], unsigned bit )
{
    return ((buf[bit >> 3] >> (7 - bit & 7)) & 1);
}

#endif
```

BOX

FUNCTION	DESCRIPTION
box_get()	Saves rectangular area of screen
box_put()	Restores saved area on screen
box_color()	Sets current colors in box
box_charfill()	Fills box with a character
box_draw()	Draws box with optional border
box_erase()	Blanks a rectangular area of screen

The BOX toolbox module provides a collection of functions for the fast manipulation of "boxes," rectangular areas of a text mode screen. These functions are useful for designing menus and dialog boxes. In fact, the MENU toolbox module, presented later in this book, uses functions from the BOX module. Take a look at MENU.C to see how easily functions in one module can call functions in another.

The BOXTEST program demonstrates all the box manipulation functions. First, the program calls *box_charfill()* to display a solid rectangular background. The *box_charfill()* function accomplishes this task more quickly than is possible with *printf()*. BOXTEST then calls *box_get()* to copy two rectangular areas of the screen to storage buffers. These areas of the screen will be restored later, after the demonstration boxes are created.

The program creates the first box with bright green text on a blue background. The *box_erase()* function is used to clear the box region and set the color attributes. BOXTEST then calls *box_draw()* twice, first to create a single-line box, and then to draw a (partially overlapping) double-line box. The resulting screen is shown on the facing page. The single-line box has the same base as the double-line box, but because its sides are shorter, it appears as a horizontal line inside the larger double-line box. This technique is useful for dividing boxes.

The program then waits for any key to be pressed, at which time it calls *box_put()* to restore the original box contents and then waits for another key.

To show the speed of the *box_erase()* and *box_draw()* functions, the BOXTEST program quickly creates 100 boxes in the central area of the screen. Each box has a randomly selected size, color, and border.

The next demonstration lets you see the speed of the *box_color()* and *box_charfill()* functions. The program creates a second group of 100 colored boxes and fills each box with a randomly chosen letter of the alphabet.

Finally, BOXTEST calls *box_put()* a second time to restore the original screen contents.

Demonstration Program: BOXTEST.C

Two header files are included at the start of this program. The first, BOX.H, provides prototypes for the functions in the BOX.C toolbox module. The second, T_COLORS.H, is used throughout this book to simplify the setting of text mode background and foreground color attributes.

```
/* ------------------------------------------------------------------
   Name:          BOXTEST.C
   Type:          Demonstration program
   Language:      Microsoft QuickC version 2
   Video:         Color or monochrome text mode

   Program list:  BOXTEST.C
                  BOX.C
                  GRAPHICS.LIB

   Variables:     i        Looping index for creating boxes
                  r1       Upper left corner of box
                  c1       Upper left corner of box
                  r2       Lower right corner of box
                  c2       Lower right corner of box
                  buf1     Buffer for saving rectangular area of
                           a text mode screen
                  buf2     Buffer for saving another rectangular area of
                           a text mode screen

   Usage:         (no command line parameters)

   Description:   Demonstrates the BOX toolbox functions
   ------------------------------------------------------------------
*/

#include <stdio.h>
#include <stdlib.h>
#include <conio.h>
#include <graph.h>
#include <malloc.h>
#include "box.h"
#include "t_colors.h"

main()
{
    unsigned i;
    unsigned r1, c1, r2, c2;
    unsigned far *buf1, far *buf2;

    /* Clear the screen */
    _clearscreen( _GCLEARSCREEN );

    /* Fill most of the screen with a background pattern */
    box_charfill( 1, 1, 23, 80, 176 );
```

(continued)

BOXTEST.C *continued*

```
/* Grab and save rectangular areas of the screen */
buf1 = box_get( 5, 5, 15, 40 );
buf2 = box_get( 1, 1, 22, 80 );

/* Set bright green on blue background */
_settextcolor( T_GREEN | T_BRIGHT );
_setbkcolor( BK_BLUE );

/* Create the first box */
box_erase( 5, 5, 15, 40 );
box_draw( 7, 5, 7, 40, 1 );
box_draw( 5, 5, 15, 40, 2 );

/* Wait for user */
_settextposition( 11, 9 );
_outtext( "Press any key to continue..." );
getch();

/* Restore the original screen contents */
box_put( buf1 );

/* Free the memory used to save the background */
_ffree( buf1 );

/* Set the normal white-on-black colors */
_settextcolor( T_WHITE );
_setbkcolor( BK_BLACK );

/* Wait for user */
_settextposition( 24, 1 );
printf( "Press any key to continue..." );
getch();

/* Create 100 single-line and double-line boxes */
for ( i = 0; i < 100; i++ )
    {
    do
        {
        r1 = rand() % 20 + 3;
        r2 = rand() % 20 + 3;
        }
    while ( r2 < r1 );
```

(continued)

BOXTEST.C *continued*

```
        do
            {
            c1 = rand() % 70 + 5;
            c2 = rand() % 70 + 5;
            }
        while ( c2 < c1 );
        _setbkcolor( (long)rand() % 16 );
        _settextcolor( rand() % 16 );
        box_erase( r1, c1, r2, c2 );
        box_draw( r1, c1, r2, c2, rand() % 2 + 1 );
        }

/* Set the normal white-on-black colors */
_settextcolor( T_WHITE );
_setbkcolor( BK_BLACK );

/* Wait for the user */
_settextposition( 23, 1 );
getch();

/* Create 100 colorful, character-filled boxes */
for ( i = 0; i < 100; i++ )
    {
    do
        {
        r1 = rand() % 20 + 3;
        r2 = rand() % 20 + 3;
        }
    while ( r2 < r1 );
    do
        {
        c1 = rand() % 70 + 5;
        c2 = rand() % 70 + 5;
        }
    while ( c2 < c1 );
    _setbkcolor( (long)rand() % 16 );
    _settextcolor( rand() % 16 );
    box_color( r1, c1, r2, c2 );
    box_charfill( r1, c1, r2, c2, (char)(rand() % 26 + 65 ));
    }
/* Set the normal white-on-black colors */
_settextcolor( T_WHITE );
_setbkcolor( BK_BLACK );
```

(continued)

BOXTEST.C *continued*

```
    /* Wait for the user */
    _settextposition( 23, 1 );
    getch();

    /* Restore the original background */
    box_put( buf2 );

    /* Free the memory */
    _ffree( buf2 );

    /* Wait for the user */
    _settextposition( 23, 1 );
    getch();

    /* Clear the screen */
    _clearscreen( _GCLEARSCREEN );
}
```

Include File: BOX.H

```
/* ------------------------------------------------------------------
    Name:           BOX.H
    Type:           Include
    Language:       Microsoft QuickC version 2
    Demonstrated:   BOX.C  BOXTEST.C MENU.C
    Description:    Prototypes and definitions for BOX.C
   ------------------------------------------------------------------
*/

#ifndef BOX_DEFINED

int far *box_get( int, int, int, int );
void box_put( int far * );
void box_color( int, int, int, int );
void box_charfill( int, int, int, int, char );
void box_draw( int, int, int, int, int );
void box_erase( int, int, int, int );

#define BOX_DEFINED
#endif
```

Include File: T_COLORS.H

The include file T_COLORS.H is used by several programs and toolbox modules in this book. In the BOX module, it provides short and long integer constants you can pass to the _settextcolor() and _setbkcolor() functions, which are provided in the QuickC graphics library.

By using these constants, you can specify colors as function arguments without needing to remember which number designates a given color or which parameters must be long integers. Be aware, however, that the parameters passed to _settextcolor() and _setbkcolor() actually refer to palette numbers. If you change the color palette entries to anything other than the default colors, these named constants won't accurately describe the colors they produce.

```
/* --- ------------------------------------------------------------ ---
    Name:          T_COLORS.H
    Type:          Include
    Language:      Microsoft QuickC version 2
    Demonstrated:  BOXTEST.C COLORS.C EDITTEST.C
                   MENU.C LOOK.C OBJECT.C
    Description:   Definitions for text mode color constants
    ------------------------------------------------------------------
*/

#ifndef T_COLORS_DEFINED

/* Standard text mode colors */
#define T_BLACK 0
#define T_BLUE 1
#define T_GREEN 2
#define T_CYAN 3
#define T_RED 4
#define T_MAGENTA 5
#define T_BROWN 6
#define T_WHITE 7

/* Modifiers that can be added to the text mode color constants */
#define T_BRIGHT 8
#define T_BLINK 16

/* Common combinations */
#define T_GRAY ( T_BLACK : T_BRIGHT )
#define T_YELLOW ( T_BROWN : T_BRIGHT )
```

(continued)

T_COLORS.H *continued*

```
/* Background text mode color constants */
#define BK_BLACK 0L
#define BK_BLUE 1L
#define BK_GREEN 2L
#define BK_CYAN 3L
#define BK_RED 4L
#define BK_MAGENTA 5L
#define BK_BROWN 6L
#define BK_WHITE 7L

#define T_COLORS_DEFINED
#endif
```

Toolbox Module: BOX.C

```
/* --------------------------------------------------------------------
    Name:           BOX.C
    Type:           Toolbox module
    Language:       Microsoft QuickC version 2
    Demonstrated:   BOXTEST.C
    Video:          Color or monochrome text module
   --------------------------------------------------------------------
*/

#include <stdio.h>
#include <stdlib.h>
#include <malloc.h>
#include <dos.h>
#include <string.h>
#include <graph.h>
#include "box.h"

static void determine_video( void );
static unsigned int video_seg = 0;
static char far *videoptr;
static int columns;
```

Function: *box_get()*

The *box_get()* function saves a rectangular area of an 80-column or 40-column text mode screen in a buffer. The four parameters define the upper left and lower right corners of the area you want to save. The function uses *malloc()* to dynamically allocate an integer buffer of the proper size. All characters and color attribute bytes in the area are saved in the buffer. The coordinates of the area are saved in the first four bytes of the buffer. These coordinates let you restore the box area exactly as saved by passing the buffer to the *box_put()* function.

You can also change any or all of the coordinates to copy a rectangular area of the screen to a second location or to reorient a box on the screen. By manipulating the width and height of the box, you could, for example, save a horizontal box and restore it vertically to provide fast vertical printing.

```
/* - - - - - - - - - - - - - - - - - - - - - - - - - - - - - - - - - -
    Function:       box_get()
    Toolbox:        BOX.C
    Demonstrated:   BOXTEST.C MENU.C

    Parameters:
      (input)       row1        Upper left corner of box
      (input)       col1        Upper left corner of box
      (input)       row2        Lower right corner of box
      (input)       col2        Lower right corner of box

    Returned:       Address of far integer buffer containing data
                    saved from the rectangular area of screen

    Variables:      i           Looping index for lines in box
                    width       Width of box area
                    height      Height of box area
                    bytes       Total number of bytes to store box data
                    buf         Address of far buffer for storage
                    bufptr      Index into storage buffer memory
                    video_off   Offset of video address for box data

    Description:    Saves contents of a rectangular area of the
                    screen in a dynamically allocated buffer
    - - - - - - - - - - - - - - - - - - - - - - - - - - - - - - - - - -
*/
```

(continued)

BOX.C *continued*

```
unsigned far *box_get( unsigned row1, unsigned col1, unsigned row2, unsigned col2 )
{
    unsigned i, width, height, bytes;
    unsigned far *buf, far *bufptr;
    unsigned video_off;

    /* Calculate the dimensions in bytes */
    width = ( col2 - col1 + 1 ) * 2;
    height = row2 - row1 + 1;
    bytes = height * width + 8;

    /* Allocate storage space */
    if (( buf = (int far *) malloc( (size_t) bytes )) == NULL)
        {
        printf( "box_get(): malloc() failed\n" );
        exit ( 0 );
        }

    /* Save the box coordinates in the buffer */
    bufptr = buf;
    *bufptr++ = row1;
    *bufptr++ = col1;
    *bufptr++ = row2;
    *bufptr++ = col2;

    /* Determine the text mode video segment and number of columns */
    determine_video();

    /* Calculate starting location in video memory */
    video_off = (unsigned) (( columns * ( row1 - 1 ) + ( col1 - 1 ) ) * 2 );

    /* Grab each line of the video */
    for ( i = 0; i < height; i++ )
        {
        movedata( video_seg, video_off,
                FP_SEG( bufptr ), FP_OFF( bufptr ), width );
        bufptr += width / 2;
        video_off += columns * 2;
        }

    /* Return the buffer */
    return ( buf );
}
```

Function: *box_put()*

The *box_put()* function restores a rectangular region of the screen. To display a saved area, pass *box_put()* the buffer returned by *box_get()*. The buffer contains the coordinates, characters, and color attributes that enable *box_put()* to restore the box area to its original state.

The buffer created by *box_get()* and passed to *box_put()* is created dynamically. You can restore the same box more than once, but if you no longer need a buffer, you should free the memory it occupies. The demonstration program BOXTEST.C illustrates the use of *_ffree()* to delete dispensable buffers.

```
/* - - - - - - - - - - - - - - - - - - - - - - - - - - - - - - - -

   Function:       box_put()
   Toolbox:        BOX.C
   Demonstrated:   BOXTEST.C MENU.C

   Parameters:
     (input)       buf      Far integer buffer previously created
                            by the function box_get()

   Returned:       (function returns nothing)

   Variables:      row1     Upper left corner of box
                   col1     Upper left corner of box
                   row2     Lower right corner of box
                   col2     Lower right corner of box
                   i        Loop index for each line of the box
                   width    Width of the box
                   height   Height of the box
                   bytes    Total number of bytes in the box
                   video_off Offset of video address for box data
                   workbuf  Index into the buffer

   Description:    Restores screen contents that were saved in a
                   buffer by a previous call to box_get()
   - - - - - - - - - - - - - - - - - - - - - - - - - - - - - - - -
*/

void box_put( unsigned far *buf )
{
    unsigned row1, col1, row2, col2;
    unsigned i, width, height, bytes;
```

(continued)

BOX.C *continued*

```
    unsigned video_off;
    unsigned far *workbuf;

    /* Get the box coordinates */
    workbuf = buf;
    row1 = *workbuf++;
    col1 = *workbuf++;
    row2 = *workbuf++;
    col2 = *workbuf++;

    /* Calculate the dimensions in bytes */
    width = ( col2 - col1 + 1 ) * 2;
    height = row2 - row1 + 1;
    bytes = height * width;

    /* Determine the text mode video segment and number of columns */
    determine_video();

    /* Calculate starting location in video memory */
    video_off = ( columns * ( row1 - 1 ) + ( col1 - 1 )) * 2;

    /* Put each line out to video */
    for ( i = 0; i < height; i++ )
        {
        movedata( FP_SEG( workbuf ), FP_OFF( workbuf ),
                  video_seg, video_off, width );
        workbuf += width / 2;
        video_off += columns * 2;
        }
    }
```

Function: *box_color()*

The *box_color()* function sets all color attributes in a rectangular area of a text mode screen to the current foreground and background colors. The characters in the area are not affected; only their color attributes are changed.

Before you call *box_color()*, use *_settextcolor()* and *_setbkcolor()* to set the current text colors.

```
/* - - - - - - - - - - - - - - - - - - - - - - - - - - - - - - -

   Function:       box_color()
   Toolbox:        BOX.C
   Demonstrated:   BOXTEST.C MENU.C

   Parameters:
     (input)       row1      Upper left corner of box
     (input)       col1      Upper left corner of box
     (input)       row2      Lower right corner of box
     (input)       col2      Lower right corner of box

   Returned:       (function returns nothing)

   Variables:      x         Looping index for each row of box
                   y         Looping index for each column of box
                   fore      Current foreground text color
                   back      Current background text color
                   attr      Attribute byte combining fore and back

   Description:    Sets the foreground and background colors for
                   all characters in a box to the current colors.
                   Characters in the box are unaffected.
   - - - - - - - - - - - - - - - - - - - - - - - - - - - - - - -
*/

void box_color( unsigned row1, unsigned col1, unsigned row2, unsigned col2 )
{
    unsigned x, y;
    unsigned fore;
    unsigned long back;
    unsigned char attr;

    /* Determine the text mode video segment and number of columns */
    determine_video();

    /* Build the attribute byte */
    fore = _gettextcolor();
    back = _getbkcolor();
    attr = (unsigned char)(( fore & 0xF ) ¦
    (((( fore & 0x10 ) >> 1 ) ¦ back ) << 4 ));

    /* Work through the box */
    for ( x = row1 - 1; x < row2; x++ )
        for ( y = col1 - 1; y < col2; y++ )
            *( videoptr + ( columns * x + y ) * 2 + 1 ) = attr;
}
```

Function: *box_charfill()*

The *box_charfill()* function fills a rectangular area of a text mode screen with a given character. One obvious use of this function is to erase a box by filling it with space characters. Less obvious uses include filling the screen with a graphics character to create a background that is shaded, lined, or hatched.

The *box_charfill()* function fills a screen area much more quickly than is possible using *printf()* or similar functions. The demonstration program BOXTEST uses *box_charfill()* to "pop up" a shaded screen filled with graphics character number 176, a semishadow block.

```
/* - - - - - - - - - - - - - - - - - - - - - - - - - - - - - - - - - - - -
   Function:      box_charfill()
   Toolbox:       BOX.C
   Demonstrated:  BOXTEST.C MENUTEST.C

   Parameters:
     (input)      row1      Upper left corner of box
     (input)      col1      Upper left corner of box
     (input)      row2      Lower right corner of box
     (input)      col2      Lower right corner of box
     (input)      c         Character used to fill the box


   Returned:      (function returns nothing)

   Variables:     x         Looping index for each row of box
                  y         Looping index for each column of box

   Description:   Fills a rectangular area of the screen with a
                  character.  Attributes are unaffected.
   - - - - - - - - - - - - - - - - - - - - - - - - - - - - - - - - - - - -
*/

void box_charfill( unsigned row1, unsigned col1, unsigned row2, unsigned col2, char c )
{
    unsigned x, y;

    /* Determine the text mode video segment and number of columns */
    determine_video();
```

(continued)

61

BOX.C *continued*

```
    /* Work through the box */
    for ( x = row1 - 1; x < row2; x++ )
        for ( y = col1 - 1; y < col2; y++ )
            *( videoptr + ( columns * x + y ) * 2 ) = c;
}
```

Function: *box_draw()*

The *box_draw()* function draws border lines around a rectangular area of a text mode screen. The *line_type* parameter controls the type of line-drawing characters used. You can choose either single-line or double-line characters for the border.

The function does not alter color attributes anywhere in the box, nor does it affect characters in the interior of the box.

```
/* - - - - - - - - - - - - - - - - - - - - - - - - - - - - - - - - - - -
    Function:       box_draw()
    Toolbox:        BOX.C
    Demonstrated:   BOXTEST.C MENU.C

    Parameters:
      (input)       row1        Upper left corner of box
      (input)       col1        Upper left corner of box
      (input)       row2        Lower right corner of box
      (input)       col2        Lower right corner of box
      (input)       line_type   Indicates single-line or double-
                                line box border (or none)

    Returned:       (function returns nothing)

    Variables:      x           Keeps track of horizontal position
                    y           Keeps track of vertical position
                    dx          Horizontal motion increment
                    dy          Vertical motion increment
                    c           Character for each part of the border

    Description:    Draws single-line or double-line box border around a box.
                    Does not affect attributes.
    - - - - - - - - - - - - - - - - - - - - - - - - - - - - - - - - - -
*/
```

(continued)

BOX.C *continued*

```
void box_draw( unsigned row1, unsigned col1, unsigned row2, unsigned col2,
               unsigned line_type )
{
    unsigned x, y, dx, dy;
    unsigned c;

    /* Determine the text mode video segment and number of columns */
    determine_video();

    /* Work around the box */
    x = col1;
    y = row1;
    dx = 1;
    dy = 0;
    do
        {

        /* Set the default character for unbordered boxes */
        c = ' ';

        /* Set the single-line drawing character */
        if ( line_type == 1 )
            if ( dx )
                c = 196;
            else
                c = 179;

        /* Set the double-line drawing character */
        else if ( line_type == 2 )
            if ( dx )
                c = 205;
            else
                c = 186;

        /* Change direction at top right corner */
        if ( dx == 1 && x == col2 )
            {
            dx = 0;
            dy = 1;
            if ( line_type == 1 )
                c = 191;
            else if ( line_type == 2 )
                c = 187;
            }
```

(continued)

BOX.C *continued*

```
        /* Change direction at bottom right corner */
        if ( dy == 1 && y == row2 )
            {
            dx = -1;
            dy = 0;
            if ( line_type == 1 )
                c = 217;
            else if ( line_type == 2 )
                c = 188;
            }

        /* Change direction at bottom left corner */
        if ( dx == -1 && x == col1 )
            {
            dx = 0;
            dy = -1;
            if ( line_type == 1 )
                c = 192;
            else if ( line_type == 2 )
                c = 200;
            }

        /* Check for top left corner */
        if ( dy == -1 && y == row1 )
            {
            if ( line_type == 1 )
                c = 218;
            else if ( line_type == 2 )
                c = 201;
            }

        /* Put new character to video */
        *( videoptr + ( columns * ( y - 1 ) + ( x - 1 )) * 2 ) = (char)c;

        /* Move to next position */
        x += dx;
        y += dy;

        }
    while ( dy != -1 || y >= row1 );
}
```

Function: *box_erase()*

The *box_erase()* function erases a rectangular area of a text mode screen. All characters are replaced with spaces, and the color attributes are all set to the current foreground and background colors.

The effect of using this function is similar to that produced by calling *box_charfill()* with a space character for the fill character, followed by a call to *box_color()*. The *box_erase()* function uses *_outtext()* in the QuickC graphics library to fill each row of the box with a string of spaces.

```
/* - - - - - - - - - - - - - - - - - - - - - - - - - - - - - - - - - -
    Function:       box_erase()
    Toolbox:        BOX.C
    Demonstrated:   BOXTEST.C MENU.C

    Parameters:
      (input)       row1        Upper left corner of box
      (input)       col1        Upper left corner of box
      (input)       row2        Lower right corner of box
      (input)       col2        Lower right corner of box

    Returned:       (function returns nothing)

    Variables:      i           Looping index for each row of the box
                    buf         String of spaces for each row

    Description:    Fills a box with spaces.  Uses the current color
                    attributes.
    - - - - - - - - - - - - - - - - - - - - - - - - - - - - - - - - -
*/

void box_erase( unsigned row1, unsigned col1, unsigned row2, unsigned col2 )
{
    unsigned i;
    char buf[81];

    /* Fill the buffer with spaces */
    sprintf( buf, "%*s", col2 - col1 + 1, "" );

    /* Put each line out to video */
    for ( i = row1; i <= row2; i++ )
```

(continued)

BOX.C *continued*

```
        {
        _settextposition( i, col1 );
        _outtext( buf );
        }
    }
}
```

Static Function: *determine_video()*

The *determine_video()* function determines the text mode video segment and fills in several static, global variables with the results. Recall that static variables retain their values for the duration of a program, and global variables are accessible by all functions in a module.

The *determine_video()* function is also declared static, which means that its visibility within a given program is limited to the module in which it's defined. Calls to *determine_video()* can be made only from within the BOX.C module.

Using static variables and a static function in this way, the program can make a single check for the video segment, yet several BOX functions can then use the information as the program progresses.

```
/* - - - - - - - - - - - - - - - - - - - - - - - - - - - - - - - - -
    Function:      determine_video()
    Note:          STATIC FUNCTION AVAILABLE ONLY TO THIS MODULE
    Language:      Microsoft QuickC
    Toolbox:       BOX.C

    Parameters:    (none)

    Returned:      (function returns nothing)

    Variables:     (none)

    Description:   Determines the text mode video segment and the
                   number of character columns currently set.
                   Fills in static variables that are available
                   only to the functions in this module.
    - - - - - - - - - - - - - - - - - - - - - - - - - - - - - - - - -
*/
```

(continued)

BOX.C *continued*

```
static void determine_video( void )
{
    if ( !video_seg )
        {
        /* Determine the text mode video segment */
        switch ( *((char far *)0x449) )
            {
            case 0:
            case 1:
            case 2:
            case 3:
                video_seg = 0xB800;
                videoptr = (char far *)0xB8000000;
                break;
            case 7:
                video_seg = 0xB000;
                videoptr = (char far *)0xB0000000;
                break;
            default:
                printf( "BOX.C: not in text mode\n" );
                exit( 0 );
            }

        /* Determine number of columns for current text mode */
        columns = *( (int far *)0x44A );
    }
}
```

CALENDAR

ROUTINE	DESCRIPTION
date_get()	Gets date from system
date_set()	Sets system date
datestr()	Makes formatted date string
date_to_julian()	Finds Julian day number
julian_to_date()	Finds date from Julian day number
validate()	Verifies a date
day_of_week()	Finds day of the week number
day_of_year()	Finds day of the year number
day_of_century()	Finds day of the century number
days_between_dates()	Finds number of days between dates
weekday_name()	String name for day of week
month_name()	String name for a month number
one_month()	String array for a month

The CALENDAR toolbox module is a collection of functions for date conversions and calculations. These functions make it easy to find the number of days between two dates, to determine the day of the week on which a given date falls, and to make other similar calculations. The function *one_month()* will even create a complete, formatted one-month calendar for display or printing.

At the heart of several of these calculations is a function that returns the Julian day number for a given date. The Julian day number lets you catalogue dates by a single large integer. A useful feature of Julian day numbers is that a simple subtraction yields the number of days between two dates. Leap years and the nonuniform pattern of days in the various months make this calculation difficult when you deal with the usual month, day, and year numbers. The *date_to_julian()* and *julian_to_date()* functions make the necessary conversions for you.

The *validate()* function uses the conversions to and from a date's Julian day number to check the validity of a specified date. A Julian day number calculated for an invalid date will reconvert to a different date from the one originally given.

The calculations are accurate for any date from January 1, 1584 to the indefinite future. The functions return 0 for dates prior to 1584.

The demonstration program, CALTEST.C, asks for your date of birth and then displays a series of calculations based on your birthdate: the corresponding Julian day number, the day of the week on which it fell, and so on. After you press a key to continue, the program uses the *one_month()* function to display monthly calendars for the month in which your birthday occurred, the current month, and the month midway between the two.

Demonstration Program: CALTEST.C

```
/* -------------------------------------------------------------
   Name:           CALTEST.C
   Type:           Demonstration program
   Language:       Microsoft QuickC version 2
   Video:          (no special video requirements)

   Program list:   CALTEST.C
                   CALENDAR.C

   Variables:      m1       Month number for first date
                   d1       Day number for first date
                   y1       Year number for first date
                   m2       Month number for second date
                   d2       Day number for second date
                   y2       Year number for second date
                   m3       Month number for third date
                   d3       Day number for third date
                   y3       Year number for third date
                   j1       Julian day number for first date
                   j2       Julian day number for second date
                   j3       Julian day number for third date
                   i        Looping index for each day of month
                   n        Number of days in month
                   wd       Day of the week number
                   month1   Calendar page for first month
                   month2   Calendar page for second month
                   month3   Calendar page for third month
```

(continued)

CALTEST.C *continued*

```
    Usage:          (no command line parameters)

  Description:    Demonstrates the CALENDAR toolbox functions
  ----------------------------------------------------------------
*/

#include <stdio.h>
#include <stdlib.h>
#include <conio.h>
#include "calendar.h"

main()
{
    char date[11];
    int m1, d1, y1;
    int m2, d2, y2;
    int m3, d3, y3;
    long j1, j2, j3;
    int i, wd;
    char month1[MON_ROW][MON_COL];
    char month2[MON_ROW][MON_COL];
    char month3[MON_ROW][MON_COL];

    /* Ask user for date of birth */
    printf( "\n\nEnter the date of your birth\n\n" );
    printf( "Month (1 to 12)..? " );
    scanf( "%2d", &m1 );
    printf( "Day (1 to 31)....? " );
    scanf( "%2d", &d1 );
    printf( "Year (ex. 1950)..? " );
    scanf( "%4d", &y1 );

    /* Convert the date to a formatted string */
    datestr( m1, d1, y1, date );
    printf( "\nYour birthday:\t\t%s\n", date );

    /* Verify that date matches reality */
    if ( !validate( m1, d1, y1 ) )
        {
        printf( "Invalid date! (Run the program again)\n" );
        exit( 0 );
        }
```

(continued)

```
/* Find astronomical Julian day number for birth date */
j1 = date_to_julian( m1, d1, y1 );
printf( "Julian day number:\t%ld\n", j1 );

/* Find day of the week */
wd = day_of_week( m1, d1, y1 );

/* Display information about birth date */
printf( "Weekday name:   \t%s\n", weekday_name( wd ));
printf( "Month name:     \t%s\n", month_name( m1 ));
printf( "Day of the year:\t%d\n", day_of_year( m1, d1, y1 ));
printf( "Day of century: \t%ld\n", day_of_century( m1, d1, y1 ));

/* Find Julian day number for 10,000 days after birth date */
j2 = j1 + 10000;

/* Convert to the date */
julian_to_date( j2, &m2, &d2, &y2 );

/* Make a formatted string from the date numbers */
datestr( m2, d2, y2, date );

/* Display the new date */
printf( "Plus 10,000 days\t%s\n", date );

/* Wait for user */
printf( "\n\nPress any key to continue... " );
getch();

/* Get today's date from the system clock */
date_get( &m2, &d2, &y2 );

/* Find the Julian day number for today */
j2 = date_to_julian( m2, d2, y2 );

/* Calculate the Julian day number for "half your life" ago */
j3 = ( j1 + j2 ) / 2;

/* Find the half-lifetime date for the user */
julian_to_date( j3, &m3, &d3, &y3 );

/* Create calendar page for month of birth */
one_month( m1, y1, month1 );
```

(continued)

CALTEST.C *continued*

```
    /* Create calendar page for current month */
    one_month( m2, y2, month2 );

    /* Create calendar page for month equidistant from the other two */
    one_month( m3, y3, month3 );

    /* Display the three one-month calendars */
    printf( "\n\n\nThe month you were born, " );
    printf( "the current month, and half your life ago...\n\n" );
    for ( i = 0; i < MON_ROW; i++ )
        printf( "%s\t%s\t%s\n", month1[i], month2[i], month3[i] );

    /* Display today's date */
    datestr( m2, d2, y2, date );
    printf( "\nToday's date\t\t%s\n", date );

    /* Give user the ugly news */
    printf( "Your age in days:\t%ld\n\n\n",
        days_between_dates( m1, d1, y1, m2, d2, y2 ));
}
```

Include File: CALENDAR.H

```
/* -------------------------------------------------------------------
    Name:           CALENDAR.H
    Type:           Include
    Language:       Microsoft QuickC version 2
    Demonstrated:   CALENDAR.C   CALTEST.C
    Description:    Prototypes and definitions for CALENDAR.C
    -------------------------------------------------------------------
*/

#ifndef CALENDAR_DEFINED

#define MON_ROW 8
#define MON_COL 23

void date_get( int *, int *, int * );
int date_set( int, int, int );
void datestr( int, int, int, char * );
```

(continued)

```
long date_to_julian( int, int, int );
void julian_to_date( long, int *, int *, int * );
int validate( int, int, int );
int day_of_week( int, int, int );
int day_of_year( int, int, int );
long day_of_century( int, int, int );
long days_between_dates( int, int, int, int, int, int );
char *weekday_name( int );
char *month_name( int );
void one_month( int, int, char [MON_ROW][MON_COL] );

#define CALENDAR_DEFINED
#endif
```

Toolbox Module: CALENDAR.C

```
/* -------------------------------------------------------------------

    Name:          CALENDAR.C
    Type:          Toolbox module
    Language:      Microsoft QuickC version 2
    Demonstrated:  CALTEST.C
    Video:         (no special video requirements)
    Description:   Implements date-manipulation functions
    -------------------------------------------------------------------
*/

#include <stdio.h>
#include <time.h>
#include <dos.h>
#include <string.h>
#include "calendar.h"

char *day_name[7] = { "Sunday", "Monday", "Tuesday", "Wednesday",
                      "Thursday", "Friday", "Saturday" };

char *mon_name[12] = { "January", "February", "March", "April",
                       "May", "June", "July", "August", "September",
                       "October", "November", "December" };
```

Function: *date_get()*

The *date_get()* function obtains the current date from the system. This function uses in-line assembly instructions to call DOS function 0x2A. An alternative way to get the system date is to call *_dos_getdate()*, which returns a structure of type *dosdate_t*. Although both methods are satisfactory, *date_get()* is more straightforward and perhaps executes a little faster.

```
/* - - - - - - - - - - - - - - - - - - - - - - - - - - - - - -

   Function:      date_get()
   Toolbox:       CALENDAR.C
   Demonstrated:  CALTEST.C

   Parameters:
     (output)      month      Month number (1 through 12)
     (output)      day        Day number (1 through 31)
     (output)      year       Year number (such as 1993)

   Returned:       (function returns nothing)

   Variables:      md         Local variable for month and day
                   ye         Local variable for year

   Description:   Gets the current date from the system clock
   - - - - - - - - - - - - - - - - - - - - - - - - - - - - - -
*/

void date_get( int *month, int *day, int *year )
{
    int md, ye;

    _asm
        {
        mov    ah, 2Ah
        int    21h
        mov    md, dx
        mov    ye, cx
        }

    *month = md >> 8;
    *day = md & 0xFF;
    *year = ye;
}
```

Function: *date_set()*

The *date_set()* function sets the system clock to the given date. This function uses in-line assembly instructions to call DOS function 0x2B. The DOS service returns 0 if it sets the date successfully, and *date_set()* returns this value to the calling function.

An alternative way to set the system date is to pass a filled-in *dos_date_t* structure to the QuickC run-time function *_dos_setdate()*. Although both methods are satisfactory, *date_set()* is more straightforward and perhaps executes a little faster.

```
/* - - - - - - - - - - - - - - - - - - - - - - - - - - - - - - - -
    Function:       date_set()
    Toolbox:        CALENDAR.C
    Demonstrated:   CALTEST.C

    Parameters:
      (input)       month    Month number (1 through 12)
      (input)       day      Day number (1 through 31)
      (input)       year     Year number (such as 1993)

    Returned:       0 if successful, nonzero if not successful

    Variables:      md       Local variable for month and day
                    result   Value returned by DOS function

    Description:    Sets the system clock to a given date
    - - - - - - - - - - - - - - - - - - - - - - - - - - - - - - - -
*/

int date_set( int month, int day, int year )
{
    int md, result;

    md = ( month << 8 ) + day;

    _asm
        {
        mov    ah, 2Bh
        mov    dx, md
        mov    cx, year
```

CALENDAR.C *continued*

```
        int     21h
        mov     result, ax
        }


    return ( result & 0xFF );
}
```

Function: *datestr()*

The *datestr()* function formats a date into a string suitable for display or printing. The function uses a format identical to that returned by the QuickC function _*strdate()*. The advantage *datestr()* affords is that it formats any date you supply, whereas _*strdate()* returns only the current system date.

```
/* - - - - - - - - - - - - - - - - - - - - - - - - - - - - - - - - -

    Function:       datestr()
    Toolbox:        CALENDAR.C
    Demonstrated:   CALTEST.C

    Parameters:
      (input)       month     Month number (1 through 12)
      (input)       day       Day number (1 through 31)
      (input)       year      Year number (such as 1993)
      (output)      str       String for returned date


    Returned:       (function returns nothing)


    Variables:      (none)


    Description:    Creates a formatted string for a given date
    - - - - - - - - - - - - - - - - - - - - - - - - - - - - - - - - -
*/

void datestr( int month, int day, int year, char *str )
{
    if ( year >= 1900 && year <= 1999 )
        year -= 1900;

    if ( year < 100 )
        sprintf( str, "%02u/%02u/%02u", month, day, year );
    else
        sprintf( str, "%02u/%02u/%04u", month, day, year );
}
```

Function: *date_to_julian()*

The *date_to_julian()* function returns the Julian day number for any date from January 1, 1584, to the indefinite future. The function returns 0 for dates that fall prior to January 1, 1584.

The Julian day number is an astronomical convention that arose from the need to simplify calculations. The Julian day number represents the number of days since January 1, 4713 B.C. Converting dates to Julian day numbers simplifies many calendar calculations.

```
/* - - - - - - - - - - - - - - - - - - - - - - - - - - - -
   Function:       date_to_julian()
   Toolbox:        CALENDAR.C
   Demonstrated:   CALTEST.C

   Parameters:
     (input)       month      Month number (1 through 12)
     (input)       day        Day number (1 through 31)
     (input)       year       Year number (such as 1993)

   Returned:       Astronomical Julian day number

   Variables:      ta         Term 1 of calculations
                   tb         Term 2 of calculations
                   tc         Term 3 of calculations

   Description:    Calculates the astronomical Julian day number
                   for a given date
   - - - - - - - - - - - - - - - - - - - - - - - - - - -
*/

long date_to_julian( int month, int day, int year )
{
    long ta, tb, tc;

    if ( year < 1584 )
        return (0L);

    if ( month > 2 )
        month -= 3;
```

(continued)

CALENDAR.C *continued*

```
    else
        {
        month += 9;
        year--;
        }

    ta = 146097 * ( year / 100 ) / 4;
    tb = 1461L * ( year % 100 ) / 4;
    tc = ( 153L * month + 2 ) / 5 + day + 1721119;

    return ( ta + tb + tc );
}
```

Function: *julian_to_date()*

The *julian_to_date()* function converts a Julian day number to month, day, and year numbers for the indicated date. The function returns 0 for all dates that fall prior to January 1, 1584.

```
/* - - - - - - - - - - - - - - - - - - - - - - - - - - - - - - - -
    Function:       julian_to_date()
    Toolbox:        CALENDAR.C
    Demonstrated:   CALTEST.C

    Parameters:
      (input)       julian    Julian day number
      (output)      month     Month number (1 through 12)
      (output)      day       Day number (1 through 31)
      (output)      year      Year number (such as 1993)

    Returned:       (function returns nothing)

    Variables:      x         Intermediate calculation results
                    y         Intermediate calculation results
                    d         Intermediate calculation results
                    m         Intermediate calculation results

    Description:    Calculates month, day, and year numbers for a
                    given Julian day number
    - - - - - - - - - - - - - - - - - - - - - - - - - - - - - - - -
```

(continued)

```
*/

void julian_to_date( long julian, int *month, int *day, int *year )
{
    long x, y, d, m;

    if ( julian < 2299604 )
        {
        *month = 0;
        *day = 0;
        *year = 0;
        }
    else
        {
        x = 4 * julian - 6884477;
        y = ( x / 146097 ) * 100;
        d = ( x % 146097 ) / 4;
        x = 4 * d + 3;
        y = ( x / 1461 ) + y;
        d = ( x % 1461 ) / 4;
        d++;
        x = 5 * d - 3;
        m = x / 153;
        m++;
        d = ( x % 153 ) / 5;
        d++;
        if ( m < 11 )
            *month = (int)( m + 2 );
        else
            *month = (int)( m - 10 );
        *day = (int)d;
        *year = (int)( y + m / 11 );
        }
}
```

Function: *validate()*

The *validate()* function checks a date to see whether it did or will exist. The function finds the Julian day number for the date and then uses that number to recalculate the date. If the original date is invalid, the calculated date won't match. The function returns 1 if the date is valid and 0 if the date is invalid. The function returns 0 for all dates that fall before January 1, 1584.

For example, the statement *validate(2, 29, 2002);* returns 0 because February 29, 2002, is an invalid date. However, the statement *validate(2, 29, 1996);* returns 1 because 1996 is a leap year.

```
/* - - - - - - - - - - - - - - - - - - - - - - - - - - - - - - - -
    Function:       validate()
    Toolbox:        CALENDAR.C
    Demonstrated:   CALTEST.C

    Parameters:
      (input)       month     Month number (1 through 12)
      (input)       day       Day number (1 through 31)
      (input)       year      Year number (such as 1993)

    Returned:       1 if given date is valid
                    0 if given date is nonexistent

    Variables:      m2        Month from Julian day number for date
                    d2        Day from Julian day number for date
                    y2        Year from Julian day number for date
                    julian    Julian day number calculated for date

    Description:    Verifies that a given date represents a date
                    that actually existed or will exist
    - - - - - - - - - - - - - - - - - - - - - - - - - - - - - - - -
*/

int validate( int month, int day, int year )
{
    int m2, d2, y2;
    long julian;

    julian = date_to_julian( month, day, year );
    julian_to_date( julian, &m2, &d2, &y2 );
    return (( month == m2 ) && ( day == d2 ) &&
            ( year == y2 ) && ( julian ));
}
```

Function: *day_of_week()*

The *day_of_week()* function returns a number that represents the day of the week on which a given date falls. The returned number is in the range 0 through 6, where 0 corresponds to Sunday, 1 corresponds to Monday, and so on. The function returns 0 for dates that fall before January 1, 1584.

You can pass this weekday number to *weekday()* to get a string containing the name of the day of the week.

```
/* - - - - - - - - - - - - - - - - - - - - - - - - - - - - - - - - - -
   Function:       day_of_week()
   Toolbox:        CALENDAR.C
   Demonstrated:   CALTEST.C

   Parameters:
     (input)       month     Month number (1 through 12)
     (input)       day       Day number (1 through 31)
     (input)       year      Year number (such as 1993)

   Returned:       Number for the day of the week
                   0 = Sunday, 1 = Monday ... 6 = Saturday
                   (Returns -1 if an error occurs)

   Variables:      julian    Julian day number for date

   Description:    Calculates the day of the week for a given date
   - - - - - - - - - - - - - - - - - - - - - - - - - - - - - - - - - -
*/

int day_of_week( int month, int day, int year )
{
    long julian;

    julian = date_to_julian( month, day, year );
    if ( julian )
        return ((int)( ++julian % 7 ));
    else
        return ( -1 );
}
```

Function: *day_of_year()*

The *day_of_year()* function returns the day of the year for a given date. The returned number is an integer in the range 1 through 366. The function returns 0 for dates that fall prior to January 1, 1584.

```
/* - - - - - - - - - - - - - - - - - - - - - - - - - - - - - - - -
    Function:       day_of_year()
    Toolbox:        CALENDAR.C
    Demonstrated:   CALTEST.C

    Parameters:
      (input)       month     Month number (1 through 12)
      (input)       day       Day number (1 through 31)
      (input)       year      Year number (such as 1993)

    Returned:       Number for the day of the year, 1 through 366
                    (Returns 0 if an error occurs)

    Variables:      j1        Julian day number for 12/31 of previous year
                    j2        Julian day number calculated for date

    Description:    Calculates the day of the year for a given date
    - - - - - - - - - - - - - - - - - - - - - - - - - - - - - - - -
*/

int day_of_year( int month, int day, int year )
{
    long j1, j2;

    if (( j2 = date_to_julian( month, day, year )) == 0 )
        return ( 0 );

    if (( j1 = date_to_julian( 12, 31, --year )) == 0 )
        return ((int)( j2 - 2299603 ));
    else
        return ((int)( j2 - j1 ));
}
```

Function: *day_of_century()*

The *day_of_century()* function returns the day of the century for a given date. The function returns a long integer in the range 1 through approximately 36,525. It returns 0 for dates that fall before January 1, 1584.

```
/* - - - - - - - - - - - - - - - - - - - - - - - - - - - - - - - - - - -

   Function:      day_of_century()
   Toolbox:       CALENDAR.C
   Demonstrated:  CALTEST.C

   Parameters:
     (input)      month     Month number (1 through 12)
     (input)      day       Day number (1 through 31)
     (input)      year      Year number (such as 1993)

   Returned:      Number for the day of the century
                  (Returns 0 if an error occurs)

   Variables:     j1        Julian day number for last day of the
                            previous century
                  j2        Julian day number calculated for date

   Description:   Calculates the day of the century for a date
   - - - - - - - - - - - - - - - - - - - - - - - - - - - - - - - - - -
*/

long day_of_century( int month, int day, int year )
{
    long j1, j2;

    if (( j2 = date_to_julian( month, day, year )) == 0 )
        return ( 0 );

    year /= 100;
    year *= 100;
    year--;

    if (( j1 = date_to_julian( 12, 31, year )) == 0 )
        return ( j2 - 2268923 );
    else
        return ( j2 - j1 );
}
```

Function: *days_between_dates()*

The *days_between_dates()* function returns the number of days between two specified dates. If either date falls before January 1, 1584, the function returns 0.

The *days_between_dates()* function simply calls *date_to_julian()* to calculate the Julian day numbers for the two dates and then returns the difference between the two numbers.

```
/* - - - - - - - - - - - - - - - - - - - - - - - - - - - - - -
   Function:        days_between_dates()
   Toolbox:         CALENDAR.C
   Demonstrated:    CALTEST.C

   Parameters:
     (input)        month1    Month number (1 through 12) for first date
     (input)        day1      Day number (1 through 31) for first date
     (input)        year1     Year number (such as 1993) for first date
     (input)        month2    Month number for second date
     (input)        day2      Day number for second date
     (input)        year2     Year number for second date

   Returned:        Number of days between two dates
                    (Returns 0 if an error occurs)

   Variables:       j1        Julian day number for first date
                    j2        Julian day number for second date

   Description:     Calculates number of days between two dates
   - - - - - - - - - - - - - - - - - - - - - - - - - - - - - -
*/

long days_between_dates( int month1, int day1, int year1,
                         int month2, int day2, int year2 )
{
    long j1, j2;

    j1 = date_to_julian( month1, day1, year1 );
    j2 = date_to_julian( month2, day2, year2 );

    if ( j1 == 0 || j2 == 0 )
        return ( 0L );
    else
        return ( j2 - j1 );
}
```

Function: *weekday_name()*

The *weekday_name()* function returns a string that contains the name of the day of the week. Call *weekday_name()* with a value in the range 0 through 6, where 0 represents Sunday, 1 represents Monday, and so on. The function returns a NULL pointer for any value outside the range 0 through 6.

Recall that the *day_of_week()* function returns a value for a given date that you can pass to *weekday_name()*.

```
/* - - - - - - - - - - - - - - - - - - - - - - - - - - - - - - -

   Function:       weekday_name()
   Toolbox:        CALENDAR.C
   Demonstrated:   CALTEST.C

   Parameters:
     (input)       weekday   Day of week number (0 through 6)

   Returned:       String containing name of the day of the week
                   (Returns NULL if an error occurs)

   Variables:      (none)

   Description:    Returns the name of the day of the week that
                   corresponds to a given weekday number
   - - - - - - - - - - - - - - - - - - - - - - - - - - - - - - -
*/

char *weekday_name( int weekday )
{
    if ( weekday >= 0 && weekday <= 6 )
        return ( day_name[weekday] );
    else
        return ( NULL );
}
```

Function: *month_name()*

The *month_name()* function returns a pointer to a string that contains the name of a month. Call *month_name()* with a number in the range 1 through 12. The function returns a NULL pointer for any value outside the range 1 through 12.

```
/* - - - - - - - - - - - - - - - - - - - - - - - - - - - - - - - - -
    Function:       month_name()
    Toolbox:        CALENDAR.C
    Demonstrated:   CALTEST.C

    Parameters:
     (input)        month     Month number (1 through 12)

    Returned:       Pointer to a string containing name of the month
                    (Returns NULL if an error occurs)

    Variables:      (none)

    Description:    Provides the name of the month that
                    corresponds to a given month number
    - - - - - - - - - - - - - - - - - - - - - - - - - - - - - - - -
*/

char *month_name( int month )
{
    if ( month >= 1 && month <= 12 )
        return ( mon_name[--month] );
    else
        return (NULL);
}
```

Function: *one_month()*

The *one_month()* function fills a character array with a complete, formatted one-month calendar page suitable for display or printing. Before you call this function, declare a two-dimensional character array using the constants MON_ROW and MON_COL, which are declared in the CALENDAR.H header file. This array provides space for the strings that *one_month()* supplies. The CALTEST program demonstrates the output of *one_month()*.

```
/* - - - - - - - - - - - - - - - - - - - - - - - - - - - - - - - -
    Function:       one_month()
    Toolbox:        CALENDAR.C
    Demonstrated:   CALTEST.C

    Parameters:
      (input)       month       Month number (1 through 12)
      (input)       year        Year number (such as 1993)
      (output)      strary      String array that returns a one-month
                                calendar layout

    Returned:       (function returns nothing)

    Variables:      j1          Julian day number for start of month
                    j2          Julian day number for start of next month
                    w1          Working string space
                    w2          Working string space
                    i           Looping index
                    j           Looping index
                    k           Index to blank part of last line
                    n           Number of days in the month
                    wday        Day of week number
                    ndx         Index to each line of calendar
                    len0        String length manipulations
                    len1        String length manipulations
                    len2        String length manipulations

    Description:    Fills a string array with a one-month
                    calendar suitable for display or printing
    - - - - - - - - - - - - - - - - - - - - - - - - - - - - - - - -
*/

void one_month( int month, int year, char strary[MON_ROW][MON_COL] )
{
    long j1, j2;
    char w1[MON_COL];
    int i, j, k, n, wday, ndx;
    int len0, len1, len2;
```

(continued)

CALENDAR.C *continued*

```
/* Blank the calendar lines */
for( i = 0; i < MON_ROW; i++ )
    for( j = 0; j < MON_COL; j++ )
        strary[i][j] = ' ';

/* Zero the length of each line */
for( i = 0; i < MON_ROW; i++ )
    strary[i][MON_COL-1] = '\0';

/* Center the month name in first line */
sprintf( w1, "%s %4d", month_name( month ), year );
len0 = strlen( w1 );
len1 = (MON_COL >> 1) - len0 / 2;
len2 = (MON_COL - 1) - len0 - len1;
sprintf( strary[0], "%*s%s%*s", len2, "", w1, len1, "" );

/* Second line is names of days of the week */
strcpy( strary[1], " Su Mo Tu We Th Fr Sa " );

/* Find day of week for first day of month */
wday = day_of_week( month, 1, year );

/* Find number of days in the month */
j1 = date_to_julian( month, 1, year );
if ( ++month > 12 )
    {
    month = 1;
    year++;
    }
j2 = date_to_julian( month, 1, year );
n = (int)( j2 - j1 );

/* Fill in day numbers for all of the month */
for ( ndx = 2, i = 1; i <= n; i++ )
    {
    j = wday * 3;
    sprintf( &strary[ndx][j], " %2d ", i);

    /* Increment day of week */
    if ( wday < 6 )
        ++wday;
```

(continued)

CALENDAR.C *continued*

```
        /* But go back from Saturday to Sunday */
        else
            {
            wday = 0;
            ndx++;
            }

        /* Fill in spaces after last day of month */
        if ( i == n )
            for ( k = wday * 3; k < MON_COL - 2; k++ )
                strary[ndx][k] = ' ';
        }
}
```

CLOCK

FUNCTION	DESCRIPTION
time_get()	Returns the system time
time_set()	Sets the system clock
delay()	Pauses for *n* seconds
timestr()	Builds formatted time string
clock_face_make()	Draws analog clock face
clock_face_update()	Redraws hands on clock face

The CLOCK toolbox module provides functions for handling time-related calculations. With these functions you can get and set the system clock; delay execution within a program; format hours, minutes, and seconds for display or printing; and create an analog clock face of any shape or size.

The demonstration program, CLOCTEST.C, temporarily sets the system time to a different hour, minute, and second, reads the new time, and resets the original time. The results of these function calls are then displayed for your review.

The program next demonstrates several time delays of increasing intervals. At the end of each time delay, CLOCTEST displays a message that marks the expiration of the delay.

During the last part of the demonstration, CLOCTEST draws three different-size analog clock faces. The time on each is updated once per second. This part of the demonstration requires a graphics adapter that provides at least the resolution of a CGA. The program uses a higher resolution mode if either an EGA or a VGA is available. Press any key to continue to step through the different clock faces. The screen on the facing page shows the largest of the three clock faces.

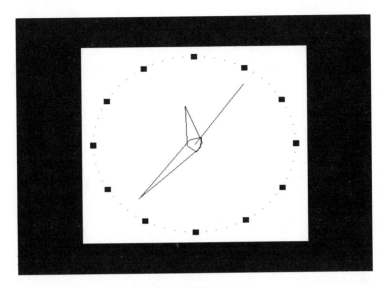

Demonstration Program: CLOCTEST.C

```
/* -----------------------------------------------------------------
    Name:         CLOCTEST.C
    Type:         Demonstration program
    Language:     Microsoft QuickC version 2
    Video:        Requires VGA, EGA, or CGA compatibility

    Program list: CLOCTEST.C
                  CLOCK.C
                  GRAPHICS.LIB

    Variables:    time       String for formatted current time
                  i          Looping index for three clock faces
                  h          Hour from the system clock
                  m          Minute from the system clock
                  s          Second from the system clock
                  hold       Last hour
                  mold       Last minute
                  sold       Last second
                  stop_flag       Signal, stop updating clock face
                  seconds         Amount of delay
                  videoconfig     Video parameters
```

(continued)

CLOCTEST.C *continued*

```
    Usage:          (no command line parameters)

    Description:    Demonstrates the CLOCK toolbox functions
    ----------------------------------------------------------------
*/

#include <stdio.h>
#include <graph.h>
#include <conio.h>
#include <stdlib.h>
#include "clock.h"

main()
{
    char time[9];
    int i;
    int h, m, s;
    int hold, mold, sold;
    int stop_flag = 0;
    double seconds;
    struct videoconfig vc;

    /* Title */
    _clearscreen( _GCLEARSCREEN );
    printf( "CLOCTEST\n\n" );

    /* Display current time using the timestr() formatting */
    time_get( &h, &m, &s );
    timestr( h, m, s, time );
    printf( "Time now... %s\n", time );

    /* Reset the system clock to different time */
    time_set( h / 2, m / 2, s / 2 );

    /* Get the new time from the system */
    time_get( &hold, &mold, &sold );

    /* Quickly reset the original time */
    time_set( h, m, s );

    /* Display the different time that was temporarily set */
    timestr( hold, mold, sold, time );
    printf( "Time set... %s\n", time );
```

(continued)

```
    /* Let user know that the clock was reset to original time */
    printf( "(original time reset)\n" );

    /* Delay several times, increasing the ticks each time */
    for ( seconds = 0.1; seconds <= 8.1; seconds *= 3.0 )
        {
        printf( "delay( %g )\n", seconds );
        delay( seconds );
        }

    /* Wait for user before continuing */
    printf( "\n\nPress any key to continue..." );
    getch();

    /* Set high resolution VGA, EGA, or CGA mode if possible */
    if ( !_setvideomode( _VRES16COLOR ))
        if ( !_setvideomode( _HRES16COLOR ))
            if ( !_setvideomode( _HRESBW ))
                {
                printf( "Failed to set VGA, EGA, or CGA graphics mode\n" );
                exit( 0 );
                }

    /* Display each of three clock faces */
    for ( i = 0; i < 3; i++ )
        {

        /* Clear the stop flag */
        stop_flag = 0;

        /* Prepare to display clock face */
        _setbkcolor( _BLUE );
        _clearscreen( _GCLEARSCREEN );
        _getvideoconfig( &vc );

        /* Display one of the three clock faces */
        switch ( i )
            {
            case 0:
                clock_face_make( vc.numxpixels * 2 / 7, vc.numypixels / 4,
                        vc.numxpixels * 5 / 7, vc.numypixels * 3 / 4 );
                break;
```

(continued)

```
            case 1:
                clock_face_make( vc.numxpixels * 2  / 11,
                                 vc.numypixels * 2 / 17,
                                 vc.numxpixels * 9 / 11,
                                 vc.numypixels * 15 / 17 );
                break;
            default:
                clock_face_make( vc.numxpixels * 4 / 11,
                                 vc.numypixels * 7 / 17,
                                 vc.numxpixels * 7 / 11,
                                 vc.numypixels * 10 / 17 );
                break;
            }

        /* Display clock faces until any key is pressed */
        while ( !stop_flag )
            {

            /* Check for a keypress */
            if ( kbhit() )
                {
                getch();
                stop_flag = 1;
                }

            /* Get current system time */
            time_get( &h, &m, &s );

            /* Redraw the clock faces only once per second */
            if ( s != sold )
                {
                hold = h;
                mold = m;
                sold = s;
                clock_face_update( h, m, s );
                }
            }
        }

    /* Restore the default video mode */
    _setvideomode( _DEFAULTMODE );
}
```

(continued)

Include File: CLOCK.H

```
/* ------------------------------------------------------------
    Name:           CLOCK.H
    Type:           Include
    Language:       Microsoft QuickC version 2
    Demonstrated:   CLOCTEST.C  CLOCK.C
    Description:    Prototypes and definitions for CLOCK.C
   ------------------------------------------------------------
*/

#ifndef CLOCK_DEFINED

void time_get( int *, int *, int * );
void time_set( int, int, int );
void delay( double );
void timestr( int, int, int, char * );
void clock_face_make( int, int, int, int );
void clock_face_update( int, int, int );

#define CLOCK_DEFINED
#endif
```

Toolbox Module: CLOCK.C

```
/* ------------------------------------------------------------
    Name:           CLOCK.C
    Type:           Toolbox module
    Language:       Microsoft QuickC version 2
    Demonstrated:   CLOCTEST.C MOUSTEST.C
    Video:          Graphics card required (CGA or better)
   ------------------------------------------------------------
*/

#include <stdio.h>
#include <time.h>
#include <dos.h>
#include <bios.h>
#include <graph.h>
#include <math.h>
#include "clock.h"
```

(continued)

CLOCK.C *continued*

```
/* Change the clock colors here if desired */
#define CLOCK_FGD_COLOR 0x00
#define CLOCK_BGD_COLOR 0xFF

/* Keeps track of clock face parameters */
int old_hour = 0;
int old_minute = 0;
int old_second = 0;
int x, y, width, height;
```

Function: *time_get()*

The *time_get()* function returns the system time. For speed and efficiency, the function uses in-line assembly code to call DOS service 2CH, which obtains the system time.

The hour and minute values are returned by the DOS Get Time function in the byte registers CH and CL. Subsequent calculations are necessary to convert each of these 8-bit values to the 16-bit values returned by the function. A similar manipulation converts the seconds value from register DH.

```
/* - - - - - - - - - - - - - - - - - - - - - - - - - - - - - - - - - -
    Function:       time_get()
    Toolbox:        CLOCK.C
    Demonstrated:   CLOCTEST.C

    Parameters:
      (output)      hour      Pointer to integer hour variable
      (output)      minute    Pointer to integer minute variable
      (output)      second    Pointer to integer second variable

    Returned:       (function returns nothing)

    Variables:      hm        Local integer for hour and minute
                    se        Local integer for second

    Description:    Gets the current time from the system clock
    - - - - - - - - - - - - - - - - - - - - - - - - - - - - - - - - - -
*/

void time_get( int * hour, int * minute, int * second )
{
```

(continued)

CLOCK.C *continued*

```
    int hm, se;

    /* Use DOS function 2CH to get the system time */
    _asm
        {
        mov    ah, 2Ch
        int    21h
        mov    hm, cx
        mov    se, dx
        }

    /* Pass time values to the referenced variables */
    *hour = hm >> 8;
    *minute = hm & 0xFF;
    *second = se >> 8;
}
```

Function: *time_set()*

The *time_set()* function sets the system clock to a given hour, minute, and second. For speed and efficiency, the function sets the time using DOS service 2DH.

```
/* - - - - - - - - - - - - - - - - - - - - - - - - - - - - - - - -
    Function:      time_set()
    Toolbox:       CLOCK.C
    Demonstrated:  CLOCTEST.C

    Parameters:
      (input)      hour      Integer hour
      (input)      minute    Integer minute
      (input)      second    Integer second

    Returned:      (function returns nothing)

    Variables:     hm        Local integer for hour and minute
                   se        Local integer for second

    Description:   Sets the system clock to the given time
    - - - - - - - - - - - - - - - - - - - - - - - - - - - - - - - -
*/
```

(continued)

CLOCK.C *continued*

```
void time_set( int hour, int minute, int second )
{
    int hm, se;

    hm = ( hour << 8 ) + minute;
    se = second << 8;

    /* Use DOS function 2DH to set the system clock */
    _asm
        {
        mov    ah, 2Dh
        mov    cx, hm
        mov    dx, se
        int    21h
        }
}
```

Function: *delay()*

The *delay()* function delays execution of a program for the indicated number of seconds.

The *seconds* parameter is a double-precision floating-point number. Note, however, that the accuracy of the delay is limited by the resolution of the system clock. Typically, the clock resolution is set to the rate of the system clock interrupt, which is approximately 18.2 ticks per second, or roughly one tick every 0.055 second. If you try to delay for an interval less than 0.055 second, the calling program still delays for a full clock tick.

```
/* - - - - - - - - - - - - - - - - - - - - - - - - - - - - - - - - - -
    Function:      delay()
    Toolbox:       CLOCK.C
    Demonstrated:  CLOCTEST.C

    Parameters:
     (input)       seconds

    Returned:      (function returns nothing)

    Variables:     say_when  Time at end of the delay
```

(continued)

CLOCK.C *continued*

```
    Description:    Delays the program for a given number of
                    seconds.  (Resolution is limited to that of
                    the system clock, or about 0.055 second.)
    - - - - - - - - - - - - - - - - - - - - - - - - - - - - - - -
*/

void delay( double seconds )
{
    clock_t say_when;

    say_when = clock() + seconds * CLK_TCK;
    while ( clock() < say_when )
        {;}
}
```

Function: *timestr()*

The *timestr()* function builds a string with hour, minute, and second values in the standard format "HH:MM:SS". Be sure to pass the function a string with sufficient space for all eight output characters plus the terminating '0' character.

```
/* - - - - - - - - - - - - - - - - - - - - - - - - - - - - - - -
    Function:       timestr()
    Toolbox:        CLOCK.C
    Demonstrated:   CLOCTEST.C

    Parameters:
        (input)     hour      Integer hour
        (input)     minute    Integer minute
        (input)     second    Integer second
        (output)    str       String address for formatted time
                              (at least 9 bytes long)


    Returned:       (function returns nothing)


    Variables:      (none)


    Description:    Formats hour, minute, and second values into
                    a string of the form "HH:MM:SS"
    - - - - - - - - - - - - - - - - - - - - - - - - - - - - - - -
*/
```

(continued)

CLOCK.C *continued*

```
void timestr( int hour, int minute, int second, char *str )
{
    /* Format the time into the character buffer */
    sprintf( str, "%02u:%02u:%02u", hour, minute, second );
}
```

Function: *clock_face_make()*

The *clock_face_make()* function creates an analog clock face in any rectangular area of a graphics mode screen. This function assumes that you have a graphics adapter available and that you have set a graphics mode. The *clock_face_make()* function calls several functions from the QuickC graphics library.

You can alter the background and foreground colors for the clock face by changing the values of the constants CLOCK_FGD_COLOR and CLOCK_BGD_COLOR, which are defined at the beginning of CLOCK.C. These constants are initially defined for drawing black hands (foreground) in a solid white rectangle (background). To use other colors, change these palette number constants.

Call this function once to create a clock face. To update the clock face, call *clock_face_update()*, which redraws the hands.

```
/* - - - - - - - - - - - - - - - - - - - - - - - - - - - - - - - - -
    Function:        clock_face_make()
    Toolbox:         CLOCK.C
    Demonstrated:    CLOCTEST.C

    Parameters:
    (input)      x1          Upper left x-coordinate of clock face
    (input)      y1          Upper left y-coordinate of clock face
    (input)      x2          Lower right x-coordinate of clock face
    (input)      y2          Lower right y-coordinate of clock face

    Returned:        (function returns nothing)
```

(continued)

CLOCK.C *continued*

```
        Variables:       x         Middle of clock face x-coordinate
                         y         Middle of clock face y-coordinate
                         width     Half of width of the clock face
                         height    Half of height of the clock face
                         mark      Hour mark and five-minute mark index
                         dx        Hour mark sizing
                         dy        Hour mark sizing
                         xt        Center coordinate of marks
                         yt        Center coordinate of marks
                         angle     Angle to marks and hands

        Description:     Draws an analog clock face in the rectangular
                         area defined by the coordinates.  This function
                         assumes that you have set a graphics mode.
        - - - - - - - - - - - - - - - - - - - - - - - - - - - - - - -
*/

void clock_face_make( int x1, int y1, int x2, int y2 )
{
    int mark;
    double dx, dy, xt, yt;
    double angle;

    /* Get the center of the clock face */
    x = ( x1 + x2 ) / 2;
    y = ( y1 + y2 ) / 2;

    /* Get the dimensions of the clock face */
    width = abs( x2 - x1 ) / 2;
    height = abs( y2 - y1 ) / 2;

    /* Determine the hour mark dimensions */
    dx = width / 40.0;
    dy = height / 40.0;

    /* Draw the rectangular clock background */
    _setcolor( CLOCK_BGD_COLOR );
    _rectangle( _GFILLINTERIOR, x - width, y - height,
                                x + width, y + height );

    /* Five-minute clock face marks */
    _setcolor( CLOCK_FGD_COLOR );
    for ( mark = 0; mark < 12; mark ++)
```

(continued)

CLOCK.C *continued*

```
       {
       angle = ( 3 - mark ) / 12.0 * 360.0 / 57.29577951;
       xt = x + .9 * width * cos( angle );
       yt = y + .9 * height * sin( angle );
       _rectangle( _GFILLINTERIOR,
                      (int)(xt - dx + .5), (int)(yt - dy + .5),
                      (int)(xt + dx + .5), (int)(yt + dy + .5) );
       }

   /* One-minute clock face marks */
   for ( mark = 0; mark < 60; mark ++ )
       {
       angle = ( 15 - mark ) / 60.0 * 360.0 / 57.29577951;
       xt = x + .9 * width * cos( angle );
       yt = y + .9 * height * sin( angle );
       _setpixel( (int)xt, (int)yt );
       }
   }
```

Function: *clock_face_update()*

The *clock_face_update()* function redraws the hands on the clock face created by *clock_face_make()*. The function first erases the old hands by redrawing them with the background color. It accesses global variables to set the time units to the previously set time. Next, *clock_face_update()* draws the hands again, this time using the foreground color and the current hour, minute, and second values.

Normally, a program would call this function once per second to update the hands on the clock face. The CLOCTEST program demonstrates one way to regulate the frequency of updates. Of course, a program can also redraw the hands less frequently than once per second.

The *clock_face_update()* function requires that your setup provide at least a CGA graphics adapter. It also assumes that a graphics mode is currently set.

```
/* - - - - - - - - - - - - - - - - - - - - - - - - - - - - - - - -
    Function:       clock_face_update()
    Toolbox:        CLOCK.C
    Demonstrated:   CLOCTEST.C

    Parameters:
      (input)       hour      Integer hour
      (input)       minute    Integer minute
      (input)       second    Integer second

    Returned:       (function returns nothing)

    Variables:      i         Loop for erasing and drawing hands
                    h         Hour
                    m         Minute
                    s         Second
                    angle     Angle to marks and hands
                    csa       Cosine of angle
                    sna       Sine of angle

    Description:    Updates the analog clock face hands.  This
                    function assumes that you have already
                    called clock_face_make().
    - - - - - - - - - - - - - - - - - - - - - - - - - - - - - - - -
*/

void clock_face_update( int hour, int minute, int second )
{
    int i;
    int h, m, s;
    double angle, csa, sna;

    /* First erase old hands, then draw new ones */
    for ( i = 0; i < 2; i++ )
        {

        if ( i )
            {
            _setcolor( CLOCK_FGD_COLOR );
            h = hour;
            m = minute;
            s = second;
            }
```

(continued)

CLOCK.C *continued*

```
        else
            {
            _setcolor( CLOCK_BGD_COLOR );
            h = old_hour;
            m = old_minute;
            s = old_second;
            }

    /* Draw the hour hand */
    if ( i !! hour != old_hour !! minute != old_minute )
        {
        angle = 1.570796327 - ( h + m / 60.0 ) * .5235987757;
        csa = cos( angle );
        sna = sin( angle );
        _moveto( (int)( x + .4 * width * csa ),
                 (int)( y - .4 * height * sna ));
        _lineto( (int)( x + .07 * width * sna ),
                 (int)( y - .07 * height * -csa ));
        _lineto( (int)( x + .08 * width * -csa ),
                 (int)( y - .08 * height * -sna ));
        _lineto( (int)( x + .07 * width * -sna ),
                 (int)( y - .07 * height * csa ));
        _lineto( (int)( x + .4 * width * csa ),
                 (int)( y - .4 * height * sna ));
        }

    /* Draw the minute hand */
    if ( i !! minute != old_minute )
        {
        angle = 1.570796327 - m * .1047197551;
        csa = cos( angle );
        sna = sin( angle );
        _moveto( (int)( x + .75 * width * csa ),
                 (int)( y - .75 * height * sna ));
        _lineto( (int)( x + .06 * width * sna ),
                 (int)( y - .06 * height * -csa ));
        _lineto( (int)( x + .09 * width * -csa ),
                 (int)( y - .09 * height * -sna ));
        _lineto( (int)( x + .06 * width * -sna ),
                 (int)( y - .06 * height * csa ));
        _lineto( (int)( x + .75 * width * csa ),
                 (int)( y - .75 * height * sna ));
        }
```

(continued)

CLOCK.C *continued*

```
      /* Draw the second hand */
      if ( i !! second != old_second )
         {
         angle = 1.570796327 - s * .1047197551;
         _moveto( x, y );
         _lineto( (int)( x + .75 * width * cos( angle )),
                  (int)( y - .75 * height * sin( angle )));
         }

      }

   /* Record current time */
   old_hour = hour;
   old_minute = minute;
   old_second = second;
}
```

COMPLEX

FUNCTION	DESCRIPTION
cstr()	Formats a complex number as a string
strc()	Converts a string to a complex number
cadd()	Adds complex numbers
csub()	Subtracts complex numbers
cmul()	Multiplies complex numbers
cdiv()	Divides complex numbers
cpow()	Raises a complex number to a complex power
croot()	Finds the complex root of a complex number
cexp()	Exponential function for complex numbers
clog()	Finds the natural log of a complex number
crec()	Calculates the reciprocal of a complex number
csqr()	Finds the square root of a complex number
complex_to_polar()	Converts a complex number to polar coordinates
polar_to_complex()	Converts polar coordinates to a complex equivalent

The COMPLEX toolbox module provides a collection of functions for working with complex numbers. These functions let you add, subtract, multiply, and divide complex numbers. Other functions convert complex numbers to and from their string representations. Several advanced calculations include finding the square root of a complex number and raising one complex number to the power of another. QuickC provides only one function for working with complex numbers, *cabs()*, which finds the magnitude of a complex number.

Notice that the COMPLEX toolbox functions generally receive and pass complex number structures by value. Although data structures are more efficiently passed by reference, that method is not especially intuitive for the calculations that the functions perform. The *complex* structure is not large, so passing and returning complex numbers by value does not impede program operation a great deal. A further advantage of returning a value is that you can pass a result directly to another function (that requires a value).

Both the *complex_to_polar()* and the *polar_to_complex()* conversion functions also appear, in slightly modified form, in the GEOMETRY toolbox module. The equivalent functions, *rectangular_to_polar()* and *polar_to_rectangular()*, deal with two-dimensional coordinates rather than complex numbers, but they are almost identical in form.

The demonstration program, COMPTEST, declares three structures of type *complex*, which is defined in MATH.H. The program initializes two of these complex numbers, *a* and *b*. It then passes these complex variables to each of the toolbox functions and displays the results.

Demonstration Program: COMPTEST.C

```
/* ------------------------------------------------------------------
    Name:           COMPTEST.C
    Type:           Demonstration program
    Language:       Microsoft QuickC
    Video:          (no special video requirements)

    Program list:   COMPTEST.C
                    COMPLEX.C

    Variables:      a           Complex number structure
                    b           Complex number structure
                    c           Complex number structure
                    str         String for formatted complex numbers

    Usage:          (no command line parameters)

    Description:    Demonstrates the COMPLEX toolbox functions
    ------------------------------------------------------------------
*/

#include <stdio.h>
#include <math.h>
#include <conio.h>
#include "complex.h"
```

(continued)

COMPTEST.C *continued*

```
main()
{
    struct complex a, b, c;
    char str[33];

    /* Set complex number a to ( 1.23 + 4.56i ) */
    a.x = 1.23;
    a.y = 4.56;

    /* Set complex number b to ( -7.65 - 4.32i ) */
    b.x = -7.65;
    b.y = -4.32;

    /* Display the component parts of the complex numbers */
    printf( "\n\n\n\n\n\n" );
    printf( "a.x = %f\t\tb.x = %f\n", a.x, b.x );
    printf( "a.y = %f\t\tb.y = %f\n\n", a.y, b.y );

    /* Display the formatted string versions of the complex numbers */
    printf( "cstr( a, str ) ...  %s\n", cstr( a, str ));
    printf( "cstr( b, str ) ...  %s\n\n", cstr( b, str ));

    /* Convert one of the strings back to a complex number */
    strc( str, &c );
    printf( "strc( str, &c ) ... c.x = %g, c.y = %g\n\n", c.x, c.y );

    /* Complex addition */
    c = cadd( a, b );
    printf( "c = cadd( a, b ) ... %s\n\n", cstr( c, str ));

    /* Complex subtraction */
    c = csub( a, b );
    printf( "c = csub( a, b ) ... %s\n\n", cstr( c, str ));

    /* Complex multiplication */
    c = cmul( a, b );
    printf( "c = cmul( a, b ) ... %s\n\n", cstr( c, str ));

    /* Complex division */
    c = cdiv( a, b );
    printf( "c = cdiv( a, b ) ... %s\n\n", cstr( c, str ));
```

(continued)

COMPTEST.C *continued*

```
    /* Wait for user before continuing */
    printf( "Press any key to continue\n\n\n" );
    getch();
    printf( "\n\n\n\n\n\n" );

    /* Complex power, raise a to the power b */
    c = cpow( a, b );
    printf( "c = cpow( a, b ) ... %s\n\n", cstr( c, str ));

    /* Complex root, find the b root of a */
    c = croot( a, b );
    printf( "c = croot( a, b ) ... %s\n\n", cstr( c, str ));

    /* Exponential function of a complex number */
    c = cexp( a );
    printf( "c = cexp( a ) ... %s\n\n", cstr( c, str ));

    /* Log of a complex number */
    c = clog( a );
    printf( "c = clog( a ) ... %s\n\n", cstr( c, str ));

    /* Reciprocal of a, or 1/a */
    c = crec( a );
    printf( "c = crec( a ) ... %s\n\n", cstr( c, str ));

    /* Square root of a */
    c = csqr( a );
    printf( "c = csqr( a ) ... %s\n\n", cstr( c, str ));

    /* Complex to polar */
    c = complex_to_polar( a );
    printf( "c = complex_to_polar( a ) ... %s\n\n", cstr( c, str ));

    /* Polar to complex */
    a = polar_to_complex( c );
    printf( "a = polar_to_complex( c ) ... %s\n\n", cstr( a, str ));
}
```

Include File: COMPLEX.H

```
/* -----------------------------------------------------------------
   Name:           COMPLEX.H
   Type:           Include
   Language:       Microsoft QuickC
   Demonstrated:   COMPLEX.C  COMPTEST.C
   Description:    Prototypes and definitions for COMPLEX.C
   -----------------------------------------------------------------
*/

#ifndef COMPLEX_DEFINED

char *cstr( struct complex, char * );
int strc( char *, struct complex * );
struct complex cadd( struct complex, struct complex );
struct complex csub( struct complex, struct complex );
struct complex cmul( struct complex, struct complex );
struct complex cdiv( struct complex, struct complex );
struct complex cpow( struct complex, struct complex );
struct complex croot( struct complex, struct complex );
struct complex cexp( struct complex );
struct complex clog( struct complex );
struct complex crec( struct complex );
struct complex csqr( struct complex );
struct complex complex_to_polar( struct complex );
struct complex polar_to_complex( struct complex );

#define COMPLEX_DEFINED
#endif
```

Toolbox Module: COMPLEX.C

```
/* -----------------------------------------------------------------
   Name:           COMPLEX.C
   Type:           Toolbox module
   Language:       Microsoft QuickC
   Demonstrated:   COMPTEST.C
   Video:          (no special video requirements)
   -----------------------------------------------------------------
*/
```

(continued)

COMPLEX.C *continued*

```
#include <math.h>
#include <stdio.h>
#include "complex.h"
```

Function: *cstr()*

The *cstr()* function formats a complex number as a string, that is suitable for display or printing. The string format is one of several that are commonly used for printing complex numbers. The format chosen here is often used, but the function can easily be modified if you require a slightly different format.

The following are examples of the strings produced:

```
( 1.23 +4.56i )
( -1.23 -4.56i )
```

```
/* - - - - - - - - - - - - - - - - - - - - - - - - - - - - - - - - - - -
   Function:       cstr()
   Toolbox:        COMPLEX.C
   Demonstrated:   COMPTEST.C

   Parameters:
     (input)       a             Structure of type complex
     (output)      str           String for formatted complex number

   Returned:       The formatted string

   Variables:      (none)

   Description:    Formats a complex number into a string
   - - - - - - - - - - - - - - - - - - - - - - - - - - - - - - - - - - -
*/

char *cstr( struct complex a, char *str )
{
    if ( a.y >= 0.0 )
        sprintf( str, "( %g +%gi )", a.x, a.y );
    else
        sprintf( str, "( %g %gi )", a.x, a.y );

    return ( str );
}
```

Function: *strc()*

The *strc()* function converts a string designation of a complex number into the equivalent complex number structure. If both the real and imaginary parts of the string convert successfully, the function returns 2, indicating the number of scanned fields. If an error occurs, the function returns 0.

The *strc()* function uses *sscanf()* to scan the string and make the conversion. The *sscanf()* function allows small variations in the exact string format, particularly in the number of spaces before and after the numbers, but *sscanf()* expects a left parenthesis character to precede the first number. See the QuickC Help facility for more information on *sscanf()*.

```
/* - - - - - - - - - - - - - - - - - - - - - - - - - - - - - - - - - - -

   Function:     strc()
   Toolbox:      COMPLEX.C
   Demonstrated: COMPTEST.C

   Parameters:
     (input)     str        String designation of a complex number
     (output)    a          Structure of type complex

   Returned:     0 if conversion failed
                 2 if both numerical fields converted correctly

   Variables:    (none)

   Description:  Converts a string designation of a complex
                 number into a complex number structure
   - - - - - - - - - - - - - - - - - - - - - - - - - - - - - - - - - - -
*/

int strc( char *str, struct complex *a )
{
    if ( sscanf( str, " ( %lg %lg", &a->x, &a->y ) == 2 )
        return ( 2 );
    else
        return ( 0 );
}
```

Function: *cadd()*

The *cadd()* function adds two complex numbers and returns the result. The function declares a third complex number, *c*, to which it assigns the result of the calculation.

```
/* - - - - - - - - - - - - - - - - - - - - - - - - - - - - - -
   Function:      cadd()
   Toolbox:       COMPLEX.C
   Demonstrated:  COMPTEST.C

   Parameters:
     (input)      a          First complex number
     (input)      b          Second complex number

   Returned:      Complex number result

   Variables:     c          Complex result

   Description:   Adds two complex numbers
   - - - - - - - - - - - - - - - - - - - - - - - - - - - - - -
*/

struct complex cadd( struct complex a, struct complex b )
{
    struct complex c;

    c.x = a.x + b.x;
    c.y = a.y + b.y;

    return ( c );
}
```

Function: *csub()*

The *csub()* function finds the difference between two complex numbers and returns the result. The function declares a third complex number structure, *c*, subtracts the second argument from the first, and assigns the difference to *c*.

```
/* - - - - - - - - - - - - - - - - - - - - - - - - - - - - - - - -
   Function:      csub()
   Toolbox:       COMPLEX.C
   Demonstrated:  COMPTEST.C

   Parameters:
     (input)      a           First complex number
     (input)      b           Second complex number

   Returned:      Complex number result

   Variables:     c           Complex result

   Description:   Subtracts two complex numbers
   - - - - - - - - - - - - - - - - - - - - - - - - - - - - - - - -
*/

struct complex csub( struct complex a, struct complex b )
{
    struct complex c;

    c.x = a.x - b.x;
    c.y = a.y - b.y;

    return ( c );
}
```

Function: *cmul()*

The *cmul()* function multiplies two complex numbers and returns the result. The function declares a third complex number structure, *c*, to which it assigns the product of the two arguments.

```
/* - - - - - - - - - - - - - - - - - - - - - - - - - - - - - - - -
   Function:      cmul()
   Toolbox:       COMPLEX.C
   Demonstrated:  COMPTEST.C

   Parameters:
     (input)      a           First complex number
     (input)      b           Second complex number

   Returned:      Complex number result
```

(continued)

COMPLEX.C *continued*

```
    Variables:      c          Complex result

    Description:    Multiplies two complex numbers
    - - - - - - - - - - - - - - - - - - - - - - - - - - - - - - - -
*/

struct complex cmul( struct complex a, struct complex b )
{
    struct complex c;

    c.x = a.x * b.x - a.y * b.y;
    c.y = a.x * b.y + a.y * b.x;

    return ( c );
}
```

Function: *cdiv()*

The *cdiv()* function divides two complex numbers and returns the result. The function divides the first argument by the second, assigns the quotient to a local complex number structure, *c*, and returns the result.

```
/* - - - - - - - - - - - - - - - - - - - - - - - - - - - - - - - -
    Function:       cdiv()
    Toolbox:        COMPLEX.C
    Demonstrated:   COMPTEST.C

    Parameters:
      (input)       a          First complex number
      (input)       b          Second complex number

    Returned:       Complex number result

    Variables:      tmp        Variable for repetitive division
                    c          Complex result

    Description:    Divides two complex numbers
    - - - - - - - - - - - - - - - - - - - - - - - - - - - - - - - -
*/
```

(continued)

COMPLEX.C *continued*

```
struct complex cdiv( struct complex a, struct complex b )
{
    double tmp;
    struct complex c;

    tmp = b.x * b.x + b.y * b.y;

    c.x = ( a.x * b.x + a.y * b.y ) / tmp;
    c.y = ( a.y * b.x - a.x * b.y ) / tmp;

    return ( c );
}
```

Function: *cpow()*

The *cpow()* function raises a complex number to the power expressed by a second complex number and returns the result. The first argument is the base, and the second is the exponent. The function calls three other routines in this module: *clog()*, *cmul()*, and *cexp()*.

```
/* - - - - - - - - - - - - - - - - - - - - - - - - - - - - - - - /* - -
    Function:       cpow()
    Toolbox:        COMPLEX.C
    Demonstrated:   COMPTEST.C

    Parameters:
      (input)       a           First complex number
      (input)       b           Second complex number

    Returned:       Complex number result

    Variables:      t1          Temporary complex number variable
                    t2          Temporary complex number variable
                    c           Complex result

    Description:    Raises complex number a to the power b
    - - - - - - - - - - - - - - - - - - - - - - - - - - - - - - - - -
*/

struct complex cpow( struct complex a, struct complex b )
```

(continued)

```
{
    struct complex t1, t2, c;

    t1 = clog( a );
    t2 = cmul( t1, b );
    c = cexp( t2 );

    return ( c );
}
```

Function: *croot()*

The *croot()* function calculates the complex root of a complex number and returns the result. The function takes two arguments, the second of which represents the root to extract from the first.

```
/* - - - - - - - - - - - - - - - - - - - - - - - - - - - - - - - - - -
    Function:       croot()
    Toolbox:        COMPLEX.C
    Demonstrated:   COMPTEST.C

    Parameters:
      (input)       a           First complex number
      (input)       b           Second complex number

    Returned:       Complex number result

    Variables:      t           Temporary complex number
                    c           Complex result

    Description:    Finds the b root of a
    - - - - - - - - - - - - - - - - - - - - - - - - - - - - - - - - - -
*/

struct complex croot( struct complex a, struct complex b )
{
    struct complex t, c;

    t = crec( b );
    c = cpow( a, t );

    return ( c );
}
```

Function: *cexp()*

The *cexp()* function calculates the exponential function of a complex number and returns the result. The exponential function raises *e* to the power specified by the function argument.

```
/* - - - - - - - - - - - - - - - - - - - - - - - - - - - - - - - - - - - - -
    Function:       cexp()
    Toolbox:        COMPLEX.C
    Demonstrated:   COMPTEST.C

    Parameters:
      (input)       a           Complex number

    Returned:       Complex number result

    Variables:      tmp         Temporary double-precision real
                    c           Complex result

    Description:    Finds the exponential function of a complex
                    number, or raises e to the power a
   - - - - - - - - - - - - - - - - - - - - - - - - - - - - - - - - - - - - -
*/

struct complex cexp( struct complex a )
{
    double tmp;
    struct complex c;

    tmp = exp( a.x );

    c.x = tmp * cos( a.y );
    c.y = tmp * sin( a.y );

    return ( c );
}
```

Function: *clog()*

The *clog()* function calculates the natural logarithm of a complex number and returns the result. The function takes a single argument, the number for which you want to find the logarithm.

```
/* - - - - - - - - - - - - - - - - - - - - - - - - - - - - - - - - -
    Function:       clog()
    Toolbox:        COMPLEX.C
    Demonstrated:   COMPTEST.C

    Parameters:
      (input)       a             Complex number

    Returned:       Complex number result

    Variables:      c             Complex result

    Description:    Finds the complex natural logarithm of a complex
                    number
    - - - - - - - - - - - - - - - - - - - - - - - - - - - - - - - - -
*/

struct complex clog( struct complex a )
{
    struct complex c;

    c.x = log( cabs( a ));
    c.y = atan2( a.y, a.x );

    return ( c );
}
```

Function: *crec()*

The *crec()* function calculates the reciprocal of a complex number and returns the result. The function finds the reciprocal of the complex number it receives as an argument.

```
/* - - - - - - - - - - - - - - - - - - - - - - - - - - - - - - - - -
    Function:       crec()
    Toolbox:        COMPLEX.C
    Demonstrated:   COMPTEST.C

    Parameters:
      (input)       a             Complex number

    Returned:       Complex number result
```

(continued)

COMPLEX.C *continued*

```
   Variables:      tmp        Temporary double-precision real
                   c          Complex result

   Description:    Calculates 1 / a, or the complex reciprocal of
                   a complex number
 - - - - - - - - - - - - - - - - - - - - - - - - - - - - - - -
*/

struct complex crec( struct complex a )
{
    double tmp;
    struct complex c;

    tmp = a.x * a.x + a.y * a.y;

    c.x = a.x / tmp;
    c.y = -a.y / tmp;

    return ( c );
}
```

Function: *csqr()*

The *csqr()* function calculates the square root of a complex number and returns the result. The function declares a complex number structure, to which it assigns the square root of the complex number it receives as its argument.

```
/* - - - - - - - - - - - - - - - - - - - - - - - - - - - - - -
   Function:       csqr()
   Toolbox:        COMPLEX.C
   Demonstrated:   COMPTEST.C

   Parameters:
    (input)        a          Complex number

   Returned:       Complex number result

   Variables:      tmp1       Temporary double-precision real
                   tmp2       Temporary double-precision real
                   c          Complex result
```

(continued)

120

COMPLEX.C *continued*

```
   Description:   Calculates the square root of a complex number
   - - - - - - - - - - - - - - - - - - - - - - - - - - - - - - - -
*/

struct complex csqr( struct complex a )
{
    double tmp1, tmp2;
    struct complex c;

    tmp1 = sqrt( cabs( a ) );
    tmp2 = atan2( a.y, a.x ) / 2.0;

    c.x = tmp1 * cos( tmp2 );
    c.y = tmp1 * sin( tmp2 );

    return ( c );
}
```

Function: *complex_to_polar()*

The *complex_to_polar()* function converts a complex number to polar notation and returns the result. The function takes a single argument, a complex number structure. The result, which is also assigned to a complex number structure, represents an equivalent value in polar notation. You must keep track of the complex numbers that are actually represented as polar coordinates.

```
/* - - - - - - - - - - - - - - - - - - - - - - - - - - - - - - - -
   Function:      complex_to_polar()
   Toolbox:       COMPLEX.C
   Demonstrated:  COMPTEST.C

   Parameters:
     (input)      a          Complex number

   Returned:      Polar notation result

   Variables:     x          Temporary double-precision real
                  y          Temporary double-precision real
                  c          Complex result
```

(continued)

COMPLEX.C *continued*

```
    Description:    Converts a complex number to its polar notation
                    equivalent
- - - - - - - - - - - - - - - - - - - - - - - - - - - - - - - - -
*/

struct complex complex_to_polar( struct complex a )
{
    double x, y;
    struct complex c;

    x = a.x;
    y = a.y;

    c.x = hypot( x, y );
    c.y = atan2( y, x );

    return ( c );
}
```

Function: *polar_to_complex()*

The *polar_to_complex()* function converts polar coordinates to a complex number and returns the result. The function takes a single argument, a complex number expressed in polar notation, and calculates an equivalent complex number. You must keep track of the complex numbers that are represented as polar coordinates.

```
/* - - - - - - - - - - - - - - - - - - - - - - - - - - - - - - -
    Function:       polar_to_complex()
    Toolbox:        COMPLEX.C
    Demonstrated:   COMPTEST.C

    Parameters:
      (input)       a           Polar notation number

    Returned:       Complex number result
```

(continued)

COMPLEX.C *continued*

```
    Variables:      radius    Temporary double-precision real
                    angle     Temporary double-precision real
                    c         Complex result

    Description:    Converts a polar number to the equivalent
                    complex number
    - - - - - - - - - - - - - - - - - - - - - - - - - - - - - -
*/

struct complex polar_to_complex( struct complex a )
{
    double radius, angle;
    struct complex c;

    radius = a.x;
    angle = a.y;

    c.x = radius * cos( angle );
    c.y = radius * sin( angle );

    return ( c );
}
```

DOSCALL

FUNCTION	DESCRIPTION
dos_version()	Gets DOS version number
oem_number()	Gets OEM serial number
serial_number()	Gets user serial number
verify()	Gets, sets, or clears verify flag
country()	Gets country-specific information and settings
case_map()	Converts characters for current country setting

The DOSCALL toolbox module provides several useful functions that exploit various operating system services. These functions supplement the set of routines in the QuickC run-time library that access the operating system, each of which is identifiable by the prefix _dos_ in the function name. The DOSCALL functions also demonstrate the convenience of using in-line assembly code for calling the operating system.

The *dos_version()* function returns the version number of DOS. Getting this information is important if a program uses features that are available only in later versions of the operating system.

The *oem_number()* and *serial_number()* functions obtain serial numbers that are optionally included by the hardware manufacturer. For IBM computers, these serial numbers generally are all 0s.

The *verify()* function lets you manipulate the state of the verify flag. Recall that the verify flag tells the operating system to verify the accuracy of operations that write to disk.

The *country()* and *case_map()* functions can help if you are writing programs to be marketed outside the United States. They show you how to obtain and apply country-specific information in your programs.

The demonstration program, DOSTEST.C, calls all of the functions DOSCALL. The program first displays the DOS version number and the serial number, if any, of your computer. DOSTEST then saves the current state of the verify flag, sets and clears the flag, and then restores its original state. The program displays the result of each step.

The demonstration concludes with a screenful of country-specific information. DOSTEST calls *country()* to fill a structure with information pertinent to the data-formatting practices in the current country. The program creates a table to present those facts. DOSTEST then calls *case_map()* to illustrate the country-specific translation of a range of characters in the IBM Extended Character Set. DOSTEST displays characters in the range 0x80 through 0xA0 in both their untranslated and translated versions.

Demonstration Program: DOSTEST.C

```
/* -----------------------------------------------------------------
   Name:            DOSTEST.C
   Type:            Demonstration program
   Language:        Microsoft QuickC version 2
   Video:           (no special video requirements)

   Program list:    DOSTEST.C
                    DOSCALL.C

   Variables:       i               Looping index
                    verify_now      State of verify flag
                    ci              Structure of type country_type

   Usage:           (no command line parameters)

   Description:     Demonstrates the DOSCALL toolbox functions
   -----------------------------------------------------------------
*/

#include <stdio.h>
#include <stdlib.h>
#include <conio.h>
#include "doscall.h"

main()
{
    int i;
    int verify_now;
    struct country_type ci;
```

(continued)

DOSTEST.C *continued*

```
    /* Show DOS version number and the optional serial number */
    printf( "\n\nDOS Version number:\t%5.2f\n", dos_version() );
    printf( "OEM number:\t\t%5d\n", oem_number() );
    printf( "Serial number:\t\t%5ld\n\n", serial_number() );

    /* Demonstrate the verify() function */
    verify_now = verify( V_GET );
    printf( "Verify flag:\t%d\n", verify_now );
    printf( "Cleared.....\t%d\n", verify( V_CLR ));
    printf( "Set.........\t%d\n", verify( V_SET ));
    printf( "Reset to....\t%d\n", verify( verify_now ));

    /* Wait for user */
    printf( "\n\nPress any key to continue\n" );
    getch();

    /* Show the country-specific information */
    country( &ci );
    printf( "\n\nCountry information...\n\n" );
    printf( "Error code:\t\t\t%d\n", ci.error_code );
    printf( "Country code:\t\t\t%d\n", ci.country_code );
    printf( "Date format:\t\t\t%s\n", ci.date_format );
    printf( "Currency symbol:\t\t%s\n", ci.currency_symbol );
    printf( "Thousands separator:\t\t%s\n", ci.thousands_separator );
    printf( "Decimal separator:\t\t%s\n", ci.decimal_separator );
    printf( "Date separator:\t\t\t%s\n", ci.date_separator );
    printf( "Time separator:\t\t\t%s\n", ci.time_separator );
    printf( "Currency symbol after amount:\t%d\n", ci.currency_symbol_last );
    printf( "Currency symbol space:\t%d\n", ci.currency_symbol_space );
    printf( "Currency decimal digits:\t%d\n", ci.currency_dec_digits );
    printf( "24-hour time:\t\t\t%d\n", ci.time_24_hours );
    printf( "Case map address (long):\t%lu\n", ci.case_map_address );
    printf( "Data list separator:\t\t%s\n", ci.data_list_separator );

    /* Translate characters 0x80 through 0xA0 */
    printf( "\nCase map...\n" );

    /* First display the untranslated set of characters */
    for ( i = 0x80; i <= 0xA0; i++ )
        printf( "%c ", i );
```

(continued)

DOSTEST.C *continued*

```
    /* Then display the translated characters for comparison */
    printf( "\n" );
    for ( i = 0x80; i <= 0xA0; i++ )
        printf( "%c ", case_map( (char)i, &ci ));
    printf( "\n" );
}
```

Include File: DOSCALL.H

```
/*-----------------------------------------------------------------
    Name:           DOSCALL.H
    Type:           Include
    Language:       Microsoft QuickC version 2
    Demonstrated:   DOSCALL.C  DOSTEST.C
    Description:    Prototypes and definitions for DOSCALL
    -----------------------------------------------------------------
*/

#ifndef DOSCALL_DEFINED

#define V_GET (-1)
#define V_SET  1
#define V_CLR  0

struct country_type
    {
    int error_code;
    int country_code;
    char date_format[6];
    char currency_symbol[5];
    char thousands_separator[2];
    char decimal_separator[2];
    char date_separator[2];
    char time_separator[2];
    int currency_symbol_last;
    int currency_symbol_space;
    int currency_dec_digits;
    int time_24_hours;
    long case_map_address;
    char data_list_separator[2];
    };
```

(continued)

DOSCALL.H *continued*

```
double dos_version( void );
int oem_number( void );
long serial_number( void );
int verify( int );
void country( struct country_type * );
char case_map( char, struct country_type * );

#define DOSCALL_DEFINED
#endif
```

Toolbox Module: DOSCALL.C

```
/* ------------------------------------------------------------------
        Name:           DOSCALL.C
        Type:           Toolbox module
        Language:       Microsoft QuickC
        Demonstrated:   DOSTEST.C
        Video:          (no special video requirements)
   ------------------------------------------------------------------
*/

#include <bios.h>
#include <dos.h>
#include <stdlib.h>
#include <stdio.h>
#include <direct.h>
#include <string.h>

#include "doscall.h"
```

Function: *dos_version()*

The *dos_version()* function returns the DOS version number. QuickC provides the global variables *_osmajor* and *_osminor*, which contain the major and minor parts of the version number. The *dos_version()* function combines the values of these two variables and returns a unique floating-point representation for any version of DOS. For example, the function returns the value 3.3 for DOS version 3.3.

```
/* - - - - - - - - - - - - - - - - - - - - - - - - - - - - - - - - - - - -
    Function:       dos_version()
    Toolbox:        DOSCALL.C
    Demonstrated:   DOSTEST.C

    Parameters:     (none)

    Returned:       DOS version number

    Variables:      (none)

    Description:    Returns the version number for DOS
    - - - - - - - - - - - - - - - - - - - - - - - - - - - - - - - - - - - -
*/

double dos_version( void )
{
    return ( _osmajor + _osminor / 100.0 );
}
```

Function: *oem_number()*

The *oem_number()* function returns an OEM (original equipment manufacturer) serial number that represents the computer product. This serial number is an optional, 8-bit integer that is assigned by the OEM. IBM computers generally return 0s.

```
/* - - - - - - - - - - - - - - - - - - - - - - - - - - - - - - - - - - - -
    Function:       oem_number()
    Toolbox:        DOSCALL.C
    Demonstrated:   DOSTEST.C

    Parameters:     (none)

    Returned:       Optional OEM serial number

    Variables:      oem        Local variable for OEM number

    Description:    Returns the optional original equipment
                    manufacturer's serial number
    - - - - - - - - - - - - - - - - - - - - - - - - - - - - - - - - - - - -
*/
```

(continued)

DOSCALL.C *continued*

```
int oem_number( void )
{
    int oem = 0;

    _asm
        {
        mov    ax, 3000h
        int    21h
        mov    bl,bh
        xor    bh,bh
        mov    oem,bx
        }

    return ( oem );
}
```

Function: *serial_number()*

The *serial_number()* function returns a long integer containing a 24-bit OEM serial number that is unique for each computer. This number is optional and OEM dependent. For IBM computers, the serial number returned is generally 0.

One possible use for this serial number is in the implementation of a straightforward copy protection mechanism. A program might check the serial number at load time and terminate at once if the current machine is not the computer on which the program was originally installed. Note, however, that any given computer manufacturer has no obligation to provide the number.

```
/* - - - - - - - - - - - - - - - - - - - - - - - - - - - - - - - - -
    Function:      serial_number()
    Toolbox:       DOSCALL.C
    Demonstrated:  DOSTEST.C

    Parameters:    (none)

    Returned:      Optional user serial number

    Variables:     s1      Local variable for serial number
                   s2      Local variable for serial number
```

(continued)

DOSCALL.C *continued*

```
   Description:    Returns the optional user serial number
   - - - - - - - - - - - - - - - - - - - - - - - - - - - - - - - - - -
*/

long serial_number( void )
{
    int s1 = 0, s2 = 0;

    _asm
        {
        mov    ax, 3000h
        int    21h
        xor    bh, bh
        mov    s1, bx
        mov    s2, cx
        }

    return (( (long)s1 << 16 ) + s2 );
}
```

Function: *verify()*

The *verify()* function gets, sets, or clears the verify state. To indicate which action you want *verify()* to perform, pass it one of the following constants: V_GET, V_SET, or V_CLR. The three constants are defined in DOSCALL.H. In all cases, the function returns the resulting state of the verify flag.

```
/* - - - - - - - - - - - - - - - - - - - - - - - - - - - - - - - - -
   Function:      verify()
   Toolbox:       DOSCALL.C
   Demonstrated:  DOSTEST.C

   Parameters:    vflag    Should be set to one of the constants
                           defined in DOSCALL.H:
                           V_GET  Get the verify state
                           V_SET  Set verify on
                           V_CLR  Set verify off


   Returned:      0 if verify is off (cleared)
                  1 if verify is on (set)
```

(continued)

DOSCALL.C *continued*

```
    Variables:       vrfy       Local variable for verify state

    Description:    Returns the state of the verify flag
    - - - - - - - - - - - - - - - - - - - - - - - - - - - - - - - -
*/

int verify( int vflag )
{
    int vrfy = vflag;

    if ( vflag != V_GET )
        _asm
            {
            mov   ax, vrfy
            mov   ah, 2Eh
            xor   dl, dl
            int   21h
            }

    /* Get the verify state */
    _asm
        {
        mov   ah, 54h
        int   21h
        xor   ah, ah
        mov   vrfy, ax
        }

    return ( vrfy );
}
```

Function: *country()*

The *country()* function calls DOS service 38H to obtain country-specific information for the currently set country. The function fills a data structure of type *country_type*, which is defined in DOSCALL.H.

Pass *country()* a pointer to the structure variable that will receive the internationalization information. The members of this structure, which are described on the following page, allow programs to adapt to users in other countries.

STRUCTURE MEMBER	DESCRIPTION
error_code	Contains the error code returned by DOS function 38H. A code of 0 indicates no error.
country_code	Country code as determined by the KEYBxx keyboard driver if one is loaded. Otherwise, the country code is OEM dependent.
date_format	String that represents the order for month, day, and year values. Possible strings are "m d y", "d m y", and "y m d".
currency_symbol	Currency symbol or denomination, expressed as a 1-character to 4-character null-terminated string, such as "$" or "Lira".
thousands_separator	Character used to separate large numbers into three-digit groups. Examples are "." and ","
decimal_separator	Character used as the decimal point for numbers. Examples are "," and "."
date_separator	Character used to separate month, day, and year values in dates. Examples are "-" and "/"
time_separator	Character used to separate hour, minute, and second numbers in displayed time. An example is ":"
currency_symbol_last	1 if currency symbol follows a monetary amount; 0 if it precedes an amount.
currency_symbol_space	1 if a space separates the currency symbol from a monetary amount; 0 if no space intervenes.
currency_dec_digits	Number of digits following the decimal point for a monetary representation.
time_24_hours	1 if 24-hour clock; 0 if 12-hour clock.
case_map_address	Address of character translation function (used by the *case_map()* function).
data_list_separator	Character used to separate items in data lists. An example is ","

```
/* - - - - - - - - - - - - - - - - - - - - - - - - - - - - - - - - - - - - -
   Function:        country()
   Toolbox:         DOSCALL.C
   Demonstrated:    DOSTEST.C

   Parameters:
     (output)       country_info    Structure of country-specific
                                    information

   Returned:        (function returns nothing)

   Variables:       ary             Buffer filled in by DOS function
                    cptr            Far pointer to ary[]
                    sg              Segment for ary[]
                    of              Offset for ary[]
                    cntry_code      Country code returned by DOS
                    error_flag      Error returned by DOS function

   Description:     Fills a structure of country-specific
                    information
   - - - - - - - - - - - - - - - - - - - - - - - - - - - - - - - - - - - - -
*/

void country( struct country_type *country_info )
{
    char ary[34];
    char far *cptr = ary;
    unsigned sg = FP_SEG( cptr );
    unsigned of = FP_OFF( cptr );

    int cntry_code = 0;
    int error_flag = 0;

    _asm
      {
            push ds
            mov  ax, 3800h
            mov  ds, sg
            mov  dx, of
            int  21h
            mov  cntry_code, bx
            mov  error_flag, 0
            jnc  done
```

(continued)

DOSCALL.C *continued*

```
            mov   error_flag, ax
        done:
            pop   ds
        }

    country_info->error_code = error_flag;
    country_info->country_code = cntry_code;

    switch ( *( (int *) &ary[0] ) )
        {
        case 0:
            strcpy( country_info->date_format, "m d y" );
            break;
        case 1:
            strcpy( country_info->date_format, "d m y" );
            break;
        case 2:
            strcpy( country_info->date_format, "y m d" );
            break;
        default:
            strcpy( country_info->date_format, "? ? ?" );
            break;
        }

    strcpy( country_info->currency_symbol, &ary[2] );
    strcpy( country_info->thousands_separator, &ary[7] );
    strcpy( country_info->decimal_separator, &ary[9] );
    strcpy( country_info->date_separator, &ary[11] );
    strcpy( country_info->time_separator, &ary[13] );
    country_info->currency_symbol_last = ary[15] & 1;
    country_info->currency_symbol_space = ( ary[15] >> 1 ) & 1;
    country_info->currency_dec_digits = ary[16];
    country_info->time_24_hours = ary[17] & 1;
    country_info->case_map_address = *( (long *) &ary[18] );
    strcpy( country_info->data_list_separator, &ary[22] );
}
```

Function: *case_map()*

The *case_map()* function translates characters from the default character set to those specified by the currently set country code. The translation affects only characters with ASCII codes in the range 0x80 through
0xFF.

Before using *case_map()*, a program must call the *country()* function, which obtains the address of the DOS translation function. This address is a member of the data structure that you pass to *case_map()*.

```
/* - - - - - - - - - - - - - - - - - - - - - - - - - - - - - -
    Function:        case_map()
    Toolbox:         DOSCALL.C
    Demonstrated:    DOSTEST.C

    Parameters:
      (input)        c              Character to be translated
      (input)        country_info   Structure of country-specific
                                    information

    Returned:        Translated character

    Variables:       new_c          Translation result
                     case_map       Pointer to DOS case map function

    Description:     Translates a character using the country-specific
                     case map function provided by DOS
    - - - - - - - - - - - - - - - - - - - - - - - - - - - - - -
*/

char case_map( char c, struct country_type *country_info )
{
    char new_c;
    void far *case_map;

    case_map = (void far *) country_info-case_map_address;

    _asm
        {
        mov  al, c
        call case_map
        mov  new_c, al
        }

    return ( new_c );
}
```

EDIT

FUNCTION	DESCRIPTION
next_word()	Finds start of next word in a string
prev_word()	Finds start of previous word in a string
delete_char()	Deletes current character in a string
insert_char()	Inserts a character in a string
insert_spaces()	Inserts one or more spaces in a string
replace()	Replaces one character in a string
editline()	Edits a string

The EDIT toolbox module is a collection of functions for editing words and characters in strings. These functions can be used as a starting point for creating a text editor program. The STRINGS and GETKEY toolbox modules contain other useful functions for editing and formatting text.

Most of the EDIT functions operate on one string and require an index into that string. The *next_word()* function increments the position index until it points to the first character of the next word in the string. The *prev_word()* function moves the pointer backward in the string so that it points to the first character of the previous word. The *delete_char()* function deletes the current character, *insert_char()* inserts a character, and *insert_spaces()* inserts one or more spaces at the current index position. The *replace()* function performs a global replacement, replacing all occurrences of a substring with another substring. The *editline()* function calls several of the other functions to provide a single-line editor suitable for data input tasks.

The EDITTEST demonstration program displays a short sample string and then calls each editing function to modify the string. The program redisplays the string after each modification so that you can study the results. EDITTEST passes a longer string to *editline()* so that you can experiment with standard editing keys and key combinations—Del, Ins, Backspace, Home, End, Left Arrow, Right Arrow, Ctrl-Left Arrow, Ctrl-Right Arrow, and Ctrl-End. Notice that the cursor shape changes when you press the Ins key to alternate between insert and overwrite typing modes.

The Up or Down Arrow key, Enter, or Esc ends the line-editing session and concludes the demonstration. You can use the mouse (as well as Right and Left Arrow keys) to move the cursor horizontally. Vertical mouse movements terminate the line-editing session.

The EDIT toolbox module uses functions from the GETKEY and MOUSEFUN modules. In particular, look at the *editline()* function for illustrations of calls to the routines in those external modules.

Demonstration Program: EDITTEST.C

```
/* ------------------------------------------------------------------
    Name:           EDITTEST.C
    Type:           Demonstration program
    Language:       Microsoft QuickC version 2
    Video:          (no special video requirements)

    Program list:   EDITTEST.C
                    EDIT.C
                    GETKEY.C
                    MOUSEFUN.C
                    GRAPHICS.LIB

    Variables:      i          Cursor position in str
                    j          Looping index
                    str        String for editing

    Usage:          (no command line parameters)

    Description:    Demonstrates the EDIT toolbox functions
    ------------------------------------------------------------------
*/

#include <stdio.h>
#include <conio.h>
#include <string.h>
#include <graph.h>

#include "edit.h"
#include "getkey.h"
#include "t_colors.h"       /* listed in BOX module */
```

(continued)

EDITTEST.C *continued*

```
main()
{
    int i = 0;
    int j;
    char str[80];
    unsigned edit_exit;

    strcpy( str, "This is a test string." );

    /* Describe situation to user */
    printf( "\n\n\n\n" );
    printf( "%s\n", str );
    printf( "^ (index starts at 0, first character of string)\n\n" );

    /* Move to fourth word (three over from first) */
    for ( j = 0; j < 3; j++ )
        i = next_word( str, i );

    /* Display the result */
    printf( "next_word() ... called three times...\n\n" );
    printf( "%s\n", str );
    for ( j = 0; j < i; j++ )
        printf( " " );
    printf( "^ (fourth word starts here)\n\n" );

    /* Describe situation to user */
    printf( "prev_word() ... called two times...\n\n" );

    /* Move back two words */
    i = prev_word( str, i );
    i = prev_word( str, i );

    /* Display the result */
    printf( "%s\n", str );
    for ( j = 0; j < i; j++ )
        printf( " " );
    printf( "^ (second word starts here)\n\n" );
```

(continued)

EDITTEST.C *continued*

```
    /* Wait for user */
    printf( "Press any key to continue" );
    getch();
    printf( "\n\n\n" );

    /* Delete five characters */
    for ( j = 0; j < 5; j++ )
        delete_char( str, i );
    printf( "delete_char() ... called five times...\n\n" );
    printf( "%s\n", str );
    for ( j = 0; j < i; j++ )
        printf( " " );
    printf( "^ (five characters were deleted here)\n\n" );

    /* Insert six characters */
    i = insert_char( str, i, 's' );
    i = insert_char( str, i, 'h' );
    i = insert_char( str, i, 'o' );
    i = insert_char( str, i, 'r' );
    i = insert_char( str, i, 't' );
    i = insert_char( str, i, ' ' );
    printf( "insert_char() ... called six times...\n\n" );
    printf( "%s\n", str );
    for ( j = 0; j < i; j++ )
        printf( " " );
    printf( "^ (next insert would be here)\n\n" );

    /* Insert three spaces */
    i -= 5;
    insert_spaces( str, i, 3 );
    printf( "insert_spaces() ... three spaces...\n\n" );
    printf( "%s\n", str );
    for ( j = 0; j < i; j++ )
        printf( " " );
    printf( "^ (three spaces inserted here)\n\n" );

    /* Replace all "s" with "sss" */
    replace( str, "s", "sss" );
    printf( "Replace all \"s\" with \"sss\" ...\n" );
    printf( "%s\n", str );
```

(continued)

EDITTEST.C *continued*

```
    /* Replace all "sss" with "x" */
    replace( str, "sss", "x" );
    printf( "\nReplace all \"sss\" with \"x\" ...\n" );
    printf( "%s\n\n", str );

    /* Wait for user */
    printf( "Press any key to continue" );
    getch();
    printf( "\n\n\n" );

    /* Edit a string */
    printf( "\n\n\n\n\n" );
    _settextposition( 21, 11 );
    _settextcolor( T_YELLOW );
    _setbkcolor( BK_BLUE );
    strcpy( str, " Edit this string, using the various editing keys. " );
    edit_exit = editline( str );
    printf( "\n\n\nKey returned from editline() ... " );
    switch ( edit_exit )
        {
        case KEY_UP:
            printf( "KEY_UP\n" );
            break;
        case KEY_DOWN:
            printf( "KEY_DOWN\n" );
            break;
        case KEY_ESCAPE:
            printf( "KEY_ESCAPE\n" );
            break;
        case KEY_ENTER:
            printf( "KEY_ENTER\n" );
            break;
        default:
            printf( "(unknown)\n" );
            break;
        }
}
```

Include File: EDIT.H

```
/* ----------------------------------------------------------------
   Name:          EDIT.H
   Type:          Include
   Language:      Microsoft QuickC
   Demonstrated:  EDIT.C  EDITTEST.C
   Description:   Prototypes and definitions for EDIT.C
   ----------------------------------------------------------------
*/

#ifndef EDIT_DEFINED

#define CURSOR_UNDERLINE  0x0707
#define CURSOR_BLOCK      0x0007
#define CURSOR_DOUBLELINE 0x0607
#define CURSOR_NONE       0x2000

int next_word( char *, int );
int prev_word( char *, int );
int delete_char( char *, int );
int insert_char( char *, int, char );
int insert_spaces( char *, int, int );
int replace( char *, char *, char * );
int editline( char * );

#define EDIT_DEFINED
#endif
```

Toolbox Module: EDIT.C

```
/* ----------------------------------------------------------------
   Name:          EDIT.C
   Type:          Toolbox module
   Language:      Microsoft QuickC
   Demonstrated:  EDITTEST.C
   Video:         (no special video requirements)
   ----------------------------------------------------------------
*/
```

(continued)

```
#include <stdio.h>
#include <stdlib.h>
#include <conio.h>
#include <string.h>
#include <graph.h>
#include "edit.h"
#include "getkey.h"
```

Function: *next_word()*

The *next_word()* function moves the position index to the start of the next word in the string and returns the new index position. Any characters other than spaces are considered parts of words. The function increments the index to the end of the current word and then over the intervening spaces to locate the first character of the next word.

A few extra lines of code handle the special cases that arise when the index reaches the end of the string or when the string contains spaces but no words.

```
/* - - - - - - - - - - - - - - - - - - - - - - - - - - - - - -
    Function:       next_word()
    Toolbox:        EDIT.C
    Demonstrated:   EDITTEST.C

    Parameters:
      (input)       str       String to be evaluated
      (input)       ndx       Character position

    Returned:       Character position of next word

    Variables:      len       Length of the string

    Description:    Finds the start of the next word in the string
    - - - - - - - - - - - - - - - - - - - - - - - - - - - - - -
*/

int next_word( char *str, int ndx )
{
    unsigned len;
```

(continued)

EDIT.C *continued*

```
    /* Get the length of the string */
    len = strlen( str );

    /* Move to end of the current word */
    while ( ndx < len && str[ndx] != ' ' )
        ndx++;

    /* Move to the start of the next word */
    while ( ndx < len && str[ndx] == ' ' )
        ndx++;

    /* If at end of string, back up to start of preceding word */
    if ( ndx == len )
        {
        ndx--;

        /* Move back over any spaces */
        while ( ndx >= 0 && str[ndx] == ' ' )
            ndx--;

        /* Move back over preceding word */
        while ( ndx >= 0 && str[ndx] != ' ' )
            ndx--;

        /* Move one step forward to start of preceding word */
        ndx++;
        }

    /* Return the new position */
    return ( ndx );
}
```

Function: *prev_word()*

The *prev_word()* function moves the position index to the start of the previous word in the string and returns the new index position. Any characters other than spaces are considered parts of words. The function decrements the index to the start of the current word and then over the intervening spaces to locate the last character of the previous word. Another loop moves the index to the start of that word.

A few extra lines of code handle the special cases that arise when the index reaches the first character of the string or when the string contains spaces but no words.

```
/* - - - - - - - - - - - - - - - - - - - - - - - - - - - - - - - - -

   Function:      prev_word()
   Toolbox:       EDIT.C
   Demonstrated:  EDITTEST.C

   Parameters:
     (input)      str        String to be evaluated
     (input)      ndx        Character position

   Returned:      Character position of previous word

   Variables:     len        Length of the string

   Description:   Finds start of the previous word in the string
   - - - - - - - - - - - - - - - - - - - - - - - - - - - - - - - - -
*/

int prev_word( char *str, int ndx )
{
    int len;

    /* Get length of the string */
    len = strlen( str );

    /* Move back over nonspace characters in current word */
    while ( ndx && str[ndx] != ' ' )
        ndx--;

    /* Move back over the spaces between words */
    while ( ndx && str[ndx] == ' ' )
        ndx--;

    /* Move back over characters in previous word */
    while ( ndx >= 0 && str[ndx] != ' ' )
        ndx--;

    /* Move to first character of the word */
    while (( ndx < len && str[ndx] == ' ' ) || ( ndx < 0 ))
        ndx++;
```

(continued)

EDIT.C *continued*

```
    /* If all spaces, then move back to start of string */
    if ( ndx == len )
        ndx = 0;

    /* Return the new position */
    return ( ndx );
}
```

Function: *delete_char()*

The *delete_char()* function deletes one character at the position indicated by the index. All succeeding characters in the string are shuffled one place to the left, causing the string length to decrease by 1. The function returns the position index, although the value of the index does not change.

```
/* - - - - - - - - - - - - - - - - - - - - - - - - - - - - - - - - -
    Function:       delete_char()
    Toolbox:        EDIT.C
    Demonstrated:   EDITTEST.C

    Parameters:
      (input)       str        String to be evaluated
      (input)       ndx        Character position

    Returned:       Character position

    Variables:      ndx_start Original index value

    Description:    Deletes one character from the string
    - - - - - - - - - - - - - - - - - - - - - - - - - - - - - - - - -
*/

int delete_char( char *str, int ndx )
{
    int ndx_start;

    /* Save current ndx */
    ndx_start = ndx;
```

(continued)

```
    /* Shuffle characters back one space */
    while ( str[ndx] )
        {
        str[ndx] = str[ndx + 1];
        ndx++;
        }

    /* Return the unchanged position */
    return ( ndx );
}
```

Function: *insert_char()*

The *insert_char()* function inserts one character at the position indicated by the index, increments the index by 1, and returns the new value. All succeeding characters are shuffled one place to the right, causing the string length to increase by 1. Be sure that you allocate enough space to the string to accommodate the increased length.

```
/* - - - - - - - - - - - - - - - - - - - - - - - - - - - - - - - - -
    Function:       insert_char()
    Toolbox:        EDIT.C
    Demonstrated:   EDITTEST.C

    Parameters:
      (input)       str       String to be evaluated
      (input)       ndx       Character position
      (input)       c         Character to be inserted

    Returned:       Next character position

    Variables:      i         Looping index

    Description:    Inserts a character into the string
    - - - - - - - - - - - - - - - - - - - - - - - - - - - - - - - - -
*/
```

(continued)

```
int insert_char( char *str, int ndx, char c )
{
    int i;

    /* Shuffle characters right one space */
    for ( i = strlen( str ) - 1; i > ndx; i-- )
        str[i] = str[i-1];

    /* Put character in new position */
    str[ndx] = c;

    /* Return next character position */
    return ( ++ndx );
}
```

Function: *insert_spaces()*

The *insert_spaces()* function inserts one or more spaces into the string at the position indicated by the index. The function increments the position index by the number of spaces inserted and returns the new value.

Notice that *insert_spaces()* also increases the length of the string by the number of spaces inserted. Be sure that you allocate enough space for the string to accommodate this increased length.

```
/* - - - - - - - - - - - - - - - - - - - - - - - - - - - - - - - -
    Function:       insert_spaces()
    Toolbox:        EDIT.C
    Demonstrated:   EDITTEST.C

    Parameters:
      (input)       str      String to be evaluated
      (input)       ndx      Character position
      (input)       n        Number of spaces

    Returned:       Next character position

    Variables:      i        Looping index

    Description:    Inserts a character into the string
    - - - - - - - - - - - - - - - - - - - - - - - - - - - - - - - -
*/
```

(continued)

EDIT.C *continued*

```
int insert_spaces( char *str, int ndx, int n )
{
    int i;

    /* Shuffle characters to the right n places */
    for ( i = strlen( str ); i >= ndx; i-- )
        str[i + n] = str[i];

    /* Put n spaces in string */
    while ( n-- )
        str[++i] = ' ';

    /* Move to the first character after the inserted spaces */
    return ( ndx + n - 1 );
}
```

Function: *replace()*

The *replace()* function performs a global find-and-replace edit of the string and returns the number of replacements made. The function finds each occurrence of the first substring and replaces it with the contents of the second substring.

The length of the resulting string depends on the relative lengths of the two substrings and on the number of replacements made. Be sure to allocate enough space for the string because the function does not check the final string length for you.

```
/* - - - - - - - - - - - - - - - - - - - - - - - - - - - - - - - - -
   Function:       replace()
   Toolbox:        EDIT.C
   Demonstrated:   EDITTEST.C

   Parameters:
     (input)       str       String to be evaluated
     (input)       substr1   Substring to find
     (input)       substr2   Substring to replace substr1

   Returned:       Number of replacements made
```

(continued)

EDIT.C *continued*

```
    Variables:      count      Count of replacements made
                    len        Length of str
                    len2       Length of substr2
                    i          Looping index
                    shift      Amount to shift for insert

    Description:    Replaces each occurrence of substr1 in str
                    with substr2
    - - - - - - - - - - - - - - - - - - - - - - - - - - - - - - -
*/

int replace( char *str, char *substr1, char *substr2 )
{
    int count = 0;
    int len, len2;
    int i, shift;

    /* Get length of replacement string */
    len2 = strlen( substr2 );

    /* Determine amount of shift for each replacement */
    shift = len2 - strlen( substr1 );

    /* Process each occurrence of substr1 in str */
    while (( str = strstr( str, substr1 )) != NULL )
        {

        /* Keep track of number of replacements */
        count++;

        /* Find current length of str */
        len = strlen( str );

        /* Shift left if substr2 is shorter than substr1 */
        if ( shift < 0 )
            {
            for ( i = abs( shift ); i < len + 1; i++ )
                str[i + shift] = str[i];
            }
```

(continued)

```
    /* Shift right if substr2 is longer than substr1 */
    else if ( shift > 0 )
        {
        for ( i = len; i; i-- )
            str[i + shift] = str[i];
        }

    /* Copy substr2 into new place in str */
    strncpy( str, substr2, len2 );

    /* Increment str pointer to character beyond replacement */
    str += len2;
    }

/* Return the number of replacements made */
return ( count );
}
```

Function: *editline()*

The *editline()* function lets the user edit a string with common editing keys. The function displays the string at the current print position on the screen, using the currently set text mode colors. EDITTEST.C shows you how to set the colors and position before you call this function.

The editing keys that *editline()* can process are those described in the following table. The function introduces other input characters into the string, except for control codes less than ASCII 32, some of which cause undesired effects on the screen.

EDITING KEY	RESULT
Right Arrow	Moves cursor one character right
Left Arrow	Moves cursor one character left
Ctrl-Right Arrow	Moves cursor to start of next word
Ctrl-Left Arrow	Moves cursor to start of preceding word
Backspace	Deletes character at left of cursor
Ins	Alternately activates overstrike and insert modes
Del	Deletes character at the cursor
Home	Moves cursor to first character in string
End	Moves cursor to last character in string
Ctrl-End	Deletes all characters from cursor to end of string

The length of the string remains constant. If necessary, the function adds spaces or drops characters at the end of the string to maintain the constant length. This makes the function easier to use for editing user input in situations in which field lengths are fixed.

The function ends whenever the user presses the Up Arrow, Down Arrow, Esc, or Enter key. The function returns the key code for the condition that terminates it.

```
/* - - - - - - - - - - - - - - - - - - - - - - - - - - - - - - - -
   Function:       editline()
   Toolbox:        EDIT.C
   Demonstrated:   EDITTEST.C

   Parameters:
     (input)       str         String to be edited

   Returned:       KEY_UP         If Cursor Up was last keypress
                   KEY_DOWN       If Cursor Down was last keypress
                   KEY_ESCAPE     If Escape was last keypress
                   KEY_ENTER      If Enter was last keypress

   Variables:      doneflag       Signals when to end the edit
                   insertflag     Insert or overstrike mode
                   index          Cursor position
                   key            Key code returned by getkey()
                   len            Length of str
                   i              Looping index
                   strpos         Original cursor position

   Description:    Displays string at the current cursor location;
                   uses the current text colors and allows user
                   to edit the string with standard editing keys
   - - - - - - - - - - - - - - - - - - - - - - - - - - - - - - - -
*/

int editline( char *str )
{
    unsigned doneflag = 0;
    int insertflag = 1, index = 0;
    int key, len, i;
    struct rccoord strpos;
```

(continued)

```
/* Get the length of the string to be edited */
len = strlen( str );

/* Record current location of the cursor */
strpos = _gettextposition();

/* Clear out any keypresses in the keyboard buffer */
while ( kbhit() )
    getch();

/* Main editing loop */
while ( !doneflag )
    {

    /* Position the cursor at the original location */
    _settextposition( strpos.row, strpos.col );

    /* Display the string */
    _outtext( str );

    /* Move cursor to current editing position */
    _settextposition( strpos.row, strpos.col + index );

    /* Set cursor type for insert or overstrike mode */
    if ( insertflag )
        _settextcursor( CURSOR_UNDERLINE );
    else
        _settextcursor( CURSOR_BLOCK );

    /* Wait for a keypress or mouse movement */
    key = getkey_or_mouse();

    /* Process each keypress */
    switch (key)
        {

        case KEY_UP:
            doneflag = key;
            break;

        case KEY_DOWN:
            doneflag = key;
            break;
```

(continued)

EDIT.C *continued*

```
        case KEY_LEFT:
            if ( index )
                index--;
            break;

        case KEY_RIGHT:
            if ( index < len - 1 )
                index++;
            break;

        case KEY_ESCAPE:
            doneflag = key;
            break;

        case KEY_CTRL_LEFT:
            index = prev_word( str, index );
            break;

        case KEY_CTRL_RIGHT:
            index = next_word( str, index );
            break;

        case KEY_END:
            for ( index = len - 1; str[index] == ' ' && index; index-- )
                {;}
            if ( index && index < len - 1 )
                index++;
            break;

        case KEY_BACKSPACE:
            if ( index )
                {
                index--;
                delete_char( str, index );
                str[len-1] = ' ';
                }
            break;

        case KEY_CTRL_END:
            for ( i = index; i < len; i++ )
                str[i] = ' ';
            break;
```

(continued)

```
            case KEY_INSERT:
                insertflag ^= 1;
                break;

            case KEY_DELETE:
                delete_char( str, index );
                str[len-1] = ' ';
                break;

            case KEY_ENTER:
                doneflag = key;
                break;

            case KEY_HOME:
                index = 0;
                break;

            default:
                if ( key >= ' ' && key < 256 )
                    {
                    if ( insertflag )
                        insert_char( str, index, (char)key );
                    else
                        str[index] = (char)key;
                    if ( index < len - 1 )
                        index++;
                    }
                break;
            }

        /* Truncate string at original length */
        str[len] = 0;
        }

    /* Return the key that caused the exit */
    return ( doneflag );
}
```

FRACTION

FUNCTION	DESCRIPTION
fadd()	Adds fractions
fsub()	Subtracts fractions
fmul()	Multiplies fractions
fdiv()	Divides fractions
reduce()	Reduces a fraction to lowest terms
gcd()	Finds the greatest common divisor
lcm()	Finds the least common multiple
frac_to_s()	Converts a fraction to a string
s_to_frac()	Converts a string to a fraction

The FRACTION toolbox module provides a collection of functions for working with fractions. The functions let you perform basic arithmetic operations with fractions and reduce fractions to lowest terms. Related functions find the greatest common divisor and least common multiple of any two long integers. Another pair of functions simplifies the conversion between a string representation of a fraction and its storage in a two-member structure.

The FRACTEST demonstration program initializes a pair of sample fractions, *a* and *b*, and shows the results of a series of calculations performed using the arithmetic functions. Notice that the result of each operation is assigned to *a*, so the value of *a* is different in subsequent calculations. FRACTEST then uses the *gcd()* and *lcm()* functions with sample long integers.

Several of the FRACTION functions are similar in design and concept to those in the COMPLEX module. To demonstrate a different approach, the FRACTION functions manipulate values by reference and return results in one of the operand structures. Compare the *fadd()* and *cadd()* functions to see this difference. The *fadd()* function expects two addresses of fractions, pointers *pa* and *pb*, and places the result in the structure referenced by *pa*. The *cadd()* function expects two values, complex numbers *a* and *b*, and returns a result in complex number *c*.

The *fraction* structure is defined in the FRACTION.H header file. The structure contains two members, which represent the numerator and denominator of the fraction. Each is defined as a long integer to allow for manipulation of large and precise fractions. The FRACTEST program shows how the addresses of these structures are passed to the functions in the FRACTION module.

Notice that *fadd()*, *fsub()*, *fmul()*, and *fdiv()* always reduce their results to lowest terms. This additional step helps prevent a chain of calculations from overflowing the numerator or denominator variable.

The *reduce()* function uses *gcd()* to reduce a fraction to lowest terms. The related *lcm()* function is included in the module for completeness.

Demonstration Program: FRACTEST.C

```
/* ------------------------------------------------------------------

   Name:          FRACTEST.C
   Type:          Demonstration program
   Language:      Microsoft QuickC
   Video:         (no special video requirements)

   Program list:  FRACTEST.C
                  FRACTION.C

   Variables:     a          First fraction
                  b          Second fraction
                  fa         String representation of fraction a
                  fb         String representation of fraction b
                  n          gcd() and lcm() results

   Usage:         (no command line parameters)

   Description:   Demonstrates the FRACTION toolbox functions
   ------------------------------------------------------------------
*/

#include <stdio.h>
#include "fraction.h"
```

(continued)

FRACTEST.C *continued*

```
main()
{
    struct fraction a, b;
    char fa[80], fb[80];
    long int n;

    /* Set fraction a to 7/8 */
    s_to_frac( " 7 / 8 ", &a );

    /* Set fraction b to 15/24 */
    s_to_frac( "15/24", &b );

    /* Display the initial values of the fractions */
    printf( "\n\n\n\n\n" );
    printf( "Fraction a: %s\n", frac_to_s( &a, fa ));
    printf( "Fraction b: %s\n", frac_to_s( &b, fb ));

    /* Add b to a */
    fadd( &a, &b );
    printf( "\na = a + b ... %s\n", frac_to_s( &a, fa ));

    /* Subtract b from a */
    fsub( &a, &b );
    printf( "\na = a - b ... %s\n", frac_to_s( &a, fa ));

    /* Multiply a by b */
    fmul( &a, &b );
    printf( "\na = a * b ... %s\n", frac_to_s( &a, fa ));

    /* Divide a by b */
    fdiv( &a, &b );
    printf( "\na = a / b ... %s\n", frac_to_s( &a, fa ));

    /* Find the greatest common divisor */
    n = gcd( 16949L, 1649L );
    printf( "\n\ngcd( 16949L, 1649L ) ... %ld\n", n );

    /* Find the least common multiple */
    n = lcm( 16949L, 1649L );
    printf( "\nlcm( 16949L, 1649L ) ... %ld\n", n );
}
```

Include File: FRACTION.H

```
/* ----------------------------------------------------------------
   Name:         FRACTION.H
   Type:         Include
   Language:     Microsoft QuickC
   Demonstrated: FRACTION.C  FRACTEST.C
   Description:  Prototypes and definitions for FRACTION.C
   ----------------------------------------------------------------
*/

#ifndef FRACTION_DEFINED

struct fraction
    {
    long int num, den;
    };

void fadd( struct fraction *, struct fraction * );
void fsub( struct fraction *, struct fraction * );
void fmul( struct fraction *, struct fraction * );
void fdiv( struct fraction *, struct fraction * );
void reduce( struct fraction * );
long int gcd( long int, long int );
long int lcm( long int, long int );
char *frac_to_s( struct fraction *, char * );
int s_to_frac( char *, struct fraction * );

#define FRACTION_DEFINED
#endif
```

Toolbox Module: FRACTION.C

```
/* ----------------------------------------------------------------
   Name:         FRACTION.C
   Type:         Toolbox module
   Language:     Microsoft QuickC
   Demonstrated: FRACTEST.C
   Video:        (no special video requirements)
   ----------------------------------------------------------------
*/
```

(continued)

FRACTION.C *continued*

```
#include <stdio.h>
#include <stdlib.h>
#include "fraction.h"
```

Function: *fadd()*

The *fadd()* function adds two fractions and returns the result in the structure that holds the first. Pass the address of each fraction variable. The function calls *reduce()* to express the sum in lowest terms.

```
/* - - - - - - - - - - - - - - - - - - - - - - - - - - - - - - - - -
    Function:       fadd()
    Toolbox:        FRACTION.C
    Demonstrated:   FRACTEST.C

    Parameters:
     (in/out)       pa          Pointer to first fraction
     (input)        pb          Pointer to second fraction

    Returned:       (function returns nothing)

    Variables:      (none)

    Description:    Adds two fractions and places sum in first
   - - - - - - - - - - - - - - - - - - - - - - - - - - - - - - - - -
*/

void fadd( struct fraction *pa, struct fraction *pb )
{
    pa->num = pa->num * pb->den + pa->den * pb->num;
    pa->den *= pb->den;

    reduce( pa );
}
```

Function: *fsub()*

The *fsub()* function subtracts two fractions and returns the result in the structure that holds the first. Pass the address of each fraction variable. The function subtracts the second fraction from the first and calls the *reduce()* function to express the result in lowest terms.

```
/* - - - - - - - - - - - - - - - - - - - - - - - - - - - - - - -
    Function:       fsub()
    Toolbox:        FRACTION.C
    Demonstrated:   FRACTEST.C

    Parameters:
      (in/out)      pa              Pointer to first fraction
      (input)       pb              Pointer to second fraction

    Returned:       (function returns nothing)

    Variables:      (none)

    Description:    Subtracts second fraction from first and
                    places difference in first
    - - - - - - - - - - - - - - - - - - - - - - - - - - - - - -
*/

void fsub( struct fraction *pa, struct fraction *pb )
{
    pa->num = pa->num * pb->den - pa->den * pb->num;
    pa->den *= pb->den;

    reduce( pa );
}
```

Function: *fmul()*

The *fmul()* function multiplies two fractions and returns the result in the structure that holds the first. Pass the address of each fraction variable. The function calls *reduce()* to express the product in lowest terms.

```
/* - - - - - - - - - - - - - - - - - - - - - - - - - - - - - - -
    Function:       fmul()
    Toolbox:        FRACTION.C
    Demonstrated:   FRACTEST.C

    Parameters:
      (in/out)      pa              Pointer to first fraction
      (input)       pb              Pointer to second fraction

    Returned:       (function returns nothing)
```

(continued)

FRACTION.C *continued*

```
    Variables:      (none)

    Description:    Multiplies two fractions and places product
                    in first
    - - - - - - - - - - - - - - - - - - - - - - - - - - - - - - - -
*/

void fmul( struct fraction *pa, struct fraction *pb )
{
    pa->num *= pb->num;
    pa->den *= pb->den;

    reduce( pa );
}
```

Function: *fdiv()*

The *fdiv()* function divides two fractions and returns the result in the structure that holds the first. Pass the address of each fraction variable. The function divides the first fraction by the second and calls *reduce()* to express the quotient in lowest terms.

```
/* - - - - - - - - - - - - - - - - - - - - - - - - - - - - - - -
    Function:       fdiv()
    Toolbox:        FRACTION.C
    Demonstrated:   FRACTEST.C

    Parameters:
      (in/out)      pa          Pointer to first fraction
      (input)       pb          Pointer to second fraction

    Returned:       (function returns nothing)

    Variables:      (none)

    Description:    Divides first fraction by second and places
                    quotient in first
    - - - - - - - - - - - - - - - - - - - - - - - - - - - - - - - -
*/
```

(continued)

```
void fdiv( struct fraction *pa, struct fraction *pb )
{
    pa->num *= pb->den;
    pa->den *= pb->num;

    reduce( pa );
}
```

Function: *reduce()*

The *reduce()* function reduces a fraction to lowest terms. Pass the address of a fraction to this function. The fractional arithmetic functions call *reduce()* to help prevent overflows and thereby maintain accuracy over successive calculations.

```
/* - - - - - - - - - - - - - - - - - - - - - - - - - - - - - - - -
    Function:       reduce()
    Toolbox:        FRACTION.C
    Demonstrated:   FRACTEST.C

    Parameters:
     (in/out)       pa          Pointer to fraction

    Returned:       (function returns nothing)

    Variables:      t           Greatest common divisor of num and den

    Description:    Reduces a fraction to its lowest terms
    - - - - - - - - - - - - - - - - - - - - - - - - - - - - - - - -
*/

void reduce( struct fraction *pa )
{
    long int t;

    t = gcd( pa->num, pa->den );

    pa->num /= t;
    pa->den /= t;
}
```

Function: *gcd()*

The *gcd()* function returns the greatest common divisor of two long integers. The greatest common divisor is the largest integer that can be divided evenly (with no remainder) into each of two given integers. The *reduce()* function calls *gcd()* in the process of reducing a fraction to its lowest terms.

```
/* - - - - - - - - - - - - - - - - - - - - - - - - - - - - - -
   Function:      gcd()
   Toolbox:       FRACTION.C
   Demonstrated:  FRACTEST.C

   Parameters:
     (input)      a          First long integer
     (input)      b          Second long integer

   Returned:      The greatest common divisor of a and b

   Variables:     c          Working variable

   Description:   Returns the greatest common divisor of two
                  long integers
   - - - - - - - - - - - - - - - - - - - - - - - - - - - - - -
*/

long int gcd( long a, long b )
{
    long int c;

    do
        {
        c = a % b;
        a = b;
        b = c;
        }
    while ( c );

    return ( a );
}
```

Function: *lcm()*

The *lcm()* function returns the least common multiple of two long integers. The least common multiple of two integers is the smallest number for which both integers are factors.

This function is closely related to the *gcd()* function, which determines the greatest common divisor of two long integers.

```
/* - - - - - - - - - - - - - - - - - - - - - - - - - - - - - - - -
    Function:       lcm()
    Toolbox:        FRACTION.C
    Demonstrated:   FRACTEST.C

    Parameters:
      (input)       a           First long integer
      (input)       b           Second long integer

    Returned:       The least common multiple of a and b

    Variables:      c           Working variable

    Description:    Returns the least common multiple of two long
                    integers
   - - - - - - - - - - - - - - - - - - - - - - - - - - - - - - - -
*/

long int lcm( long a, long b )
{
    long int c;

    c = gcd( a, b );

    return ( labs( a * b / c ));
}
```

Function: *frac_to_s()*

The *frac_to_s()* function converts a fraction from storage as a structure of type *fraction* to a string representation. This string contains two integers separated with a slash character (/) and is suitable for display or printing. Be sure to allocate enough space for the string variable to accommodate the largest fractions your program might create.

```
/* - - - - - - - - - - - - - - - - - - - - - - - - - - - - - - - - - -
     Function:        frac_to_s()
     Toolbox:         FRACTION.C
     Demonstrated:    FRACTEST.C

     Parameters:
       (input)        pa          Pointer to fraction
       (output)       str         String representation of the fraction

     Returned:        The string representation of the fraction

     Variables:       (none)

     Description:     Formats a fraction into a string representation
   - - - - - - - - - - - - - - - - - - - - - - - - - - - - - - - - - -
*/

char * frac_to_s( struct fraction *pa, char *str )
{
    sprintf( str, "%ld/%ld", pa->num, pa->den );
    return ( str );
}
```

Function: *s_to_frac()*

The *s_to_frac()* function converts a string representation of a fraction to a structure variable of type *fraction*. The string should contain two integers separated with a slash character (/).

The *s_to_frac()* function returns 2 if the translation to a fraction is successful; it returns 0 if the translation fails. This return code is actually the same error code returned by *sscanf()*, which is used to scan and translate the string.

```
/* - - - - - - - - - - - - - - - - - - - - - - - - - - - - - - - - - -
     Function:        s_to_frac()
     Toolbox:         FRACTION.C
     Demonstrated:    FRACTEST.C

     Parameters:
       (input)        str         String representation of a fraction
       (output)       pa          Pointer to fraction
```

(continued)

FRACTION.C *continued*

```
    Returned:        2  if the string was successfully converted
                     0  if conversion failed


    Variables:       (none)


    Description:     Scans a string and converts it to a fraction
    - - - - - - - - - - - - - - - - - - - - - - - - - - - - - - - -
*/

int s_to_frac( char *str, struct fraction *pa )
{
    if ( sscanf( str, " %ld / %ld", &pa->num, &pa->den ) == 2 )
        return( 2 );
    else
        return ( 0 );
}
```

GAME

FUNCTION	DESCRIPTION
array_fill()	Fills array with sequential integers
array_shuffle()	Shuffles elements of integer array
card_name()	Generates string name of playing card
dice()	Rolls *n* dice and returns the sum
shuffle_str()	Shuffles characters in a string
shuffle_rand()	Randomly seeds random number generator

The GAME toolbox module provides a collection of functions that perform some common game-programming tasks. With these functions you can shuffle and deal from a deck of playing cards, randomly rearrange the characters in a string, or roll one or more dice.

The GAME functions are useful in a wide variety of programs. For example, *array_shuffle()* provides a fast, efficient way to shuffle the contents of an integer array. The technique can easily be extended for any situation in which you need to randomize the order of the elements in a list of any type—the numbers to be called in a bingo game, for instance. The *shuffle_rand()* function shows how to use the system time to seed the QuickC random number generator; you can apply the same technique to many tasks that require an unpredictable sequence of random numbers.

The GAMETEST program demonstrates all the functions in this module. It creates a 54-element integer array named *deck* and fills it with the numbers 0 through 53. The integers represent the 52 cards of a standard deck of playing cards, plus 2 jokers. The program calls *array_fill()* to initialize the array, and then it uses *array_shuffle()* to shuffle the order of the numbers in the array. With the deck effectively shuffled, GAMETEST displays, or "deals," the first seven cards and uses the *card_name()* function to convert each integer to the name of the card it represents.

GAMETEST uses another function, *shuffle_str()*, which is similar to *array_shuffle()*, to shuffle the characters in a string. The program displays the contents of the string before and after they are shuffled.

Finally, GAMETEST rolls a pair of dice several times and displays the total for each roll. Notice that with two dice the totals should average 7.

Demonstration Program: GAMETEST.C

```
/* -----------------------------------------------------------------
    Name:           GAMETEST.C
    Type:           Demonstration program
    Language:       Microsoft QuickC
    Video:          (no special video requirements)

    Program list:   GAMETEST.C
                    GAME.C

    Variables:      i           Looping index
                    deck        Array representing a deck of cards
                    str         String to be shuffled
                    card        Name of card in the deck

    Usage:          (no command line parameters)

    Description:    Demonstrates the GAME toolbox functions
   ------------------------------------------------------------------
*/

#include <stdio.h>
#include <string.h>
#include "game.h"

main()
{
    int i;
    int deck[54];
    char str[80];
    char card[20];
```

(continued)

GAMETEST.C *continued*

```
    /* Shuffle the random numbers */
    shuffle_rand();

    /* Fill the deck with card numbers */
    array_fill( deck, 0, 53, 0 );

    /* Shuffle the deck */
    array_shuffle( deck, 0, 53 );

    /* Deal first seven cards from the deck */
    printf( "\nFirst seven cards from a shuffled deck...\n\n" );
    for ( i = 0; i < 7; i++ )
        printf( "%s\n", card_name( deck[i], card ));

    /* Demonstrate string shuffling */
    strcpy( str, "This string is going to get shuffled" );
    printf( "\n\nString shuffling...\n\n%s\n", str );
    shuffle_str( str );
    printf( "%s\n\n\n", str );

    /* Roll some dice */
    printf( "Rolling a pair of dice, several times...\n" );
    for ( i = 0; i < 17; i++ )
        printf( "%d ", dice( 2 ));

    /* All done */
    printf( "\n\n" );
}
```

Include File: GAME.H

```
/* -----------------------------------------------------------------
    Name:           GAME.H
    Type:           Include
    Language:       Microsoft QuickC
    Demonstrated:   GAME.C  GAMETEST.C
    Description:    Prototypes and definitions for GAME.C
   -----------------------------------------------------------------
*/
```

(continued)

```
#ifndef GAME_DEFINED

void array_fill( int *, int, int, int );
void array_shuffle( int *, int, int );
char * card_name( int, char * );
int dice( int );
void shuffle_str( char * );
void shuffle_rand(void);

#define GAME_DEFINED
#endif
```

Toolbox Module: GAME.C

```
/* ---------------------------------------------------------------
    Name:           GAME.C
    Type:           Toolbox module
    Language:       Microsoft QuickC
    Demonstrated:   GAMETEST.C
    Video:          (no special video requirements)
   ---------------------------------------------------------------
*/

#include <stdio.h>
#include <stdlib.h>
#include <string.h>
#include <time.h>
#include "game.h"
```

Function: *array_fill()*

The *array_fill()* function fills all or part of an integer array with sequential integers. The function expects four parameters: the array to be filled, the first element to be filled, the last element to be filled, and the starting integer for the fill.

The GAMETEST demonstration program uses *array_fill()* to initialize a complete array that represents a deck of cards. Another program might declare an integer array *years[1000]* that contains lists of years. If the array elements from 90 through 99 are to contain year numbers 1770 through 1779, the following call puts these numbers into the array:

```
array_fill( years, 90, 99, 1770 );
```

```
/* - - - - - - - - - - - - - - - - - - - - - - - - - - - - - - - -

   Function:       array_fill()
   Toolbox:        GAME.C
   Demonstrated:   GAMETEST.C

   Parameters:
     (in/out)      array     Array of integers to be filled
     (input)       start     Index to first array element to fill
     (input)       finish    Index to last array element to fill
     (input)       n         Number to put in first array element

   Returned:       (function returns nothing)

   Variables:      i         Looping index

   Description:    Fills part or all of an integer array with
                   sequential integers, starting with n
   - - - - - - - - - - - - - - - - - - - - - - - - - - - - - - - -
*/

void array_fill( int *array, int start, int finish, int n )
{
    int i;

    /* Fill each array element with sequential integers */
    for ( i = start; i <= finish; i++ )
        array[i] = n++;
}
```

Function: *array_shuffle()*

The *array_shuffle()* function randomly reorders the elements of an integer array. The function expects three parameters: the array to be shuffled, the first element to be shuffled, and the last element to be shuffled.

The GAMETEST demonstration program uses *array_shuffle()* to shuffle the 54 card numbers stored in the array *deck*. The function swaps each element of the array with a randomly selected second element. This technique guarantees that each element is shuffled and that each element is equally likely to end up in any of the array positions.

```
/* - - - - - - - - - - - - - - - - - - - - - - - - - - - - - - - -

    Function:       array_shuffle()
    Toolbox:        GAME.C
    Demonstrated:   GAMETEST.C

    Parameters:
      (in/out)      array     Array of integers to be shuffled
      (input)       start     First array element to be shuffled
      (input)       finish    Last array element to be shuffled

    Returned:       (function returns nothing)

    Variables:      i         Looping index, each element
                    j         Random element to swap with element i
                    count     Number of array elements to shuffle
                    t         Temporary swapping variable

    Description:    Shuffles the contents of part or all of an
                    integer array
    - - - - - - - - - - - - - - - - - - - - - - - - - - - - - - - -
*/

void array_shuffle( int *array, int start, int finish )
{
    int i, j, count, t;

    /* Determine the number of array entries to shuffle */
    count = finish - start + 1;

    /* Shuffle each element with a randomly selected element */
    for ( i = start; i <= finish; i++ )
        {
        j = rand() % count + start;
        t = array[i];
        array[i] = array[j];
        array[j] = t;
        }
}
```

Function: *card_name()*

The *card_name()* function fills a string with the name of a playing card represented by an integer. The function associates integers from 0 through 51 with cards in the standard deck, and it matches any number outside this range with the string "Joker". This makes it easy to include 2 jokers in your deck by using integers from 0 to 53.

Pass a string that has been dimensioned to at least 18 characters. The longest card name created is "Queen of Diamonds", which contains 18 characters including the terminating '\0'. The string is filled in with the card name, and the string address is returned by the function call.

```
/* - - - - - - - - - - - - - - - - - - - - - - - - - - - - - - - - -
   Function:      card_name()
   Toolbox:       GAME.C
   Demonstrated:  GAMETEST.C

   Parameters:
     (input)      n          Number from 0 to 51 (or more)
     (output)     card       String where card name is put

   Returned:      card is returned by the function

   Variables:     (none)

   Description:   Fills the string with the name of one of the
                  52 cards that make up a standard card deck. Returns
                  "Joker" for numbers out of the range 0 through 51.
   - - - - - - - - - - - - - - - - - - - - - - - - - - - - - - - - -
*/

char *card_name( int n, char *card )
{
    /* Determine the card number or face name */
    switch ( n % 13 )
        {
        case 0:
            strcpy( card, "Ace" );
            break;
        case 1:
        case 2:
        case 3:
        case 4:
```

(continued)

```
        case 5:
        case 6:
        case 7:
        case 8:
        case 9:
            card[0] = (char)('0' + ( n % 13 ));
            card[1] = '0';
            break;
        case 10:
            strcpy( card, "Jack" );
            break;
        case 11:
            strcpy( card, "Queen" );
            break;
        case 12:
            strcpy( card, "King" );
            break;
        }

    /* Add the suit name */
    switch ( n / 13 )
        {
        case 0:
            strcat( card, " of Spades" );
            break;
        case 1:
            strcat( card, " of Clubs" );
            break;
        case 2:
            strcat( card, " of Hearts" );
            break;
        case 3:
            strcat( card, " of Diamonds" );
            break;
        default:
            strcpy( card, "Joker" );
            break;
        }

    /* Return the name of the card */
    return ( card );
}
```

Function: *dice()*

The *dice()* function returns the total number of dots showing after a roll of a specified number of dice. This function uses the QuickC random number generator to generate a pseudorandom integer from 1 through 6 for each die. The function returns the sum of these random numbers.

Be sure to call *shuffle_rand()* at the start of any program that uses the *dice()* function. Otherwise, your program will generate the same sequence of random numbers every time you run it.

```
/* - - - - - - - - - - - - - - - - - - - - - - - - - - - - - - - - - - - - -
    Function:      dice()
    Toolbox:       GAME.C
    Demonstrated:  GAMETEST.C

    Parameters:
     (input)       n          Number of dice to be rolled

    Returned:      Total of dots showing on the n dice

    Variables:     i          Looping index
                   total      Sum of the dice

    Description:   Rolls n dice, sums the number of dots showing,
                   and returns this total
    - - - - - - - - - - - - - - - - - - - - - - - - - - - - - - - - - - -
*/

int dice( int n )
{
    int i, total = 0;

    /* Sum each of the n dice into total */
    for ( i = 0; i < n; i++ )
        total += ( rand() % 6 + 1 );

    /* Return the total of all the dice */
    return ( total );
}
```

Function: *shuffle_str()*

The *shuffle_str()* function randomly reorders the characters in a string. This function is similar to *array_shuffle()* in operation, but it shuffles characters rather than integers. The function can easily determine the length of the string, so the only argument you need to supply is the string itself.

The *shuffle_str()* function would be useful for creating or solving anagrams, or for word games in which the order of the letters has been randomized.

```
/* - - - - - - - - - - - - - - - - - - - - - - - - - - - - - - - - -
    Function:       shuffle_str()
    Toolbox:        GAME.C
    Demonstrated:   GAMETEST.C

    Parameters:
     (in/out)       str       String of characters to be shuffled

    Returned:       (function returns nothing)

    Variables:      i         Looping index, each character of str
                    j         Random character to swap with char i
                    len       Length of the string
                    t         Temporary swapping variable

    Description:    Randomly shuffles the characters in a string
    - - - - - - - - - - - - - - - - - - - - - - - - - - - - - - - - -
*/

void shuffle_str( char *str )
{
    int i, j, len, t;

    /* Determine the length of the string */
    len = strlen( str );

    /* Shuffle each character with a randomly selected character */
    for ( i = 0; i < len; i++ )
        {
        j = rand() % len;
        t = str[i];
        str[i] = str[j];
        str[j] = (char)t;
        }
}
```

Function: *shuffle_rand()*

The *shuffle_rand()* function randomly sets the starting point for the QuickC random number sequence. The function uses the system time to seed the random numbers, thereby creating a different sequence every second. The RANDOMS toolbox module offers a different method of generating pseudorandom numbers.

```
/* - - - - - - - - - - - - - - - - - - - - - - - - - - - - - /*
    Function:       shuffle_rand()
    Toolbox:        GAME.C
    Demonstrated:   GAMETEST.C

    Parameters:     (none)

    Returned:       (function returns nothing)

    Variables:      (none)

    Description:    Uses the system clock to seed the sequence of
                    pseudorandom numbers
    - - - - - - - - - - - - - - - - - - - - - - - - - - - - - -
*/

void shuffle_rand( void )
{
    /* Use the system time to seed the random numbers */
    srand( (unsigned)time( NULL ));
}
```

GEOMETRY

FUNCTION	DESCRIPTION
polar_to_rect()	Converts polar to rectangular notation
rect_to_polar()	Converts rectangular to polar notation
distance()	Finds the distance between two points
direction()	Finds the angle from point to point
translate()	Shifts an x,y point
rotate()	Rotates a point around the origin
angle_between()	Finds the angle defined by three points
area()	Calculates the area defined by three points
equidistant()	Finds the point equidistant from three points
translate_3d()	Shifts an x,y,z point
distance_3d()	Finds the distance between x,y,z points
angle_between_3d()	Finds the angle defined by three space points
area_3d()	Finds the area defined by three space points
volume_3d()	Finds the volume defined by four points
xyz_to_cyl()	Converts Cartesian to cylindrical notation
xyz_to_sph()	Converts Cartesian to spherical notation
cyl_to_xyz()	Converts cylindrical to Cartesian notation
cyl_to_sph()	Converts cylindrical to spherical notation
sph_to_xyz()	Converts spherical to Cartesian notation
sph_to_cyl()	Converts spherical to cylindrical notation

The GEOMETRY toolbox module provides a collection of functions you can use in two-dimensional and three-dimensional analytical geometry. The module includes functions for rectangular-to-polar and polar-to-rectangular conversions in two dimensions. Similar functions for three-dimensional calculations provide conversions between rectangular, cylindrical, and spherical coordinate notations. Other functions find the distance between points, the angles formed by connected points, the area defined by three points, and the volume defined by four points in space.

The GEOMTEST program demonstrates the functions in this module. The program declares sets of points in both two-dimensional and three-dimensional coordinate systems; the declarations reference the structure definitions in GEOMETRY.H. GEOMTEST then passes sample points to the module functions and displays the results.

The measurements that are manipulated in this module are declared as double-precision floating-point variables. You can change the structure definitions in GEOMETRY.H if you prefer to use the shorter *float* variables for coordinates.

Demonstration Program: GEOMTEST.C

```
/* ------------------------------------------------------------------
    Name:          GEOMTEST.C
    Type:          Demonstration program
    Language:      Microsoft QuickC
    Video:         (no special video requirements)

    Program list:  GEOMTEST.C
                   GEOMETRY.C

    Variables:     p1          Two-dimensional point
                   p2          Two-dimensional point
                   p3          Two-dimensional point
                   p4          Two-dimensional point
                   q1          Three-dimensional point
                   q2          Three-dimensional point
                   q3          Three-dimensional point
                   q4          Three-dimensional point

    Usage:         (no command line parameters)

    Description:   Demonstrates the GEOMETRY toolbox functions
   ------------------------------------------------------------------
*/

#include <stdio.h>
#include <conio.h>
#include "geometry.h"

main()
{
    struct coord_2d p1, p2, p3, p4;
    struct coord_3d q1, q2, q3, q4;
```

(continued)

GEOMTEST.C *continued*

```
    printf( "\n\nTwo-dimensional functions...\n\n" );

    /* Set and display the first point */
    p1.x = 3.0;
    p1.y = 4.0;
    printf( "p1 = %f, %f\n", p1.x, p1.y );

    /* Set and display the second point */
    p2.x = -3.0;
    p2.y = 7.0;
    printf( "p2 = %f, %f\n", p2.x, p2.y );

    /* Set and display the third point */
    p3.x = 5.0;
    p3.y = 9.0;
    printf( "p3 = %f, %f\n", p3.x, p3.y );

    /* Convert first point from rectangular to polar notation */
    rect_to_polar( &p1 );
    printf( "\nrect_to_polar, p1 = %f, %f\n", p1.x, p1.y );

    /* Then convert it from polar to rectangular notation */
    polar_to_rect( &p1 );
    printf( "polar_to_rect, p1 = %f, %f\n", p1.x, p1.y );

    /* Find the point equidistant from three points */
    printf( "\nRadius of circle touching p1, p2, and p3 = %f\n",
            equidistant( &p1, &p2, &p3, &p4 ));
    printf( "Center of circle touching p1, p2, and p3 = %f, %f\n",
            p4.x, p4.y);

    /* Find the distance between two points */
    printf( "\nDistance p1 to p2 = %f\n", distance( &p1, &p2 ));

    /* Find the angular direction of point 2 from point 1 */
    printf( "Direction p1 to p2 = %f\n", direction( &p1, &p2 ));

    /* Find the angle formed by connecting point 1 to 2 to 3 */
    printf( "\nAngle at p1 to p2 to p3 = %f\n",
            angle_between( &p1, &p2, &p3 ));
```

(continued)

GEOMTEST.C *continued*

```
/* Find area of the triangle defined by points 1, 2, and 3 */
printf( "Area at p1 to p2 to p3 = %f\n\n",
        area( &p1, &p2, &p3 ));

/* Shift the first point 2 to the right and up 3 */
translate( &p1, 2.0, 3.0 );
printf( "p1 translated by 2, 3 = %f, %f\n", p1.x, p1.y );

/* Rotate first point around origin by 1.23 radians */
rotate( &p1, 1.23 );
printf( "Then rotated around origin by 1.23 radians = %f, %f\n",
        p1.x, p1.y );

/* Wait for user */
printf( "\nPress any key to continue... " );
getch();

printf( "\n\nThree-dimensional functions...\n\n" );

/* Set and display the first three-dimensional point */
q1.x = 3.0;
q1.y = 4.0;
q1.z = 5.0;
printf( "q1 = %f, %f, %f\n", q1.x, q1.y, q1.z );

/* Set and display the second three-dimensional point */
q2.x = 6.0;
q2.y = 7.0;
q2.z = 2.0;
printf( "q2 = %f, %f, %f\n", q2.x, q2.y, q2.z );

/* Set and display the third three-dimensional point */
q3.x = -3.0;
q3.y = 4.0;
q3.z = 3.0;
printf( "q3 = %f, %f, %f\n", q3.x, q3.y, q3.z );

/* Set and display the fourth three-dimensional point */
q4.x = 7.0;
q4.y = 7.0;
q4.z = 4.0;
printf( "q4 = %f, %f, %f\n", q4.x, q4.y, q4.z );
```

(continued)

```
/* Find the distance from point 1 to point 2 */
printf( "\nDistance q1 to q2 = %f\n", distance_3d( &q1, &q2 ));

/* Find the angle formed by connecting point 1 to 2 to 3 */
printf( "\nAngle at q1 to q2 to q3 = %f\n",
        angle_between_3d( &q1, &q2, &q3 ));

/* Find the area formed by connecting point 1 to 2 to 3 */
printf( "Area at q1 to q2 to q3 = %f\n\n",
        area_3d( &q1, &q2, &q3 ));

/* Find the volume defined by the four points */
printf( "Volume q1, q2, q3, q4 = %f\n",
        volume_3d( &q1, &q2, &q3, &q4 ));

/* Shift the first space point */
translate_3d( &q1, 1.0, 2.0, 3.0 );
printf( "q1 translated by 1, 2, 3 = %f, %f, %f\n",
        q1.x, q1.y, q1.z );

/* Display the first x,y,z point */
printf( "\nq1 xyz = %f, %f, %f (x, y, z)\n",
        q1.x, q1.y, q1.z );

/* Convert from Cartesian to cylindrical notation */
xyz_to_cyl( &q1 );
printf( "q1 cyl = %f, %f, %f (radius, theta, z)\n",
        q1.x, q1.y, q1.z );

/* Convert from cylindrical to spherical notation */
cyl_to_sph( &q1 );
printf( "q1 sph = %f, %f, %f (rho, theta, phi)\n",
        q1.x, q1.y, q1.z );

/* Convert from spherical to cylindrical notation */
sph_to_cyl( &q1 );
printf( "q1 cyl = %f, %f, %f (radius, theta, z)\n",
        q1.x, q1.y, q1.z );

/* Convert from cylindrical to Cartesian notation */
cyl_to_xyz( &q1 );
printf( "q1 xyz = %f, %f, %f (x, y, z)\n",
        q1.x, q1.y, q1.z );
```

(continued)

GEOMTEST.C *continued*

```
    /* Convert from Cartesian to spherical notation */
    xyz_to_sph( &q1 );
    printf( "q1 sph = %f, %f, %f (rho, theta, phi)\n",
            q1.x, q1.y, q1.z );

    /* Convert from spherical to Cartesian notation */
    sph_to_xyz( &q1 );
    printf( "q1 xyz = %f, %f, %f (x, y, z)\n",
            q1.x, q1.y, q1.z );
}
```

Include File: GEOMETRY.H

```
/* -------------------------------------------------------------------
    Name:           GEOMETRY.H
    Type:           Include
    Language:       Microsoft QuickC
    Demonstrated:   GEOMETRY.C  GEOMTEST.C
    Description:    Prototypes and definitions for GEOMETRY.C
   -------------------------------------------------------------------
*/

#ifndef GEOMETRY_DEFINED

#define PI 3.141592653589793

/* Analytical geometry two-dimensional coordinate structure */
struct coord_2d
    {
    double x, y;
    };

/* Analytical geometry three-dimensional coordinate structure */
struct coord_3d
    {
    double x, y, z;
    };

/* Two-dimensional function prototypes */
void polar_to_rect( struct coord_2d * );
void rect_to_polar( struct coord_2d * );
double distance( struct coord_2d *, struct coord_2d * );
```

(continued)

GEOMETRY.H *continued*

```
double direction( struct coord_2d *, struct coord_2d * );
void translate( struct coord_2d *, double, double );
void rotate( struct coord_2d *, double );

double angle_between
    (
    struct coord_2d *,
    struct coord_2d *,
    struct coord_2d *
    );

double area
    (
    struct coord_2d *,
    struct coord_2d *,
    struct coord_2d *
    );

double equidistant
    (
    struct coord_2d *,
    struct coord_2d *,
    struct coord_2d *,
    struct coord_2d *
    );

/* Three-dimensional function prototypes */
void translate_3d( struct coord_3d *, double, double, double );
double distance_3d( struct coord_3d *, struct coord_3d * );

double angle_between_3d
    (
    struct coord_3d *,
    struct coord_3d *,
    struct coord_3d *
    );

double area_3d
    (
    struct coord_3d *,
    struct coord_3d *,
    struct coord_3d *
    );
```

(continued)

185

```
double volume_3d
    (
    struct coord_3d *,
    struct coord_3d *,
    struct coord_3d *,
    struct coord_3d *
    );

void xyz_to_cyl( struct coord_3d * );
void xyz_to_sph( struct coord_3d * );
void cyl_to_xyz( struct coord_3d * );
void cyl_to_sph( struct coord_3d * );
void sph_to_xyz( struct coord_3d * );
void sph_to_cyl( struct coord_3d * );

#define GEOMETRY_DEFINED
#endif
```

Toolbox Module: GEOMETRY.C

```
/* ------------------------------------------------------------------
    Name:           GEOMETRY.C
    Type:           Toolbox module
    Language:       Microsoft QuickC
    Demonstrated:   GEOMTEST.C
    Video:          (no special video requirements)
    ------------------------------------------------------------------
*/

#include <math.h>
#include "geometry.h"
```

Function: *polar_to_rect()*

The *polar_to_rect()* function converts a two-dimensional point from polar notation (*magnitude, angle*) to rectangular coordinates (*x, y*). The angle must be expressed in radians.

```
/* - - - - - - - - - - - - - - - - - - - - - - - - - - - - - - - - - - -
    Function:       polar_to_rect()
    Toolbox:        GEOMETRY.C
    Demonstrated:   GEOMTEST.C

    Parameters:
      (in/out)      coord     Two-dimensional point coordinates

    Returned:       (function returns nothing)

    Variables:      radius    Distance from origin
                    angle     Direction of point from origin

    Description:    Converts point notation from polar to rectangular
    - - - - - - - - - - - - - - - - - - - - - - - - - - - - - - - - -
*/

void polar_to_rect( struct coord_2d *coord )
{
    double radius, angle;

    radius = coord->x;
    angle = coord->y;

    coord->x = radius * cos( angle );
    coord->y = radius * sin( angle );
}
```

Function: *rect_to_polar()*

The *rect_to_polar()* function converts a two-dimensional point from rectangular coordinates (*x*, *y*) to polar notation (*magnitude*, *angle*). The angle is expressed in radians.

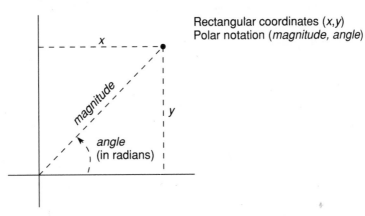

Rectangular coordinates (*x*,*y*)
Polar notation (*magnitude*, *angle*)

```
/* - - - - - - - - - - - - - - - - - - - - - - - - - - - - - - - - -

   Function:       rect_to_polar()
   Toolbox:        GEOMETRY.C
   Demonstrated:   GEOMTEST.C

   Parameters:
    (in/out)       coord      Two-dimensional point coordinates

   Returned:       (function returns nothing)

   Variables:      x          Cartesian x-coordinate
                   y          Cartesian y-coordinate

   Description:    Converts point notation from rectangular to polar
   - - - - - - - - - - - - - - - - - - - - - - - - - - - - - - - - -
*/

void rect_to_polar( struct coord_2d *coord )
{
    double x, y;

    x = coord->x;
    y = coord->y;

    coord->x = hypot( x, y );
    coord->y = atan2( y, x );
}
```

Function: *distance()*

The *distance()* function returns the distance between two points. The function calls the QuickC run-time function *hypot()*, which finds the hypotenuse of a right triangle using the Pythagorean theorem. To provide arguments for *hypot()*, the *distance()* function calculates the difference between the x-coordinates and between the y-coordinates of the two points.

```
/* - - - - - - - - - - - - - - - - - - - - - - - - - - - - - - - -

   Function:       distance()
   Toolbox:        GEOMETRY.C
   Demonstrated:   GEOMTEST.C
```

(continued)

GEOMETRY.C *continued*

```
    Parameters:
       (input)       coord1    First x,y point
       (input)       coord2    Second x,y point

    Returned:        Distance from point 1 to point 2

    Variables:       dx        Change in x from point 1 to point 2
                     dy        Change in y from point 1 to point 2

    Description:     Calculates the distance between two x,y points
    - - - - - - - - - - - - - - - - - - - - - - - - - - - - - -
*/

double distance( struct coord_2d *coord1, struct coord_2d *coord2 )
{
    double dx, dy;

    dx = coord2->x - coord1->x;
    dy = coord2->y - coord1->y;

    return ( hypot( dx, dy ));
}
```

Function: *direction()*

The *direction()* function calculates the angular direction from one point to another. The angle is measured counterclockwise in radians from the x-axis.

```
/* - - - - - - - - - - - - - - - - - - - - - - - - - - - - - - -
   Function:       direction()
   Toolbox:        GEOMETRY.C
   Demonstrated:   GEOMTEST.C

   Parameters:
      (input)       coord1    First x,y point
      (input)       coord2    Second x,y point

   Returned:        Direction from point 1 to point 2
```

(continued)

GEOMETRY.C *continued*

```
    Variables:      dx          Change in x from point 1 to point 2
                    dy          Change in y from point 1 to point 2

    Description:    Calculates the direction in radians from one x,y
                    point to another
- - - - - - - - - - - - - - - - - - - - - - - - - - - - - - - - - -
*/

double direction( struct coord_2d *coord1, struct coord_2d *coord2 )
{
    double dx, dy;

    dx = coord2->x - coord1->x;
    dy = coord2->y - coord1->y;

    return ( atan2( dy, dx ));
}
```

Function: *translate()*

The *translate()* function translates, or shifts the location of, a point in the x,y plane by adding translation amounts to the x-coordinate and the y-coordinate.

```
/* - - - - - - - - - - - - - - - - - - - - - - - - - - - - - - - - -
    Function:       translate()
    Toolbox:        GEOMETRY.C
    Demonstrated:   GEOMTEST.C

    Parameters:
      (in/out)      coord       An x,y point to be translated
      (input)       x           Amount to add to x-coordinate
      (input)       y           Amount to add to y-coordinate

    Returned:       (function returns nothing)

    Variables:      (none)

    Description:    Translates an x,y point by adding variables x and y
                    to the x-coordinate and the y-coordinate
- - - - - - - - - - - - - - - - - - - - - - - - - - - - - - - - -
*/
```

(continued)

GEOMETRY.C *continued*

```
void translate( struct coord_2d *coord, double x, double y )
{
    coord->x += x;
    coord->y += y;
}
```

Function: *rotate()*

The *rotate()* function rotates a point around the origin. Pass the amount of rotation as an angle expressed in radians. If the rotation angle is positive, the function rotates the point counterclockwise.

```
/* - - - - - - - - - - - - - - - - - - - - - - - - - - - - - - -
    Function:       rotate()
    Toolbox:        GEOMETRY.C
    Demonstrated:   GEOMTEST.C

    Parameters:
      (in/out)      coord      An x,y point to be rotated
      (input)       angle      Radians to rotate point around origin

    Returned:       (function returns nothing)

    Variables:      t1         Starting x-coordinate
                    t2         Starting y-coordinate
                    csa        Cosine of the negative of the angle
                    sna        Sine of the negative of the angle

    Description:    Rotates an x,y point around the origin by an
                    angle, expressed in radians
    - - - - - - - - - - - - - - - - - - - - - - - - - - - - - - -
*/

void rotate( struct coord_2d *coord, double angle )
{
    double t1, t2;
    double csa, sna;

    csa = cos( -angle );
    sna = sin( -angle );
```

(continued)

GEOMETRY.C *continued*

```
    t1 = coord->x;
    t2 = coord->y;

    coord->x = t1 * csa + t2 * sna;
    coord->y = t2 * csa - t1 * sna;
}
```

Function: *angle_between()*

The *angle_between()* function returns the angle formed by connecting three points in the x,y plane. The vertex of the angle is the second point, and the angle is measured counterclockwise from the first point around to the third.

```
/* - - - - - - - - - - - - - - - - - - - - - - - - - - - - - - - - -
    Function:       angle_between()
    Toolbox:        GEOMETRY.C
    Demonstrated:   GEOMTEST.C

    Parameters:
     (input)        coord1      First x,y point
     (input)        coord2      Second x,y point
     (input)        coord3      Third x,y point

    Returned:       Angle at second point, defined by three points

    Variables:      ang21       Direction from point 2 to point 1
                    ang23       Direction from point 2 to point 3

    Description:    Calculates the angle formed by three x,y points.
                    The angle is expressed in radians and is
                    measured counterclockwise from point 1 to point 3.
    - - - - - - - - - - - - - - - - - - - - - - - - - - - - - - - - -
*/

double angle_between( struct coord_2d *coord1,
                      struct coord_2d *coord2,
                      struct coord_2d *coord3 )
```

(continued)

GEOMETRY.C *continued*

```
{
    double ang21, ang23;

    ang21 = atan2( coord1->y - coord2->y, coord1->x - coord2->x );
    ang23 = atan2( coord3->y - coord2->y, coord3->x - coord2->x );

    if ( ang23 < ang21 )
        ang23 += PI + PI;

    return ( ang23 - ang21 );
}
```

Function: *area()*

The *area()* function returns the area of a triangle formed by connecting three points in the x,y plane. Areas of other polygons can be determined by summing the areas of component triangles.

```
/* - - - - - - - - - - - - - - - - - - - - - - - - - - - - - - - -
    Function:       area()
    Toolbox:        GEOMETRY.C
    Demonstrated:   GEOMTEST.C

    Parameters:
       (input)      coord1    First x,y point
       (input)      coord2    Second x,y point
       (input)      coord3    Third x,y point

    Returned:       Area of triangle defined by three x,y points

    Variables:      sideA     Distance from point 1 to point 2
                    sideB     Distance from point 2 to point 3
                    sideC     Distance from point 3 to point 1
                    p         Temporary variable, area calculation

    Description:    Calculates the area of a triangle defined by
                    three x,y points
    - - - - - - - - - - - - - - - - - - - - - - - - - - - - - - - -
*/
```

(continued)

GEOMETRY.C *continued*

```
double area( struct coord_2d *coord1,
             struct coord_2d *coord2,
             struct coord_2d *coord3 )
{
    double sideA, sideB, sideC;
    double p;

    sideA = distance( coord1, coord2 );
    sideB = distance( coord2, coord3 );
    sideC = distance( coord3, coord1 );

    p = (sideA + sideB + sideC) / 2.0;

    return ( sqrt( p * (p - sideA) * (p - sideB) * (p - sideC) ));
}
```

Function: *equidistant()*

The *equidistant()* function finds the point in the x,y plane that is equidistant from three given points. This point is the center of a circle that passes through the three given points. The function assigns the coordinates of the equidistant point to the fourth parameter and returns the distance from the new point to each of the other three points. This distance is the radius of the circle defined by the three points.

```
/* - - - - - - - - - - - - - - - - - - - - - - - - - - - - - - - - - -
    Function:       equidistant()
    Toolbox:        GEOMETRY.C
    Demonstrated:   GEOMTEST.C

    Parameters:
     (input)        coord1    First x,y point
     (input)        coord2    Second x,y point
     (input)        coord3    Third x,y point
     (output)       coord4    Point equidistant from the other three

    Returned:       Distance from point 4 to any of the other three
```

(continued)

GEOMETRY.C *continued*

```
      Variables:       x0        Temporary x variable for swapping points
                       y0        Temporary y variable for swapping points
                       x1        Point 1, x-coordinate
                       y1        Point 1, y-coordinate
                       x2        Point 2, x-coordinate
                       y2        Point 2, y-coordinate
                       x3        Point 3, x-coordinate
                       y3        Point 3, y-coordinate
                       dx12      Change in x from point 1 to point 2
                       dx13      Change in x from point 1 to point 3
                       dy12      Change in y from point 1 to point 2
                       dy13      Change in y from point 1 to point 3
                       t1        Intermediate calculation results
                       t2        Intermediate calculation results
                       t3        Intermediate calculation results
                       t4        Intermediate calculation results
                       tries     Count of attempts to get nonvertical
                                 points

    Description:       Finds the point that is equidistant from three
                       given x,y points
    - - - - - - - - - - - - - - - - - - - - - - - - - - - - - - -
*/

double equidistant( struct coord_2d *coord1,
                    struct coord_2d *coord2,
                    struct coord_2d *coord3,
                    struct coord_2d *coord4 )
{
    double x0, y0;
    double x1, y1, x2, y2, x3, y3;
    double dx12, dx13, dy12, dy13;
    double t1, t2, t3, t4;
    int tries = 2;

    /* Copy three points into working variables */
    x1 = coord1->x;
    y1 = coord1->y;
    x2 = coord2->x;
    y2 = coord2->y;
    x3 = coord3->x;
    y3 = coord3->y;
```

(continued)

GEOMETRY.C *continued*

```
    /* Rotate the points until point 1 is at unique x-coordinate */
    do
        {
        dx12 = x2 - x1;
        dx13 = x3 - x1;
        if ( dx12 == 0.0 || dx13 == 0.0 )
            {
            x0 = x1;
            y0 = y1;
            x1 = x2;
            y1 = y2;
            x2 = y3;
            y2 = y3;
            x3 = x0;
            y3 = y0;
            tries--;
            if ( !tries )
                return ( HUGE_VAL );
            }
        else
            tries = 0;
        }
    while ( tries );

    /* Get the y distances from point 1 to each of the others */
    dy12 = y2 - y1;
    dy13 = y3 - y1;

    /* Make sure the three points aren't in a straight line */
    if ( dy12 * dx13 == dx12 * dy13 )
        return ( HUGE_VAL );

    /* Calculate the equidistant point */
    t1 = (dx12 * (x1 + x2) + dy12 * (y1 + y2)) / dx12 / 2.0;
    t2 = (dx13 * (x1 + x3) + dy13 * (y1 + y3)) / dx13 / 2.0;

    t3 = dy12 / dx12;
    t4 = dy13 / dx13;

    coord4->y = (t2 - t1) / (t4 - t3);
    coord4->x = t2 - t4 * coord4->y;

    /* Return the distance from the new point to each of the others */
    return ( hypot( x1 - coord4->x, y1 - coord4->y ));
}
```

Function: *translate_3d()*

The *translate_3d()* function translates, or shifts the location of, a point in space by adding values to the x-coordinate, y-coordinate, and z-coordinate.

```
/* - - - - - - - - - - - - - - - - - - - - - - - - - - - - - - - - -
   Function:        translate_3d()
   Toolbox:         GEOMETRY.C
   Demonstrated:    GEOMTEST.C

   Parameters:
     (in/out)       coord      x,y,z point to be translated
     (input)        x          Amount to shift the x-coordinate
     (input)        y          Amount to shift the y-coordinate
     (input)        z          Amount to shift the z-coordinate

   Returned:        (function returns nothing)

   Variables:       (none)

   Description:     Shifts an x,y,z point in space by adding variables
                    x, y and z to the coordinates
   - - - - - - - - - - - - - - - - - - - - - - - - - - - - - - - -
*/

void translate_3d( struct coord_3d *coord,
                   double x, double y, double z )
{
    coord->x += x;
    coord->y += y;
    coord->z += z;
}
```

Function: *distance_3d()*

The *distance_3d()* function returns the distance between two given points in space. This function is similar to the *distance()* function, except that it must apply the Pythagorean theorem twice. The function *distance_3d()* combines the calculations in one equation.

```
/* - - - - - - - - - - - - - - - - - - - - - - - - - - - - - - -
    Function:       distance_3d()
    Toolbox:        GEOMETRY.C
    Demonstrated:   GEOMTEST.C

    Parameters:
      (input)       coord1    First x,y,z point
      (input)       coord2    Second x,y,z point

    Returned:       Distance between the two points

    Variables:      dx        Change in x from point 1 to point 2
                    dy        Change in y from point 1 to point 2
                    dz        Change in z from point 1 to point 2

    Description:    Calculates the straight line distance between
                    two points in space
    - - - - - - - - - - - - - - - - - - - - - - - - - - - - - - -
*/

double distance_3d( struct coord_3d *coord1, struct coord_3d *coord2 )
{
    double dx, dy, dz;

    dx = coord2->x - coord1->x;
    dy = coord2->y - coord1->y;
    dz = coord2->z - coord1->z;

    return ( sqrt( dx * dx + dy * dy + dz * dz ));
}
```

Function: *angle_between_3d()*

The *angle_between_3d()* function finds the acute angle formed by connecting three given points in space. The vertex of the angle is the second point, and the result is expressed in radians.

```
/* - - - - - - - - - - - - - - - - - - - - - - - - - - - - - - -
    Function:       angle_between_3d()
    Toolbox:        GEOMETRY.C
    Demonstrated:   GEOMTEST.C
```

(continued)

GEOMETRY.C *continued*

```
    Parameters:
      (input)        coord1      First x,y,z point
      (input)        coord2      Second x,y,z point
      (input)        coord3      Third x,y,z point

    Returned:        Angle formed by the three points

    Variables:       dx21        Change in x from point 2 to point 1
                     dy21        Change in y from point 2 to point 1
                     dz21        Change in z from point 2 to point 1
                     dx23        Change in x from point 2 to point 3
                     dy23        Change in y from point 2 to point 3
                     dz23        Change in z from point 2 to point 3
                     mag0        Intermediate calculation results
                     mag1        Intermediate calculation results
                     mag2        Intermediate calculation results

    Description:     Calculates the angle formed by connecting three
                     points in space
    - - - - - - - - - - - - - - - - - - - - - - - - - - - - - - -
*/

double angle_between_3d( struct coord_3d *coord1,
                         struct coord_3d *coord2,
                         struct coord_3d *coord3 )
{
    double dx21, dy21, dz21;
    double dx23, dy23, dz23;
    double mag0, mag1, mag2;

    dx21 = coord1->x - coord2->x;
    dy21 = coord1->y - coord2->y;
    dz21 = coord1->z - coord2->z;

    dx23 = coord3->x - coord2->x;
    dy23 = coord3->y - coord2->y;
    dz23 = coord3->z - coord2->z;

    mag0 = dx21 * dx23 + dy21 * dy23 + dz21 * dz23;
    mag1 = sqrt( dx21 * dx21 + dy21 * dy21 + dz21 * dz21 );
    mag2 = sqrt( dx23 * dx23 + dy23 * dy23 + dz23 * dz23 );

    return ( acos( mag0 / mag1 / mag2 ));
}
```

Function: *area_3d()*

The *area_3d()* function returns the area of a triangle formed by connecting three given points in space.

```
/* - - - - - - - - - - - - - - - - - - - - - - - - - - - - - - - - - -
    Function:       area_3d()
    Toolbox:        GEOMETRY.C
    Demonstrated:   GEOMTEST.C

    Parameters:
      (input)       coord1    First x,y,z point
      (input)       coord2    Second x,y,z point
      (input)       coord3    Third x,y,z point

    Returned:       Area of the triangle defined by three x,y,z points

    Variables:      s1        Distance from point 1 to point 2
                    s2        Distance from point 2 to point 3
                    s3        Distance from point 3 to point 1
                    p         Intermediate calculation result

    Description:    Calculates the area of a triangle defined by
                    three points in space
    - - - - - - - - - - - - - - - - - - - - - - - - - - - - - - - - - -
*/

double area_3d( struct coord_3d *coord1,
                struct coord_3d *coord2,
                struct coord_3d *coord3 )
{
    double s1, s2, s3;
    double p;

    s1 = distance_3d( coord1, coord2 );
    s2 = distance_3d( coord2, coord3 );
    s3 = distance_3d( coord3, coord1 );

    p = ( s1 + s2 + s3 ) / 2.0;

    return ( sqrt( p * (p - s1) * (p - s2) * (p - s3) ));
}
```

Function: *volume_3d()*

The *volume_3d()* function returns the volume defined by connecting four given points in space.

```
/* - - - - - - - - - - - - - - - - - - - - - - - - - - - - - - - - - - - -
   Function:      volume_3d()
   Toolbox:       GEOMETRY.C
   Demonstrated:  GEOMTEST.C

   Parameters:
     (input)      coord1    First x,y,z point
     (input)      coord2    Second x,y,z point
     (input)      coord3    Third x,y,z point
     (input)      coord4    Fourth x,y,z point

   Returned:      Volume defined by four points in space

   Variables:     x1        Point 1, x-coordinate
                  y1        Point 1, y-coordinate
                  z1        Point 1, z-coordinate
                  x2        Point 2, x-coordinate
                  y2        Point 2, y-coordinate
                  z2        Point 2, z-coordinate
                  x3        Point 3, x-coordinate
                  y3        Point 3, y-coordinate
                  z3        Point 3, z-coordinate
                  x4        Point 4, x-coordinate
                  y4        Point 4, y-coordinate
                  z4        Point 4, z-coordinate
                  t1        Intermediate calculation results
                  t2        Intermediate calculation results
                  t3        Intermediate calculation results
                  t4        Intermediate calculation results
                  t5        Intermediate calculation results
                  t6        Intermediate calculation results
                  t7        Intermediate calculation results
                  t8        Intermediate calculation results

   Description:   Calculates the volume defined by four points in
                  space
   - - - - - - - - - - - - - - - - - - - - - - - - - - - - - - - - - - - -
*/
```

(continued)

GEOMETRY.C *continued*

```c
double volume_3d( struct coord_3d *coord1,
                  struct coord_3d *coord2,
                  struct coord_3d *coord3,
                  struct coord_3d *coord4 )
{
    double x1, y1, z1;
    double x2, y2, z2;
    double x3, y3, z3;
    double x4, y4, z4;
    double t1, t2, t3, t4, t5, t6, t7, t8;

    x1 = coord1->x;
    y1 = coord1->y;
    z1 = coord1->z;

    x2 = coord2->x;
    y2 = coord2->y;
    z2 = coord2->z;

    x3 = coord3->x;
    y3 = coord3->y;
    z3 = coord3->z;

    x4 = coord4->x;
    y4 = coord4->y;
    z4 = coord4->z;

    t1 = x2 * y3 * z4 + y2 * z3 * x4 + z2 * x3 * y4;
    t2 = x2 * z3 * y4 + y2 * x3 * z4 + z2 * y3 * x4;

    t3 = x1 * y3 * z4 + y1 * z3 * x4 + z1 * x3 * y4;
    t4 = x1 * z3 * y4 + y1 * x3 * z4 + z1 * y3 * x4;

    t5 = x1 * y2 * z4 + y1 * z2 * x4 + z1 * x2 * y4;
    t6 = x1 * z2 * y4 + y1 * x2 * z4 + z1 * y2 * x4;

    t7 = x1 * y2 * z3 + y1 * z2 * x3 + z1 * x2 * y3;
    t8 = x1 * z2 * y3 + y1 * x2 * z3 + z1 * y2 * x3;

    return ( (t1 - t2 - t3 + t4 + t5 - t6 - t7 + t8) / 6.0 );
}
```

Function: *xyz_to_cyl()*

The *xyz_to_cyl()* function and the remaining functions presented in this module convert a set of spacial coordinates from one type of notation to another.

The *xyz_to_cyl()* function converts the coordinates of a point from Cartesian to cylindrical notation. The figure below shows a point located with each of these types of notation, as well as a third type, spherical notation.

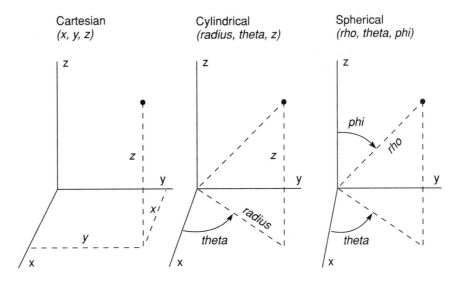

Cartesian
(x, y, z)

Cylindrical
(radius, theta, z)

Spherical
(rho, theta, phi)

```
/* - - - - - - - - - - - - - - - - - - - - - - - - - - - - - -
    Function:      xyz_to_cyl()
    Toolbox:       GEOMETRY.C
    Demonstrated:  GEOMTEST.C

    Parameters:
     (in/out)      coord    Three-dimensional point to be converted

    Returned:      (function returns nothing)

    Variables:     x        X-coordinate for point
                   y        Y-coordinate for point
```

(continued)

GEOMETRY.C *continued*

```
    Description:    Converts a space point from Cartesian to
                    cylindrical notation
- - - - - - - - - - - - - - - - - - - - - - - - - - - - - - - -
*/

void xyz_to_cyl( struct coord_3d *coord )
{
    double x, y;

    x = coord->x;
    y = coord->y;
    coord->x = hypot( x, y );
    coord->y = atan2( y, x );
}
```

Function: *xyz_to_sph()*

The *xyz_to_sph()* function converts the coordinates of a point from Cartesian to spherical notation. (See illustration, page 203.)

```
/* - - - - - - - - - - - - - - - - - - - - - - - - - - - - - - -
    Function:       xyz_to_sph()
    Toolbox:        GEOMETRY.C
    Demonstrated:   GEOMTEST.C

    Parameters:
      (in/out)      coord       Three-dimensional point to be converted

    Returned:       (function returns nothing)

    Variables:      x           X-coordinate for point
                    y           Y-coordinate for point
                    z           Z-coordinate for point

    Description:    Converts a space point from Cartesian to
                    spherical notation
- - - - - - - - - - - - - - - - - - - - - - - - - - - - - - - -
*/

void xyz_to_sph( struct coord_3d *coord )
{
    double x, y, z;
```

(continued)

```
    x = coord->x;
    y = coord->y;
    z = coord->z;

    coord->x = hypot( hypot( x, y ), z );     /* rho */
    coord->y = atan2( y, x );                 /* theta */
    coord->z = acos( z / coord->x );          /* phi */
}
```

Function: *cyl_to_xyz()*

The *cyl_to_xyz()* function converts the coordinates of a point from cylindrical to Cartesian notation. (See illustration, page 203.)

```
/* - - - - - - - - - - - - - - - - - - - - - - - - - - - - - - -
    Function:       cyl_to_xyz()
    Toolbox:        GEOMETRY.C
    Demonstrated:   GEOMTEST.C

    Parameters:
      (in/out)      coord      Three-dimensional point to be converted

    Returned:       (function returns nothing)

    Variables:      radius     Cylindrical notation, radius
                    theta      Cylindrical notation, theta
                    z          Z-coordinate for point

    Description:    Converts a space point from cylindrical to
                    Cartesian notation
    - - - - - - - - - - - - - - - - - - - - - - - - - - - - - - -
*/

void cyl_to_xyz( struct coord_3d *coord )
{
    double radius, theta;

    radius = coord->x;
    theta = coord->y;

    coord->x = radius * cos( theta );
    coord->y = radius * sin( theta );
}
```

Function: *cyl_to_sph()*

The *cyl_to_sph()* function converts the coordinates of a point from cylindrical to spherical notation. (See illustration, page 203.)

```
/* - - - - - - - - - - - - - - - - - - - - - - - - - - - - - - - - -
    Function:       cyl_to_sph()
    Toolbox:        GEOMETRY.C
    Demonstrated:   GEOMTEST.C

    Parameters:
      (in/out)      coord     Three-dimensional point to be converted

    Returned:       (function returns nothing)

    Variables:      radius    Cylindrical notation, radius
                    theta     Cylindrical notation, theta
                    z         Z-coordinate for point

    Description:    Converts a space point from cylindrical to
                    spherical notation
    - - - - - - - - - - - - - - - - - - - - - - - - - - - - - - - - -
*/

void cyl_to_sph( struct coord_3d *coord )
{
    double radius, theta, z;

    radius = coord->x;
    z = coord->z;

    coord->x = hypot( radius, z );       /* rho */
    coord->z = acos( z / coord->x );   /* phi */
}
```

Function: *sph_to_xyz()*

The *sph_to_xyz()* function converts the coordinates of a point from spherical to Cartesian notation. (See illustration, page 203.)

```
/* - - - - - - - - - - - - - - - - - - - - - - - - - - - - - - -
    Function:       sph_to_xyz()
    Toolbox:        GEOMETRY.C
    Demonstrated:   GEOMTEST.C

    Parameters:
     (in/out)       coord      Three-dimensional point to be converted

    Returned:       (function returns nothing)

    Variables:      rho        Spherical notation, rho
                    cos_theta  Cosine of spherical notation theta
                    sin_theta  Sine of spherical notation theta
                    cos_phi    Cosine of spherical notation phi
                    sin_phi    Sine of spherical notation phi

    Description:    Converts a space point from spherical to
                    Cartesian notation
    - - - - - - - - - - - - - - - - - - - - - - - - - - - - - - -
*/

void sph_to_xyz( struct coord_3d *coord )
{
    double rho;
    double cos_theta, sin_theta;
    double cos_phi, sin_phi;

    rho = coord->x;

    cos_theta = cos( coord->y );
    sin_theta = sin( coord->y );

    cos_phi = cos( coord->z );
    sin_phi = sin( coord->z );

    coord->x = rho * cos_theta * sin_phi;
    coord->y = rho * sin_theta * sin_phi;
    coord->z = rho * cos_phi;
}
```

Function: *sph_to_cyl()*

The *sph_to_cyl()* function converts the coordinates of a point from
spherical to cylindrical notation. (See illustration, page 203.)

```
/* - - - - - - - - - - - - - - - - - - - - - - - - - - - - - - - - - -
    Function:       sph_to_cyl()
    Toolbox:        GEOMETRY.C
    Demonstrated:   GEOMTEST.C

    Parameters:
     (in/out)       coord      Three-dimensional point to be converted

    Returned:       (function returns nothing)

    Variables:      rho        Spherical notation, rho
                    phi        Spherical notation, phi

    Description:    Converts a space point from spherical to
                    cylindrical notation
    - - - - - - - - - - - - - - - - - - - - - - - - - - - - - - - - - -
*/

void sph_to_cyl( struct coord_3d *coord )
{
    double rho, phi;

    rho = coord->x;
    phi = coord->z;

    coord->x = rho * sin( phi );      /* radius */
    coord->z = rho * cos( phi );      /* z */
}
```

GETKEY

FUNCTION	DESCRIPTION
getkey()	Obtains key code for any key
getkey_or_mouse()	Obtains key code or mouse equivalent

The GETKEY toolbox module provides a systematic way to get input from the keyboard and mouse. The *getkey()* function returns a unique unsigned integer for every key on the keyboard. The *getkey_or_mouse()* function also returns equivalent key code numbers for detected mouse movement and button presses. For example, when you move the mouse left, the function returns the key code for the Left Arrow key; and if you press the left mouse button, the function returns the key code for the Enter key.

Several of the most frequently used key codes are defined in the GETKEY.H header file. To improve the readability of your programs, use these constants in routines that call the GETKEY functions.

GETKTEST.C demonstrates the two GETKEY functions. The first demonstration obtains keyboard input only. The program displays the key code or the associated constant identifier for the keys you press. The second demonstration calls *getkey_or_mouse()* to report mouse movements and button presses in addition to keypresses. The GETKEY functions detect keyboard activity whether or not a mouse is installed.

Demonstration Program: GETKTEST.C

```
/* -----------------------------------------------------------------
    Name:           GETKTEST.C
    Type:           Demonstration program
    Language:       Microsoft QuickC
    Video:          (no special video requirements)

    Program list:   GETKTEST.C
                    GETKEY.C
                    MOUSEFUN.C
```

(continued)

GETKTEST.C *continued*

```
    Variables:      key        Key code
                    i          Looping index

    Usage:          (no command line parameters)

    Description:    Demonstrates the GETKEY toolbox functions
    ----------------------------------------------------------------
*/

#include <stdio.h>
#include "getkey.h"

main()
{
    unsigned key;
    int i;

    for ( i = 0; i < 2; i++ )
        {

        if ( i == 0 )
            {
            printf( "\n\nPress any keys ...\n" );
            printf( "(press Esc to quit)...\n\n" );
            }
        else
            {
            printf( "\n\nNow press any keys or use the mouse...\n\n" );
            printf( "(press Esc or right mouse button to quit)...\n\n" );
            }

        do
            {
            if ( i == 0 )
                key = getkey();
            else
                key = getkey_or_mouse();

            if ( key == KEY_F1         ) printf( "KEY_F1       " );
            if ( key == KEY_F2         ) printf( "KEY_F2       " );
            if ( key == KEY_F3         ) printf( "KEY_F3       " );
            if ( key == KEY_F4         ) printf( "KEY_F4       " );
            if ( key == KEY_F5         ) printf( "KEY_F5       " );
```

(continued)

GETKTEST.C *continued*

```
          if ( key == KEY_F6        ) printf( "KEY_F6        " );
          if ( key == KEY_F7        ) printf( "KEY_F7        " );
          if ( key == KEY_F8        ) printf( "KEY_F8        " );
          if ( key == KEY_F9        ) printf( "KEY_F9        " );
          if ( key == KEY_F10       ) printf( "KEY_F10       " );
          if ( key == KEY_SHIFT_F1  ) printf( "KEY_SHIFT_F1  " );
          if ( key == KEY_SHIFT_F2  ) printf( "KEY_SHIFT_F2  " );
          if ( key == KEY_SHIFT_F3  ) printf( "KEY_SHIFT_F3  " );
          if ( key == KEY_SHIFT_F4  ) printf( "KEY_SHIFT_F4  " );
          if ( key == KEY_SHIFT_F5  ) printf( "KEY_SHIFT_F5  " );
          if ( key == KEY_SHIFT_F6  ) printf( "KEY_SHIFT_F6  " );
          if ( key == KEY_SHIFT_F7  ) printf( "KEY_SHIFT_F7  " );
          if ( key == KEY_SHIFT_F8  ) printf( "KEY_SHIFT_F8  " );
          if ( key == KEY_SHIFT_F9  ) printf( "KEY_SHIFT_F9  " );
          if ( key == KEY_SHIFT_F10 ) printf( "KEY_SHIFT_F10 " );
          if ( key == KEY_CTRL_F1   ) printf( "KEY_CTRL_F1   " );
          if ( key == KEY_CTRL_F2   ) printf( "KEY_CTRL_F2   " );
          if ( key == KEY_CTRL_F3   ) printf( "KEY_CTRL_F3   " );
          if ( key == KEY_CTRL_F4   ) printf( "KEY_CTRL_F4   " );
          if ( key == KEY_CTRL_F5   ) printf( "KEY_CTRL_F5   " );
          if ( key == KEY_CTRL_F6   ) printf( "KEY_CTRL_F6   " );
          if ( key == KEY_CTRL_F7   ) printf( "KEY_CTRL_F7   " );
          if ( key == KEY_CTRL_F8   ) printf( "KEY_CTRL_F8   " );
          if ( key == KEY_CTRL_F9   ) printf( "KEY_CTRL_F9   " );
          if ( key == KEY_CTRL_F10  ) printf( "KEY_CTRL_F10  " );
          if ( key == KEY_ALT_F1    ) printf( "KEY_ALT_F1    " );
          if ( key == KEY_ALT_F2    ) printf( "KEY_ALT_F2    " );
          if ( key == KEY_ALT_F3    ) printf( "KEY_ALT_F3    " );
          if ( key == KEY_ALT_F4    ) printf( "KEY_ALT_F4    " );
          if ( key == KEY_ALT_F5    ) printf( "KEY_ALT_F5    " );
          if ( key == KEY_ALT_F6    ) printf( "KEY_ALT_F6    " );
          if ( key == KEY_ALT_F7    ) printf( "KEY_ALT_F7    " );
          if ( key == KEY_ALT_F8    ) printf( "KEY_ALT_F8    " );
          if ( key == KEY_ALT_F9    ) printf( "KEY_ALT_F9    " );
          if ( key == KEY_ALT_F10   ) printf( "KEY_ALT_F10   " );
          if ( key == KEY_INSERT    ) printf( "KEY_INSERT    " );
          if ( key == KEY_HOME      ) printf( "KEY_HOME      " );
          if ( key == KEY_PGUP      ) printf( "KEY_PGUP      " );
          if ( key == KEY_DELETE    ) printf( "KEY_DELETE    " );
          if ( key == KEY_END       ) printf( "KEY_END       " );
          if ( key == KEY_PGDN      ) printf( "KEY_PGDN      " );
          if ( key == KEY_UP        ) printf( "KEY_UP        " );
          if ( key == KEY_LEFT      ) printf( "KEY_LEFT      " );
```

(continued)

```
            if ( key == KEY_DOWN        ) printf( "KEY_DOWN       " );
            if ( key == KEY_RIGHT       ) printf( "KEY_RIGHT      " );
            if ( key == KEY_ENTER       ) printf( "KEY_ENTER      " );
            if ( key == KEY_ESCAPE      ) printf( "KEY_ESCAPE     " );
            if ( key == KEY_BACKSPACE   ) printf( "KEY_BACKSPACE  " );
            if ( key == KEY_TAB         ) printf( "KEY_TAB        " );
            if ( key == KEY_SHIFT_TAB   ) printf( "KEY_SHIFT_TAB  " );
            if ( key == KEY_CTRL_LEFT   ) printf( "KEY_CTRL_LEFT  " );
            if ( key == KEY_CTRL_RIGHT  ) printf( "KEY_CTRL_RIGHT" );
            if ( key == KEY_CTRL_HOME   ) printf( "KEY_CTRL_HOME  " );
            if ( key == KEY_CTRL_PGUP   ) printf( "KEY_CTRL_PGUP  " );
            if ( key == KEY_CTRL_PGDN   ) printf( "KEY_CTRL_PGDN  " );
            if ( key == KEY_CTRL_END    ) printf( "KEY_CTRL_END   " );
            if ( key == KEY_CTRL_ENTER  ) printf( "KEY_CTRL_ENTER" );
            printf( "\t%u\n", key );
            }
        while ( key != KEY_ESCAPE );
        }
}
```

Include File: GETKEY.H

```
/* ------------------------------------------------------------------
   Name:          GETKEY.H
   Type:          Include
   Language:      Microsoft QuickC
   Demonstrated:  GETKEY.C  GETKTEST.C
   Description:   Prototypes and definitions for GETKEY.C
   ------------------------------------------------------------------
*/

#ifndef GETKEY_DEFINED

#define KEY_F1        15104
#define KEY_F2        15360
#define KEY_F3        15616
#define KEY_F4        15872
#define KEY_F5        16128
#define KEY_F6        16384
#define KEY_F7        16640
```

(continued)

GETKEY.H *continued*

```
#define KEY_F8          16896
#define KEY_F9          17152
#define KEY_F10         17408
#define KEY_SHIFT_F1    21504
#define KEY_SHIFT_F2    21760
#define KEY_SHIFT_F3    22016
#define KEY_SHIFT_F4    22272
#define KEY_SHIFT_F5    22528
#define KEY_SHIFT_F6    22784
#define KEY_SHIFT_F7    23040
#define KEY_SHIFT_F8    23296
#define KEY_SHIFT_F9    23552
#define KEY_SHIFT_F10   23808
#define KEY_CTRL_F1     24064
#define KEY_CTRL_F2     24320
#define KEY_CTRL_F3     24576
#define KEY_CTRL_F4     24832
#define KEY_CTRL_F5     25088
#define KEY_CTRL_F6     25344
#define KEY_CTRL_F7     25600
#define KEY_CTRL_F8     25856
#define KEY_CTRL_F9     26112
#define KEY_CTRL_F10    26368
#define KEY_ALT_F1      26624
#define KEY_ALT_F2      26880
#define KEY_ALT_F3      27136
#define KEY_ALT_F4      27392
#define KEY_ALT_F5      27648
#define KEY_ALT_F6      27904
#define KEY_ALT_F7      28160
#define KEY_ALT_F8      28416
#define KEY_ALT_F9      28672
#define KEY_ALT_F10     28928
#define KEY_INSERT      20992
#define KEY_HOME        18176
#define KEY_PGUP        18688
#define KEY_DELETE      21248
#define KEY_END         20224
#define KEY_PGDN        20736
#define KEY_UP          18432
#define KEY_LEFT        19200
#define KEY_DOWN        20480
#define KEY_RIGHT       19712
```

(continued)

```
#define KEY_ENTER          13
#define KEY_ESCAPE         27
#define KEY_BACKSPACE       8
#define KEY_TAB             9
#define KEY_SHIFT_TAB    3840
#define KEY_CTRL_LEFT   29440
#define KEY_CTRL_RIGHT  29696
#define KEY_CTRL_HOME   30464
#define KEY_CTRL_PGUP   33792
#define KEY_CTRL_PGDN   30208
#define KEY_CTRL_END    29952
#define KEY_CTRL_ENTER     10

unsigned int getkey( void );
unsigned int getkey_or_mouse( void );

#define GETKEY_DEFINED
#endif
```

Toolbox Module: GETKEY.C

```
/* -----------------------------------------------------------------
   Name:         GETKEY.C
   Type:         Toolbox module
   Language:     Microsoft QuickC
   Demonstrated: GETKTEST.C COLORS.C LOOK.C MENUTEST.C OBJECT.C
   Video:        (no special video requirements)
   -----------------------------------------------------------------
*/

#include <conio.h>
#include "mousefun.h"
#include "getkey.h"

#define HORZ_COUNTS 30
#define VERT_COUNTS 20

static int mouse_flag = 0;
```

Function: *getkey()*

The *getkey()* function returns a unique, unsigned integer key code for each key. This key code matches the expected ASCII value for alphanumeric keys, but for function keys and other editing keys, the function returns a (left-shifted) scan code. The GETKEY.H header file defines the codes for many nonalphanumeric keys.

Notice that keys that return extended scan codes do so by returning a zero byte followed immediately by a nonzero byte. The *getkey()* function handles extended scan codes by calling *getch()* twice and combining the results.

```
/* - - - - - - - - - - - - - - - - - - - - - - - - - - - - - - - - -

   Function:      getkey()
   Toolbox:       GETKEY.C
   Demonstrated:  GETKTEST.C

   Parameters:    (none)

   Returned:      Unsigned integer key code

   Variables:     key       Value returned by getch()

   Description:   Returns an unsigned integer that corresponds to
                  a keypress
   - - - - - - - - - - - - - - - - - - - - - - - - - - - - - - - - -
*/

unsigned getkey( void )
{
    unsigned key;

    if (( key = getch() ) == 0 )
        key = getch() << 8;

    return ( key );
}
```

Function: *getkey_or_mouse()*

The *getkey_or_mouse()* function returns a unique, unsigned integer key code for every keypress and an equivalent key code for a mouse motion or a mouse button press. The key code returned for a keypress is the same as that returned by the *getkey()* function. When the mouse is

215

moved up, down, left, or right, the function returns the key code for
the appropriate arrow key. The left mouse button returns the same
code as that generated by the Enter key, and the right button returns
the code for the Escape key.

```
/* - - - - - - - - - - - - - - - - - - - - - - - - - - - - - - - -

   Function:        getkey_or_mouse()
   Toolbox:         GETKEY.C
   Demonstrated:    GETKTEST.C

   Parameters:      (none)

   Returned:        Unsigned integer key code

   Variables:       key       Value returned by getch()
                    status    Mouse status
                    buttons   Number of mouse buttons
                    horz      Horizontal mouse position
                    vert      Vertical mouse position
                    presses   Number of mouse button presses
                    horz_pos  Mouse position at last button press
                    vert_pos  Mouse position at last button press
                    tot_horz  Accumulated horizontal mouse motion
                    tot_vert  Accumulated vertical mouse motion

   Description:     Returns an unsigned integer that corresponds to a
                    keypress; also detects mouse motion and converts
                    it to equivalent keypresses
   - - - - - - - - - - - - - - - - - - - - - - - - - - - - - - - -
*/

unsigned getkey_or_mouse( void )
{
    unsigned key;
    int status, buttons;
    int horz, vert;
    int presses, horz_pos, vert_pos;
    int tot_horz, tot_vert;

    /* Set the mouse motion counters to 0 */
    tot_horz = tot_vert = 0;
```

(continued)

216

```
    /* Clear out the mouse button press counts */
    mouse_press( LBUTTON, &status, &presses, &horz_pos, &vert_pos );
    mouse_press( RBUTTON, &status, &presses, &horz_pos, &vert_pos );

    /* Loop starts here, watches for keypress or mouse activity */
    while ( 1 )
        {

        switch ( mouse_flag )
            {

            /* If this is first iteration, check for existence of mouse */
            case 0:
                mouse_reset( &status, &buttons );
                if ( status == 0 )
                    mouse_flag = -1;
                else
                    mouse_flag = 1;
                break;

            /* If mouse does not exist, ignore monitoring functions */
            case -1:
                break;

            /* Check for mouse activity */
            case 1:

                /* Accumulate mouse motion counts */
                mouse_motion( &horz, &vert );
                tot_horz += horz;
                tot_vert += vert;

                /* Check for enough horizontal motion */
                if ( tot_horz < -HORZ_COUNTS )
                    return ( KEY_LEFT );
                if ( tot_horz > HORZ_COUNTS )
                    return ( KEY_RIGHT );

                /* Check for enough vertical motion */
                if ( tot_vert < -VERT_COUNTS )
                    return ( KEY_UP );
                if ( tot_vert > VERT_COUNTS )
                    return ( KEY_DOWN );
```

(continued)

217

GETKEY.C *continued*

```
                /* Check for mouse left button presses */
                mouse_press( LBUTTON, &status, &presses,
                                        &horz_pos, &vert_pos );
                if ( presses )
                    return ( KEY_ENTER );

                /* Check for mouse right button presses */
                mouse_press( RBUTTON, &status, &presses,
                                        &horz_pos, &vert_pos );
                if ( presses )
                    return ( KEY_ESCAPE );
                break;
            }

    /* Check for keyboard input */
    if ( kbhit() )
        {
        if (( key = getch() ) == 0 )
            key = getch() << 8;

        return ( key );
        }
    }
}
```

GRAPHICS

FUNCTION	DESCRIPTION
collision()	Detects collisions between graphics objects
bresenham()	Calculates coordinates of points in a line segment
triangle()	Draws outlined or solid triangles
polygon()	Draws outlined or solid polygons

The GRAPHICS toolbox module provides a sampling of functions to enhance graphics output. The GRAPHICS functions provide useful capabilities and suggest methods for developing similar functions of your own. The *collision()* function, for example, detects the collision or near collision between a given figure and any pixels that are not part of the background. You might want to modify the function to detect collisions only of specific color combinations. You might also find the Bresenham line-drawing algorithm, presented in the *bresenham()* function, useful for developing your own figure-drawing algorithms. The *triangle()* function in this module uses *bresenham()* to find the left and right edges of a triangle. In addition, the *polygon()* function uses *bresenham()* indirectly to fill a series of triangular regions within a polygon.

The GRAPHICS functions are demonstrated in GRAPTEST.C. The program draws a set of triangles, both outlined and solid. GRAPTEST then demonstrates the *polygon()* function, with which it draws and then fills a hexagon. To show the *collision()* function in action, the program sets a square "ball" in motion within a rectangular region that contains several solid objects. If the ball encounters any graphics pixels other than those that constitute the background, the ball bounces away. You can easily see how you might use the *collision()* function to create many types of games.

Demonstration Program: GRAPTEST.C

```
/* ------------------------------------------------------------------
    Name:           GRAPTEST.C
    Type:           Demonstration program
    Language:       Microsoft QuickC
    Video:          Requires CGA or better graphics capability

    Program list:   GRAPTEST.C
                    GRAPHICS.C
                    GRAPHICS.LIB

    Variables:      i         Looping index
                    j         Looping index
                    x1        Triangle corner coordinate
                    y1        Triangle corner coordinate
                    x2        Triangle corner coordinate
                    y2        Triangle corner coordinate
                    x3        Triangle corner coordinate
                    y3        Triangle corner coordinate
                    x         Ball coordinate for collision check
                    y         Ball coordinate for collision check
                    dx        Change in x for each ball movement
                    dy        Change in y for each ball movement
                    tnum      Bounce direction control

    Usage:          (no command line parameters)

    Description:    Demonstrates the GRAPHICS toolbox functions
   ------------------------------------------------------------------
*/

#include <stdio.h>
#include <stdlib.h>
#include <conio.h>
#include <graph.h>
#include <malloc.h>
#include <time.h>
#include "graphics.h"

#define BALLX 5
#define BALLY 5
#define DELAY 500
```

(continued)

GRAPTEST.C *continued*

```c
char far ball[500];
char far back[500];
long far n;

main()
{
    int i, j;
    int x1, y1, x2, y2, x3, y3;
    int x, y, dx, dy, tnum = 0;

    /* Define a polygon */
    int xybuf[6][2] =
        {
        { 259, 100 }, { 210, 34 }, { 110, 34 },
        { 61, 100 }, { 110, 186 }, { 210, 186 },
        };

    /* Set a graphics mode */
     if ( _setvideomode( _MRES256COLOR ) == 0 )
         if ( _setvideomode( _MRES16COLOR ) == 0 )
             if ( _setvideomode( _MRES4COLOR ) == 0 )
                 {
                 printf( "This program requires VGA, EGA, or CGA\n" );
                 exit( 1 );
                 };

    /* Shuffle the random numbers */
    srand( (unsigned)time( NULL ) );

    /* Draw several triangle outlines */
    for ( i = 0; i < 7; i++ )
        {
        x1 = rand() % 320;
        y1 = rand() % 200;
        x2 = rand() % 320;
        y2 = rand() % 200;
        x3 = rand() % 320;
        y3 = rand() % 200;
        _setcolor( rand() % 3 + 1 );
        triangle( LINED, x1, y1, x2, y2, x3, y3 );
        }
```

(continued)

GRAPTEST.C *continued*

```
    printf( "LINED Triangles\n" );
    printf( "Press any key to continue..." );
    getch();
    _clearscreen( _GCLEARSCREEN );

    /* Draw several solid triangles */
    for ( i = 0; i < 7; i++ )
        {
        x1 = rand() % 320;
        y1 = rand() % 200;
        x2 = rand() % 320;
        y2 = rand() % 200;
        x3 = rand() % 320;
        y3 = rand() % 200;
        _setcolor( rand() % 3 + 1 );
        triangle( SOLID, x1, y1, x2, y2, x3, y3 );
        }
    printf( "SOLID Triangles\n" );
    printf( "Press any key to continue..." );
    getch();
    _clearscreen( _GCLEARSCREEN );

    /* Draw the polygon outline */
    _setcolor( 3 );
    polygon( LINED, 6, xybuf );
    printf( "LINED Polygon\n" );
    printf( "Press any key to continue..." );
    getch();
    _clearscreen( _GCLEARSCREEN );

    /* Draw a solid polygon */
    _setcolor( 2 );
    polygon( SOLID, 6, xybuf );
    printf( "SOLID Polygon\n" );
    printf( "Press any key to continue..." );
    getch();
    _clearscreen( _GCLEARSCREEN );

    /* Draw background for the collision detection */
    _setcolor( 3 );
    _rectangle( _GBORDER, 10, 10, 310, 190 );
```

(continued)

```
     _floodfill( 0, 0, 3 );
     _setcolor( 1 );
     _rectangle( _GFILLINTERIOR, 80, 40, 100, 70 );
     _rectangle( _GFILLINTERIOR, 60, 140, 90, 170 );
     _setcolor( 2 );
     _rectangle( _GFILLINTERIOR, 180, 120, 250, 140 );
     _rectangle( _GFILLINTERIOR, 180, 40, 250, 80 );

     /* Set initial conditions for collision detection */
     x = 160;
     y = 100;
     dx = 1;
     dy = 1;
     _setcolor( 3 );
     _getimage( 0, 0, BALLX, BALLY, ball );

     /* Draw the ball at the center of the screen to start */
     _putimage( x, y, ball, _GXOR );
     n = _imagesize( 0, 0, BALLX, BALLY );
     printf( "collision()..." );

     /* Drift and bounce */
     while ( !kbhit() )
         {

         /* Change value of DELAY to speed up or slow the ball */
         for ( i = 0; i < DELAY; i++ )
             { ; }

         /* Erase the ball at the current location */
         _putimage( x, y, ball, _GXOR );

         /* Change the location */
         x += dx;
         y += dy;

         /* Grab the background so we can check for collision */
         _getimage( x, y, x + BALLX, y + BALLY, back );

         /* Draw the ball at the new location */
         _putimage( x, y, ball, _GXOR );
```

(continued)

GRAPTEST.C *continued*

```
        /* Is there a collision here? */
        if ( collision( ball, back, n ) )
            {

            /* Erase the ball at the collision point */
            _putimage( x, y, ball, _GXOR );

            /* Shift back to the previous point */
            x -= dx;
            y -= dy;

            /* Redraw the ball at the previous position */
            _putimage( x, y, ball, _GXOR );

            /* Modify the test for which way to bounce */
            if ( ++tnum > 3 )
                tnum = 0;

            /* Bounce in appropriate direction */
            switch ( tnum )
                {
                case 1:
                    dx = -dx;
                    break;
                case 2:
                    dx = -dx;
                    dy = -dy;
                    break;
                case 3:
                    dy = -dy;
                    break;
                default:
                    dx = -dx;
                    dy = -dy;
                    break;
                }
            }
        /* No collision detected */
        else
            tnum = 0;
        }

    /* Reset default video mode */
    _setvideomode( _DEFAULTMODE );
}
```

Include File: GRAPHICS.H

```
/* --------------------------------------------------------------
   Name:          GRAPHICS.H
   Type:          Include
   Language:      Microsoft QuickC
   Demonstrated:  GRAPHICS.C  GRAPTEST.C
   Description:   Prototypes and definitions for GRAPHICS.C
   --------------------------------------------------------------
*/

#ifndef GRAPHICS_DEFINED

#define FALSE 0
#define TRUE !FALSE
#define LINED 0
#define SOLID 1

int collision( char far *, char far *, long );
int *bresenham( int, int, int, int );
void triangle(int, int, int, int, int, int, int);
void polygon( int, int, int [][2] );

#define GRAPHICS_DEFINED
#endif
```

Toolbox Module: GRAPHICS.C

```
/* --------------------------------------------------------------
   Name:          GRAPHICS.C
   Type:          Toolbox module
   Language:      Microsoft QuickC
   Demonstrated:  GRAPTEST.C
   Video:         Requires CGA or better graphics capability
   --------------------------------------------------------------
*/

#include <stdio.h>
#include <stdlib.h>
#include <graph.h>
#include <malloc.h>
#include <time.h>
#include "graphics.h"
```

Function: *collision()*

The collision of two graphics objects forms the basis of many types of computer graphics games. The *collision()* function is a fast, simple technique for detecting and displaying such an event.

The function regards an "object" as a rectangular area of the graphics screen that you have saved in a buffer by calling the QuickC function *_getimage()*. (If you are unfamiliar with the *_getimage()* and *_putimage()* graphics functions, see the QuickC documentation. The demonstration program ANIMATE.C, accessed through QuickC's help system, demonstrates these functions.)

Call the *collision()* function with the addresses of two identical-size object buffers and their size (in bytes). One buffer contains an object to be placed on the screen, and the other contains the screen contents at the target location. In the two buffers, a pixel with color value 0 belongs to the background, and a pixel with nonzero color bits is distinct from the background. The *collision()* function tests for bytes that are nonzero in the same position in both buffers, an indication that nonbackground pixels either are intersecting or are very close together.

```
/* - - - - - - - - - - - - - - - - - - - - - - - - - - - - - - - -
   Function:      collision()
   Toolbox:       GRAPHICS.C
   Demonstrated:  GRAPTEST.C

   Parameters:
     (input)      buf1     Graphics object via _getimage()
     (input)      buf2     Graphics object via _getimage()
     (input)      buf_siz  Size of the graphics buffers

   Returned:      TRUE if collision, FALSE if no collision

   Variables:     i        Looping variable

   Description:   Checks for collision of two graphics objects
   - - - - - - - - - - - - - - - - - - - - - - - - - - - - - - - -
*/
```

(continued)

GRAPHICS.C *continued*

```
int collision( char far *buf1, char far *buf2, long buf_siz )
{
    int i;

    /* Look for nonbackground bytes in each array */
    for ( i = 3; i < (int)buf_siz; i++ )
        if ( buf1[i] && buf2[i] )
            return ( TRUE );

    /* No collision detected */
    return ( FALSE );
}
```

Function: *bresenham()*

Bresenham's algorithm is a method for drawing straight lines using only integer math. This algorithm is at the core of many sophisticated graphics functions, including those provided with QuickC.

The slope of a line is the ratio of *y* steps to *x* steps. Bresenham's algorithm uses this fact to determine where the pixels along the line shift up, down, left, or right. If the slope of the line is greater than 1, then the line is more vertical than horizontal, in which case the function increments the y-coordinate for every point it calculates along the line. A calculation of relative step counts determines whether a corresponding *x* value should also be incremented. If the line is more horizontal than vertical, the function increments through the *x* values and determines where changes in the *y* values occur. The *bresenham()*

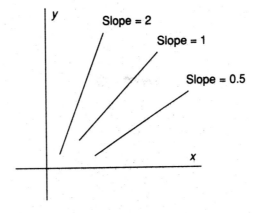

function uses this method to find x-coordinates and y-coordinates for all pixels along the line between the two specified points.

The *bresenham()* function expects the coordinates for the endpoints of a line segment. The function allocates enough memory for a buffer of (integer) coordinates along the line and returns the address of the buffer. The calling routine can then process these coordinates as they are needed but should free the memory after the coordinates are used. The *triangle()* function in this module uses *bresenham()* and then calls *free()* to release the memory allocated for the buffer.

The buffer of coordinates that *bresenham()* returns is an integer array. The first element contains the number of x,y coordinate pairs stored in the array. For example, consider the following call to *bresenham()* to find the coordinates along a line connecting the points (1,1) and (3,3):

```
int *buf;
buf = bresenham( 1, 1, 3, 3 );
```

The memory allocated for *buf* is 14 bytes; the contents of *buf* are shown in the following table:

ELEMENT	VALUE	DESCRIPTION
buf[0]	3	Three points to follow
buf[1]	1	X-coordinate
buf[2]	1	Y-coordinate
buf[3]	2	X-coordinate
buf[4]	2	Y-coordinate
buf[5]	3	X-coordinate
buf[6]	3	Y-coordinate

```
/* - - - - - - - - - - - - - - - - - - - - - - - - - - - - - - - - -
   Function:      bresenham()
   Toolbox:       GRAPHICS.C
   Demonstrated:  GRAPTEST.C

   Parameters:
     (input)      x1      X-coordinate for first point
     (input)      y1      Y-coordinate for first point
```

(continued)

GRAPHICS.C *continued*

```
        (input)      x2        X-coordinate for second point
        (input)      y2        Y-coordinate for second point

     Returned:           Integer buffer containing points on line

     Variables:   xi        X increment direction
                  yi        Y increment direction
                  dx        Relative change in x-coordinate
                  dy        Relative change in y-coordinate
                  xp        Current point along the line
                  yp        Current point along the line
                  cx        Accumulated x increments
                  cy        Accumulated y increments
                  buf       Pointer to returned buffer
                  ndx       Index into buf for each coordinate
                  i         Looping index

     Description:    Builds a table of coordinates that form a line
                     connecting two given points
     - - - - - - - - - - - - - - - - - - - - - - - - - - - - - -
*/

int *bresenham( int x1, int y1, int x2, int y2 )
{
    unsigned xi, yi, dx, dy, xp, yp, cx, cy;
    int *buf;
    int ndx = 1;
    int i;

    /* Right to left from first point to second? */
    if ( x2 < x1 )
        {
        dx = x1 - x2;
        xi = -1;
        }

    /* Must be left to right from first point to second */
    else
        {
        dx = x2 - x1;
        xi = 1;
        }
```

(continued)

GRAPHICS.C *continued*

```
/* Is first y-coordinate greater than second? */
if ( y2 < y1 )
    {
    dy = y1 - y2;
    yi = -1;
    }

/* Second y-coordinate must be greater than first */
else
    {
    dy = y2 - y1;
    yi = 1;
    }

/* Set the working point to the first point */
xp = x1;
yp = y1;

/* Is the line more vertical than horizontal? */
if ( dx < dy )
    {

    /* Start with the accumulated count at halfway point */
    cy = dy >> 1;

    /* Allocate memory for the buffer */
    buf = (int *)malloc( ((y2 - y1 + yi) * yi) * 4 + 2 );
    if ( buf == NULL )
        {
        printf( "Not enough memory for bresenham()\n" );
        exit( 1 );
        }

    /* Until we get to the last point */
    while ( yp != y2 )
        {

        /* Put the current point in the buffer */
        buf[ndx++] = xp;
        buf[ndx++] = yp;
```

(continued)

```
            /* Accumulate the relative counts */
            cy += dx;
            yp += yi;

            /* Is it time to change x-coordinate? */
            if ( dy < cy )
                {

                /* Reset the accumulating count */
                cy -= dy;

                /* Change the x-coordinate */
                xp += xi;
                }
            }
        }

/* Line must be more horizontal than vertical */
else
    {

    /* Start with the accumulated count at halfway point */
    cx = dx >> 1;

    /* Allocate memory for the buffer */
    buf = (int *)malloc( ((x2 - x1 + xi) * xi) * 4 + 2 );
    if ( buf == NULL )
        {
        printf( "Not enough memory for bresenham()\n" );
        exit( 1 );
        }

    /* Until we get to the last point */
    while ( xp != x2 )
        {

        /* Put the current point in the buffer */
        buf[ndx++] = xp;
        buf[ndx++] = yp;
```

(continued)

GRAPHICS.C *continued*

```
            /* Accumulate the relative counts */
            cx += dy;
            xp += xi;

            /* Is it time to change y-coordinate? */
            if ( dx < cx )
                {

                /* Reset the accumulating count */
                cx -= dx;

                /* Change the y-coordinate */
                yp += yi;
                }
            }
        }

    /* Save the last point in the buffer */
    buf[ndx++] = x2;
    buf[ndx++] = y2;

    /* Save the number of points at head of buffer */
    buf[0] = ndx >> 1;

    /* Return the buffer */
    return ( buf );

}
```

Function: *triangle()*

The *triangle()* function draws an outlined triangle or a solid triangle. Pass the constant LINED to draw only the three lines that form the triangle. Pass SOLID to fill the triangle with a given color. These constants are defined in the GRAPHICS.H header file, which you should include in any program that calls the functions in the GRAPHICS module.

The QuickC graphics library provides functions for drawing solid rectangles and for flooding an area with a color. The _rectangle() function is limited, however, to drawing rectangles, and _floodfill() offers limited speed. The *triangle()* function efficiently draws and optionally fills a triangular region of the screen. You can also use *triangle()* to draw more complicated shapes, provided that they can be broken up into a collection of triangles. (See the *polygon()* function for an example of this technique.)

The *triangle()* function first finds the minimum and maximum y-coordinates and x-coordinates of the triangle to be drawn. The goal is to draw horizontal lines from the left edge of the triangle to the right edge at every y-coordinate that falls within the triangle. The function calls *bresenham()* three times to determine all the coordinates of the sides of the triangle. For *y* values that lie within the triangle, the function compares side coordinates to determine the *x* values that are farthest left and farthest right. The *triangle()* function uses the resulting table of left and right coordinate pairs to draw horizontal lines that fill the triangle.

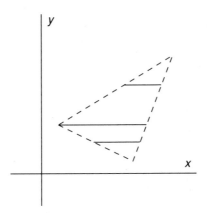

```
/* - - - - - - - - - - - - - - - - - - - - - - - - - - - - - - - - - /* - - -

    Function:        triangle()
    Toolbox:         GRAPHICS.C
    Demonstrated:    GRAPTEST.C

    Parameters:
      (input)        type       LINED (outline) or SOLID (filled)
      (input)        x1         X-coordinate at first point
      (input)        y1         Y-coordinate at first point
      (input)        x2         X-coordinate at second point
      (input)        y2         Y-coordinate at second point
      (input)        x3         X-coordinate at third point
      (input)        y3         Y-coordinate at third point
```

(continued)

GRAPHICS.C *continued*

```
    Returned:       (function returns nothing)

    Variables:      buf12      Points along line from point 1 to 2
                    buf23      Points along line from point 2 to 3
                    buf13      Points along line from point 1 to 3
                    xleft      Points along left side of triangle
                    xright     Points along right side of triangle
                    i          Looping index
                    ymin       Minimum y point of triangle
                    ymax       Maximum y point of triangle
                    xmin       Minimum x point of triangle
                    xmax       Maximum x point of triangle
                    x          X-coordinates along triangle edges
                    y          Y-coordinates along triangle edges
                    numy       Number of y-coordinates in triangle

    Description:    Draws a triangle, optionally filled in
    - - - - - - - - - - - - - - - - - - - - - - - - - - - - - - - -
*/

void triangle( int type, int x1, int y1, int x2, int y2, int x3, int y3 )
{
    int *buf12, *buf23, *buf13;
    int *xleft, *xright;
    int i, ymin, ymax, xmin, xmax;
    int x, y, numy;

    if ( type == LINED )

        /* Draw only the outline */
        {
        _moveto( x1, y1 );
        _lineto( x2, y2 );
        _lineto( x3, y3 );
        _lineto( x1, y1 );
        }

    else

        /* Fill in solid area */
        {
```

(continued)

```
        /* Determine minimum and maximum y-coordinates */
        ymin = ymax = y1;
        ymin = ( y2 < ymin ) ? y2 : ymin;
        ymin = ( y3 < ymin ) ? y3 : ymin;
        ymax = ( y2 > ymax ) ? y2 : ymax;
        ymax = ( y3 > ymax ) ? y3 : ymax;

        /* Determine minimum and maximum x-coordinates */
        xmin = xmax = x1;
        xmin = ( x2 < xmin ) ? x2 : xmin;
        xmin = ( x3 < xmin ) ? x3 : xmin;
        xmax = ( x2 > xmax ) ? x2 : xmax;
        xmax = ( x3 > xmax ) ? x3 : xmax;

        /* Calculate line coordinates for the triangle sides */
        buf12 = bresenham( x1, y1, x2, y2 );
        buf23 = bresenham( x2, y2, x3, y3 );
        buf13 = bresenham( x1, y1, x3, y3 );

        /* Build arrays for x values at all possible y values */
        numy = ymax - ymin + 1;
        xleft = (int *)malloc( (size_t)( numy * 2 ));
        xright = (int *)malloc( (size_t)( numy * 2 ));

        /* Fill arrays with starting values */
        for ( i = 0; i < numy; i++ )
            {
            xleft[i] = xmax;
            xright[i] = xmin;
            }

        /* Put coordinates for first triangle side into arrays */
        for ( i = 0; i < buf12[0]; i++ )
            {
            x = buf12[i+i+1];
            y = buf12[i+i+2] - ymin;
            if ( x < xleft[y] )
                xleft[y] = x;
            if ( x > xright[y] )
                xright[y] = x;
            }
```

(continued)

GRAPHICS.C *continued*

```
      /* Put coordinates for second triangle side into arrays */
      for ( i = 0; i < buf23[0]; i++ )
          {
          x = buf23[i+i+1];
          y = buf23[i+i+2] - ymin;
          if ( x < xleft[y] )
              xleft[y] = x;
          if ( x > xright[y] )
              xright[y] = x;
          }

      /* Put coordinates for third triangle side into arrays */
      for ( i = 0; i < buf13[0]; i++ )
          {
          x = buf13[i+i+1];
          y = buf13[i+i+2] - ymin;
          if ( x < xleft[y] )
              xleft[y] = x;
          if ( x > xright[y] )
              xright[y] = x;
          }

      /* Now we can fill the triangle efficiently */
      for ( i = 0; i < numy; i++ )
          {
          _moveto( xleft[i], ymin + i );
          _lineto( xright[i], ymin + i );
          }

      /* Free some memory */
      free( buf12 );
      free( buf23 );
      free( buf13 );
      free( xleft );
      free( xright );
      }
  }
```

Function: *polygon()*

The *polygon()* function draws an outlined or a solid polygon. Pass the constant LINED to draw only the lines that form the polygon. Pass SOLID to fill the polygon with a given color. These constants are defined in the GRAPHICS.H header file, which you should include in any program that calls the functions in the GRAPHICS module.

The *polygon()* function creates a solid figure by making multiple calls to the *triangle()* function. The first point in the passed x,y buffer is always used as one corner of the triangles. To fill each triangular piece of the polygon, sequential pairs of polygon coordinates are passed to *triangle()* along with the coordinates of the first point.

Notice that the order of the points in the x,y buffer can be important for some concave polygons. Each triangular piece of the polygon uses the first point as one of the corners. The angular direction from this first point to the others should always increase or decrease consistently from point to point. If the angular direction backtracks for a point, one of the vertices will end up inside the solid filled area. Usually, selecting a different order for the points will solve this problem. For example, in the polygon below, point A would be an appropriate point to pass first, but point B would not.

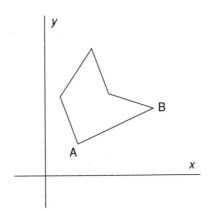

```
/* - - - - - - - - - - - - - - - - - - - - - - - - - - - - - - - -

   Function:      polygon()
   Toolbox:       GRAPHICS.C
   Demonstrated:  GRAPTEST.C

   Parameters:
     (input)      type      LINED (outline) or SOLID (filled)
     (input)      n         Number of points defining polygon
     (input)      xybuf     Array of n polygon coordinates

   Returned:      (function returns nothing)

   Variables:     x         X-coordinates
                  y         Y-coordinates
                  i         Looping index

   Description:   Draws a polygon, optionally filled in
   - - - - - - - - - - - - - - - - - - - - - - - - - - - - - - - -
*/

void polygon( int type, int n, int xybuf[][2] )
{
    int x, y, i;

    /* Not a solid fill situation? */
    if ( type == LINED || n < 3 )
        {

        /* Move to the last point in the list */
        n--;
        _moveto( ( x = xybuf[n][0] ), ( y = xybuf[n][1] ));

        /* Draw to each previous point */
        while ( --n >= 0 )
            _lineto( xybuf[n][0], xybuf[n][1] );

        /* Connect the first and last points */
        _lineto( x, y );
        }

    /* Fill in triangular areas */
    else
        {
```

(continued)

```
        /* Fill triangles, each having first point as a vertex */
        for ( i = 0; i <= n - 2; i++ )
            triangle( SOLID, xybuf[0][0], xybuf[0][1],
                             xybuf[i][0], xybuf[i][1],
                             xybuf[i+1][0], xybuf[i+1][1] );
        }
}
```

MENU

FUNCTION	DESCRIPTION
menu_box_lines()	Sets the border lines 0, 1, or 2
menu_box_shadow()	Sets the shadow on or off
menu_back_color()	Sets the background color
menu_line_color()	Sets the menu outline color
menu_title_color()	Sets the title color
menu_text_color()	Sets the menu text color
menu_prompt_color()	Sets the text color for prompts
menu_hilight_letter()	Sets the highlighted character color
menu_hilight_text()	Sets the highlighted text color
menu_hilight_back()	Sets the highlighted background color
menu_bar()	Creates a bar menu
menu_drop()	Creates a drop menu
menu_message()	Creates a message box
menu_erase()	Erases a displayed menu

The MENU toolbox module provides functions for creating menu bars, pull-down menus, and message boxes. Supporting functions let you control the color attributes for various parts of the menus, the box outline characters, and the use of shadows.

The *menu_bar()* function pops up a single horizontal line of choices. The *menu_drop()* function displays a vertical list of strings from which to choose. The *menu_message()* function simply places a (non-interactive) message on the screen. When these functions return to the calling program, the pop-up menu or box remains on the screen. The functions return a buffer address that can be passed to *menu_erase()* at any time. As a result, you can create multiple, overlapping pop-up menus and message boxes. To restore the original background, however, the calling program must erase the menu and message boxes in the opposite order from that in which it created them.

The MENUTEST.C program demonstrates the MENU functions by creating menus that let you modify the menus themselves. This program provides a handy utility for experimenting with the various color, shadow, and line parameter combinations. You can immediately assess the effect of each change to the appearance of the menus and boxes. The figure below shows the output of the MENUTEST program and identifies many of the elements you can create and modify with the functions in this module.

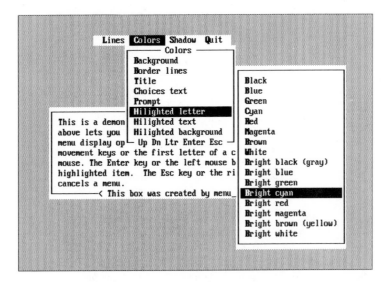

Look at MENUTEST.C to see how the text within menus and message boxes is created. The contents of *info_box*, for example, are defined as an array of strings. The first string in the list, *"Instructions"*, is the title line. The last string is the prompt line, which is displayed at the bottom edge of the box. All other strings are displayed in the interior of the box. To mark the end of the list, place a NULL pointer after the last string in each array definition. The *menu_bar()* function expects a single string of words separated by spaces.

Demonstration Program: MENUTEST.C

```
/* -----------------------------------------------------------------
   Name:           MENUTEST.C
   Type:           Demonstration program
   Language:       Microsoft QuickC version 2
   Video:          (no special video requirements)

   Program list:   MENUTEST.C
                   MENU.C
                   BOX.C
                   MOUSEFUN.C
                   GETKEY.C
                   GRAPHICS.LIB


   Variables:      info_box        Message box definition
                   bar_main        Menu bar definition
                   drop_lines      Menu of outline types
                   drop_colors     Menu for selecting color area
                   drop_t_colors   Menu of foreground colors
                   drop_bk_colors  Menu of background colors
                   drop_shadow     Menu for shadow control
                   drop_quit       Menu for quitting
                   n               First level drop menu selection
                   n1              Second level drop menu selection
                   bar_choice      Bar menu selection
                   first_time      Signals first time through menus
                   quit_flag       Signals to exit from function
                   save_info_box       Buffer for background save
                   save_bar_main       Buffer for background save
                   save_drop_colors    Buffer for background save

   Usage:          (no command line parameters)

   Description:    Demonstrates the MENU toolbox functions
   -----------------------------------------------------------------
*/

#include <stdio.h>
#include <graph.h>
#include "menu.h"
#include "box.h"
#include "t_colors.h"
```

(continued)

MENUTEST.C *continued*

```
char *info_box[] =
    {
    " Instructions ",
    "This is a demonstration of the MENU functions.  The menu bar",
    "above lets you select and try out the many combinations of",
    "menu display options.  To access a menu, press the cursor",
    "movement keys or the first letter of a choice or move your",
    "mouse.  The Enter key or the left mouse button selects the",
    "highlighted item.  The Esc key or the right mouse button",
    "cancels a menu.",
    "< This box was created by menu_message() >",
    NULL
    };

char *bar_main = "  Lines   Colors   Shadow   Quit  ";

char *drop_lines[] =
    {
    " Box Outline ",
    "Single line",
    "Double line",
    "No lines",
    " Select ",
    NULL
    };

char *drop_colors[] =
    {
    " Colors ",
    "Background",
    "Border lines",
    "Title",
    "Choices text",
    "Prompt",
    "Highlighted letter",
    "Highlighted text",
    "Highlighted background",
    " Up Dn Ltr Enter Esc ",
    NULL
    };
```

(continued)

MENUTEST.C *continued*

```
char *drop_t_colors[] =
    {
    "",  /* No title */
    "Black",
    "Blue",
    "Green",
    "Cyan",
    "Red",
    "Magenta",
    "Brown",
    "White",
    "Bright black (gray)",
    "Bright blue",
    "Bright green",
    "Bright cyan",
    "Bright red",
    "Bright magenta",
    "Bright brown (yellow)",
    "Bright white",
    "",  /* No prompt */
    NULL
    };

char *drop_bk_colors[] =
    {
    "",
    "Black",
    "Blue",
    "Green",
    "Cyan",
    "Red",
    "Magenta",
    "Brown",
    "White",
    "",
    NULL
    };

char *drop_shadow[] =
    {
    " Menu Shadow Control ",
    "Shadow off",
    "Shadow on",
    "",
```

(continued)

244

MENUTEST.C *continued*

```
    NULL
    };

char *drop_quit[] =
    {
    " Quit? ",
    "No",
    "Yes",
    "",
    NULL
    };

main()
{
    int n, n1;
    int bar_choice = 1;
    int first_time = 1;
    int quit_flag = 0;
    int far *save_info_box;
    int far *save_bar_main;
    int far *save_drop_colors;

    /* Initialize video */
    _setvideomode( _TEXTC80 );
    _clearscreen( _GCLEARSCREEN );

    /* Fill the background */
    box_charfill( 1, 1, 25, 80, 178 );

    /* Main loop begins here */
    while ( !quit_flag )
        {

        /* Erase the info box and main menu bar if not first time */
        if ( !first_time )
            {
            menu_erase( save_info_box );
            menu_erase( save_bar_main );
            }
        else
            first_time = 0;

        /* Display the information box */
        save_info_box = menu_message( 10, 8, info_box );
```

(continued)

MENUTEST.C *continued*

```
        /* The main menu bar */
        save_bar_main = menu_bar( 3, 18, bar_main, &bar_choice );
        switch( bar_choice )
            {
            case 1:
                menu_erase( menu_drop( 4, 18, drop_lines, &n ));
                if ( n )
                    menu_box_lines( n );
                break;
            case 2:
                save_drop_colors = menu_drop( 4, 25, drop_colors, &n );
                if ( n > 1 && n < 8 )
                    {
                    menu_erase( menu_drop( 6, 50, drop_t_colors, &n1 ));
                    n1--;
                    switch( n )
                        {
                        case 2:
                            menu_line_color( n1 );
                            break;
                        case 3:
                            menu_title_color( n1 );
                            break;
                        case 4:
                            menu_text_color( n1 );
                            break;
                        case 5:
                            menu_prompt_color( n1 );
                            break;
                        case 6:
                            menu_hilight_letter( n1 );
                            break;
                        case 7:
                            menu_hilight_text( n1 );
                            break;
                        }
                    }
                else if ( n == 1 || n == 8 )
                    {
                    menu_erase( menu_drop( 6, 50, drop_bk_colors, &n1 ));
                    n1--;
                    switch( n )
                        {
```

(continued)

MENUTEST.C *continued*

```
                        case 1:
                            menu_back_color( (long int)n1 );
                            break;
                        case 8:
                            menu_hilight_back( (long int)n1 );
                            break;
                        }
                    }
                menu_erase( save_drop_colors );
                break;
            case 3:
                menu_erase( menu_drop( 4, 33, drop_shadow, &n ));;
                if ( n )
                    menu_box_shadow( --n );
                break;
            case 4:
                menu_erase( menu_drop( 4, 41, drop_quit, &n ));;
                if ( n == 2 )
                    quit_flag = 1;
                break;
            default:
                /* (We'll ignore the Esc keypress at this level) */
                break;
            }
        }

    /* Clear screen before quitting */
    _clearscreen( _GCLEARSCREEN );
}
```

Include File: MENU.H

```
/* -------------------------------------------------------------------
    Name:          MENU.H
    Type:          Include
    Language:      Microsoft QuickC
    Demonstrated:  MENU.C  MENUTEST.C
    Description:   Prototypes and definitions for MENU.C
   -------------------------------------------------------------------
*/
```

(continued)

MENU.H *continued*

```
#ifndef MENU_DEFINED

void menu_box_lines( int );
void menu_box_shadow( int );
void menu_back_color( long int );
void menu_line_color( int );
void menu_title_color( int );
void menu_text_color( int );
void menu_prompt_color( int );
void menu_hilight_letter( int );
void menu_hilight_text( int );
void menu_hilight_back( long int );
int far *menu_bar( int, int, char *, int * );
int far *menu_drop( int, int, char **, int * );
int far *menu_message( int, int, char ** );
void menu_erase( int far * );

#define MENU_DEFINED
#endif
```

Toolbox Module: MENU.C

```
/* --------------------------------------------------------------------
   Name:          MENU.C
   Type:          Toolbox module
   Language:      Microsoft QuickC
   Demonstrated:  MENUTEST.C
   Video:         (no special video requirements)
   --------------------------------------------------------------------
*/

#include <graph.h>
#include <stdio.h>
#include <ctype.h>
#include <string.h>
#include <malloc.h>
#include "box.h"
#include "mousefun.h"
#include "getkey.h"
#include "t_colors.h"
#include "menu.h"
```

(continued)

MENU.C *continued*

```
/* Default menu colors */
static int c_lines = T_BLACK;
static int c_title = T_BLACK;
static int c_text = T_BLACK;
static int c_prompt = T_BLACK;
static int c_hitext = T_WHITE;
static int c_hiletter = T_WHITE ! T_BRIGHT;
static long int c_back = BK_WHITE;
static long int c_hiback = BK_BLACK;

/* Default border lines and shadow control */
static int mb_lines = 1;
static int mb_shadow = 1;
```

Function: *menu_box_lines()*

The *menu_box_lines()* function defines the outline style for the menu and message boxes. The outline can be a single line, a double line, or no line at all, as specified by a parameter (1, 2, or 0). The function creates the single-line or double-line borders from the graphics characters in the IBM extended character set.

```
/* - - - - - - - - - - - - - - - - - - - - - - - - - - - - - - - -

   Function:       menu_box_lines()
   Toolbox:        MENU.C
   Demonstrated:   MENUTEST.C

   Parameters:
     (input)       line_type           0, 1, or 2 (outline)

   Returned:       (function returns nothing)

   Variables:      (none)

   Description:    Sets the box outline type.  Selects single-line or
                   double-line border (or none)
   - - - - - - - - - - - - - - - - - - - - - - - - - - - - - - - -
*/

void menu_box_lines( int line_type )
{
    mb_lines = line_type;
}
```

Function: *menu_box_shadow()*

The *menu_box_shadow()* function controls the use of shadows for the menu or dialog boxes. Pass 0 if you do not want the shadows to appear; pass 1 to have them displayed. The function projects the shadows below and to the right of the boxes, in the same way that shadows are created for the pull-down menus you use in QuickC itself.

The shadow effect is produced by a change in the color attributes for the characters in the shadow. Notice that the function changes all the color attributes within the shadow to gray foreground text on a black background; as a result, the characters that fall into the shadow remain readable.

The shadow area is part of the background saved by the menu functions. When a program calls the *menu_erase()* function to restore the background, the shadowed area is restored as well.

```
/* - - - - - - - - - - - - - - - - - - - - - - - - - - - - - - - -
    Function:        menu_box_shadow()
    Toolbox:         MENU.C
    Demonstrated:    MENUTEST.C

    Parameters:
      (input)        on_off              Shadow control

    Returned:        (function returns nothing)

    Variables:       (none)

    Description:     Sets the menu box shadow control to on or off.
                     0 = off; nonzero = on.
    - - - - - - - - - - - - - - - - - - - - - - - - - - - - - - - -
*/

void menu_box_shadow( int on_off )
{
    mb_shadow = on_off;
}
```

Function: *menu_back_color()*

The *menu_back_color()* function sets the background color for the menu and message boxes. Separate functions are provided for setting foreground colors. The background color applies to all parts of the boxes and menus except the shadow and the currently highlighted selection.

```
/* - - - - - - - - - - - - - - - - - - - - - - - - - - - - - /*
   Function:      menu_back_color()
   Toolbox:       MENU.C
   Demonstrated:  MENUTEST.C

   Parameters:
     (input)      back               Background color

   Returned:      (function returns nothing)

   Variables:     (none)

   Description:   Sets the background color for boxes
   - - - - - - - - - - - - - - - - - - - - - - - - - - - - -
*/

void menu_back_color( long back )
{
    c_back = back;
}
```

Function: *menu_line_color()*

The *menu_line_color()* function sets the color for the box outline characters. These characters constitute the single-line or double-line border of the menu or message boxes. The background for the border is the same as the background for the rest of the box. If the box has no outline character, the *menu_line_color()* selection has no effect on the appearance of the menu and message boxes.

```
/* - - - - - - - - - - - - - - - - - - - - - - - - - - - - - - - - - - - - - -
   Function:       menu_line_color()
   Toolbox:        MENU.C
   Demonstrated:   MENUTEST.C
   Parameters:
     (input)       lines                   Border line color

   Returned:       (function returns nothing)

   Variables:      (none)

   Description:    Sets the box outline color
   - - - - - - - - - - - - - - - - - - - - - - - - - - - - - - - - - - - - - -
*/

void menu_line_color( int lines )
{
    c_lines = lines;
}
```

Function: *menu_title_color()*

The *menu_title_color()* function sets the foreground color for the text displayed in the title line of the menu or dialog boxes. The background is the same as for the rest of the box. If you pass a zero-length string ("") for the title, the *menu_title_color()* function has no effect on the appearance of the menus.

```
/* - - - - - - - - - - - - - - - - - - - - - - - - - - - - - - - - - - - - -
   Function:       menu_title_color()
   Toolbox:        MENU.C
   Demonstrated:   MENUTEST.C

   Parameters:
     (input)       title                   Title text color

   Returned:       (function returns nothing)

   Variables:      (none)

   Description:    Sets the text color for the title
   - - - - - - - - - - - - - - - - - - - - - - - - - - - - - - - - - - - - - -
*/
```

(continued)

```
void menu_title_color( int title )
{
    c_title = title;
}
```

Function: *menu_text_color()*

The *menu_text_color()* function sets the foreground color for the text displayed in the interior of menu or message boxes. To set the background color, use the *menu_back_color()* function. The *menu_text_color()* function sets the color of all the text inside boxes except the title, the prompt line, and the currently selected item in a menu.

```
/* - - - - - - - - - - - - - - - - - - - - - - - - - - - - - - - - - - -
    Function:       menu_text_color()
    Toolbox:        MENU.C
    Demonstrated:   MENUTEST.C

    Parameters:
      (input)       text                 Menu text color

    Returned:       (function returns nothing)

    Variables:      (none)

    Description:    Sets the menu box text color
    - - - - - - - - - - - - - - - - - - - - - - - - - - - - - - - - - - -
*/

void menu_text_color( int text )
{
    c_text = text;
}
```

Function: *menu_prompt_color()*

The *menu_prompt_color()* function sets the foreground color for the prompt at the bottom of a menu or message box. The background is the same as that for the rest of the box. If the prompt line is a zero-length string, this function has no effect on the appearance of the menu or message box.

```
/* - - - - - - - - - - - - - - - - - - - - - - - - - - - - - - - - -
    Function:       menu_prompt_color()
    Toolbox:        MENU.C
    Demonstrated:   MENUTEST.C

    Parameters:
     (input)        prompt                  Menu prompt line color

    Returned:       (function returns nothing)

    Variables:      (none)        .

    Description:    Sets the menu box prompt line text color
 - - - - - - - - - - - - - - - - - - - - - - - - - - - - - - - - - -
*/

void menu_prompt_color( int prompt )
{
    c_prompt = prompt;
}
```

Function: *menu_hilight_letter()*

The *menu_hilight_letter()* function sets the foreground color for the first letter of all menu options in both menu bars and pull-down menus. The foreground color for the first letter does not change when that option is selected and highlighted.

```
/* - - - - - - - - - - - - - - - - - - - - - - - - - - - - - - - - -
    Function:       menu_hilight_letter()
    Toolbox:        MENU.C
    Demonstrated:   MENUTEST.C

    Parameters:
     (input)        hiletter                Highlighted letter color

    Returned:       (function returns nothing)

    Variables:      (none)

    Description:    Sets highlighted character color for menu options
 - - - - - - - - - - - - - - - - - - - - - - - - - - - - - - - - - -
*/
```

(continued)

MENU.C *continued*

```
void menu_hilight_letter( int hiletter )
{
    c_hiletter = hiletter;
}
```

Function: *menu_hilight_text()*

The *menu_hilight_text()* function sets the foreground color for the text of the currently selected menu option. This setting affects all characters except the first letter of each choice. The *menu_back_color()* and *menu_text_color()* functions control the color settings for nonselected menu options.

```
/* - - - - - - - - - - - - - - - - - - - - - - - - - - - - - - - -
   Function:       menu_hilight_text()
   Toolbox:        MENU.C
   Demonstrated:   MENUTEST.C

   Parameters:
     (input)       hitext              Highlighted text color

   Returned:       (function returns nothing)

   Variables:      (none)

   Description:    Sets highlighted text color for menu options
   - - - - - - - - - - - - - - - - - - - - - - - - - - - - - - - -
*/

void menu_hilight_text( int hitext )
{
    c_hitext = hitext;
}
```

Function: *menu_hilight_back()*

The *menu_hilight_back()* function sets the background color for the currently selected and highlighted menu item. This setting affects the background for all characters in the currently selected menu item, including that for the first letter of each option. When items are not selected, the foreground and background colors revert to those set with *menu_back_color()* and *menu_text_color()*.

```
/* - - - - - - - - - - - - - - - - - - - - - - - - - - - - - - - - - -
   Function:        menu_hilight_back()
   Toolbox:         MENU.C
   Demonstrated:    MENUTEST.C

   Parameters:
    (input)         hiback               Highlighted line background

   Returned:        (function returns nothing)

   Variables:       (none)

   Description:     Sets the background color for the highlighted line
                    in the menu box
   - - - - - - - - - - - - - - - - - - - - - - - - - - - - - - - - - -
*/

void menu_hilight_back( long hiback )
{
    c_hiback = hiback;
}
```

Function: *menu_bar()*

The *menu_bar()* function creates a horizontal menu bar and waits for the user to select a word. The function places the number of the selected word in a variable. It returns the address of a buffer that contains that portion of the previous screen hidden by the menu.

The menu bar does not disappear when *menu_bar()* returns. Menus therefore remain visible while submenus are displayed. To restore the previous screen, pass the pointer returned by *menu_bar()* to the *menu_erase()* function. Be sure that the order in which you eventually erase the menus is the reverse of that in which you created them.

The menu bar is a string, or character array, of words separated by one or more spaces. The *menu_bar()* function changes the appearance of the menu in response to input from the keyboard or mouse. Pressing arrow keys or moving the mouse left or right shifts the location of the highlight bar from option to option. Pressing the first letter of a menu option moves the highlight bar to the next menu option that begins with the given letter. Pressing the Home or End keys moves the highlight bar to the first or last selection. Pressing the Enter key or clicking the left mouse button selects the currently highlighted option. To escape from the menu without selecting an option, either press the Esc key or click the right mouse button.

The default color selection is limited to monochrome attributes and is suitable for just about any type of monitor. To change the colors, use the other MENU functions. Note that including the header file T_COLORS.H, as was done in MENUTEST.C and in MENU.C, gives you access to a set of convenient constants for identifying background and foreground colors.

```
/* - - - - - - - - - - - - - - - - - - - - - - - - - - - - - /*

   Function:      menu_bar()
   Toolbox:       MENU.C
   Demonstrated:  MENUTEST.C

   Parameters:
     (input)      row         Screen row to locate menu bar
     (input)      col         Screen column to locate menu bar
     (input)      string      String of menu bar selections
     (output)     choice      Number of item selected by user

   Returned:      Buffer used to restore the background

   Variables:     len         Length of menu string
                  fore        Saves current foreground color
                  maxchoice   Number of choices
                  i           Looping index
                  j           Looping index
                  cpos        Current position in the menu
                  quit_flag   Signals to exit function
                  savebuf     Buffer containing background
                  fstr        Foreground color attributes
                  lastc       Last character checked
                  thisc       Current character checked
                  bstr        Background color attributes
                  key         Key code from getkey_or_mouse()
                  back        Saves current background color
                  oldpos      Saves the cursor position

   Description:   Creates a pop-up menu bar
   - - - - - - - - - - - - - - - - - - - - - - - - - - - - -
*/
```

(continued)

MENU.C *continued*

```
int far *menu_bar( int row, int col, char *string, int *choice )
{
    int len;
    int fore;
    int maxchoice;
    int i, j;
    int cpos;
    int quit_flag = 0;
    int far *savebuf;
    int fstr[81];
    char lastc, thisc;
    long int bstr[81];
    unsigned key;
    long int back;
    struct rccoord oldpos;

    /* Save the current color settings */
    fore = _gettextcolor();
    back = _getbkcolor();

    /* Save the current cursor position */
    oldpos = _gettextposition();

    /* Calculate the string length only once */
    len = strlen( string );

    /* Save the menu background */
    if ( mb_shadow )
        savebuf = box_get( row, col, row + 1, col + len + 1 );
    else
        savebuf = box_get( row, col, row, col + len - 1 );

    /* Put the menu bar on the screen */
    _settextposition( row, col );
    _outtext( string );

    /* Cast a shadow */
    if ( mb_shadow )
        {
        _settextcolor( T_GRAY );
        _setbkcolor( BK_BLACK );
        box_color( row + 1, col + 2, row + 1, col + len + 1 );
        }
```

(continued)

MENU.C *continued*

```
    /* Initialize choice if necessary */
    if ( *choice < 1 )
        *choice = 1;

    /* Process each keypress */
    while ( !quit_flag )
        {

        /* Determine the color attributes */
        j = 0;
        maxchoice = 0;
        lastc = 0;
        for ( i = 0; i < len; i++ )
            {
            thisc = string[i];
            if ( lastc == ' ' && thisc == ' ' && i < len - 1 )
                {
                j++;
                maxchoice++;
                }
            if ( j == *choice && i < len - 1 )
                {
                fstr[i] = c_hitext;
                bstr[i] = c_hiback;
                }
            else
                {
                fstr[i] = c_text;
                bstr[i] = c_back;
                }
            if ( isupper( thisc ) )
                {
                fstr[i] = c_hiletter;
                if ( j == *choice )
                    cpos = i;
                }
            lastc = thisc;
            }

        /* Put the attributes to video */
        for ( i = 0; i < len; i++ )
            {
            _settextcolor( fstr[i] );
```

(continued)

MENU.C *continued*

```
            _setbkcolor( bstr[i] );
            box_color( row, col + i, row, col + i );
            }

    /* Put cursor at appropriate position */
    _settextposition( row, col + cpos );

    key = getkey_or_mouse();

    /* Convert to uppercase */
    if ( key >= 'a' && key <= 'z' )
        key -= 32;

    /* Check for alpha key */
    if ( key >= 'A' && key <= 'Z' )
        {
        for ( i = 0; i < len; i++ )
            {
            if ( ++cpos >= len )
                {
                cpos = 0;
                *choice = 0;
                }
            if ( isupper( string[cpos] ))
                *choice += 1;
            if ( string[cpos] == (char)key )
                break;
            }
        }

    /* Check for control keys */
    switch( key )
        {
        case KEY_LEFT:
            if ( *choice > 1 )
                *choice -= 1;
            break;
        case KEY_RIGHT:
            if ( *choice < maxchoice )
                *choice += 1;
            break;
        case KEY_HOME:
            *choice = 1;
            break;
```

(continued)

MENU.C *continued*

```
              case KEY_END:
                  *choice = maxchoice;
                  break;
              case KEY_ESCAPE:
              case KEY_UP:
                  *choice = 0;
                  quit_flag = 1;
                  break;
              case KEY_ENTER:
              case KEY_DOWN:
                  quit_flag = 1;
                  break;
              }
          }

      /* Restore original conditions */
      _settextposition( oldpos.row, oldpos.col );
      _settextcolor( fore );
      _setbkcolor( back );
      return ( savebuf );
  }
```

Function: *menu_drop()*

The *menu_drop()* function creates a pull-down menu and waits for the user to choose an option with either the keyboard or a mouse. The function places the number of the selected item in a variable. It returns the address of a buffer that contains that portion of the previous screen hidden by the menu.

The pull-down menu does not disappear from the screen when *menu_drop()* returns. Menus therefore remain visible while submenus are displayed. To restore the previous screen, pass the pointer returned by *menu_drop()* to the *menu_erase()* function. Be sure that the order in which you eventually erase the menus is the reverse of that in which you created them.

The menu text consists of an array of strings, the last of which is the NULL pointer. The function sizes the menu box to accommodate the number of strings and the length of the longest string. The appearance of the menu changes in response to input from the keyboard or mouse. Pressing the arrow keys or moving the mouse up or down shifts the location of the highlight bar from option to option. To highlight the first or last selection, press the Home key or the End key. Pressing the first letter of a menu option moves the highlight bar to the next menu option that begins with the given letter. Pressing the Enter key or clicking the left mouse button selects the currently highlighted option. To escape from the menu without selecting an option, either press the Esc key or click the right mouse button.

The default color selection is limited to monochrome attributes and is suitable for just about any type of monitor. To change the colors, use the other MENU functions. Note that including the header file T_COLORS.H, as was done in MENUTEST.C and in MENU.C, gives you access to a set of convenient constants for identifying the background and foreground colors.

```
/* - - - - - - - - - - - - - - - - - - - - - - - - - - - - - - - - - - - - -

    Function:      menu_drop()
    Toolbox:       MENU.C
    Demonstrated:  MENUTEST.C

    Parameters:
      (input)      row        Screen row to locate menu bar
      (input)      col        Screen column to locate menu bar
      (input)      strary     String array of menu selections
      (output)     choice     Number of item selected by user

    Returned:      Buffer used to restore the background

    Variables:     n          Number of strings in menu
                   len        Length of menu string
                   fore       Saves current foreground color
                   tmpcol     Column to start title and prompt
                   maxchoice  Number of choices
                   i          Looping index
                   quit_flag  Signals to exit function
                   savebuf    Buffer containing background
                   key        Key code from getkey_or_mouse()
                   back       Saves current background color
                   oldpos     Saves the cursor position

    Description:   Creates a pop-up pull-down menu
    - - - - - - - - - - - - - - - - - - - - - - - - - - - - - - - - - - - - -
*/
```

(continued)

```
int far *menu_drop( int row, int col, char **strary, int *choice )
{
    int n = 0;
    int len = 0;
    int fore;
    int tmpcol;
    int maxchoice;
    int i;
    int quit_flag = 0;
    int far *savebuf;
    unsigned key;
    long int back;
    struct rccoord oldpos;

    /* Save the current color settings */
    fore = _gettextcolor();
    back = _getbkcolor();

    /* Save the current cursor position */
    oldpos = _gettextposition();

    /* Determine the number of strings in the menu */
    while ( strary[n] != NULL )
        n++;

    /* Set the maximum choice number */
    maxchoice = n - 2;

    /* Determine the maximum menu string length */
    for ( i = 0; i < n; i++ )
        if ( strlen( strary[i] ) > len )
            len = strlen( strary[i] );

    /* Save the menu background */
    if ( mb_shadow )
        savebuf = box_get( row, col, row + n, col + len + 5 );
    else
        savebuf = box_get( row, col, row + n - 1, col + len + 3 );

    /* Create the menu box */
    _settextcolor( c_lines );
    _setbkcolor( c_back );
```

(continued)

MENU.C *continued*

```
    box_erase( row, col, row + n - 1, col + len + 3 );
    box_draw( row, col, row + n - 1, col + len + 3, mb_lines );

    /* Cast a shadow */
    if ( mb_shadow )
        {
        _settextcolor( T_GRAY );
        _setbkcolor( BK_BLACK );
        box_color( row + n, col + 2, row + n, col + len + 3 );
        box_color( row + 1, col + len + 4, row + n, col + len + 5 );
        }

    /* Put the title at the top */
    tmpcol = col + ( len - strlen( strary[0] ) + 4 ) / 2;
    _settextposition( row, tmpcol );
    _settextcolor( c_title );
    _setbkcolor( c_back );
    _outtext( strary[0] );

    /* Print the choices */
    _settextcolor( c_text );
    for ( i = 1; i <= maxchoice; i++ )
        {
        _settextposition( row + i, col + 2 );
        _outtext( strary[i] );
        }

    /* Put the prompt at the bottom */
    tmpcol = col + ( len - strlen( strary[n - 1] ) + 4 ) / 2;
    _settextposition( row + n - 1, tmpcol );
    _settextcolor( c_prompt );
    _outtext( strary[n - 1] );

    /* Initialize choice */
    *choice = 1;

    /* Process each keypress */
    while ( !quit_flag )
        {

        /* Determine and set the color attributes */
        for ( i = 1; i <= maxchoice; i++ )
```

(continued)

```
            {
        if ( i == *choice )
            {
            _setbkcolor( c_hiback );
            _settextcolor( c_hiletter );
            box_color( row + i, col + 1, row + i, col + 2 );
            _settextcolor( c_hitext );
            box_color( row + i, col + 3, row + i, col + len + 2 );
            }
        else
            {
            _setbkcolor( c_back );
            _settextcolor( c_hiletter );
            box_color( row + i, col + 1, row + i, col + 2 );
            _settextcolor( c_text );
            box_color( row + i, col + 3, row + i, col + len + 2 );
            }
        }

    /* Put cursor at appropriate position */
    _settextposition( row + *choice, col + 2 );

    key = getkey_or_mouse();

    /* Convert to uppercase */
    if ( key >= 'a' && key <= 'z' )
        key -= 32;

    /* Check for alpha key */
    if ( key >= 'A' && key <= 'Z' )
        {
        for ( i = 1; i <= maxchoice; i++ )
            {
            *choice += 1;
            if ( *choice > maxchoice )
                *choice = 1;
            if ( strary[*choice][0] == (char)key )
                break;
            }
        }
```

(continued)

MENU.C *continued*

```
            /* Check for control keys */
            switch( key )
                {
                case KEY_UP:
                    if ( *choice > 1 )
                        *choice -= 1;
                    break;
                case KEY_DOWN:
                    if ( *choice < maxchoice )
                        *choice += 1;
                    break;
                case KEY_HOME:
                    *choice = 1;
                    break;
                case KEY_END:
                    *choice = maxchoice;
                    break;
                case KEY_ESCAPE:
                    *choice = 0;
                    quit_flag = 1;
                    break;
                case KEY_ENTER:
                    quit_flag = 1;
                    break;
                }
            }

        /* Restore original conditions */
        _settextposition( oldpos.row, oldpos.col );
        _settextcolor( fore );
        _setbkcolor( back );
        return ( savebuf );
    }
```

Function: *menu_message()*

The *menu_message()* function pops up a box for displaying text lines. This function is similar to *menu_drop()*, but it does not highlight any text, and it returns immediately instead of waiting for the user to select an item.

The function returns the address of a buffer that contains all the information necessary for restoring the original screen contents. The message boxes can remain visible while menus or other message boxes are displayed. At the appropriate time, the program can erase them by passing the returned address to *menu_erase()*. Be sure the order in which you eventually erase the message boxes and menus is the reverse of that in which you created them.

Make color selections for your message boxes as you do for menus. Of course, the color selections for highlighted items do not affect the message boxes. The first string in the message is the title, and the last string is the prompt line. Other functions in this module enable you to set the foreground colors for the title and prompt line to distinguish them from the main text in the message box.

```
/* - - - - - - - - - - - - - - - - - - - - - - - - - - - - - - - - - - - - - - -
    Function:        menu_message()
    Toolbox:         MENU.C
    Demonstrated:    MENUTEST.C

    Parameters:
      (input)        row        Screen row to locate message box
      (input)        col        Screen column to locate message box
      (input)        strary     String array of message text

    Returned:        Buffer used to restore the background

    Variables:       n            Number of strings in message
                     len          Length of longest message string
                     fore         Saves current foreground color
                     tmpcol       Column to start title and prompt
                     i            Looping index
                     savebuf      Buffer containing background
                     key          Key code from getkey_or_mouse()
                     back         Saves current background color
                     oldpos       Saves the cursor position

    Description:     Creates a pop-up message box
    - - - - - - - - - - - - - - - - - - - - - - - - - - - - - - - - - - - - - -
*/

int far *menu_message( int row, int col, char **strary )
{
    int n = 0;
    int len = 0;
    int fore;
    int tmpcol;
```

(continued)

MENU.C *continued*

```
    int i;
    int far *savebuf;
    unsigned key;
    long int back;
    struct rccoord oldpos;

    /* Save the current color settings */
    fore = _gettextcolor();
    back = _getbkcolor();

    /* Save the current cursor position */
    oldpos = _gettextposition();

    /* Determine the number of strings in the message */
    while ( strary[n] != NULL )
        n++;

    /* Determine the maximum message string length */
    for ( i = 0; i < n; i++ )
        if ( strlen( strary[i] ) > len )
            len = strlen( strary[i] );

    /* Save the message background */
    if ( mb_shadow )
        savebuf = box_get( row, col, row + n, col + len + 5 );
    else
        savebuf = box_get( row, col, row + n - 1, col + len + 3 );

    /* Create the information box */
    _settextcolor( c_lines );
    _setbkcolor( c_back );
    box_erase( row, col, row + n - 1, col + len + 3 );
    box_draw( row, col, row + n - 1, col + len + 3, mb_lines );

    /* Cast a shadow */
    if ( mb_shadow )
        {
        _settextcolor( T_GRAY );
        _setbkcolor( BK_BLACK );
        box_color( row + n, col + 2, row + n, col + len + 3 );
        box_color( row + 1, col + len + 4, row + n, col + len + 5 );
        }
```

(continued)

MENU.C *continued*

```
      /* Put the title at the top */
      tmpcol = col + ( len - strlen( strary[0] ) + 4 ) / 2;
      _settextposition( row, tmpcol );
      _settextcolor( c_title );
      _setbkcolor( c_back );
      _outtext( strary[0] );

      /* Print the text */
      _settextcolor( c_text );
      for ( i = 1; i < n - 1; i++ )
          {
          _settextposition( row + i, col + 2 );
          _outtext( strary[i] );
          }

      /* Put the prompt at the bottom */
      tmpcol = col + ( len - strlen( strary[n - 1] ) + 4 ) / 2;
      _settextposition( row + n - 1, tmpcol );
      _settextcolor( c_prompt );
      _outtext( strary[n - 1] );

      /* Restore original conditions */
      _settextposition( oldpos.row, oldpos.col );
      _settextcolor( fore );
      _setbkcolor( back );
      return ( savebuf );
   }
```

Function: *menu_erase()*

The *menu_erase()* function restores the screen contents underneath a menu bar, pull-down menu, or message box. The function requires a single parameter: the buffer address returned by the function that created the menu or message box. The buffer contains the screen locations, character codes, and all attributes necessary for restoring the screen to its previous state.

Menus and dialog boxes often overlap each other. Be sure that the order in which you erase them is the reverse of that in which you created them. That is, erase the most recently created box before you erase any boxes that it covers.

The functions that create menus and message boxes allocate memory for the restore buffers. The *menu_erase()* function frees this memory and returns it to the memory pool.

```
/* - - - - - - - - - - - - - - - - - - - - - - - - - - - - - - - -
    Function:       menu_erase()
    Toolbox:        MENU.C
    Demonstrated:   MENUTEST.C

    Parameters:
      (input)       buf       Buffer for restoring background

    Returned:       (function returns nothing)

    Variables:      (none)

    Description:    Restores the background behind a bar menu,
                    pull-down menu, or message box
    - - - - - - - - - - - - - - - - - - - - - - - - - - - - - - - -
*/

void menu_erase( int far *buf )
{
    box_put( buf );
    _ffree( buf );
}
```

MONEY

FUNCTION	DESCRIPTION
round()	Rounds a decimal number
dollar()	Formats dollar amounts
monthly_payment()	Calculates a monthly loan payment

The MONEY toolbox module provides a sampling of functions for working with monetary amounts. Each function provides a starting point for developing many similar functions.

The *round()* function rounds decimal numbers to a specified precision. If your program performs dollar calculations, for example, you would want it to round numbers to the hundredths place, the −2 power of 10. The *round()* function is also useful for scientific and engineering calculations, in which values must commonly be rounded to a given precision.

To help with printing or display, the *dollar()* function formats dollar amounts as strings of a fixed length.

The *monthly_payment()* function is handy for the most common type of loan, one that is amortized at a fixed rate over a fixed number of months. You can easily modify this function to perform similar financial calculations.

The MONETEST.C program demonstrates each of the functions in this module. The program output shows the result of rounding a large number at various decimal places, displays a formatted table of dollar amounts to illustrate the use of the *dollar()* function, and calculates the monthly payment on a typical fixed-interest house loan.

Demonstration Program: MONETEST.C

```
/* -----------------------------------------------------------------
   Name:        MONETEST.C
   Type:        Demonstration program
   Language:    Microsoft QuickC
   Video:       (no special video requirements)
```

(continued)

MONETEST.C *continued*

```
     Program list:    MONETEST.C
                      MONEY.C

     Variables:       x              A large number for rounding
                      y              The number after rounding
                      principal      Amount of loan
                      interest       Annual interest rate of loan
                      payment        Monthly payment on loan
                      months         Number of months to pay on loan
                      i              Looping index
                      n              Decimal place for rounding
                      buf            Formatted dollar representation

     Usage:           (no command line parameters)

     Description:     Demonstrates the MONEY toolbox functions
     ------------------------------------------------------------------
*/

#include <stdio.h>
#include "money.h"

main()
{
    double x, y;
    double principal, interest, payment;
    int months, i, n;
    char buf[80];

    /* Show rounding at various decimal places */
    x = 1234567.7654;
    printf("\nx = %12.4f\n",x);
    for ( n = -3; n < 3; n++ )
        {
        y = round( x, n );
        printf( "round( x, %d) = %12.4f\n", n, y );
        }

    /* Show dollar amounts formatted in 15-character string */
    printf( "\ndollar( x, 15, buf )...\n" );
    for ( i = 0; i < 5; i++ )
```

(continued)

MONETEST.C *continued*

```
        {
        /* First, positive dollar amounts */
        dollar( x, 15, buf );
        printf( "%s\t\t", buf );

        /* Next, negative values */
        dollar( -x, 15, buf );
        printf( "%s\n", buf );

        /* Make the dollar amount smaller each time */
        x /= 10.0;
        }

    /* Show a simple house loan calculation */
    printf( "\nLoan...\n" );
    principal = 75000.00;
    interest = 11.5;
    months = 360;
    payment = monthly_payment( principal, months, interest );
    printf( "principal:\t%9.2f\n", principal );
    printf( "interest:\t%9.2f\n", interest );
    printf( "months:\t\t%9d\n", months );
    printf( "payment:\t%9.2f\n", payment );
}
```

Include File: MONEY.H

```
/* -------------------------------------------------------------------
    Name:          MONEY.H
    Type:          Include
    Language:      Microsoft QuickC
    Demonstrated:  MONEY.C  MONETEST.C
    Description:   Prototypes and definitions for MONEY.C
    -------------------------------------------------------------------
*/
```

(continued)

MONEY.H *continued*

```
#ifndef MONEY_DEFINED

double round( double, int );
void dollar( double, int, char * );
double monthly_payment( double, int, double );

#define MONEY_DEFINED
#endif
```

Toolbox Module: MONEY.C

```
/* ------------------------------------------------------------------
    Name:           MONEY.C
    Type:           Toolbox module
    Language:       Microsoft QuickC
    Demonstrated:   MONETEST.C
    Video:          (no special video requirements)
    ------------------------------------------------------------------
*/

#include <stdio.h>
#include <math.h>
#include <string.h>

# include "money.h"
```

Function: *round()*

The *round()* function rounds a number to a given decimal place. Indicate the decimal place in the second parameter as a power of ten. For example, to round a number to the nearest whole number, specify the power of ten as 0. To round dollar amounts two digits to the right of the decimal point, pass −2 for the power of ten. The MONETEST demonstration program shows the result of rounding a number to various decimal places.

```
/* - - - - - - - - - - - - - - - - - - - - - - - - - - - - - - - -
   Function:      round()
   Toolbox:       MONEY.C
   Demonstrated:  MONETEST.C

   Parameters:
     (input)      amount         Number to round
     (input)      power_of_ten   Place at which to round

   Returned:      The amount rounded to the indicated place

   Variables:     pten      10 raised to power_of_ten
                  intpart   Integer part of number divided by pten
                  halfsign  Plus or minus 0.5 for accurate rounding

   Description:   Rounds a double to the given power-of-ten place
   - - - - - - - - - - - - - - - - - - - - - - - - - - - - - - - -
*/

double round( double amount, int power_of_ten )
{
    double pten, intpart, halfsign;

    pten = pow( 10.0, (double)power_of_ten );
    halfsign = ( amount < 0.0 ) ? -0.5 : 0.5;
    modf( amount / pten + halfsign, &intpart );
    return ( intpart * pten );
}
```

Function: *dollar()*

The *dollar()* function formats a dollar amount as a string suitable for printing or display. The function inserts a comma before every third digit to the left of the decimal point and right justifies the string contents within the field length indicated in the second parameter. This right justification causes decimal points to align when several monetary values are printed or displayed in a column.

```
/* - - - - - - - - - - - - - - - - - - - - - - - - - - - - - - - - -

   Function:       dollar()
   Toolbox:        MONEY.C
   Demonstrated:   MONETEST.C

   Parameters:
     (input)       amount       Dollar amount
     (input)       len          Desired length of string result
     (input)       dollarstr    String to store formatted amount

   Returned:       (function returns nothing)

   Variables:      buf          Temporary working string space
                   i            Index into buf
                   j            Index into dollarstr
                   k            Length of dollarstr
                   t            Character under test

   Description:    Formats a dollar amount into a right-justified
                   string; adds commas every third digit
   - - - - - - - - - - - - - - - - - - - - - - - - - - - - - - - - -
*/

void dollar( double amount, int len, char *dollarstr )
{
    char buf[40];
    int i, j, k, t;

    /* Format dollar amount with no commas */
    sprintf( dollarstr, "%.2f", amount );

    /* Shuffle characters into buf, adding commas */
    k = strlen( dollarstr );
    for ( i = j = 0; k >= 0; k-- )
        {
        t = buf[i++] = dollarstr[j++];
        if (( k % 3 ) == 1 && k > 4 && t != '-' )
            buf[i++] = ',';
        }

    /* Move into dollarstr, flush with right end of the string */
    sprintf( dollarstr, "%*s", len, buf );
}
```

Function: *monthly_payment()*

The *monthly_payment()* function calculates the amount of the monthly payment for a simple loan. This calculation covers the most common type of loan, one in which a dollar amount (principal) is to be repaid over a given number of months at a fixed annual interest rate.

The MONETEST program shows the payment amount calculated for a 30-year (360-month) house loan of $75,000 at an annual interest rate of 11.5 percent. Notice that you pass the interest rate to the function as a percentage (11.5) rather than converting it to a decimal equivalent (0.115) yourself.

```
/* - - - - - - - - - - - - - - - - - - - - - - - - - - - - - - - - - -
   Function:      monthly_payment()
   Toolbox:       MONEY.C
   Demonstrated:  MONETEST.C

   Parameters:
     (input)      principal           Amount of loan
     (input)      months              Number of monthly payments
     (input)      annual_interest     Annual interest rate

   Returned:      Monthly payment for the loan

   Variables:     tmp                 Intermediate calculation
                  monthly_interest    Monthly interest rate

   Description:   Calculates a simple loan payment amount
   - - - - - - - - - - - - - - - - - - - - - - - - - - - - - - - - -
*/

double monthly_payment( double principal, int months,
                        double annual_interest )
{
    double tmp, monthly_interest;

    monthly_interest = annual_interest / 1200.0;
    tmp = 1.0 - pow(( monthly_interest + 1.0 ), (double)( -months ));
    return ( round( monthly_interest * principal / tmp, -2 ));
}
```

MOUSEFUN

FUNCTION	DESCRIPTION
mouse_reset()	Resets the mouse parameters
mouse_show()	Makes the cursor visible
mouse_hide()	Makes the cursor invisible
mouse_status()	Gets the mouse status
mouse_setpos()	Sets the cursor position
mouse_press()	Gets the button presses
mouse_release()	Gets the button releases
mouse_sethorz()	Sets the horizontal motion limits
mouse_setvert()	Sets the vertical motion limits
mouse_setgcurs()	Sets the graphics cursor shape
mouse_settcurs()	Sets the text mode cursor
mouse_motion()	Gets the mouse motion
mouse_setratios()	Sets the mickey/pixel ratios
mouse_condoff()	Sets the conditional off region
mouse_setdouble()	Sets the double speed threshold
mouse_storage()	Determines the mouse state size
mouse_save()	Saves the mouse state in a buffer
mouse_restore()	Restores the saved mouse state
mouse_setsensitivity()	Sets the mouse sensitivity
mouse_getsensitivity()	Gets the mouse sensitivity
mouse_setmaxrate()	Sets the interrupt rate
mouse_setpage()	Sets the video page for the mouse
mouse_getpage()	Gets the video page for the mouse
mouse_setlang()	Sets the language for messages
mouse_getlang()	Gets the language for messages
mouse_getversion()	Gets the mouse driver version

The MOUSEFUN toolbox module provides a collection of functions for accessing and using your mouse. Most of these functions work in any video mode, but a few require at least CGA graphics capability.

The MOUSEFUN functions show how easily you can take advantage of powerful in-line assembly code. All the functions were originally written using the QuickC library functions *int86()* and *int86x()* and were later rewritten using the *_asm* statement. The rewritten functions are smaller and more straightforward, and they run faster.

Several other modules and programs in this book use MOUSEFUN functions to add mouse capability. The MENU.C module, for example, calls *getkey_or_mouse()*, which in turn calls several mouse functions. The MENUTEST.C program lets you see the MOUSEFUN functions at work— they enable you to use a mouse to choose items on pull-down menus.

The MOUSTEST.C program demonstrates all the functions in this toolbox module. A good way to understand each function is to proceed function by function through the MOUSTEST program, stopping at each demonstration to read the relevant function description.

The first demonstration, for example, resets the mouse parameters with *mouse_reset()* and displays the values of two variables that the function sets—the mouse status and the number of mouse buttons.

In a later demonstration, MOUSTEST shows a series of graphics mode mouse cursors. The data structures for these cursors are defined in the MOUSEFUN.H header file. The MOUSGCRS.C utility presented in Part III lets you design your own graphics mode cursors.

Several functions in this module use virtual screen coordinates to indicate the mouse cursor position. The virtual screen coordinates are not necessarily the same as the graphics mode or text mode screen coordinates. The virtual screen is scaled to 640 horizontal units for all modes, including standard text modes, and to 200 vertical units for most modes, the exceptions being some of the newer EGA and VGA modes. In particular, graphics modes with vertical resolutions of 350 or 480 pixels have mouse virtual screens with 350 or 480 vertical units.

This toolbox module includes all but a few of the functions provided by the mouse driver. If you want to dig into mouse programming in more detail, an excellent source of information is *Microsoft Mouse Programmer's Reference,* published by Microsoft Press. The book covers all the mouse functions in detail and provides programming examples for all the major programming languages.

Demonstration Program: MOUSTEST.C

```
/* -------------------------------------------------------------------
   Name:           MOUSTEST.C
   Type:           Demonstration program
   Language:       Microsoft QuickC version 2
   `Video:          Requires CGA or better graphics capability

   Program list:   MOUSTEST.C
                   MOUSEFUN.C
                   CLOCK.C
                   GRAPHICS.LIB

   Variables:      leftb           Left button status
                   rightb          Right button status
                   horz            Horizontal mouse position
                   vert            Vertical mouse position
                   i               Looping index
                   status          Mouse reset status
                   buttons         Number of mouse buttons
                   presses         Number of button presses
                   releases        Number of button releases
                   row             Row for drawing background
                   col             Columns for drawing background
                   mouse_type      Type of mouse
                   irq_num         Interrupt request type
                   threshold       Double speed threshold
                   page            Video page
                   lang            Language number for messages
                   bufsize         Size for mouse storage buffer
                   buf             Mouse state storage buffer
                   version         Mouse driver version number

   Usage:          (no command line parameters)

   Description:    Demonstrates the MOUSEFUN toolbox functions
   -------------------------------------------------------------------
*/

#include <stdio.h>
#include <stdlib.h>
#include <conio.h>
#include <graph.h>
#include <malloc.h>
#include "mousefun.h"
#include "clock.h"
```

(continued)

MOUSTEST.C *continued*

```c
main()
{
    int leftb = 0, rightb = 0, horz = 0, vert = 0;
    int i, status, buttons, presses, releases;
    int row, col;
    int mouse_type, irq_num;
    int threshold, page, lang;
    unsigned bufsize;
    char *buf;
    double version;

    /* Demonstrate mouse_reset() */
    _clearscreen( _GCLEARSCREEN );
    printf( "mouse_reset( &status, &buttons ); ...\n" );
    mouse_reset( &status, &buttons );
    printf( "status = %d, buttons = %d\n\n", status, buttons );

    /* Demonstrate mouse_show() */
    printf( "mouse_show();\n\n" );
    printf( "Press any key to continue" );
    mouse_show();
    getch();

    /* Demonstrate mouse_hide() */
    mouse_hide();
    _clearscreen( _GCLEARSCREEN );
    printf( "mouse_hide();\n\n" );
    printf( "Press any key to continue" );
    getch();

    /* Demonstrate mouse_status() */
    _clearscreen( _GCLEARSCREEN );
    printf( "(Press both mouse buttons simultaneously to continue)\n\n" );
    printf( "mouse_status( &leftb, &rightb, &horz, &vert );\n" );
    mouse_show();
    while ( !(leftb & rightb) )
        {
        mouse_status( &leftb, &rightb, &horz, &vert );
        printf( "Left button: %1d\t", leftb );
        printf( "Right button: %1d\t\t", rightb );
        printf( "x, y position: %4d,%4d\r", horz, vert );
        if ( kbhit() ) getch();
        }
```

(continued)

MOUSTEST.C *continued*

```
/* Demonstrate mouse_setpos() */
mouse_hide();
_clearscreen( _GCLEARSCREEN );
printf( "mouse_setpos( x, y );\n" );
mouse_show();
for ( i = 0; i < 200; i += 8 )
    {
    mouse_setpos( i, i );
    delay( .1 );
    }
for ( i = 0; i < 200; i += 8 )
    {
    mouse_setpos( i, 200 - i );
    delay( .1 );
    }

/* Demonstrate mouse_press() */
mouse_hide();
_clearscreen( _GCLEARSCREEN );
printf( "(Click right button at upper left corner to continue)\n\n" );
printf( "mouse_press( button, &status, &presses, &horz, &vert );\n\n" );
mouse_show();
leftb = rightb = 0;
while ( horz | vert )
    {
    mouse_press( LBUTTON, &leftb, &presses, &horz, &vert );
    _settextposition( 4, 1 );
    printf( "Left button: status, presses, x, y...\t" );
    printf( "%5d, %5d, %5d, %5d\n", leftb, presses, horz, vert );
    mouse_press( RBUTTON, &rightb, &presses, &horz, &vert );
    printf( "Right button: status, presses, x, y...\t" );
    printf( "%5d, %5d, %5d, %5d\n", rightb, presses, horz, vert );
    if ( kbhit() ) getch();
    delay( 1.0 );
    }

/* Demonstrate mouse_release() */
mouse_hide();
_clearscreen( _GCLEARSCREEN );
printf( "(Click right button at upper right corner to continue)\n\n" );
printf( "mouse_release( button, &status, &release, &horz, &vert );\n\n" );
mouse_show();
```

(continued)

MOUSTEST.C *continued*

```
    leftb = rightb = 0;
    while (( horz != 632 ) ¦ vert )
        {
        mouse_release( LBUTTON, &leftb, &releases, &horz, &vert );
        _settextposition( 4, 1 );
        printf( "Left button: status, releases, x, y...\t" );
        printf( "%5d, %5d, %5d, %5d\n", leftb, releases, horz, vert );
        mouse_release( RBUTTON, &rightb, &releases, &horz, &vert );
        printf( "Right button: status, releases, x, y...\t" );
        printf( "%5d, %5d, %5d, %5d\n", rightb, releases, horz, vert );
        if ( kbhit() ) getch();
        delay( 1.0 );
        }

    /* Demonstrate mouse_sethorz() */
    mouse_hide();
    _clearscreen( _GCLEARSCREEN );
    mouse_sethorz( 160, 480 );

    /* Demonstrate mouse_setvert() */
    mouse_setvert( 50, 150 );
    printf( "mouse_sethorz( 160, 480 );\nmouse_setvert( 50, 150 );\n\n" );
    printf( "Press any key to continue" );
    for ( row = 7; row < 20; row++ )
        for ( col = 21; col < 62; col++ )
            {
            _settextposition( row, col );
            putchar( 176 );
            }
    mouse_show();
    getch();
    mouse_hide();
    mouse_sethorz( 0, 632 );
    mouse_setvert( 0, 192 );

    /* Demonstrate mouse_setgcurs() */
    _setvideomode( _HRESBW );
    _clearscreen( _GCLEARSCREEN );
    printf( "Press any key to continue\n\n" );
    printf( "mouse_setgcurs( struct graphics_cursor far * );" );
    mouse_show();
    mouse_setgcurs( &gcursor_hand );
    getch();
```

(continued)

MOUSTEST.C *continued*

```
    mouse_setgcurs( &gcursor_check );
    getch();
    mouse_setgcurs( &gcursor_hour );
    getch();
    mouse_setgcurs( &gcursor_jet );
    getch();
    mouse_setgcurs( &gcursor_left );
    getch();
    mouse_setgcurs( &gcursor_plus );
    getch();
    mouse_setgcurs( &gcursor_up );
    getch();
    mouse_setgcurs( &gcursor_x );
    getch();
    mouse_setgcurs( &gcursor_default );
    mouse_hide();

    /* Demonstrate mouse_settcurs() */
    _setvideomode( _DEFAULTMODE );
    _clearscreen( _GCLEARSCREEN );
    printf( "Press any key to continue\n\n" );
    printf( "mouse_settcurs( SOFT_TEXT_CURSOR, 0x1234, 0x7654 );\n" );
    mouse_settcurs( SOFT_TEXT_CURSOR, 0x1234, 0x7654 );
    mouse_show();
    getch();
    mouse_hide();
    _clearscreen( _GCLEARSCREEN );
    printf( "Press any key to continue\n\n" );
    printf( "mouse_settcurs( HARD_TEXT_CURSOR, 3, 7 );\n" );
    mouse_settcurs( HARD_TEXT_CURSOR, 3, 7 );
    mouse_show();
    getch();
    mouse_hide();
    mouse_settcurs( HARD_TEXT_CURSOR, 7, 7 );
    _clearscreen( _GCLEARSCREEN );
    printf( "Press any key to continue\n\n" );
    printf( "mouse_settcurs( SOFT_TEXT_CURSOR, 0xFFFF, 0x7700 );\n" );
    mouse_settcurs( SOFT_TEXT_CURSOR, 0xFFFF, 0x7700 );
    mouse_show();
    getch();
    mouse_hide();
```

(continued)

```
    /* Demonstrate mouse_motion() */
    _clearscreen( _GCLEARSCREEN );
    printf( "Click left button to continue\n\n" );
    printf( "mouse_motion( &horz_mickeys, &vert_mickeys );\n" );
    mouse_show();
    mouse_press( LBUTTON, &status, &presses, &horz, &vert );
    presses = 0;
    while ( !presses )
        {
        mouse_motion( &horz, &vert );
        printf( "Horizontal mickeys: %5d\t", horz );
        printf( "Vertical mickeys: %5d\r", vert );
        delay( .5 );
        if ( kbhit() ) getch();
        mouse_press( LBUTTON, &status, &presses, &horz, &vert );
        }

    /* Demonstrate mouse_setratios() */
    mouse_hide();
    _clearscreen( _GCLEARSCREEN );
    printf( "Press any key to continue\n\n" );
    printf( "mouse_setratios( 32, 32 );" );
    mouse_setratios( 32, 32 );
    mouse_show();
    getch();
    mouse_hide();
    mouse_setratios( 8, 16 );

    /* Demonstrate mouse_condoff() */
    mouse_setpos( 600, 150 );
    _clearscreen( _GCLEARSCREEN );
    printf( "Press any key to continue\n\n" );
    printf( "(Move cursor to upper left corner to make it disappear)\n" );
    printf( "mouse_condoff( 0, 0, 100, 30 );" );
    mouse_show();
    mouse_condoff( 0, 0, 100, 30 );
    getch();
    mouse_hide();

    /* Demonstrate mouse_setdouble() */
    _clearscreen( _GCLEARSCREEN );
    printf( "Press any key to continue\n\n" );
    printf( "mouse_setdouble( 9999 );" );
```

(continued)

MOUSTEST.C *continued*

```
    mouse_setdouble( 9999 );
    mouse_show();
    mouse_show();
    getch();
    mouse_hide();
    printf( "\n\nmouse_setdouble( 1 );" );
    mouse_setdouble( 1 );
    mouse_show();
    getch();
    mouse_hide();
    mouse_setdouble( 64 );

    /* Demonstrate mouse_storage() */
    _setvideomode( _HRESBW );
    _clearscreen( _GCLEARSCREEN );
    printf( "mouse_storage( &bufsize );\n" );
    mouse_storage( &bufsize );

    /* Allocate storage space */
    if (( buf = malloc( bufsize )) == NULL)
        {
        printf( "Failed to allocate mouse state storage\n" );
        exit( 0 );
        }

    /* Demonstrate mouse_save() */
    printf( "mouse_save( buf );\n\n" );
    mouse_show();
    delay( 2.0 );
    mouse_save( buf );
    mouse_hide();

    /* Demonstrate mouse_restore() */
    printf( "Press any key to restore mouse state" );
    mouse_setgcurs( &gcursor_hand );
    mouse_show();
    getch();
    mouse_hide();
    mouse_restore( buf );
    printf( "\n\nPress any key to continue" );
    mouse_show();
    getch();
```

(continued)

MOUSTEST.C *continued*

```
    /* Demonstrate mouse_getsensitivity() */
    _setvideomode( _DEFAULTMODE );
    _clearscreen( _GCLEARSCREEN );
    printf( "mouse_getsensitivity( &horz, &vert, &threshold );\n\n" );
    mouse_getsensitivity( &horz, &vert, &threshold );
    printf( "horz:      %5d\n", horz );
    printf( "vert:      %5d\n", vert );
    printf( "threshold: %5d\n\n\n", threshold );
    printf( "Press any key to continue" );
    mouse_show();
    getch();
    mouse_hide();

    /* Demonstrate mouse_setsensitivity() */
    _clearscreen( _GCLEARSCREEN );
    printf( "mouse_setsensitivity( 90, 90, 10 );\n\n" );
    mouse_setsensitivity( 90, 90, 10 );
    printf( "Press any key to continue" );
    mouse_show();
    getch();
    mouse_hide();
    mouse_setsensitivity( horz, vert, threshold );

    /* Demonstrate mouse_setmaxrate() */
    _clearscreen( _GCLEARSCREEN );
    printf( "mouse_setmaxrate( 200 );\n\n" );
    mouse_setmaxrate( 200 );
    printf( "Press any key to continue" );
    mouse_show();
    getch();
    mouse_hide();
    mouse_setmaxrate( 50 );

    /* Demonstrate mouse_setpage() */
    _setvideomode( _DEFAULTMODE );
    _setvisualpage( 1 );
    _setactivepage( 1 );
    _clearscreen( _GCLEARSCREEN );
    printf( "Active and visual page is now 1...\n\n" );
    printf( "mouse_setpage( 1 );\n" );
    mouse_setpage( 1 );
```

(continued)

MOUSTEST.C *continued*

```
    /* Demonstrate mouse_getpage() */
    mouse_getpage( &page );
    printf( "mouse_getpage( &page ); ... page: %d\n\n", page );
    printf( "Press any key to continue" );
    mouse_show();
    getch();
    mouse_hide();
    _setvisualpage( 0 );
    _setactivepage( 0 );
    mouse_setpage( 0 );

    /* Demonstrate mouse_setlang() */
    _clearscreen( _GCLEARSCREEN );
    printf( "mouse_setlang( SPANISH ); ...  Works correctly only\n" );
    printf( "if international version of the mouse driver installed." );
    mouse_setlang( SPANISH );

    /* Demonstrate mouse_getlang() */
    mouse_getlang( &lang );
    printf( "\n\n\nmouse_getlang( &lang ); ... lang: " );
    switch( lang )
        {
        case ENGLISH:
            printf( "English\n\n" );
            break;
        case FRENCH:
            printf( "French\n\n" );
            break;
        case DUTCH:
            printf( "Dutch\n\n" );
            break;
        case GERMAN:
            printf( "German\n\n" );
            break;
        case SWEDISH:
            printf( "Swedish\n\n" );
            break;
        case FINNISH:
            printf( "Finnish\n\n" );
            break;
        case SPANISH:
            printf( "Spanish\n\n" );
            break;
```

(continued)

MOUSTEST.C *continued*

```
            case PORTUGUESE:
                printf( "Portuguese\n\n" );
                break;
            case ITALIAN:
                printf( "Italian\n\n" );
                break;
            default:
                printf( "Unknown\n\n" );
                break;
        }
    printf( "Press any key to continue" );
    getch();
    mouse_setlang( 0 );

    /* Demonstrate mouse_getversion() */
    _clearscreen( _GCLEARSCREEN );
    mouse_getversion( &version, &mouse_type, &irq_num );
    printf( "mouse_getversion( &version, &mouse_type, &irq_num );\n\n" );
    printf( "Mouse driver version: %7.2f\n", version );
    printf( "Mouse type: " );
    switch( mouse_type )
        {
        case MOUSE_BUS:
            printf( "Bus mouse\n" );
            break;
        case MOUSE_SERIAL:
            printf( "Serial mouse\n" );
            break;
        case MOUSE_INPORT:
            printf( "InPort mouse\n" );
            break;
        case MOUSE_PS2:
            printf( "PS/2 mouse\n" );
            break;
        case MOUSE_HP:
            printf( "Hewlett-Packard mouse\n" );
            break;
        default:
            printf( "Unknown\n" );
            break;
        }
    if ( irq_num )
        printf( "Mouse IRQ type: Mouse interrupt\n" );
```

(continued)

MOUSTEST.C *continued*

```
    else
        printf( "Mouse IRQ type: PS/2\n" );

    /* All done */
    printf( "Press any key to continue" );
    getch();
    _clearscreen( _GCLEARSCREEN );
}
```

Include File: MOUSEFUN.H

```
/* -------------------------------------------------------------------
    Name:           MOUSEFUN.H
    Type:           Include
    Language:       Microsoft QuickC version 2
    Demonstrated:   MOUSEFUN.C  MOUSTEST.C
    Description:    Prototypes and definitions for MOUSEFUN.C
    -------------------------------------------------------------------
*/

#ifndef MOUSEFUN_DEFINED

#define LBUTTON 0
#define RBUTTON 1

#define SOFT_TEXT_CURSOR 0
#define HARD_TEXT_CURSOR 1

#define ENGLISH     0
#define FRENCH      1
#define DUTCH       2
#define GERMAN      3
#define SWEDISH     4
#define FINNISH     5
#define SPANISH     6
#define PORTUGUESE 7
#define ITALIAN     8

#define MOUSE_BUS    1
#define MOUSE_SERIAL 2
```

(continued)

MOUSEFUN.H *continued*

```
#define MOUSE_INPORT 3
#define MOUSE_PS2    4
#define MOUSE_HP     5

#define IRQ_PS2 0

/* Structure definition for graphics mode mouse cursors */
struct graphics_cursor
    {
    int screen_mask[16];
    int cursor_mask[16];
    int hot_spot_x;
    int hot_spot_y;
    };

void mouse_reset( int *, int * );                       /* Function  0 */
void mouse_show();                                      /* Function  1 */
void mouse_hide();                                      /* Function  2 */
void mouse_status( int *, int *, int *, int * );        /* Function  3 */
void mouse_setpos( int, int );                          /* Function  4 */
void mouse_press( int, int *, int *, int *, int * );    /* Function  5 */
void mouse_release( int, int *, int *, int *, int * );  /* Function  6 */
void mouse_sethorz( int, int );                         /* Function  7 */
void mouse_setvert( int, int );                         /* Function  8 */
void mouse_setgcurs( struct graphics_cursor far * );    /* Function  9 */
void mouse_settcurs( int, int, int );                   /* Function 10 */
void mouse_motion( int *, int * );                      /* Function 11 */
void mouse_setratios( int, int );                       /* Function 15 */
void mouse_condoff( int, int, int, int );               /* Function 16 */
void mouse_setdouble( int );                            /* Function 19 */
void mouse_storage( int * );                            /* Function 21 */
void mouse_save( char far * );                          /* Function 22 */
void mouse_restore( char far * );                       /* Function 23 */
void mouse_setsensitivity( int, int, int );             /* Function 26 */
void mouse_getsensitivity( int *, int *, int * );       /* Function 27 */
void mouse_setmaxrate( int );                           /* Function 28 */
void mouse_setpage( int );                              /* Function 29 */
void mouse_getpage( int * );                            /* Function 30 */
void mouse_setlang( int );                              /* Function 34 */
void mouse_getlang( int * );                            /* Function 35 */
void mouse_getversion( double *, int *, int * );        /* Function 36 */
```

(continued)

MOUSEFUN.H *continued*

```
/* Default graphics mode cursor */
static struct graphics_cursor far gcursor_default =
    {

    /*   screen mask  */
    0xCFFF,    /* 1100111111111111 */
    0xC7FF,    /* 1100011111111111 */
    0xC3FF,    /* 1100001111111111 */
    0xC1FF,    /* 1100000111111111 */
    0xC0FF,    /* 1100000011111111 */
    0xC07F,    /* 1100000001111111 */
    0xC03F,    /* 1100000000111111 */
    0xC01F,    /* 1100000000011111 */
    0xC00F,    /* 1100000000001111 */
    0xC007,    /* 1100000000000111 */
    0xC07F,    /* 1100000001111111 */
    0xC43F,    /* 1100010000111111 */
    0xCC3F,    /* 1100110000111111 */
    0xFE1F,    /* 1111111000011111 */
    0xFE1F,    /* 1111111000011111 */
    0xFF1F,    /* 1111111100011111 */

    /*   cursor mask  */
    0x0000,    /* 0000000000000000 */
    0x1000,    /* 0001000000000000 */
    0x1800,    /* 0001100000000000 */
    0x1C00,    /* 0001110000000000 */
    0x1E00,    /* 0001111000000000 */
    0x1F00,    /* 0001111100000000 */
    0x1F80,    /* 0001111110000000 */
    0x1FC0,    /* 0001111111000000 */
    0x1FE0,    /* 0001111111100000 */
    0x1F00,    /* 0001111100000000 */
    0x1B00,    /* 0001101100000000 */
    0x1180,    /* 0001000110000000 */
    0x0180,    /* 0000000110000000 */
    0x00C0,    /* 0000000011000000 */
    0x00C0,    /* 0000000011000000 */
    0x0000,    /* 0000000000000000 */

    /* hot spot x,y */
    02, 00
    };
```

(continued)

MOUSEFUN.H *continued*

```
/* Graphics mode cursor, pointing hand */
static struct graphics_cursor far gcursor_hand =
    {

    /*  screen mask  */
    0xE1FF,    /* 1110000111111111 */
    0xE1FF,    /* 1110000111111111 */
    0xE1FF,    /* 1110000111111111 */
    0xE1FF,    /* 1110000111111111 */
    0xE1FF,    /* 1110000111111111 */
    0xE000,    /* 1110000000000000 */
    0xE000,    /* 1110000000000000 */
    0xE000,    /* 1110000000000000 */
    0x0000,    /* 0000000000000000 */
    0x0000,    /* 0000000000000000 */
    0x0000,    /* 0000000000000000 */
    0x0000,    /* 0000000000000000 */
    0x0000,    /* 0000000000000000 */
    0x0000,    /* 0000000000000000 */
    0x0000,    /* 0000000000000000 */
    0x0000,    /* 0000000000000000 */

    /*  cursor mask  */
    0x1E00,    /* 0001111000000000 */
    0x1200,    /* 0001001000000000 */
    0x1200,    /* 0001001000000000 */
    0x1200,    /* 0001001000000000 */
    0x1200,    /* 0001001000000000 */
    0x13FF,    /* 0001001111111111 */
    0x1249,    /* 0001001001001001 */
    0x1249,    /* 0001001001001001 */
    0xF249,    /* 1111001001001001 */
    0x9001,    /* 1001000000000001 */
    0x9001,    /* 1001000000000001 */
    0x9001,    /* 1001000000000001 */
    0x8001,    /* 1000000000000001 */
    0x8001,    /* 1000000000000001 */
    0x8001,    /* 1000000000000001 */
    0xFFFF,    /* 1111111111111111 */

    /* hot spot x,y */
    05, 00
    };
```

(continued)

MOUSEFUN.H *continued*

```
/* Graphics mode cursor, check mark */
static struct graphics_cursor far gcursor_check =
    {

    /*  screen mask  */
    0xFFF0,     /* 1111111111110000 */
    0xFFE0,     /* 1111111111100000 */
    0xFFC0,     /* 1111111111000000 */
    0xFF81,     /* 1111111110000001 */
    0xFF03,     /* 1111111100000011 */
    0x0607,     /* 0000011000000111 */
    0x000F,     /* 0000000000001111 */
    0x001F,     /* 0000000000011111 */
    0xC03F,     /* 1100000000111111 */
    0xF07F,     /* 1111000001111111 */
    0xFFFF,     /* 1111111111111111 */
    0xFFFF,     /* 1111111111111111 */
    0xFFFF,     /* 1111111111111111 */
    0xFFFF,     /* 1111111111111111 */
    0xFFFF,     /* 1111111111111111 */
    0xFFFF,     /* 1111111111111111 */

    /*  cursor mask  */
    0x0000,     /* 0000000000000000 */
    0x0006,     /* 0000000000000110 */
    0x000C,     /* 0000000000001100 */
    0x0018,     /* 0000000000011000 */
    0x0030,     /* 0000000000110000 */
    0x0060,     /* 0000000001100000 */
    0x70C0,     /* 0111000011000000 */
    0x1D80,     /* 0001110110000000 */
    0x0700,     /* 0000011100000000 */
    0x0000,     /* 0000000000000000 */
    0x0000,     /* 0000000000000000 */
    0x0000,     /* 0000000000000000 */
    0x0000,     /* 0000000000000000 */
    0x0000,     /* 0000000000000000 */
    0x0000,     /* 0000000000000000 */
    0x0000,     /* 0000000000000000 */

    /* hot spot x,y */
    06, 07
    };
```

(continued)

```
/* Graphics mode cursor, hour glass */
static struct graphics_cursor far gcursor_hour =
    {

    /*  screen mask  */
    0x0000,    /* 0000000000000000 */
    0x0000,    /* 0000000000000000 */
    0x0000,    /* 0000000000000000 */
    0x8001,    /* 1000000000000001 */
    0xC003,    /* 1100000000000011 */
    0xE007,    /* 1110000000000111 */
    0xF00F,    /* 1111000000001111 */
    0xE007,    /* 1110000000000111 */
    0xC003,    /* 1100000000000011 */
    0x8001,    /* 1000000000000001 */
    0x0000,    /* 0000000000000000 */
    0x0000,    /* 0000000000000000 */
    0x0000,    /* 0000000000000000 */
    0x0000,    /* 0000000000000000 */
    0x0000,    /* 0000000000000000 */
    0x0000,    /* 0000000000000000 */

    /*  cursor mask  */
    0x0000,    /* 0000000000000000 */
    0x7FFE,    /* 0111111111111110 */
    0x6006,    /* 0110000000000110 */
    0x300C,    /* 0011000000001100 */
    0x1818,    /* 0001100000011000 */
    0x0C30,    /* 0000110000110000 */
    0x0660,    /* 0000011001100000 */
    0x03C0,    /* 0000001111000000 */
    0x0660,    /* 0000011001100000 */
    0x0C30,    /* 0000110000110000 */
    0x1998,    /* 0001100110011000 */
    0x33CC,    /* 0011001111001100 */
    0x67E6,    /* 0110011111100110 */
    0x7FFE,    /* 0111111111111110 */
    0x0000,    /* 0000000000000000 */
    0x0000,    /* 0000000000000000 */

    /* hot spot x,y */
    07, 07
    };
```

(continued)

MOUSEFUN.H *continued*

```
/* Graphics mode cursor, jet aircraft */
static struct graphics_cursor far gcursor_jet =
    {

    /*  screen mask  */
    0xFFFF,     /* 1111111111111111 */
    0xFEFF,     /* 1111111011111111 */
    0xFC7F,     /* 1111110001111111 */
    0xF83F,     /* 1111100000111111 */
    0xF83F,     /* 1111100000111111 */
    0xF83F,     /* 1111100000111111 */
    0xF01F,     /* 1111000000011111 */
    0xE00F,     /* 1110000000001111 */
    0xC007,     /* 1100000000000111 */
    0x8003,     /* 1000000000000011 */
    0x8003,     /* 1000000000000011 */
    0xF83F,     /* 1111100000111111 */
    0xF83F,     /* 1111100000111111 */
    0xF01F,     /* 1111000000011111 */
    0xE00F,     /* 1110000000001111 */
    0xFFFF,     /* 1111111111111111 */

    /*  cursor mask  */
    0x0000,     /* 0000000000000000 */
    0x0000,     /* 0000000000000000 */
    0x0100,     /* 0000000100000000 */
    0x0380,     /* 0000001110000000 */
    0x0380,     /* 0000001110000000 */
    0x0380,     /* 0000001110000000 */
    0x07C0,     /* 0000011111000000 */
    0x0FE0,     /* 0000111111100000 */
    0x1FF0,     /* 0001111111110000 */
    0x3FF8,     /* 0011111111111000 */
    0x638C,     /* 0110001110001100 */
    0x0380,     /* 0000001110000000 */
    0x0380,     /* 0000001110000000 */
    0x07C0,     /* 0000011111000000 */
    0x0C60,     /* 0000110001100000 */
    0x0000,     /* 0000000000000000 */

    /* hot spot x,y */
    07, 01
    };
```

(continued)

MOUSEFUN.H *continued*

```
/* Graphics mode cursor, left pointing arrow */
static struct graphics_cursor far gcursor_left =
    {

    /*  screen mask  */
    0xFE1F,    /* 1111111000011111 */
    0xF01F,    /* 1111000000011111 */
    0x0000,    /* 0000000000000000 */
    0x0000,    /* 0000000000000000 */
    0x0000,    /* 0000000000000000 */
    0xF01F,    /* 1111000000011111 */
    0xFE1F,    /* 1111111000011111 */
    0xFFFF,    /* 1111111111111111 */
    0xFFFF,    /* 1111111111111111 */
    0xFFFF,    /* 1111111111111111 */
    0xFFFF,    /* 1111111111111111 */
    0xFFFF,    /* 1111111111111111 */
    0xFFFF,    /* 1111111111111111 */
    0xFFFF,    /* 1111111111111111 */
    0xFFFF,    /* 1111111111111111 */
    0xFFFF,    /* 1111111111111111 */

    /*  cursor mask  */
    0x0000,    /* 0000000000000000 */
    0x00C0,    /* 0000000011000000 */
    0x07C0,    /* 0000011111000000 */
    0x7FFE,    /* 0111111111111110 */
    0x07C0,    /* 0000011111000000 */
    0x00C0,    /* 0000000011000000 */
    0x0000,    /* 0000000000000000 */
    0x0000,    /* 0000000000000000 */
    0x0000,    /* 0000000000000000 */
    0x0000,    /* 0000000000000000 */
    0x0000,    /* 0000000000000000 */
    0x0000,    /* 0000000000000000 */
    0x0000,    /* 0000000000000000 */
    0x0000,    /* 0000000000000000 */
    0x0000,    /* 0000000000000000 */
    0x0000,    /* 0000000000000000 */

    /* hot spot x,y */
    00, 03
    };
```

(continued)

MOUSEFUN.H *continued*

```
/* Graphics mode cursor, plus sign */
static struct graphics_cursor far gcursor_plus =
   {

   /*  screen mask  */
   0xFC3F,    /* 1111110000111111 */
   0xFC3F,    /* 1111110000111111 */
   0xFC3F,    /* 1111110000111111 */
   0x0000,    /* 0000000000000000 */
   0x0000,    /* 0000000000000000 */
   0x0000,    /* 0000000000000000 */
   0xFC3F,    /* 1111110000111111 */
   0xFC3F,    /* 1111110000111111 */
   0xFC3F,    /* 1111110000111111 */
   0xFFFF,    /* 1111111111111111 */
   0xFFFF,    /* 1111111111111111 */
   0xFFFF,    /* 1111111111111111 */
   0xFFFF,    /* 1111111111111111 */
   0xFFFF,    /* 1111111111111111 */
   0xFFFF,    /* 1111111111111111 */
   0xFFFF,    /* 1111111111111111 */

   /*  cursor mask  */
   0x0000,    /* 0000000000000000 */
   0x0180,    /* 0000000110000000 */
   0x0180,    /* 0000000110000000 */
   0x0180,    /* 0000000110000000 */
   0x7FFE,    /* 0111111111111110 */
   0x0180,    /* 0000000110000000 */
   0x0180,    /* 0000000110000000 */
   0x0180,    /* 0000000110000000 */
   0x0000,    /* 0000000000000000 */
   0x0000,    /* 0000000000000000 */
   0x0000,    /* 0000000000000000 */
   0x0000,    /* 0000000000000000 */
   0x0000,    /* 0000000000000000 */
   0x0000,    /* 0000000000000000 */
   0x0000,    /* 0000000000000000 */
   0x0000,    /* 0000000000000000 */

   /* hot spot x,y */
   07, 04
   };
```

(continued)

MOUSEFUN.H *continued*

```
/* Graphics mode cursor, up pointing arrow */
static struct graphics_cursor far gcursor_up =
    {

    /*   screen mask   */
    0xF9FF,    /* 1111100111111111 */
    0xF0FF,    /* 1111000011111111 */
    0xE07F,    /* 1110000001111111 */
    0xE07F,    /* 1110000001111111 */
    0xC03F,    /* 1100000000111111 */
    0xC03F,    /* 1100000000111111 */
    0x801F,    /* 1000000000011111 */
    0x801F,    /* 1000000000011111 */
    0x000F,    /* 0000000000001111 */
    0x000F,    /* 0000000000001111 */
    0xF0FF,    /* 1111000011111111 */
    0xF0FF,    /* 1111000011111111 */
    0xF0FF,    /* 1111000011111111 */
    0xF0FF,    /* 1111000011111111 */
    0xF0FF,    /* 1111000011111111 */
    0xF0FF,    /* 1111000011111111 */

    /*   cursor mask   */
    0x0000,    /* 0000000000000000 */
    0x0600,    /* 0000011000000000 */
    0x0F00,    /* 0000111100000000 */
    0x0F00,    /* 0000111100000000 */
    0x1F80,    /* 0001111110000000 */
    0x1F80,    /* 0001111110000000 */
    0x3FC0,    /* 0011111111000000 */
    0x3FC0,    /* 0011111111000000 */
    0x7FE0,    /* 0111111111100000 */
    0x0600,    /* 0000011000000000 */
    0x0600,    /* 0000011000000000 */
    0x0600,    /* 0000011000000000 */
    0x0600,    /* 0000011000000000 */
    0x0600,    /* 0000011000000000 */
    0x0600,    /* 0000011000000000 */
    0x0000,    /* 0000000000000000 */

    /* hot spot x,y */
    05, 00
    };
```

(continued)

MOUSEFUN.H *continued*

```
/* Graphics mode cursor, X mark */
static struct graphics_cursor far gcursor_x =
    {

    /*  screen mask  */
    0x07E0,     /* 0000011111100000 */
    0x0180,     /* 0000000110000000 */
    0x0000,     /* 0000000000000000 */
    0xC003,     /* 1100000000000011 */
    0xF00F,     /* 1111000000001111 */
    0xC003,     /* 1100000000000011 */
    0x0000,     /* 0000000000000000 */
    0x0180,     /* 0000000110000000 */
    0x03C0,     /* 0000001111000000 */
    0xFFFF,     /* 1111111111111111 */
    0xFFFF,     /* 1111111111111111 */
    0xFFFF,     /* 1111111111111111 */
    0xFFFF,     /* 1111111111111111 */
    0xFFFF,     /* 1111111111111111 */
    0xFFFF,     /* 1111111111111111 */
    0xFFFF,     /* 1111111111111111 */

    /*  cursor mask  */
    0x0000,     /* 0000000000000000 */
    0x700E,     /* 0111000000001110 */
    0x1C38,     /* 0001110000111000 */
    0x0660,     /* 0000011001100000 */
    0x03C0,     /* 0000001111000000 */
    0x0660,     /* 0000011001100000 */
    0x1C38,     /* 0001110000111000 */
    0x700E,     /* 0111000000001110 */
    0x0000,     /* 0000000000000000 */
    0x0000,     /* 0000000000000000 */
    0x0000,     /* 0000000000000000 */
    0x0000,     /* 0000000000000000 */
    0x0000,     /* 0000000000000000 */
    0x0000,     /* 0000000000000000 */
    0x0000,     /* 0000000000000000 */
    0x0000,     /* 0000000000000000 */
```

(continued)

```
    /* hot spot x,y */
    07, 04
    };

#define MOUSEFUN_DEFINED
#endif
```

Toolbox Module: MOUSEFUN.C

```
/* -----------------------------------------------------------------
    Name:           MOUSEFUN.C
    Type:           Toolbox module
    Language:       Microsoft QuickC version 2
    Demonstrated:   MOUSTEST.C COLORS.C LOOK.C MENUTEST.C
                    MOUSGCRS.C OBJECT.C
    Video:          Some functions require CGA or better graphics
    -----------------------------------------------------------------
*/

#include <dos.h>
#include "mousefun.h"
```

Function: *mouse_reset()*

The *mouse_reset()* function resets all mouse parameters to default values. For example, it sets the cursor position to the middle of the screen, the sensitivity and double speed threshold to normal, and the graphics cursor to the standard arrow.

If the function finds and resets the mouse, it sets the status to −1. If the mouse is not installed, the function sets the status to 0. The *mouse_reset()* function is normally called only once, at the start of any program that uses the mouse.

Note that the mouse cursor will not be visible after a call to *mouse_reset()*. Call *mouse_show()* to make the cursor visible.

```
/* - - - - - - - - - - - - - - - - - - - - - - - - - - - - - - - - - - -
    Function:       mouse_reset()
    Toolbox:        MOUSEFUN.C
    Demonstrated:   MOUSTEST.C

    Parameters:
      (output)      status    Status of the mouse
      (output)      buttons   Number of mouse buttons

    Returned:       (function returns nothing)

    Variables:      m1        Local variable for register ax
                    m2        Local variable for register bx

    Description:    Resets the mouse and verifies its existence
    - - - - - - - - - - - - - - - - - - - - - - - - - - - - - - - - - -
*/

void mouse_reset( int *status, int *buttons )
{
    int m1, m2;

    _asm
        {
        xor    ax, ax
        int    33h
        mov    m1, ax
        mov    m2, bx
        }

    *status = m1;
    *buttons = m2;
}
```

Function: *mouse_show()*

The *mouse_show()* function makes the mouse cursor visible. A call to *mouse_show()* will not make the cursor visible if the program has not reset the mouse.

An internal cursor counter keeps track of the number of times that a program calls *mouse_hide()* and *mouse_show()*. When *mouse_reset()* is called to reset the mouse parameters, this counter is set to −1. When the program calls *mouse_show()*, the function adds 1 to the counter, which then has a value of 0. The mouse cursor becomes visible only when the value of the counter is 0.

Each call to *mouse_hide()* subtracts 1 from the counter. For this reason, a program that makes *n* calls to *mouse_hide()* must make *n* calls to *mouse_show()* for the cursor to become visible again. Note, however, that the counter does not increment above 0, which means that one call to *mouse_hide()* is always sufficient to make the cursor invisible.

```
/* - - - - - - - - - - - - - - - - - - - - - - - - - - - - - - - - -
   Function:       mouse_show()
   Toolbox:        MOUSEFUN.C
   Demonstrated:   MOUSTEST.C

   Parameters:     (none)

   Returned:       (function returns nothing)

   Variables:      (none)

   Description:    Makes the mouse cursor visible
   - - - - - - - - - - - - - - - - - - - - - - - - - - - - - - - - -
*/

void mouse_show( void )
{
    _asm
        {
        mov   ax, 1
        int   33h
        }
}
```

Function: *mouse_hide()*

The *mouse_hide()* function removes the mouse cursor from the screen. Two functions, *mouse_hide()* and *mouse_show()*, work together to control the visibility of the cursor. See the *mouse_show()* function for an explanation of the internal cursor counter.

Whenever a program writes text or graphics to the screen, it should first hide the mouse cursor by calling *mouse_hide()*. Immediately after it updates the screen, the program should call *mouse_show()* to redisplay the cursor. This sequence of function calls prevents the cursor pixels from interfering with the screen graphics.

```
/* - - - - - - - - - - - - - - - - - - - - - - - - - - - - - - - - - - - /* - -

    Function:       mouse_hide()
    Toolbox:        MOUSEFUN.C
    Demonstrated:   MOUSTEST.C

    Parameters:     (none)

    Returned:       (function returns nothing)

    Variables:      (none)

    Description:    Makes the mouse cursor invisible
    - - - - - - - - - - - - - - - - - - - - - - - - - - - - - - - - - - - -
*/

void mouse_hide( void )
{
    _asm
        {
        mov    ax, 2
        int    33h
        }
}
```

Function: *mouse_status()*

The *mouse_status()* function gets the current position of the mouse and the instantaneous state of the mouse buttons.

The function returns the horizontal and vertical positions of the mouse in virtual screen units. It returns the *left_button* and *right_button* variables as 1 if the associated button is pressed at the moment the function is called; they are returned as 0 if the associated buttons are not pressed.

```
/* - - - - - - - - - - - - - - - - - - - - - - - - - - - - - - - -
    Function:        mouse_status()
    Toolbox:         MOUSEFUN.C
    Demonstrated:    MOUSTEST.C

    Parameters:
      (output)       left_button     State of the left button
      (output)       right_button    State of the right button
      (output)       horz_pos        Horizontal position of the cursor
      (output)       vert_pos        Vertical position of the cursor

    Returned:        (function returns nothing)

    Variables:       m2        Local variable for register bx
                     m3        Local variable for register cx
                     m4        Local variable for register dx

    Description:     Gets the current state of the mouse buttons and
                     the mouse cursor position
    - - - - - - - - - - - - - - - - - - - - - - - - - - - - - - - -
*/

void mouse_status( int *left_button, int *right_button,
                   int *horz_pos, int *vert_pos )
{
    int m2, m3, m4;

    _asm
        {
        mov    ax, 3
        int    33h
        mov    m2, bx
        mov    m3, cx
        mov    m4, dx
        }

    *left_button = m2 & 1;
    *right_button = ( m2 >> 1 ) & 1;
    *horz_pos = m3;
    *vert_pos = m4;
}
```

Function: *mouse_setpos()*

The *mouse_setpos()* function sets the mouse cursor position. The function interprets the horizontal and vertical positions as virtual screen coordinates. The cursor immediately jumps to the new position on the screen.

```
/* - - - - - - - - - - - - - - - - - - - - - - - - - - - - - - -
    Function:       mouse_setpos()
    Toolbox:        MOUSEFUN.C
    Demonstrated:   MOUSTEST.C

    Parameters:
      (input)       horizontal      Horizontal position
      (input)       vertical        Vertical position

    Returned:       (function returns nothing)

    Variables:      (none)

    Description:    Sets the mouse cursor to the indicated position
    - - - - - - - - - - - - - - - - - - - - - - - - - - - - - - -
*/

void mouse_setpos( int horizontal, int vertical )
{
    _asm
        {
        mov    ax, 4
        mov    cx, horizontal
        mov    dx, vertical
        int    33h
        }
}
```

Function: *mouse_press()*

The *mouse_press()* function gets information that pertains to the pressing of either mouse button. Pass LBUTTON or RBUTTON in the first parameter to get information for either the left or right mouse button. These two constants are defined in the MOUSEFUN.H header file.

When the function returns, the variable *presses* contains the number of times the given mouse button was pressed since the last time *mouse_press()* was called or since the mouse parameters were reset. The *horz_pos* and *vert_pos* variables receive the position of the mouse at the most recent button press, which might not be the current mouse position.

```
/* - - - - - - - - - - - - - - - - - - - - - - - - - - - - - - -
    Function:      mouse_press()
    Toolbox:       MOUSEFUN.C
    Demonstrated:  MOUSTEST.C

    Parameters:
      (input)      button    Left or right button
      (output)     status    Status of the button
      (output)     presses   Number of button presses
      (output)     horz_pos  Horizontal position at last press
      (output)     vert_pos  Vertical position at last press

    Returned:      (function returns nothing)

    Variables:     m1        Local variable for register ax
                   m2        Local variable for register bx
                   m3        Local variable for register cx
                   m4        Local variable for register dx

    Description:   Gets button press information
    - - - - - - - - - - - - - - - - - - - - - - - - - - - - - - -
*/

void mouse_press( int button, int *status, int *presses,
                  int *horz_pos, int *vert_pos )
{
    int m1, m2, m3, m4;

    _asm
        {
        mov    ax, 5
        mov    bx, button
        int    33h
        mov    m1, ax
        mov    m2, bx
        mov    m3, cx
        mov    m4, dx
        }
```

(continued)

```
    if ( button == LBUTTON )
        *status = m1 & 1;
    else
        *status = ( m1 >> 1 ) & 1;
    *presses = m2;
    *horz_pos = m3;
    *vert_pos = m4;
}
```

Function: *mouse_release()*

The *mouse_release()* function gets information pertaining to the release of either mouse button. Pass LBUTTON or RBUTTON in the first parameter to get information for either the left or right button. These two constants are defined in the MOUSEFUN.H header file.

When the function returns, the variable *releases* contains the number of times the given mouse button was released since the last time this function was called or since the mouse was reset. The *horz_pos* and *vert_pos* variables receive the position of the mouse at the most recent button release, which might not be the current mouse position.

```
/* - - - - - - - - - - - - - - - - - - - - - - - - - - - - - - - - -
    Function:       mouse_release()
    Toolbox:        MOUSEFUN.C
    Demonstrated:   MOUSTEST.C

    Parameters:
      (input)       button    Left or right button
      (output)      status    Status of the button
      (output)      releases  Number of button releases
      (output)      horz_pos  Horizontal position at last release
      (output)      vert_pos  Vertical position at last release

    Returned:       (function returns nothing)

    Variables:      m1        Local variable for register ax
                    m2        Local variable for register bx
                    m3        Local variable for register cx
                    m4        Local variable for register dx
```

(continued)

MOUSEFUN.C *continued*

```
    Description:    Gets button release information
    - - - - - - - - - - - - - - - - - - - - - - - - - - - - - -
*/

void mouse_release( int button, int *status, int *releases,
                    int *horz_pos, int *vert_pos )
{
    int m1, m2, m3, m4;

    _asm
        {
        mov    ax, 6
        mov    bx, button
        int    33h
        mov    m1, ax
        mov    m2, bx
        mov    m3, cx
        mov    m4, dx
        }

    if ( button == LBUTTON )
        *status = m1 & 1;
    else
        *status = ( m1 >> 1 ) & 1;

    *releases = m2;
    *horz_pos = m3;
    *vert_pos = m4;
}
```

Function: *mouse_sethorz()*

The *mouse_sethorz()* function sets the minimum and maximum horizontal positions for the mouse cursor. The function interprets the positions as virtual screen units and limits cursor motion to the given range.

When you reset the mouse parameters, the minimum and maximum horizontal positions are set to 0 and 640 (the edges of the screen in virtual screen units).

```
/* - - - - - - - - - - - - - - - - - - - - - - - - - - - - - - - -
    Function:       mouse_sethorz()
    Toolbox:        MOUSEFUN.C
    Demonstrated:   MOUSTEST.C

    Parameters:
      (input)       horz_min  Minimum horizontal cursor position
      (input)       horz_max  Maximum horizontal cursor position

    Returned:       (function returns nothing)

    Variables:      (none)

    Description:    Sets minimum and maximum horizontal mouse
                    cursor positions
    - - - - - - - - - - - - - - - - - - - - - - - - - - - - - - -
*/

void mouse_sethorz( int horz_min, int horz_max )
{
    _asm
        {
        mov   ax, 7
        mov   cx, horz_min
        mov   dx, horz_max
        int   33h
        }
}
```

Function: *mouse_setvert()*

The *mouse_setvert()* function sets the minimum and maximum vertical positions for the mouse cursor. The function interprets the positions in virtual screen units and limits cursor motion to the given range.

When you reset the mouse parameters, the minimum and maximum vertical positions are set to the edges of the screen.

```
/* - - - - - - - - - - - - - - - - - - - - - - - - - - - - - - - - -
   Function:        mouse_setvert()
   Toolbox:         MOUSEFUN.C
   Demonstrated:    MOUSTEST.C

   Parameters:
     (input)        vert_min  Minimum vertical cursor position
     (input)        vert_max  Maximum vertical cursor position

   Returned:        (function returns nothing)

   Variables:       (none)

   Description:     Sets minimum and maximum vertical mouse cursor
                    positions
   - - - - - - - - - - - - - - - - - - - - - - - - - - - - - - - - -
*/

void mouse_setvert( int vert_min, int vert_max )
{
    _asm
        {
        mov   ax, 8
        mov   cx, vert_min
        mov   dx, vert_max
        int   33h
        }
}
```

Function: *mouse_setgcurs()*

The *mouse_setgcurs()* function sets the shape of the mouse cursor for graphics mode. The cursor is defined as a data structure in the MOUSEFUN.H header file, which also defines several common graphics cursor shapes.

The MOUSTEST.C demonstration program displays each cursor defined in MOUSEFUN.H and shows how to use it in other programs. In Part III of this book, the MOUSGCRS.C utility lets you create your own graphics mode cursors.

Each graphics mode mouse cursor is defined as a rectangular area, 16 by 16 bits. The mouse driver uses this bit pattern to modify screen pixels in a manner dependent on the current graphics mode.

As you can see from the *graphics_cursor* structure in MOUSEFUN.H, the appearance of the cursor is determined by two bit masks—a screen mask and a cursor mask. To update the graphics cursor on the screen, the mouse driver processes first the screen mask and then the cursor mask. Each 1 bit in the screen mask allows the original screen pixel to remain untouched, and each 0 bit sets the associated pixel to the 0 palette entry (the background color, often black). The cursor mask bits are then processed over the same region of the screen. Each 0 bit leaves the screen pixel untouched, and each 1 bit causes the highest numbered palette entry to be set (usually white).

Notice that the graphics cursor pixels are always a single color, the color currently set for the highest number in the palette. By default, the highest palette entry is always white, but you can change this color by calling the QuickC function *_remappalette()* or *_remapallpalette()*.

The last two members of the *graphics_cursor* structure locate the hot spot on the screen. This is the point in the cursor array to which the icon on the screen is pointing. The hot spot x and y values are relative to the upper left corner of the 16-by-16 cursor pixel region. The hot spot on the pointing hand cursor, for example, is specified by the values 05 and 00, which locate it at the tip of the extended index finger.

```
/* - - - - - - - - - - - - - - - - - - - - - - - - - - - - - - - - -
     Function:        mouse_setgcurs()
     Toolbox:         MOUSEFUN.C
     Demonstrated:    MOUSTEST.C

     Parameters:
       (input)        cursor     Structure defining a graphics cursor

     Returned:        (function returns nothing)

     Variables:       cursor_seg     Segment of the cursor structure
                      cursor_off     Offset of the cursor structure
                      hotx           Hot spot x value
                      hoty           Hot spot y value

     Description:     Creates a graphics mode mouse cursor
     - - - - - - - - - - - - - - - - - - - - - - - - - - - - - - - -
*/
```

(continued)

MOUSEFUN.C *continued*

```
void mouse_setgcurs( struct graphics_cursor far *cursor )
{
    unsigned cursor_seg = FP_SEG( cursor );
    unsigned cursor_off = FP_OFF( cursor );
    int hotx = cursor->hot_spot_x;
    int hoty = cursor->hot_spot_y;
    _asm
        {
        mov    ax, 9
        mov    bx, hotx
        mov    cx, hoty
        mov    es, cursor_seg
        mov    dx, cursor_off
        int    33h
        }
}
```

Function: *mouse_settcurs()*

The *mouse_settcurs()* function sets one of the two types of text mode mouse cursors. Pass SOFT_TEXT_CURSOR or HARD_TEXT_CURSOR in the first parameter to set either the software cursor or the hardware cursor. These constants are defined in the MOUSEFUN.H header file, which should be included in any program that uses the MOUSEFUN toolbox module.

If you specify the software cursor, the *screen_mask* and *cursor_mask* parameters define the way in which on-screen character cells are modified when the cursor is placed on the screen. In text mode, 16 bits of video memory determine the appearance of each character. Half of these bits identify the ASCII character code, and half specify the background and foreground color attributes for the character. To update the mouse cursor, the mouse software first performs a logical AND operation between the screen mask and the 16 bits of screen data for the character. It then performs a logical XOR operation with the cursor mask and the result of the AND operation. The default screen and cursor mask values are 0xFFFF and 0x7700, which cause the character to remain unchanged but invert its color attributes.

If you specify the hardware cursor, the values passed in *screen_mask* and *cursor_mask* actually represent the start and stop scan lines for a block cursor. The hardware cursor is the cursor you see at the DOS prompt. It consists of a group of scan lines that blink in a character cell. The *mouse_settcurs()* function lets you control the number and placement of the scan lines that form the cursor.

```
/* - - - - - - - - - - - - - - - - - - - - - - - - - - - - - - - - - -
   Function:        mouse_settcurs()
   Toolbox:         MOUSEFUN.C
   Demonstrated:    MOUSTEST.C

   Parameters:
     (input)        cursor_select   Hardware or software cursor
     (input)        screen_mask     Screen mask (or start scan line)
     (input)        cursor_mask     Cursor mask (or end scan line)

   Returned:        (function returns nothing)

   Variables:       (none)

   Description:     Sets the text mode hardware or software cursor
   - - - - - - - - - - - - - - - - - - - - - - - - - - - - - - - - - -
*/

void mouse_settcurs( int cursor_select, int screen_mask, int cursor_mask )
{
    _asm
       {
       mov   ax, 10
       mov   bx, cursor_select
       mov   cx, screen_mask
       mov   dx, cursor_mask
       int   33h
       }
}
```

Function: *mouse_motion()*

The *mouse_motion()* function gets the horizontal and vertical mouse motion counts (mickeys) since the last call to this function. The mouse driver accumulates the counts internally. Two hundred mickeys represent an inch of mouse motion.

```
/* - - - - - - - - - - - - - - - - - - - - - - - - - - - - - - - -
    Function:       mouse_motion()
    Toolbox:        MOUSEFUN.C
    Demonstrated:   MOUSTEST.C
    Parameters:
      (output)      horz_mickeys    Horizontal mickeys
      (output)      vert_mickeys    Vertical mickeys

    Returned:       (function returns nothing)

    Variables:      m3        Local variable for register cx
                    m4        Local variable for register dx

    Description:    Gets the accumulated mouse motion counts
                    (mickeys) since the last call to this function
    - - - - - - - - - - - - - - - - - - - - - - - - - - - - - - - -
*/

void mouse_motion( int *horz_mickeys, int *vert_mickeys )
{
    int m3, m4;

    _asm
        {
        mov     ax, 11
        int     33h
        mov     m3, cx
        mov     m4, dx
        }

    *horz_mickeys = m3;
    *vert_mickeys = m4;
}
```

Function: *mouse_setratios()*

The *mouse_setratios()* function sets the horizontal and vertical ratios of mickeys to pixels. These ratios specify the number of mickeys for every 8 virtual screen pixels.

The default horizontal ratio is 8 mickeys to 8 virtual screen pixels. The default vertical ratio is 16 mickeys to every 8 virtual screen pixels.

The *mouse_setsensitivity()* function provides another method of setting the mouse sensitivity. The approach taken by that function is somewhat more intuitive than that taken in *mouse_setratios()*.

```
/* - - - - - - - - - - - - - - - - - - - - - - - - - - - - - - - - - -
    Function:        mouse_setratios()
    Toolbox:         MOUSEFUN.C
    Demonstrated:    MOUSTEST.C

    Parameters:
      (output)       horizontal      Horizontal mickey/pixel ratio
      (output)       vertical        Vertical mickey/pixel ratio

    Returned:        (function returns nothing)

    Variables:       (none)

    Description:     Sets the mickey/pixel ratios for mouse motion
    - - - - - - - - - - - - - - - - - - - - - - - - - - - - - - - - - -
*/

void mouse_setratios( int horizontal, int vertical )
{
    _asm
        {
        mov    ax, 15
        mov    cx, horizontal
        mov    dx, vertical
        int    33h
        }
}
```

Function: *mouse_condoff()*

The *mouse_condoff()* function defines a region on the screen within which the mouse cursor disappears. If the cursor is in the region when you call this function, it is immediately hidden. If you move the cursor into the region after you call the function, it disappears at that time. The effect is canceled by a call to *mouse_show()*, whether the cursor is still visible or is hidden.

The *mouse_condoff()* function lets you update a portion of the screen without necessarily having to hide the cursor. The cursor disappears only if it occupies the region being updated. Hiding the cursor prevents interaction between the cursor pixels and the updated pixels on the screen.

This function is similar in concept to *mouse_hide()* but more efficient for advanced applications that require fast screen updates.

```
/* - - - - - - - - - - - - - - - - - - - - - - - - - - - - - - - -
    Function:       mouse_condoff()
    Toolbox:        MOUSEFUN.C
    Demonstrated:   MOUSTEST.C

    Parameters:
      (input)       x1        Upper left corner of region
      (input)       y1        Upper left corner of region
      (input)       x2        Lower right corner of region
      (input)       y2        Lower right corner of region

    Returned:       (function returns nothing)


    Variables:      (none)


    Description:    Sets a region for conditionally turning off the
                    mouse cursor
    - - - - - - - - - - - - - - - - - - - - - - - - - - - - - - - -
*/

void mouse_condoff( int x1, int y1, int x2, int y2 )
{
    _asm
        {
        mov    ax, 16
        mov    cx, x1
        mov    dx, y1
        mov    si, x2
        mov    di, y2
        int    33h
        }
}
```

Function: *mouse_setdouble()*

The *mouse_setdouble()* function sets the double speed threshold for the mouse. This threshold defines the mouse velocity at which cursor motion on the screen doubles. It allows quick movement of the cursor across relatively great distances on the screen without inhibiting fine control at slower velocities. The function interprets the threshold in mickeys per second.

To disable the double speed threshold, pass the function an unattainably large value for mickeys per second, such as 10000.

317

```
/* - - - - - - - - - - - - - - - - - - - - - - - - - - - - - - - - - -
   Function:       mouse_setdouble()
   Toolbox:        MOUSEFUN.C
   Demonstrated:   MOUSTEST.C

   Parameters:
     (input)       mickeys_per_second   Double speed threshold

   Returned:       (function returns nothing)

   Variables:      (none)

   Description:    Sets the mouse double speed threshold
   - - - - - - - - - - - - - - - - - - - - - - - - - - - - - - - - - -
*/

void mouse_setdouble( int mickeys_per_second )
{
    _asm
        {
        mov    ax, 19
        mov    dx, mickeys_per_second
        int    33h
        }
}
```

Function: *mouse_storage()*

The *mouse_storage()* function determines the number of bytes required to save the current state of the mouse. With this information, a program can allocate space for a buffer and pass its address to *mouse_save()* to save the mouse state. The program can restore the mouse state by calling the *mouse_restore()* function.

```
/* - - - - - - - - - - - - - - - - - - - - - - - - - - - - - - - - - -
   Function:       mouse_storage()
   Toolbox:        MOUSEFUN.C
   Demonstrated:   MOUSTEST.C

   Parameters:
     (output)      buffer_size    Bytes for saving mouse state
```

(continued)

MOUSEFUN.C *continued*

```
    Returned:        (function returns nothing)

    Variables:       m2          Local variable for register bx

    Description:     Determines the number of bytes required for
                     saving the current state of the mouse
    - - - - - - - - - - - - - - - - - - - - - - - - - - - - - -
*/

void mouse_storage( int *buffer_size )
{
    int m2;

    _asm
        {
        mov   ax, 21
        int   33h
        mov   m2, bx
        }

    *buffer_size = m2;
}
```

Function: *mouse_save()*

The *mouse_save()* function saves the entire state of the mouse, which includes such factors as cursor position, visibility, sensitivity, and cursor type. You must pass the function a buffer big enough to contain all the information required to restore the mouse state. Use the *mouse_storage()* function to determine the minimum size for the buffer.

After you save the mouse state, you can call another program or modify the mouse cursor and its behavior. Later, you can restore the mouse state by passing the buffer to the *mouse_restore()* function.

```
/* - - - - - - - - - - - - - - - - - - - - - - - - - - - - - - - -
    Function:        mouse_save()
    Toolbox:         MOUSEFUN.C
    Demonstrated:    MOUSTEST.C

    Parameters:
      (in/out)       buffer      Buffer for saving mouse state
```

(continued)

MOUSEFUN.C *continued*

```
   Returned:        (function returns nothing)

   Variables:       buffer_seg     Segment of the buffer
                    buffer_off     Offset of the buffer

   Description:     Saves the current state of the mouse
   - - - - - - - - - - - - - - - - - - - - - - - - - - - - - - - -
*/

void mouse_save( char far *buffer )
{
    unsigned buffer_seg = FP_SEG( buffer );
    unsigned buffer_off = FP_OFF( buffer );

    _asm
        {
        mov    ax, 22
        mov    es, buffer_seg
        mov    dx, buffer_off
        int    33h
        }
}
```

Function: *mouse_restore()*

The *mouse_restore()* function restores the state of the mouse. The function receives a buffer that has been previously filled with mouse state information by a call to *mouse_save()*. The cursor position, visibility, sensitivity, cursor type, and other similar information are restored to the conditions at the moment you called *mouse_save()*.

```
/* - - - - - - - - - - - - - - - - - - - - - - - - - - - - - - - -
   Function:        mouse_restore()
   Toolbox:         MOUSEFUN.C
   Demonstrated:    MOUSTEST.C

   Parameters:
    (input)         buffer     Buffer for restoring the mouse state

   Returned:        (function returns nothing)
```

(continued)

MOUSEFUN.C *continued*

```
    Variables:      buffer_seg      Segment of the buffer
                    buffer_off      Offset of the buffer

    Description:    Restores the current state of the mouse
    - - - - - - - - - - - - - - - - - - - - - - - - - - - - -
*/

void mouse_restore( char far *buffer )
{
    unsigned buffer_seg = FP_SEG( buffer );
    unsigned buffer_off = FP_OFF( buffer );

    _asm
        {
        mov     ax, 23
        mov     es, buffer_seg
        mov     dx, buffer_off
        int     33h
        }
}
```

Function: *mouse_setsensitivity()*

The *mouse_setsensitivity()* function sets the mouse motion sensitivity and double speed threshold. This function duplicates the combined effects of the *mouse_setratios()* and *mouse_setdouble()* functions, but it operates in a more intuitive way.

When you call the function, you simply set its three parameters to values in the range 1 through 100. This range represents a relative scale in which the default values are all 50. To increase the speed of horizontal cursor movement from its default speed, for example, pass the function a larger number, such as 60 or 70, in the *horz* parameter.

```
/* - - - - - - - - - - - - - - - - - - - - - - - - - - - - -
    Function:       mouse_setsensitivity()
    Toolbox:        MOUSEFUN.C
    Demonstrated:   MOUSTEST.C

    Parameters:
      (input)       horz      Relative horizontal sensitivity
```

(continued)

MOUSEFUN.C *continued*

```
      (input)        vert      Relative vertical sensitivity
      (input)        threshold Relative double speed threshold

   Returned:         (function returns nothing)

   Variables:        (none)

   Description:      Sets the mouse sensitivity and double speed
                     threshold
   - - - - - - - - - - - - - - - - - - - - - - - - - - - - - - - -
*/

void mouse_setsensitivity( int horz, int vert, int threshold )
{
   _asm
      {
      mov   ax, 26
      mov   bx, horz
      mov   cx, vert
      mov   dx, threshold
      int   33h
      }
}
```

Function: *mouse_getsensitivity()*

The *mouse_getsensitivity()* function gets the current relative scale factors for mouse sensitivity and double speed threshold. These values are the same as those set with *mouse_setsensitivity()*. Default values are all 50.

```
/* - - - - - - - - - - - - - - - - - - - - - - - - - - - - - - -
   Function:      mouse_getsensitivity()
   Toolbox:       MOUSEFUN.C
   Demonstrated:  MOUSTEST.C

   Parameters:
      (output)       horz      Relative horizontal sensitivity
      (output)       vert      Relative vertical sensitivity
      (output)       threshold Relative double speed threshold

   Returned:         (function returns nothing)
```

(continued)

MOUSEFUN.C *continued*

```
    Variables:      (none)

    Description:    Gets the mouse sensitivity and double speed
                    threshold
    - - - - - - - - - - - - - - - - - - - - - - - - - - - -
*/

void mouse_getsensitivity( int *horz, int *vert, int *threshold )
{
    int m2, m3, m4;

    _asm
        {
        mov    ax, 27
        int    33h
        mov    m2, bx
        mov    m3, cx
        mov    m4, dx
        }

    *horz = m2;
    *vert = m3;
    *threshold = m4;
}
```

Function: *mouse_setmaxrate()*

The *mouse_setmaxrate()* function sets the mouse interrupt rate. This function works only with the InPort mouse to set the rate at which the mouse driver polls the status of the mouse. If you don't have an InPort mouse, this function has no effect.

Faster interrupt rates provide smoother cursor movement in graphics applications, whereas slower rates might let the application run faster.

```
/* - - - - - - - - - - - - - - - - - - - - - - - - - - - - - - - - - -
    Function:        mouse_setmaxrate()
    Toolbox:         MOUSEFUN.C
    Demonstrated:    MOUSTEST.C

    Parameters:
      (input)        interrupts_per_second    Interrupt rate

    Returned:        (function returns nothing)

    Variables:       rate      Number for range of interrupt rates

    Description:     Sets the interrupt rate (InPort mouse only)
    - - - - - - - - - - - - - - - - - - - - - - - - - - - - - - - - -
*/

void mouse_setmaxrate( int interrupts_per_second )
{
    int rate;

    if ( interrupts_per_second <= 0 )
        rate = 0;
    else if ( interrupts_per_second > 0 && interrupts_per_second <= 30 )
        rate = 1;
    else if ( interrupts_per_second > 30 && interrupts_per_second <= 50 )
        rate = 2;
    else if ( interrupts_per_second > 50 && interrupts_per_second <= 100 )
        rate = 3;
    else
        rate = 4;

    _asm
        {
        mov    ax, 28
        mov    bx, rate
        int    33h
        }
}
```

Function: *mouse_setpage()*

The *mouse_setpage()* function sets the video page in which the mouse cursor is visible. Use this function in conjunction with the QuickC functions *_setactivepage()* and *_setvisualpage()* to allow the mouse to be active on any given page of video memory.

```
/* - - - - - - - - - - - - - - - - - - - - - - - - - - - - - - - - -
    Function:      mouse_setpage()
    Toolbox:       MOUSEFUN.C
    Demonstrated:  MOUSTEST.C

    Parameters:
      (input)      crt_page  Video page for mouse cursor

    Returned:      (function returns nothing)

    Variables:     (none)

    Description:   Sets the video page where mouse cursor appears
    - - - - - - - - - - - - - - - - - - - - - - - - - - - - - - - -
*/

void mouse_setpage( int crt_page )
{
    _asm
        {
        mov   ax, 29
        mov   bx, crt_page
        int   33h
        }
}
```

Function: *mouse_getpage()*

The *mouse_getpage()* function gets the current video page in which the
mouse cursor is active. To change the video page in which the mouse is
active, use the *mouse_setpage()* function.

```
/* - - - - - - - - - - - - - - - - - - - - - - - - - - - - - - - - -
    Function:      mouse_getpage()
    Toolbox:       MOUSEFUN.C
    Demonstrated:  MOUSTEST.C

    Parameters:
      (output)     crt_page  Video page for mouse cursor

    Returned:      (function returns nothing)
```

(continued)

MOUSEFUN.C *continued*

```
    Variables:      m2        Local variable for register bx

    Description:    Gets the video page in which mouse cursor appears
    - - - - - - - - - - - - - - - - - - - - - - - - - - - - - - - - -
*/

void mouse_getpage( int *crt_page )
{
    int m2;

    _asm
        {
        mov     ax, 30
        int     33h
        mov     m2, bx
        }

    *crt_page = m2;
}
```

Function: *mouse_setlang()*

The *mouse_setlang()* function specifies the language for mouse driver messages and prompts. This function works only with the international version of the mouse driver and has no effect with the domestic version. The language numbers are defined as constants in the MOUSEFUN.H header file.

```
/* - - - - - - - - - - - - - - - - - - - - - - - - - - - - - - - - -
    Function:       mouse_setlang()
    Toolbox:        MOUSEFUN.C
    Demonstrated:   MOUSTEST.C

    Parameters:
      (input)       language  Language number

    Returned:       (function returns nothing)

    Variables:      (none)
```

(continued)

MOUSEFUN.C *continued*

```
    Description:    Sets the language for mouse driver messages
    - - - - - - - - - - - - - - - - - - - - - - - - - - - - - - - -
*/

void mouse_setlang( int language )
{
    _asm
        {
        mov    ax, 34
        mov    bx, language
        int    33h
        }
}
```

Function: *mouse_getlang()*

The *mouse_getlang()* function gets the current language for mouse
driver messages and prompts. This function always returns ENGLISH
with the domestic version of the mouse driver. The language numbers
are defined as constants in the MOUSEFUN.H header file.

```
/* - - - - - - - - - - - - - - - - - - - - - - - - - - - - - - - -
    Function:       mouse_getlang()
    Toolbox:        MOUSEFUN.C
    Demonstrated:   MOUSTEST.C

    Parameters:
     (output)       language  Language number

    Returned:       (function returns nothing)

    Variables:      (none)

    Description:    Gets the language for mouse driver messages
    - - - - - - - - - - - - - - - - - - - - - - - - - - - - - - -
*/

void mouse_getlang( int *language )
{
    int m2;
```

(continued)

MOUSEFUN.C *continued*

```
    _asm
        {
        mov    ax, 35
        int    33h
        mov    m2, bx
        }

    *language = m2;
}
```

Function: *mouse_getversion()*

The *mouse_getversion()* function gets the mouse driver version number, the mouse type, and the interrupt request type. The version number is a double-precision floating-point number in standard version notation.

The mouse types and interrupt request types are defined as constants in the MOUSEFUN.H header file. The demonstration program MOUSTEST.C shows how you can use these constants.

```
/* - - - - - - - - - - - - - - - - - - - - - - - - - - - - - - - - -
    Function:      mouse_getversion()
    Toolbox:       MOUSEFUN.C
    Demonstrated:  MOUSTEST.C

    Parameters:
      (output)     version       Mouse driver version number
      (output)     mouse_type    Type of mouse
      (output)     irq_num       Interrupt request type


    Returned:      (function returns nothing)

    Variables:     m2     Local variable for register bx
                   m3     Local variable for register cx
                   maj    Major part of version number
                   min    Minor part of version number


    Description:   Gets the mouse driver version number, mouse type,
                   and interrupt request type
    - - - - - - - - - - - - - - - - - - - - - - - - - - - - - - - - -
*/
```

(continued)

MOUSEFUN.C *continued*

```
void mouse_getversion( double *version, int *mouse_type, int *irq_num )
{
    int m2, m3;
    int maj, min;

    _asm
        {
        mov    ax, 36
        int    33h
        mov    m2, bx
        mov    m3, cx
        }

    maj = ( m2 >> 12 ) * 10 + (( m2 >> 8 ) & 0xf );
    min = (( m2 >> 4 ) & 0xf ) * 10 + ( m2 & 0xf );
    *version = maj + min / 100.0;
    *mouse_type = m3 >> 8;
    *irq_num = m3 & 0xff;
}
```

PROBSTAT

FUNCTION	DESCRIPTION
arithmetic_mean()	Finds the arithmetic mean of a *double* array
geometric_mean()	Finds the geometric mean of a *double* array
harmonic_mean()	Finds the harmonic mean of a *double* array
quadratic_mean()	Finds the quadratic mean of a *double* array
combinations()	Calculates the number of possible combinations
permutations()	Calculates the number of possible permutations
factorial()	Calculates the factorial of an integer

The PROBSTAT toolbox module provides a collection of functions for probability and statistics calculations. One set of functions determines mean values of four types for an array of double-precision floating-point numbers. Two other functions return the number of possible combinations and the number of possible permutations of n things taken r at a time.

One additional function, *factorial()*, calculates the factorial of an integer. This function also provides an example of recursion: It calls itself repeatedly, as needed. Although recursive functions can be unnecessarily slow, the technique can simplify some types of calculations.

The PROBTEST.C program demonstrates the functions in this module. It creates an array of five double-precision numbers and uses this set of values to calculate the various means. PROBTEST then demonstrates the three probability functions using typical values so that the results can easily be verified.

Demonstration Program: PROBTEST.C

```
/* -------------------------------------------------------------------

   Name:            PROBTEST.C
   Type:            Demonstration program
   Language:        Microsoft QuickC
   Video:           (no special video requirements)

   Program list:    PROBTEST.C
                    PROBSTAT.C

   Variables:       i         Looping index for printing array
                    cnt       Count of the array entries
                    ary       Array of sample values

   Usage:           (no command line parameters)

   Description:     Demonstrates the PROBSTAT toolbox functions
   -------------------------------------------------------------------
*/

#include <stdio.h>
#include "probstat.h"

main()
{
    int i, cnt = 5;
    double ary[] = { 1.23, 4.56, 7.89, 3.45, 6.78 };

    /* Print the array contents */
    printf( "\n\nary[] = " );
    for ( i = 0; i < cnt; i++ )
        printf( "%7.2f", ary[i] );
    printf( "\n\n" );

    /* Print the results from each function */
    printf( "arithmetic_mean( ary ) = %g\n", arithmetic_mean( cnt, ary ));
    printf( "geometric_mean( ary ) = %g\n", geometric_mean( cnt, ary ));
    printf( "harmonic_mean( ary ) = %g\n", harmonic_mean( cnt, ary ));
    printf( "quadratic_mean( ary ) = %g\n\n", quadratic_mean( cnt, ary ));
    printf( "combinations( 17L, 3L ) = %g\n", combinations( 17L, 3L ));
    printf( "permutations( 17L, 3L ) = %g\n", permutations( 17L, 3L ));
    printf( "factorial( 7 ) = %g\n\n", factorial( 7 ));
}
```

Include File: PROBSTAT.H

```
/* ------------------------------------------------------------
    Name:          PROBSTAT.H
    Type:          Include
    Language:      Microsoft QuickC
    Demonstrated:  PROBSTAT.C  PROBTEST.C
    Description:   Prototypes and definitions for PROBSTAT.C
   ------------------------------------------------------------
*/

#ifndef PROBSTAT_DEFINED

double arithmetic_mean( int, double * );
double geometric_mean( int, double * );
double harmonic_mean( int, double * );
double quadratic_mean( int, double * );
double combinations( unsigned long, unsigned long );
double permutations( unsigned long, unsigned long );
double factorial( int );

#define PROBSTAT_DEFINED
#endif
```

Toolbox Module: PROBSTAT.C

```
/* ------------------------------------------------------------
    Name:          PROBSTAT.C
    Type:          Toolbox module
    Language:      Microsoft QuickC
    Demonstrated:  PROBTEST.C
    Video:         (no special video requirements)
   ------------------------------------------------------------
*/

#include <math.h>
#include "probstat.h"
```

Function: *arithmetic_mean()*

The *arithmetic_mean()* function calculates the arithmetic mean of an array of numbers. The function receives two parameters—the number of elements in the array and an array of type *double*.

The return value is the result of dividing the sum of the elements by the total number of elements.

```
/* - - - - - - - - - - - - - - - - - - - - - - - - - - - - - -

   Function:      arithmetic_mean()
   Toolbox:       PROBSTAT.C
   Demonstrated:  PROBTEST.C

   Parameters:
     (input)      n           Number of array values
     (input)      ary         Array of double-precision numbers

   Returned:      Arithmetic mean

   Variables:     i           Looping index
                  sum         Total sum of the array values

   Description:   Returns the arithmetic mean of an array
   - - - - - - - - - - - - - - - - - - - - - - - - - - - - - -
*/

double arithmetic_mean( int n, double *ary )
{
    int i;
    double sum = 0.0;

    for ( i = 0; i < n; i++ )
        sum += ary[i];

    return ( sum / n );
}
```

Function: *geometric_mean()*

The *geometric_mean()* function returns the geometric mean of an array of numbers. The function receives two parameters—the number of elements in the array and an array of type *double*.

To calculate the geometric mean, the function multiplies all *n* values together and then finds the *n*th root of the result.

```
/* - - - - - - - - - - - - - - - - - - - - - - - - - - - - - - - -
    Function:        geometric_mean()
    Toolbox:         PROBSTAT.C
    Demonstrated:    PROBTEST.C

    Parameters:
      (input)        n          Number of array values
      (input)        ary        Array of double-precision numbers

    Returned:        Geometric mean

    Variables:       i          Looping index
                     prod       Product of the array values

    Description:     Returns the geometric mean of an array
    - - - - - - - - - - - - - - - - - - - - - - - - - - - - - - -
*/

double geometric_mean( int n, double *ary )
{
    int i;
    double prod = 1.0;

    for ( i = 0; i < n; i++ )
        prod *= ary[i];

    return ( pow( prod, 1.0 / n ));
}
```

Function: *harmonic_mean()*

The *harmonic_mean()* function returns the harmonic mean of an array of numbers. The function receives two parameters—the number of elements in the array and an array of type *double*.

To calculate the harmonic mean, the function sums the inverse of all *n* values and divides the result into *n*.

```
/* - - - - - - - - - - - - - - - - - - - - - - - - - - - - - - - - -
    Function:       harmonic_mean()
    Toolbox:        PROBSTAT.C
    Demonstrated:   PROBTEST.C

    Parameters:
      (input)       n           Number of array values
      (input)       ary         Array of double-precision numbers

    Returned:       Harmonic mean

    Variables:      i           Looping index
                    sum         Sum of the inverse of the array values

    Description:    Returns the harmonic mean of an array
    - - - - - - - - - - - - - - - - - - - - - - - - - - - - - - -
*/

double harmonic_mean( int n, double *ary )
{
    int i;
    double sum = 0.0;

    for ( i = 0; i < n; i++ )
        sum += 1.0 / ary[i];

    return ( n / sum );
}
```

Function: *quadratic_mean()*

The *quadratic_mean()* function calculates the quadratic mean of an array of numbers. The function receives two parameters—the number of elements in the array and an array of type *double*.

To calculate the quadratic mean, the function sums the squares of all n values, divides the result by n, and finds the square root of the quotient.

```
/* - - - - - - - - - - - - - - - - - - - - - - - - - - - - - - - - - -

    Function:       quadratic_mean()
    Toolbox:        PROBSTAT.C
    Demonstrated:   PROBTEST.C

    Parameters:
      (input)       n           Number of array values
      (input)       ary         Array of double-precision numbers

    Returned:       Quadratic mean

    Variables:      i           Looping index
                    sum         Sum of the squares of the array values

    Description:    Returns the quadratic mean of an array
    - - - - - - - - - - - - - - - - - - - - - - - - - - - - - - - - - -
*/

double quadratic_mean( int n, double *ary )
{
    int i;
    double sum = 0.0;

    for ( i = 0; i < n; i++ )
        sum += ary[i] * ary[i];

    return ( sqrt( sum / n ) );
}
```

Function: *combinations()*

The *combinations()* function returns the number of possible combinations of *n* things taken *r* at a time. Both parameters, *n* and *r*, are unsigned long integers.

```
/* - - - - - - - - - - - - - - - - - - - - - - - - - - - - - - -

    Function:       combinations()
    Toolbox:        PROBSTAT.C
    Demonstrated:   PROBTEST.C

    Parameters:
      (input)       n           Number of things
      (input)       r           Number of things per combination

    Returned:       Combinations of n things taken r at a time

    Variables:      k           Difference between n and r
                    i           Looping index
                    t           Temporary swapping variable
                    result      Working result variable

    Description:    Returns the possible combinations for n things
                    taken r at a time
    - - - - - - - - - - - - - - - - - - - - - - - - - - - - - - -
*/

double combinations( unsigned long n, unsigned long r )
{
    long k, i, t;
    double result = 1.0;

    k = n - r;
    if ( r > k )
        {
        t = r;
        r = k;
        k = t;
        }
    for ( i = 1; i <= r; i++ )
        {
        result *= n--;
        result /= i;
        }
    return ( result );
}
```

Function: *permutations()*

The *permutations()* function returns the number of permutations of *n* things taken *r* at a time. Both parameters, *n* and *r*, are unsigned long integers.

```
/* - - - - - - - - - - - - - - - - - - - - - - - - - - - - - - - - - -
    Function:       permutations()
    Toolbox:        PROBSTAT.C
    Demonstrated:   PROBTEST.C

    Parameters:
      (input)       n          Number of things
      (input)       r          Number of things taken together

    Returned:       Permutations of n things taken r at a time

    Variables:      i          Looping index
                    result     Working result variable

    Description:    Returns the possible permutations for n things
                    taken r at a time
    - - - - - - - - - - - - - - - - - - - - - - - - - - - - - - - - -
*/

double permutations( unsigned long n, unsigned long r )
{
    long i;
    double result = 1.0;

    for ( i = n - r + 1; i <= n; i++ )
        result *= (double)i;

    return ( result );
}
```

Function: *factorial()*

The *factorial()* function returns the factorial of *n*. The factorial of an integer is the product of the integers 1 through *n*. This function finds the factorial by using recursion, a process by which a function calls itself. If you calculate the factorial of a number that is less than or equal to 1, the function returns 1 as the result. If you calculate the factorial of a number *n* that is greater than 1, the function returns a value that is *n* times the factorial of *n*–1.

Typically, the *factorial()* function calls itself several times, with intermediate results pending the result of the next call to *factorial()*. Eventually, the passed parameter is 1, and all the pending calculations are subsequently satisfied.

```
/* - - - - - - - - - - - - - - - - - - - - - - - - - - - - - - -
    Function:       factorial()
    Toolbox:        PROBSTAT.C
    Demonstrated:   PROBTEST.C

    Parameters:
      (input)       n           Number for which to find factorial

    Returned:       Factorial of n

    Variables:      (none)

    Description:    Returns the factorial of n
    - - - - - - - - - - - - - - - - - - - - - - - - - - - - - - -
*/

double factorial( int n )
{
    if ( n > 1 )
        return ( n * factorial( n - 1 ));
    else
        return ( 1.0 );
}
```

RANDOMS

FUNCTION	DESCRIPTION
rand_shuffle()	Initializes random numbers
rand_long()	Returns a random long integer
rand_short()	Returns a random short integer
rand_frac()	Returns a random fraction 0 through 1
rand_int_range()	Returns a random integer in a range
rand_double()	Returns a random *double* in a range
rand_normal()	Returns a random *double*, normal distribution
rand_exponential()	Returns a random *double*, exponential distribution
rand_long_buf()	Fills a buffer with random long integers

The RANDOMS toolbox module provides a collection of functions for generating pseudorandom numbers. At the heart of these routines are two techniques described in *The Art of Computer Programming,* Vol. 2, *Semi-Numerical Algorithms,* by Donald Knuth. The *rand_long()* function combines the two techniques. The underlying algorithm is extremely fast and involves no multiplication or division. The function simply adds unsigned long integers in a table (ignoring overflow) and uses a table-shuffling technique to increase the randomness of the sequence.

Several other RANDOMS functions use the long integers returned by *rand_long()* to create other types of random numbers. For example, *rand_frac()* returns fractional numbers, or double-precision floating-point values in the range 0 through 1.

For programs that use a large number of pseudorandom values, the *rand_long_buf()* function fills a buffer with pseudorandom long integers. The CIPHER program, presented later in this book, uses this function to generate 1000 pseudorandom numbers with each call.

The RANDTEST.C program demonstrates each function in this module. The first half of the program generates and displays short lists of the various types of pseudorandom numbers. The second half of the program generates a series of histograms and scatter plots of the various types of pseudorandom numbers. This part of the demonstration requires at least CGA graphics capability.

To initialize the sequence of random numbers, call *rand_shuffle()* at the start of any program that uses other RANDOMS functions. The *rand_shuffle()* function accepts any string of reasonable length as the key string, or seed, for initializing the sequence. A given string always generates the same sequence; however, even a minor change to the key string causes *rand_shuffle()* to generate an entirely different sequence. (Repeatability is an important feature for the CIPHER utility, which uses this module.) If you pass a zero-length string to *rand_shuffle()*, the function uses the system date and time to generate a key string, and hence a unique pseudorandom sequence for every second.

Demonstration Program: RANDTEST.C

```
/* -------------------------------------------------------------
    Name:          RANDTEST.C
    Type:          Demonstration program
    Language:      Microsoft QuickC
    Video:         Second half of the program requires at least CGA

    Program list:  RANDTEST.C
                   RANDOMS.C
                   GRAPHICS.LIB

    Variables:     key        Key string entered by user
                   i          Looping index
                   j          Looping index
                   x          X pixel location for plotting
                   y          Array of pixel heights for plotting
                   esc_flag   Signal that Esc key was pressed
                   buf        Array to be filled with randoms

    Usage:         (no command line parameters)

    Description:   Demonstrates the RANDOMS toolbox functions
    -------------------------------------------------------------
*/

#include <stdio.h>
#include <stdlib.h>
#include <graph.h>
#include <conio.h>
#include "randoms.h"
```

(continued)

RANDTEST.C *continued*

```
main()
{
    char key[255];
    int i, j;
    int x, y[320];
    int esc_flag = 0;
    long buf[8];

    printf( "\n\n\nEnter a key string for randomizing,\n" );
    printf( "or just press Enter to use system date and time...\n\n" );

    /* Initialize key string to zero length */
    key[0] = '\0';

    /* Obtain a string, whitespace and all, delimited with Enter key */
    scanf( "%[^\n]", key );

    /* Initialize the random number generator */
    rand_shuffle( key );

    printf( "\n\nrand_short() ...\n" );
    for ( i = 0; i < 8; i++ )
        printf( "%u\t", rand_short() );

    printf( "\n\nrand_long() ...\n" );
    for ( i = 0; i < 8; i++ )
        printf( "%lu\t", rand_long() );

    printf( "\n\nrand_frac() ...\n" );
    for ( i = 0; i < 8; i++ )
        printf( "%f\t", rand_frac() );

    printf( "\n\nrand_long_buf( 8, buf ) ...\n" );
    rand_long_buf( 8, buf );
    for ( i = 0; i < 8; i++ )
        printf( "%lu\t", buf[i] );

    printf( "\n\n\nPress any key to continue\n\n" );
    getch();

    printf( "\n\nrand_int_range( -10, 10 ) ...\n" );
    for ( i = 0; i < 8; i++ )
        printf( "%d\t", rand_int_range( -10, 10 ));
```

(continued)

RANDTEST.C *continued*

```
    printf( "\n\nrand_double( -10.0, 10.0 ) ...\n" );
    for ( i = 0; i < 8; i++ )
        printf( "%f\t", rand_double( -10.0, 10.0 ));

    printf( "\n\nrand_normal( 50.0, 10.0 ) ...\n" );
    for ( i = 0; i < 8; i++ )
        printf( "%f\t", rand_normal( 50.0, 10.0 ));

    printf( "\n\nrand_exponential( 10.0 ) ...\n" );
    for ( i = 0; i < 8; i++ )
        printf( "%f\t", rand_exponential( 10.0 ));

    printf( "\n\n\nPress any key to continue" );
    getch();

    /* Set a graphics mode */
    if ( _setvideomode( _MRES256COLOR ) == 0 )
        if ( _setvideomode( _MRES16COLOR ) == 0 )
            if ( _setvideomode( _MRES4COLOR ) == 0 )
                {
                printf( "Graphics mode demonstrations " );
                printf( "require VGA, EGA, or CGA\n" );
                exit( 1 );
                };

    printf( "Accumulated uniform distribution\n" );
    printf( "(Press Esc to end each test)" );

    for ( i = 0; i < 320; i++ )
        y[i] = 0;

    while ( !esc_flag )
        {
        x = rand_short() % 320;
        y[x]++;
        _setpixel( x, 199 - y[x] );
        if ( kbhit() )
            esc_flag = ( getch() == 27 );
        }

    _clearscreen( _GCLEARSCREEN );
    esc_flag = 0;
```

(continued)

RANDTEST.C *continued*

```
    printf( "Random pixels\n" );

    while ( !esc_flag )
        {
        _setpixel( rand_short() % 320, rand_short() % 200 );
        if ( kbhit() )
            esc_flag = ( getch() == 27 );
        }

    _clearscreen( _GCLEARSCREEN );
    esc_flag = 0;

    printf( "Normal distribution\nmean = 160, std deviation = 50\n" );

    for ( i = 0; i < 320; i++ )
        y[i] = 0;

    while ( !esc_flag )
        {
        x = (int)rand_normal( 160.0, 50.0 );
        if ( x >= 0 && x <= 319 )
            {
            y[x]++;
            _setpixel( x, 199 - y[x] );
            if ( kbhit() )
                esc_flag = ( getch() == 27 );
            }
        }

    _clearscreen( _GCLEARSCREEN );
    esc_flag = 0;

    printf( "Exponential distribution\nmean = 100\n" );

    for ( i = 0; i < 320; i++ )
        y[i] = 0;

    while ( !esc_flag )
        {
        x = (int)rand_exponential( 100.0 );
        if ( x >= 0 && x <= 319 )
            {
```

(continued)

344

RANDTEST.C *continued*

```
            y[x]++;
            _setpixel( x, 199 - y[x] );
            if ( kbhit() )
                esc_flag = ( getch() == 27 );
            }
        }

    _setvideomode( _DEFAULTMODE );
    _clearscreen( _GCLEARSCREEN );
}
```

Include File: RANDOMS.H

```
/* -------------------------------------------------------------------
    Name:          RANDOMS.H
    Type:          Include
    Language:      Microsoft QuickC
    Demonstrated:  RANDOMS.C  RANDTEST.C
    Description:   Prototypes and definitions for RANDOMS.C
    -------------------------------------------------------------------
*/

#ifndef RANDOMS_DEFINED

void rand_shuffle( char * );
unsigned long rand_long( void );
unsigned short rand_short( void );
double rand_frac( void );
int rand_int_range( int, int );
double rand_double( double, double );
double rand_normal( double, double );
double rand_exponential( double );
void rand_long_buf( int, long * );

#define RANDOMS_DEFINED
#endif
```

Toolbox Module: RANDOMS.C

```
/* ----------------------------------------------------------------
   Name:           RANDOMS.C
   Type:           Toolbox module
   Language:       Microsoft QuickC
   Demonstrated:   RANDTEST.C CIPHER.C
   Video:          (no special video requirements)
   ----------------------------------------------------------------
*/

#include <time.h>
#include <math.h>
#include <string.h>
#include "randoms.h"

#define TWOPI   6.283185307179586
#define MAXLONG 4294967295.0

struct rand_array
    {
    unsigned long *ptr1;
    unsigned long *ptr2;
    unsigned long table[55];
    unsigned long shuff[45];
    unsigned long last;
    } r;
```

Function: *rand_shuffle()*

The *rand_shuffle()* function initializes the sequence of pseudorandom numbers from which the other RANDOMS functions obtain values.

Pass the function any string to serve as the initialization key. Any given string always generates the same sequence. If you pass a zero-length string, *rand_shuffle()* generates its own key string using the date and time supplied by the system clock. This method causes the function to generate a unique sequence for every second.

The *rand_shuffle()* function works by filling the random number generation table and the shuffling table with long integers generated from the key string. To "warm up" the generator, the function generates and then discards a sequence of almost a thousand pseudorandom long integers.

```
/* - - - - - - - - - - - - - - - - - - - - - - - - - - - - - - - -

   Function:       rand_shuffle()
   Toolbox:        RANDOMS.C
   Demonstrated:   RANDTEST.C

   Parameters:
    (input)        key        String to use as a key

   Returned:       (function returns nothing)

   Variables:      i          Looping index
                   j          Looping index
                   tmp        Intermediate temporary results
                   ky         Key array

   Description:    Shuffles the pseudorandom number sequence.
                   Initializes a unique but repeatable sequence
                   for every unique key string.
   - - - - - - - - - - - - - - - - - - - - - - - - - - - - - - - -
*/

void rand_shuffle( char *key )
{
    int i, j;
    unsigned long tmp = 817171717;

    union
        {
        char keystr[200];
        long keylng[50];
        } ky;

    /* Fill the key array with starting numbers */
    for ( i = 0; i < 50; i++ )
        ky.keylng[i] = 123456 + i * 997;

    /* Use system date and time if key string is zero length */
    if (( j = strlen( key )) == 0 )
        {
        _strdate( ky.keystr );
        _strtime( &ky.keystr[8] );
        }
```

(continued)

RANDOMS.C *continued*

```
    /* Otherwise, mix the key string into the key array */
    else
        for ( i = 0; i < j; i++ )
            ky.keystr[i % 200] ^= key[i];

    /* Use the key array to initialize the table */
    for ( i = 0; i < 55; i++ )
        tmp = r.table[i] = (( tmp << 3 ) ^ ky.keylng[i % 50] ) | i;

    /* Use the key array to initialize the shuffle table */
    for ( i = 0; i < 45; i++ )
        tmp = r.shuff[i] = (( tmp << 3 ) ^ ky.keylng[i] ) | i;

    /* Initialize pointers into the table */
    r.ptr1 = r.table + 54;
    r.ptr2 = r.table + 23;

    /* Initialize the "last" random number */
    r.last = 0;

    /* Warm it up */
    for ( i = 0; i < 997; i++ )
        rand_long();
}
```

Function: *rand_long()*

The *rand_long()* function generates and returns a pseudorandom unsigned long integer. This function is exceptionally fast because it requires no multiplication, division, or floating-point operations. The sequence has an extremely long cycle and provides very good random numbers.

Each call to the function updates a globally accessible table of 55 unsigned long integers. The function adds two values from the table and assigns the sum to the first value, ignoring the overflow. The indexes pointing into the table are shifted to the next values. The function then uses the result of this summation to extract and replace a return value from a 45-element shuffle table.

You must call *rand_shuffle()* once before you use *rand_long()*. This call initializes the tables and indexes. If you do not call *rand_shuffle()*, the result of calling *rand_long()* is unpredictable.

```
/* - - - - - - - - - - - - - - - - - - - - - - - - - - - - - - -
    Function:       rand_long()
    Toolbox:        RANDOMS.C
    Demonstrated:   RANDTEST.C

    Parameters:     (none)

    Returned:       Pseudorandom unsigned long integer

    Variables:      tmp      Temporary accumulating variable
                    shuffptr Pointer into shuffle table

    Description:    Returns a pseudorandom unsigned long integer
    - - - - - - - - - - - - - - - - - - - - - - - - - - - - - - -
*/

unsigned long rand_long( void )
{
    unsigned long tmp, *shuffptr;

    /* Add two table entries */
    tmp = ( *r.ptr1 += *r.ptr2 );

    /* Decrement first index, keeping in table range 0 through 54 */
    if ( r.ptr1 > r.table )
        r.ptr1--;
    else
        r.ptr1 = r.table + 54;

    /* Decrement second index, keeping in table range 0 through 54 */
    if ( r.ptr2 > r.table )
        r.ptr2--;
    else
        r.ptr2 = r.table + 54;

    /* Use last random number to index into shuffle table */
    shuffptr = r.shuff + ( r.last % 45 );

    /* Grab from the shuffle table */
    r.last = *shuffptr;

    /* Put the new random number in the shuffle table */
    *shuffptr = tmp;

    /* Return the number grabbed from the shuffle table */
    return ( r.last );
}
```

Function: *rand_short()*

The *rand_short()* function returns a pseudorandom unsigned short integer. This function works by masking out the high-order bytes of a pseudorandom long integer returned by the *rand_long()* function.

Call the *rand_shuffle()* function to initialize the sequence of pseudorandom numbers before you use *rand_short()*.

```
/* - - - - - - - - - - - - - - - - - - - - - - - - - - - - - -

   Function:      rand_short()
   Toolbox:       RANDOMS.C
   Demonstrated:  RANDTEST.C

   Parameters:    (none)

   Returned:      Pseudorandom unsigned short integer

   Variables:     (none)

   Description:   Returns a pseudorandom unsigned short integer
   - - - - - - - - - - - - - - - - - - - - - - - - - - - - - -
*/

unsigned short rand_short( void )
{
    return ( rand_long() & 0xFFFF );
}
```

Function: *rand_frac()*

The *rand_frac()* function returns a pseudorandom fractional floating-point number in the range 0 through 1. To produce a value in this range, the function divides an unsigned long integer value obtained from *rand_long()* by the largest possible unsigned long integer (the constant MAXLONG defined near the beginning of RANDOMS.C). Note that the function can return the exact values 0.0 or 1.0.

Call the *rand_shuffle()* function to initialize the sequence of pseudorandom numbers before you use *rand_frac()*.

```
/* - - - - - - - - - - - - - - - - - - - - - - - - - - - - - - - -

    Function:        rand_frac()
    Toolbox:         RANDOMS.C
    Demonstrated:    RANDTEST.C


    Parameters:      (none)


    Returned:        Pseudorandom double in the range 0.0 through 1.0


    Variables:       (none)


    Description:     Returns a pseudorandom positive double in the
                     range 0.0 through 1.0
    - - - - - - - - - - - - - - - - - - - - - - - - - - - - - - - -
*/

double rand_frac( void )
{
    return ( rand_long() / MAXLONG );
}
```

Function: *rand_int_range()*

The *rand_int_range()* function returns a pseudorandom integer in a given range. The function uses a long integer returned by *rand_long()* to generate a pseudorandom number in the inclusive range specified by two parameters, *a* and *b.*

Call the *rand_shuffle()* function to initialize the sequence of pseudorandom numbers before you use *rand_int_range().*

```
/* - - - - - - - - - - - - - - - - - - - - - - - - - - - - - - - -

    Function:        rand_int_range()
    Toolbox:         RANDOMS.C
    Demonstrated:    RANDTEST.C


    Parameters:      a          Minimum integer in range
                     b          Maximum integer in range


    Returned:        Pseudorandom integer in the range a through b


    Variables:       (none)
```

(continued)

351

RANDOMS.C *continued*

```
    Description:    Returns a pseudorandom integer in the range
                    a through b
 - - - - - - - - - - - - - - - - - - - - - - - - - - - - - - - -
*/

int rand_int_range( int a, int b )
{
    return ( (int)( rand_long() % ( b - a + 1 ) + a ));
}
```

Function: *rand_double()*

The *rand_double()* function returns a pseudorandom double-precision floating-point number in a given range. The function uses a long integer returned by *rand_long()* to generate a pseudorandom number in the inclusive range specified by two parameters, *a* and *b*.

Call the *rand_shuffle()* function to initialize the sequence of pseudorandom numbers before you use *rand_double()*.

```
/* - - - - - - - - - - - - - - - - - - - - - - - - - - - - - - -
    Function:       rand_double()
    Toolbox:        RANDOMS.C
    Demonstrated:   RANDTEST.C

    Parameters:     double_a  Minimum double in range
                    double_b  Maximum double in range

    Returned:       Pseudorandom double in the range double_a
                    through double_b

    Variables:      (none)

    Description:    Returns a pseudorandom double in the range
                    double_a through double_b
 - - - - - - - - - - - - - - - - - - - - - - - - - - - - - - - -
*/

double rand_double( double double_a, double double_b )
{
    return (( rand_long() / MAXLONG ) *
            ( double_b - double_a ) + double_a );
}
```

Function: *rand_normal()*

The *rand_normal()* function returns a pseudorandom double-precision floating-point number with a normal distribution defined by a given mean and standard deviation. The function uses long integers returned by *rand_long()* to generate a normalized pseudorandom number, which is then modified by the given mean and standard deviation values to produce a number with the expected probability.

Call the *rand_shuffle()* function to initialize the sequence of pseudorandom numbers before you use *rand_normal()*.

```
/* - - - - - - - - - - - - - - - - - - - - - - - - - - - - - - /* - -
    Function:       rand_normal()
    Toolbox:        RANDOMS.C
    Demonstrated:   RANDTEST.C

    Parameters:     mean       Mean of the distribution
                    std_dev    Standard deviation of the distribution

    Returned:       Pseudorandom double with a normal distribution

    Variables:      u1         Pseudorandom in the range 0.0 through 1.0
                    u2         Pseudorandom in the range 0.0 through 1.0
                    x          Normalized normal distribution number

    Description:    Returns a pseudorandom double with a normal
                    distribution defined by a given mean and
                    standard deviation
    - - - - - - - - - - - - - - - - - - - - - - - - - - - - - - - - -
*/

double rand_normal( double mean, double std_dev )
{
    double u1, u2, x;

    u1 = rand_long() / MAXLONG;
    u2 = rand_long() / MAXLONG;

    x = sqrt( -2.0 * log( u1 )) * cos( TWOPI * u2 );

    return ( mean + std_dev * x );
}
```

Function: *rand_exponential()*

The *rand_exponential()* function returns double-precision numbers with an exponential distribution defined by the given mean. To generate these values, the function modifies pseudorandom unsigned long integers returned by *rand_long()*.

Call the *rand_shuffle()* function to initialize the sequence of pseudorandom numbers before you use *rand_exponential()*.

```
/* - - - - - - - - - - - - - - - - - - - - - - - - - - - - - - -

    Function:       rand_exponential()
    Toolbox:        RANDOMS.C
    Demonstrated:   RANDTEST.C

    Parameters:     mean      Mean of the distribution

    Returned:       Pseudorandom double with an exponential
                    distribution

    Variables:      (none)

    Description:    Returns a pseudorandom double with an
                    exponential distribution defined by a given mean
    - - - - - - - - - - - - - - - - - - - - - - - - - - - - - -
*/

double rand_exponential( double mean )
{
    return ( -mean * log( rand_long() / MAXLONG ));
}
```

Function: *rand_long_buf()*

The *rand_long_buf()* function fills a buffer with pseudorandom long integers. The first parameter indicates the number of values to generate, and the second parameter is the address of the buffer to fill. The function uses the same algorithm as that provided in the *rand_long()* function but duplicates the steps to eliminate the overhead of calling *rand_long()* to create each value.

This function is handy for programs that require a long list of random numbers.

```
/* - - - - - - - - - - - - - - - - - - - - - - - - - - - - - - - - - -

   Function:      rand_long_buf()
   Toolbox:       RANDOMS.C
   Demonstrated:  RANDTEST.C CIPHER.C

   Parameters:    n        Size of the buffer to be filled
                  buf      Long integer buffer to be filled

   Returned:      (function returns nothing)

   Variables:     tmp      Retains calculated random long value
                  shuffptr Pointer into the shuffle table

   Description:   Fills a buffer with pseudorandom long integers
   - - - - - - - - - - - - - - - - - - - - - - - - - - - - - - - - - -
*/

void rand_long_buf( int n, long *buf )
{
    unsigned long tmp, *shuffptr;

    /* Loop through all buffer locations */
    while ( n )
        {

        /* Add two table entries */
        tmp = ( *r.ptr1 += *r.ptr2 );

        /* Decrement first index, keeping in table range 0 through 54 */
        if ( r.ptr1 > r.table )
            r.ptr1--;
        else
            r.ptr1 = r.table + 54;

        /* Decrement second index, keeping in table range 0 through 54 */
        if ( r.ptr2 > r.table )
            r.ptr2--;
        else
            r.ptr2 = r.table + 54;

        /* Use last random number to index into shuffle table */
        shuffptr = r.shuff + ( r.last % 45 );
```

(continued)

RANDOMS.C *continued*

```
        /* Grab from the shuffle table */
        r.last = *shuffptr;

        /* Put the new random number in the shuffle table */
        *shuffptr = tmp;

        /* And put it in the return buffer */
        buf[--n] = r.last;

        }
    }
```

SOUND

FUNCTION	DESCRIPTION
speaker_toggle()	Toggles the speaker on and off
sound()	Starts a tone of a given frequency
silence()	Stops the tone generation
wait_ticks()	Delays execution for a given number of clock ticks
warble()	Generates a three-tone warble
weird()	Generates a variable-tone waveform
siren()	Generates a rising and falling tone
white_noise()	Generates random speaker pulses
note()	Generates a tone of given frequency and duration

The SOUND toolbox module provides a variety of functions for creating and controlling sound effects. The module illustrates two fundamentally different ways to control the speaker in an IBM PC: pulsing the speaker directly and modifying a sound by means of the timer hardware.

The *speaker_toggle()* function pulses, or toggles, the speaker on and off to create sound waves. This function shows how you can generate sounds by reading and writing I/O port values.

The *sound()* function uses the second method for controlling the speaker. It manipulates the internal timer to generate a tone from the speaker. The tone can persist while the computer goes on with other tasks. Use the *silence()* function to end the sound. The *note()* function uses this second method to generate a musical note.

The *warble()*, *weird()*, and *siren()* functions demonstrate a few of the sound effects you can generate. Each of these functions has timing and looping constants that you can change to create wildly different effects. Use the functions as starting points for further experimentation.

Some of the techniques presented in these functions are useful for programming tasks other than sound generation. For example, the *white_noise()* function employs a simple but useful technique for generating pseudorandom integers. The random numbers in the sequence are in the range 0 through 65,536 and are ideal for generating white noise. You can use the technique for similar purposes, although you should not use it to produce statistically random values.

The *wait_ticks()* function lets you delay a program for a given number of clock ticks. To explore clock functions at greater length, refer to the CLOCK toolbox module.

The SOUNTEST.C program is a simple recital in which various SOUND functions are called. The program displays the current call on the screen and waits for a keypress from the user before starting the next demonstration. Functions in the module that are not explicitly called, such as *sound()* or *silence()*, are used within the execution of other functions.

Demonstration Program: SOUNTEST.C

```
/* ----------------------------------------------------------------
   Name:          SOUNTEST.C
   Type:          Demonstration program
   Language:      Microsoft QuickC
   Video:         (no special video requirements)

   Program list:  SOUNTEST.C
                  SOUND.C

   Variables:     (none)

   Usage:         (no command line parameters)

   Description:   Demonstrates the SOUND toolbox functions
   ----------------------------------------------------------------
*/

#include <stdio.h>
#include <conio.h>
#include "sound.h"

main()
{
    printf( "\n\nPress any key to start each sound effect...\n" );
    getch();
    printf( "warble( 5 );\n" );
```

(continued)

SOUNTEST.C *continued*

```
    warble( 5 );
    getch();
    printf( "weird( 5 );\n" );
    weird( 5 );
    getch();
    printf( "white_noise( 40 );\n" );
    white_noise( 40 );
    getch();
    printf( "siren( 5 );\n" );
    siren( 5 );
    getch();
    printf( "note( 330, 5 );\n" );
    note( 330, 5 );
    printf( "note( 294, 5 );\n" );
    note( 294, 5 );
    printf( "note( 264, 5 );\n" );
    note( 264, 5 );
    printf( "note( 294, 5 );\n" );
    note( 294, 5 );
    printf( "note( 330, 5 );\n" );
    note( 330, 5 );
    printf( "note( 330, 5 );\n" );
    note( 330, 5 );
    printf( "note( 330, 5 );\n" );
    note( 330, 5 );
}
```

Include File: SOUND.H

```
/* -------------------------------------------------------------------
    Name:           SOUND.H
    Type:           Include
    Language:       Microsoft QuickC
    Demonstrated:   SOUND.C  SOUNTEST.C
    Description:    Prototypes and definitions for SOUND.C
    -------------------------------------------------------------------
*/

#ifndef SOUND_DEFINED
```

(continued)

SOUND.H *continued*

```
void sound( int );
void silence( void );
void speaker_toggle( void );
void wait_ticks( unsigned int );
void warble( int );
void weird( int );
void siren( int );
void white_noise( int );
void note( int, int );

#define SOUND_DEFINED
#endif
```

Toolbox Module: SOUND.C

```
/* -----------------------------------------------------------------
    Name:           SOUND.C
    Type:           Toolbox module
    Language:       Microsoft QuickC
    Demonstrated:   SOUNTEST.C
    Video:          (no special video requirements)
   -----------------------------------------------------------------
*/

#include <conio.h>
#include <time.h>
#include "sound.h"

static unsigned control;
static int control_flag = 1;
```

Function: *speaker_toggle()*

The *speaker_toggle()* function pulses the speaker alternately on and off. The module declares a static variable *control_flag* that reflects the state of the speaker. This flag enables each call to *speaker_toggle()* to reverse the signal to the speaker.

This function creates sounds in a way that is fundamentally different from that used in the *sound()* function. The *speaker_toggle()* function requires more direct controlling action by your program because each half of every sound wave requires a call to this function. Also, because the system interrupts the CPU regularly (and irregularly), you'll hear glitches in the sound quality during the interrupt-processing moments. For example, the clock interrupt happens about 18.2 times per second, producing a noticeable background clicking noise. This function is useful for creating white noise and other special sound effects.

```
/* - - - - - - - - - - - - - - - - - - - - - - - - - - - - - - - -
    Function:       speaker_toggle()
    Toolbox:        SOUND.C
    Demonstrated:   SOUNTEST.C

    Parameters:     (none)

    Returned:       (function returns nothing)

    Variables:      (none)

    Description:    Pulses the speaker on or off with each call
    - - - - - - - - - - - - - - - - - - - - - - - - - - - - - - -
*/

void speaker_toggle( void )
{
    if ( control_flag )
        {
        control = inp( 0x61 );
        control_flag = 0;
        }
    outp( 0x61, ( inp( 0x61 ) & 0xFE ) ^ 2 );
}
```

Function: *sound()*

The *sound()* function starts a tone or changes the current tone to a given frequency. The function divides the frequency into a special constant and uses the result to provide values for the ports that control the timer chip in the IBM PC. These values cause the timer to oscillate at a frequency that generates the intended output from the speaker.

The tone continues even after the *sound()* function returns. The calling program can continue with other tasks while the tone is sounding. Any program that calls *sound()* should call the *silence()* function to turn off the sound.

Notice that if a tone is currently being generated, the *sound()* function can access only the ports necessary for changing the frequency in the timer. This approach allows smooth transitions from frequency to frequency, as demonstrated by the *siren()* function.

```
/* - - - - - - - - - - - - - - - - - - - - - - - - - - - - - - - - - -
    Function:       sound()
    Toolbox:        SOUND.C
    Demonstrated:   SOUNTEST.C

    Parameters:
     (input)        frequency       Frequency of generated tone

    Returned:       (function returns nothing)

    Variables:      divisor         Timer value for given frequency

    Description:    Sets a tone at a given frequency
    - - - - - - - - - - - - - - - - - - - - - - - - - - - - - - - - -
*/

void sound( int frequency )
{
    unsigned divisor;

    divisor = (unsigned)( 1193180L / frequency );
    if ( control_flag )
        {
        outp( 0x43, 0xB6 );
        outp( 0x42, divisor % 256 );
        outp( 0x42, divisor / 256 );
        control = inp( 0x61 );
        control_flag = 0;
        }
    else
        {
        divisor = (unsigned)( 1193180L / frequency );
        outp( 0x42, divisor % 256 );
        outp( 0x42, divisor / 256 );
        }
    outp( 0x61, control | 3 );
}
```

Function: *silence()*

The *silence()* function terminates the tone previously set by the *sound()* function.

```
/* - - - - - - - - - - - - - - - - - - - - - - - - - - - - - - - - - - - -
   Function:       silence()
   Toolbox:        SOUND.C
   Demonstrated:   SOUNTEST.C

   Parameters:     (none)

   Returned:       (function returns nothing)

   Variables:      (none)

   Description:    Turns off the tone generator
   - - - - - - - - - - - - - - - - - - - - - - - - - - - - - - - - - - - -
*/

void silence( void )
{
    outp( 0x61, control );
    control_flag = 1;
}
```

Function: *wait_ticks()*

The *wait_ticks()* function delays execution of a program for a given number of clock ticks. Clock ticks occur approximately 18.2 times a second; with each tick, the system interrupts the computer to update the system time and to perform other housekeeping chores. The system time returned by the QuickC *clock()* function is accurate only to the nearest clock tick, so clock ticks become a convenient unit to count.

The *wait_ticks()* function is useful in any program that requires a fixed interval of time. The *warble()* function calls it to provide a short but noticeable duration for each of three frequencies.

```
/* - - - - - - - - - - - - - - - - - - - - - - - - - - - - - - - -

   Function:      wait_ticks()
   Toolbox:       SOUND.C
   Demonstrated:  SOUNTEST.C

   Parameters:
     (input)      ticks          Number of clock ticks

   Returned:      (function returns nothing)

   Variables:     now            Time as returned by sound()

   Description:   Delays for a given number of clock ticks
   - - - - - - - - - - - - - - - - - - - - - - - - - - - - - - - -
*/

void wait_ticks( unsigned ticks )
{
    clock_t now;

    do
        {
        now = clock();
        while ( clock() == now )
            { ; }
        }
    while ( --ticks );
}
```

Function: *warble()*

The *warble()* function creates a warbling sound by toggling three tones in succession. Each frequency has a duration of one clock tick, or about 1/18.2 of a second. The function expects one parameter, which indicates the number of times to cycle through the warbling sound.

By changing the frequencies specified in the function itself, you can create quite different sound effects.

```
/* - - - - - - - - - - - - - - - - - - - - - - - - - - - - - - - - - - -
    Function:      warble()
    Toolbox:       SOUND.C
    Demonstrated:  SOUNTEST.C

    Parameters:
      (input)      count      Number of warble cycles

    Returned:      (function returns nothing)

    Variables:     (none)

    Description:   Creates a three-tone warble
    - - - - - - - - - - - - - - - - - - - - - - - - - - - - - - - - - - -
*/

void warble( int count )
{
    do
        {
        sound( 500 );
        wait_ticks( 1 );
        sound( 2000 );
        wait_ticks( 1 );
        sound( 1000 );
        wait_ticks( 1 );
        sound( 750 );
        wait_ticks( 1 );
        }
    while ( --count );

    silence();
}
```

Function: *weird()*

The *weird()* function creates a sound effect that might have come from
an old science fiction movie. Feel free to experiment with the looping
ranges and increments to create a wide range of similar sounds.

```
/* - - - - - - - - - - - - - - - - - - - - - - - - - - - - - - - -

    Function:      weird()
    Toolbox:       SOUND.C
    Demonstrated:  SOUNTEST.C

    Parameters:    count      Number of sound generation cycles

    Returned:      (function returns nothing)

    Variables:     i          Looping index
                   j          Tone frequency

    Description:   Creates a modulated sound
    - - - - - - - - - - - - - - - - - - - - - - - - - - - - - - -
*/

void weird( int count )
{
    int i, j;

    sound( 50 );
    do
        for ( i = 50; i < 1200; i += 100 )
            for ( j = i; j < i + 1200; j += 5 )
                sound( j );
    while ( --count );

    silence();
}
```

Function: *siren()*

The *siren()* function produces a sound similar to that of a squad car siren. The function calls *sound()* with a series of increasing frequency values and then with a series of decreasing values to impart a sliding effect to the generated tones.

```
/* - - - - - - - - - - - - - - - - - - - - - - - - - - - - - - -
    Function:       siren()
    Toolbox:        SOUND.C
    Demonstrated:   SOUNTEST.C

    Parameters:     count     Number of sound generation cycles

    Returned:       (function returns nothing)

    Variables:      i         Looping index

    Description:    Creates a sound whose frequency rises and falls
    - - - - - - - - - - - - - - - - - - - - - - - - - - - - - - -
*/

void siren( int count )
{
    int i;

    sound( 50 );
    do
        {
        for ( i = 50; i < 2000; i++ )
            sound( i );
        for ( i = 2000; i > 50; i-- )
            sound( i );
        }
    while ( --count );

    silence();
}
```

Function: *white_noise()*

The *white_noise()* function generates white noise, sound composed of a wide range of frequencies. The result is a hissing noise, like static on the radio or ocean surf.

To create this sound, the function toggles the speaker at randomly spaced points in time. A simple pseudorandom integer generator provides a varying delay count between each toggle of the speaker. The *white_noise()* function demonstrates the use of *speaker_toggle()* to exercise direct control of the speaker.

```
/* - - - - - - - - - - - - - - - - - - - - - - - - - - - - - - - -

    Function:       white_noise()
    Toolbox:        SOUND.C
    Demonstrated:   SOUNTEST.C

    Parameters:     ticks     Number of clock ticks

    Returned:       (function returns nothing)

    Variables:      i         Looping index
                    rndm      Pseudorandom unsigned integer
                    now       Time as returned by clock()

    Description:    Generates white noise, a wide-ranging multifrequency
                    sound
    - - - - - - - - - - - - - - - - - - - - - - - - - - - - - - -
*/

void white_noise( int ticks )
{
    unsigned i, rndm;
    clock_t now;

    do
        {
        now = clock();
        while ( clock() == now )
            {
            speaker_toggle();
            rndm = rndm * 317 + 21317;
            for ( i = rndm & 0xFF; i; i-- )
                {;}
            }
        }
    while ( --ticks );

    silence();
}
```

Function: *note()*

The *note()* function generates a musical note, a tone with a given frequency and duration. The function calls the *sound()* function to start the tone, *wait_ticks()* to time its duration, and *silence()* to terminate it.

```
/* - - - - - - - - - - - - - - - - - - - - - - - - - - - - - - - -
   Function:       note()
   Toolbox:        SOUND.C
   Demonstrated:   SOUNTEST.C

   Parameters:     frequency     Frequency of the tone
                   ticks         Number of clock ticks

   Returned:       (function returns nothing)

   Variables:      (none)

   Description:    Creates a tone given its frequency and duration
   - - - - - - - - - - - - - - - - - - - - - - - - - - - - - - - -
*/

void note( int frequency, int ticks )
{
    sound( frequency );
    wait_ticks( ticks );
    silence();
}
```

STRINGS

FUNCTION	DESCRIPTION
s_ltrm()	Trims spaces from the left end of a string
s_rtrm()	Trims spaces from the right end of a string
s_trm()	Trims spaces from both ends of a string
s_rot()	Rotates characters left or right
s_ljust()	Left justifies a string
s_rjust()	Right justifies a string
s_center()	Centers a string
s_lrjust()	Justifies a string on both left and right margins
s_shuffle()	Randomizes character order
s_fill()	Fills a string using a second string
s_split()	Splits a string between words

The STRINGS toolbox module provides an assortment of functions that enhance the string-handling capabilities of QuickC.

All the STRINGS functions receive a string as a parameter, modify it in place, and then return the location of the modified string. Several functions create temporary string space in which to do their work and return NULL if the memory allocation fails.

The demonstration program, STRITEST.C, shows you how to use the STRINGS functions. The program defines and displays a sample string and then passes a copy of this string to each function in this module. STRITEST displays the syntax of each function call and the string the function returns.

Demonstration Program: STRITEST.C

```c
/* -------------------------------------------------------------------
   Name:          STRITEST.C
   Type:          Demonstration program
   Language:      Microsoft QuickC
   Video:         (no special video requirements)

   Program list:  STRITEST.C
                  STRINGS.C

   Variables:     txt0     Sample string for demonstrations
                  txt      Working copy of original string
                  txt2     Remainder of txt after s_split()

   Usage:         (no command line parameters)

   Description:   Demonstrates the STRINGS toolbox functions
   -------------------------------------------------------------------
*/

#include <stdio.h>
#include <string.h>

#include "strings.h"

main()
{
    char *txt0 = "  This is a short demonstration string.      ";
    char txt[80], txt2[80];

    printf( "\n\nOriginal string:\t\"%s\"\n", txt0 );

    strcpy( txt, txt0 );
    s_ltrm( txt );
    printf( "s_ltrm( txt ):\t\t\"%s\"\n", txt );

    strcpy( txt, txt0 );
    s_rtrm( txt );
    printf( "s_rtrm( txt ):\t\t\"%s\"\n", txt );

    strcpy( txt, txt0 );
    s_trm( txt );
    printf( "s_trm( txt ):\t\t\"%s\"\n", txt );
```

(continued)

STRITEST.C *continued*

```
      strcpy( txt, txt0 );
      s_rot( txt, 7 );
      printf( "s_rot( txt, 7 ):\t\"%s\"\n", txt );

      strcpy( txt, txt0 );
      s_rot( txt, -7 );
      printf( "s_rot( txt, -7 ):\t\"%s\"\n", txt );

      strcpy( txt, txt0 );
      s_ljust( txt );
      printf( "s_ljust( txt ):\t\t\"%s\"\n", txt );

      strcpy( txt, txt0 );
      s_rjust( txt );
      printf( "s_rjust( txt ):\t\t\"%s\"\n", txt );

      strcpy( txt, txt0 );
      s_center( txt );
      printf( "s_center( txt ):\t\"%s\"\n", txt );

      strcpy( txt, txt0 );
      s_lrjust( txt );
      printf( "s_lrjust( txt ):\t\"%s\"\n", txt );

      strcpy( txt, txt0 );
      s_shuffle( txt );
      printf( "s_shuffle( txt ):\t\"%s\"\n", txt );

      s_fill( txt, "xyz", 17 );
      printf( "s_fill( txt, \"xyz\", 17 ):\t\"%s\"\n", txt );

      strcpy( txt, txt0 );
      s_split( txt, txt2, 16 );
      printf( "s_split( txt, txt2, 16 )...\n\"%s\"\n\"%s\"\n", txt, txt2 );

      strcpy( txt, txt0 );
      s_split( txt, txt2, 17 );
      printf( "s_split( txt, txt2, 17 )...\n\"%s\"\n\"%s\"\n", txt, txt2 );

}
```

Include File: STRINGS.H

```
/* ------------------------------------------------------------------
     Name:          STRINGS.H
     Type:          Include
     Language:      Microsoft QuickC
     Demonstrated:  STRINGS.C  STRITEST.C
     Description:   Prototypes and definitions for STRINGS.C
   ------------------------------------------------------------------
*/

#ifndef STRINGS_DEFINED

char *s_ltrm( char * );
char *s_rtrm( char * );
char *s_trm( char * );
char *s_rot( char *, int );
char *s_ljust( char * );
char *s_rjust( char * );
char *s_center( char * );
char *s_lrjust( char * );
char *s_shuffle( char * );
char *s_fill( char *, char *, unsigned int );
char *s_split( char *, char *, unsigned int );

#define STRINGS_DEFINED
#endif
```

Toolbox Module: STRINGS.C

```
/* ------------------------------------------------------------------
     Name:          STRINGS.C
     Type:          Toolbox module
     Language:      Microsoft QuickC
     Demonstrated:  STRITEST.C
     Video:         (no special video requirements)
   ------------------------------------------------------------------
*/

#include <stdio.h>
#include <stdlib.h>
```

(continued)

STRINGS.C *continued*

```
#include <string.h>
#include <malloc.h>
#include <ctype.h>

#include "strings.h"
```

Function: *s_ltrm()*

The *s_ltrm()* function removes spaces from the beginning of a string and returns the modified string. The function shifts the string contents to the left until no spaces remain at the left side of the string.

```
/* - - - - - - - - - - - - - - - - - - - - - - - - - - - - - - - - - -
    Function:        s_ltrm()
    Toolbox:         STRINGS.C
    Demonstrated:    STRITEST.C

    Parameters:
      (in/out)       s1          String to be modified

    Returned:        The modified string

    Variables:       i           First nonspace character
                     j           Looping index
                     len         Length of the string

    Description:     Trims spaces from left end of a string
    - - - - - - - - - - - - - - - - - - - - - - - - - - - - - - - - - -
*/

char *s_ltrm( char *s1 )
{
    unsigned i = 0, j = 0, len;

    /* Get length of string */
    len = strlen( s1 );

    /* Find first nonspace character */
    while ( i < len && s1[i] == ' ' )
        i++;
```

(continued)

```
    /* Shuffle the characters */
    while ( i <= len )
        s1[j++] = s1[i++];

    /* Return the string */
    return ( s1 );
}
```

Function: *s_rtrm()*

The *s_rtrm()* function trims spaces from the end of a string and returns the modified string. The function replaces each space at the right end of the string with a null character, '0'. These substitutions effectively shorten the string.

```
/* - - - - - - - - - - - - - - - - - - - - - - - - - - - - - -
    Function:      s_rtrm()
    Toolbox:       STRINGS.C
    Demonstrated:  STRITEST.C

    Parameters:
      (in/out)     s1         String to be modified

    Returned:      The modified string

    Variables:     len        Length of the string

    Description:   Trims spaces from right end of a string
    - - - - - - - - - - - - - - - - - - - - - - - - - - - - - -
*/

char *s_rtrm( char *s1 )
{
    unsigned len;

    /* Get length of the string */
    len = strlen( s1 );

    /* Chop off trailing spaces */
    while( s1[--len] == ' ' )
        s1[len] = '\0';
```

(continued)

STRINGS.C *continued*

```
    /* Return the string */
    return ( s1 );
}
```

Function: *s_trm()*

The *s_trm()* function trims spaces from both ends of a string and returns the modified string. The function calls *s_ltrm()* and *s_rtrm()* to remove the spaces.

```
/* - - - - - - - - - - - - - - - - - - - - - - - - - - - - - - - -

    Function:       s_trm()
    Toolbox:        STRINGS.C
    Demonstrated:   STRITEST.C

    Parameters:
      (in/out)      s1          String to be modified

    Returned:       The modified string

    Variables:      (none)

    Description:    Trims spaces from both ends of a string
    - - - - - - - - - - - - - - - - - - - - - - - - - - - - - - - -
*/

char *s_trm( char *s1 )
{
    /* Trim the right end of the string */
    s_rtrm( s1 );

    /* Trim the left end of the string */
    s_ltrm( s1 );

    /* Return the string */
    return ( s1 );
}
```

Function: *s_rot()*

The *s_rot()* function rotates the contents of a string by n character places and returns the modified string. If n is positive, the function rotates the characters to the right; if n is negative, the rotation occurs to the left.

The function allocates memory for temporary working space and returns NULL if it can't allocate the necessary space.

```
/* - - - - - - - - - - - - - - - - - - - - - - - - - - - - - - - - - -
    Function:       s_rot()
    Toolbox:        STRINGS.C
    Demonstrated:   STRITEST.C

    Parameters:
      (in/out)      s1          String to be modified
                    n           Number of places to rotate

    Returned:       The modified string

    Variables:      i           Looping index
                    len         Length of the string
                    tmp         Working copy of the string

    Description:    Rotates characters in a string n places.  If n
                    is positive, rotation occurs to the right; if
                    negative, rotation occurs to the left.
    - - - - - - - - - - - - - - - - - - - - - - - - - - - - - - - - -
*/

char *s_rot( char *s1, int n )
{
    int i, len;
    char *tmp;

    /* Get the length of the string */
    len = strlen( s1 );

    /* Change the sign of n */
    n = (-n);

    /* Make sure n is less than length of s1 */
    if ( n >= len )
        n %= len;
```

(continued)

STRINGS.C *continued*

```
    /* Make sure n is positive */
    if ( n < 0 )
        {
        n %= len;
        n += len;
        }

    /* Get a temporary copy of the string */
    if (( tmp = strdup( s1 )) == NULL )
        return ( NULL );

    /* Move 'em */
    for ( i = 0; i < len; i++ )
        {
        *s1++ = *( tmp + n );
        if ( ++n >= len )
            n -= len;
        }

    /* Delete the temporary string copy */
    free( tmp );

    /* Return the string */
    return ( s1 );
}
```

Function: *s_ljust()*

The *s_ljust()* function left justifies a string and returns the modified string. The function does not change the string length, but it moves spaces at the beginning of the string to the end of the string until the first character in the string is a nonspace character.

```
/* - - - - - - - - - - - - - - - - - - - - - - - - - - - - - - - -

   Function:      s_ljust()
   Toolbox:       STRINGS.C
   Demonstrated:  STRITEST.C

   Parameters:
     (in/out)     s1         String to be modified
```

(continued)

```
    Returned:        The modified string

    Variables:       i         Looping index
                     len1      Length of the string before trim
                     len2      Length of the string after trim

    Description:     Justifies string to left.  Leading spaces are
                     moved to the end of the string.
    - - - - - - - - - - - - - - - - - - - - - - - - - - - - - -
*/

char *s_ljust( char *s1 )
{
    unsigned i, len1, len2;

    /* Get the starting string length */
    len1 = strlen( s1 );

    /* Trim spaces from left */
    s_ltrm( s1 );

    /* Get new string length */
    len2 = strlen( s1 );

    /* Pad on right to original length */
    for ( i = len2; i < len1; i++ )
        s1[i] = ' ';

    /* Return the string */
    return ( s1 );
}
```

Function: *s_rjust()*

The *s_rjust()* function right justifies a string. The function does not change the string length, but it moves spaces at the end of the string to the beginning of the string until the last character in the string is a nonspace character.

```
/* - - - - - - - - - - - - - - - - - - - - - - - - - - - - - - - -
    Function:       s_rjust()
    Toolbox:        STRINGS.C
    Demonstrated:   STRITEST.C

    Parameters:
     (in/out)       s1          String to be modified

    Returned:       The modified string

    Variables:      i           Looping index
                    len1        Length of the string before trim
                    len2        Length of the string after trim
                    dlen        Difference in the string lengths

    Description:    Right justifies string.  Moves trailing
                    spaces to the start of the string.
    - - - - - - - - - - - - - - - - - - - - - - - - - - - - - - - -
*/

char *s_rjust( char *s1 )
{
    unsigned i, len1, len2, dlen;

    /* Get the starting string length */
    len1 = strlen( s1 );

    /* Trim spaces from right */
    s_rtrm( s1 );

    /* Get new string length */
    len2 = strlen( s1 );

    /* Get the difference in lengths */
    dlen = len1 - len2;

    /* Shift string to right */
    while ( len2 )
        s1[--len1] = s1[--len2];

    /* Pad on left with spaces */
    for ( i = 0; i < dlen; i++ )
        s1[i] = ' ';

    /* Return the string */
    return ( s1 );
}
```

Function: *s_center()*

The *s_center()* function centers a string. The function does not change the string length. It effectively rotates the string left or right until the number of spaces at each end is the same or differs by only 1.

```
/* - - - - - - - - - - - - - - - - - - - - - - - - - - - - - - - - -
    Function:      s_center()
    Toolbox:       STRINGS.C
    Demonstrated:  STRITEST.C

    Parameters:
     (in/out)      s1          String to be modified

    Returned:      The modified string

    Variables:     i           Count of spaces on left end
                   j           Count of spaces on right end
                   len         Length of the string

    Description:   Centers a string by balancing spaces on each end
    - - - - - - - - - - - - - - - - - - - - - - - - - - - - - - - -
*/

char *s_center( char *s1 )
{
    int i = 0, j, len;

    /* Get the starting string length */
    len = strlen( s1 );

    /* Count spaces on left */
    while ( s1[i] == ' ' && i < len )
        i++;

    /* Count spaces on right */
    j = len - 1;
    while ( s1[j] == ' ' && j )
        j--;

    /* Rotate string to center it */
    s_rot( s1, ( len - j - i - 1 ) / 2 );

    /* Return the string */
    return ( s1 );
}
```

Function: *s_lrjust()*

The *s_lrjust()* function justifies a string on both the left and right ends. The function does not change the string length. It shuffles space characters until it achieves a nearly equal distribution between words. The resulting string begins and ends with nonspace characters.

This function is commonly used in word-processing programs to format entire paragraphs so that the words at the ends of each line are flush with the left and right margins.

```
/* - - - - - - - - - - - - - - - - - - - - - - - - - - - - - - - -
    Function:       s_lrjust()
    Toolbox:        STRINGS.C
    Demonstrated:   STRITEST.C

    Parameters:
      (in/out)      s1          String to be modified

    Returned:       The modified string

    Variables:      i           Looping index
                    len         Length of the string
                    spc         Number of spaces in the string
                    wrd         Number of words in the string
                    spcflg      Indicates run of spaces
                    minspc      Minimum number of spaces between words
                    extraspc    Number of extra spaces to insert
                    tmp         Temporary working string
                    wrk         Temporary working string
                    pad         Temporary working string

    Description:    Justifies a string by adding and removing spaces
                    so that the spacing is even and so that no spaces
                    remain at either end
    - - - - - - - - - - - - - - - - - - - - - - - - - - - - - - - -
*/

char *s_lrjust( char *s1 )
{
    unsigned i, len;
    unsigned spc = 0, wrd = 0, spcflg = 1;
    unsigned minspc, extraspc;
    char *tmp, *wrk, *pad;
```

(continued)

```
    /* Get the starting string length */
    len = strlen( s1 );

    /* Count words and spaces in string */
    for ( i = 0; i < len; i++ )
        if ( s1[i] == ' ' )
            {
            spc++;
            spcflg = 1;
            }
        else
            if ( spcflg )
                {
                wrd++;
                spcflg = 0;
                }

    /* If fewer than two words or no spaces, go no further */
    if ( wrd < 2 || !spc )
        return ( s1 );

    /* Calculate minimum spaces between words */
    minspc = spc / ( wrd - 1 );

    /* Get a string for the minimum spaces */
    if (( pad = (char *)malloc( (size_t)( minspc + 1 ))) == NULL )
        return ( NULL );

    /* Fill the pad string with spaces */
    pad[minspc] = '\0';
    for ( i = 0; i < minspc; i++ )
        pad[i] = ' ';

    /* Calculate number of extra spaces */
    extraspc = spc - ( wrd - 1 ) * minspc;

    /* Get a temporary string for deciding extra spaces */
    if (( tmp = (char *)malloc( (size_t)wrd )) == NULL )
        return ( NULL );
```

(continued)

STRINGS.C *continued*

```
    /* Fill tmp with 1s and 0s to represent extra spaces */
    tmp[wrd - 1] = '\0';
    for ( i = 0; i < wrd - 1; i++ )
        if ( i < extraspc )
            tmp[i] = '1';
        else
            tmp[i] = '0';

    /* Shuffle the order of the 1s and 0s */
    s_shuffle( tmp );

    /* Get working copy of the string */
    if (( wrk = strdup( s1 )) == NULL )
        return ( NULL );

    /* Get first word into new s1 */
    strcpy( s1, strtok( wrk, " " ));

    /* Build rest of string */
    for ( i = 0; i < wrd - 1; i++ )
        {

        /* Add minimum spaces */
        strcat( s1, pad );

        /* Add spare space if indicated */
        if ( tmp[i] == '1' )
            strcat( s1, " " );

        /* Get next word */
        strcat( s1, strtok( NULL, " " ));
        }

    /* Delete the working strings */
    free( wrk );
    free( tmp );
    free( pad );

    /* Return the string */
    return ( s1 );
}
```

Function: *s_shuffle()*

The *s_shuffle()* function shuffles the characters in a string. The function uses *rand()* to randomize the order of the characters in a string.

The *s_ljust()* function uses *s_shuffle()* to distribute at random the extra spaces between words as a string is justified. You might also use *s_shuffle()* for word games.

```
/* - - - - - - - - - - - - - - - - - - - - - - - - - - - - - - - - - -
   Function:      s_shuffle()
   Toolbox:       STRINGS.C
   Demonstrated:  STRITEST.C

   Parameters:
    (in/out)      s1         String to be modified

   Returned:      The modified string

   Variables:     i          Looping index
                  j          Random character index
                  k          Swapping variable
                  len        Length of the string

   Description:   Shuffle a string by randomizing character order
   - - - - - - - - - - - - - - - - - - - - - - - - - - - - - - - - - -
*/

char *s_shuffle( char *s1 )
{
    unsigned i, j, k, len;

    /* Get the length of the string */
    len = strlen( s1 );

    /* Randomize the order of the characters */
    for ( i = 0; i < len; i++ )
        {
        j = rand() % len;
        k = (unsigned)s1[i];
        s1[i] = s1[j];
        s1[j] = (char)k;
        }

    /* Return the string */
    return ( s1 );
}
```

Function: *s_fill()*

The *s_fill()* function fills a string to length *n* with characters from a fill string and returns the modified string. The function concatenates the contents of the fill string (repeatedly, if necessary) until a given length is achieved. A terminating null character is added to the end of the resulting string.

The function is useful for filling a string with spaces or with any other pattern of characters.

```
/* - - - - - - - - - - - - - - - - - - - - - - - - - - - - - - - -
    Function:       s_fill()
    Toolbox:        STRINGS.C
    Demonstrated:   STRITEST.C

    Parameters:
      (in/out)      s1          String to be modified
      (input)       fill        String to use for filling
      (input)       len         Desired length of string

    Returned:       The modified string

    Variables:      i           Looping index
                    j           Random character index
                    flen        Length of the fill string

    Description:    Fills a string to the given length by using
                    multiple copies of the fill string
    - - - - - - - - - - - - - - - - - - - - - - - - - - - - - - - -
*/
char *s_fill( char *s1, char *fill, unsigned len )
{
    unsigned i, j, flen;

    /* Get the length of the fill string */
    flen = strlen( fill );

    /* Work through string */
    for ( i = j = 0; i < len; i++ )
        {
        s1[i] = fill[j++];
        if ( j == flen )
            j = 0;
        }
```

(continued)

STRINGS.C *continued*

```
    /* Terminate the string */
    s1[len] = '\0';

    /* Return the string */
    return ( s1 );
}
```

Function: *s_split()*

The *s_split()* function splits a string between words to produce a string whose length is less than or equal to a given value n. This is a useful formatting task, one that is commonly required in word-processing programs.

The *s_split()* function returns the first part of the string and places the remaining part in the string specified in the second parameter. Be sure to declare the second string of sufficient size to accommodate the remainder of the first string after the split. To break the string into several strings with a length less than n, you can call the function repeatedly.

To place the break between words, *s_split()* searches the string for a space character, beginning at the nth position and proceeding toward the start of the string.

```
/* - - - - - - - - - - - - - - - - - - - - - - - - - - - - - -
    Function:       s_split()
    Toolbox:        STRINGS.C
    Demonstrated:   STRITEST.C

    Parameters:
      (in/out)      s1         String to be split
      (output)      s2         Returns rest of the string
      (input)       n          Maximum length of split first string

    Returned:       The original string, truncated

    Variables:      len        Length of the string

    Description:    Splits a string between words
    - - - - - - - - - - - - - - - - - - - - - - - - - - - - - -
*/
```

(continued)

STRINGS.C *continued*

```
char *s_split( char *s1, char *s2, unsigned n )
{
    unsigned len;

    /* Get the length of the string */
    len = strlen( s1 );

    /* If string is short enough, we're almost done */
    if ( n >= len )
        {
        s2[0] = '\0';
        return ( s1 );
        }

    /* Find last space character before the split */
    while ( s1[n] != ' ' && n )
        n--;

    /* If no space found then don't split */
    if ( !n )
        {
        s2[0] = '\0';
        return ( s1 );
        }

    /* Make the split */
    strcpy( s2, &s1[n + 1] );

    /* Trim spaces from end of first string */
    while ( s1[n] == ' ' )
        s1[n--] = '\0';

    /* Return the first string */
    return ( s1 );
}
```

UTILITIES

ABOUT
THE UTILITIES

The utility programs in this part of the book are tools for working with files, directories, and QuickC source code. Although most of the utilities perform standard tasks, some provide unusual capabilities. For example, the OUT program can be valuable for creating batch files that send escape code control sequences to the printer and to ANSI.SYS.

Some of the utilities call toolbox functions presented in Part II. The CIPHER program, for example, uses random numbers generated by functions in the RANDOMS toolbox module. The program list in the comment block at the start of each utility program indicates which toolbox module or modules are required.

Syntax and Wildcards

The command syntax for each utility is presented in the source file header and in the descriptive text that precedes each listing. In the text, syntax statements use a few simple conventions. Formal elements (as opposed to literally typed elements) are shown in italics. A gray background indicates an optional entry, and a parameter with an underscore arrow can be replaced with multiple entries. The following sample illustrates these conventions:

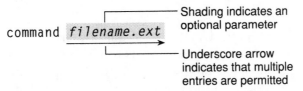

command *filename.ext*

Shading indicates an optional parameter

Underscore arrow indicates that multiple entries are permitted

Wildcard expansion is a useful feature in many utilities that operate on one or more files. For example, the DETAB utility opens a file and replaces tabs with a specified number of space characters. The DETAB utility lets you use wildcard characters to specify filenames on the command line. The command *DETAB 4 WORDS.C* replaces tabs with spaces aligned at every fourth column in the file WORDS.C; however, the command *DETAB 4 *.C* takes advantage of the wildcard-expanding capability of DETAB to replace the tabs in all C source files in the current directory. The CIPHER and REFRESH utilities provide further illustrations of wildcard processing.

Two details are critical when you compile and link a program that uses wildcard expansion. First, remember to create a program list for the program that contains the file SETARGV.OBJ. (You can enter the full path to SETARGV.OBJ in the program list, or you can copy the file into the current working directory.) Second, you must turn off the Extended Dictionary flag before you compile the program. To check the status of this flag, choose Make from the Options menu and then choose Linker Flags. If an *X* appears beside the Extended Dictionary flags, tab to that option and press the Spacebar to clear it.

I/O Redirection

Some of the utilities in Part III are written as filters, programs that process a stream of data from standard input and send the results to standard output. The WORDS program is a utility that counts and reports the total number of words from standard input. When you run WORDS, it counts all the words you type at the keyboard until you press Ctrl-Z. By default, the program displays the word count on the screen.

The DOS redirection operators often enable you to use filters more effectively. For example, you can use the input redirection operator (<) to make a file, rather than the keyboard, the source of input for a program. Likewise, you can use the output redirection operator (>) to send program output to a file or to a printer. For example, the command

```
C>words < words.c > prn
```

sends the word count in WORDS.C to your printer.

Another type of redirection lets you use the pipe operator (¦) to send the output of one program directly to the input of another. For example, DOS provides a filter program named SORT that alphabetically sorts the input lines. To sort a file of names and then count the number of words in the sorted output, you could enter the command

```
C>type names.txt ¦ sort ¦ words
```

DOS pipes the NAMES.TXT file into the SORT filter, redirects the result into the WORDS utility, and displays the final word count.

BASE

SYNTAX

base *number*

number is a value expressed in binary, octal, hexadecimal, or ASCII format.

The BASE program converts an integer from one common number base to its equivalent in each of the other common numeric systems. You can represent the value to be converted in decimal, octal, hexadecimal, or ASCII form, and the program will display equivalent values for all three bases and the ASCII character associated with the equivalent binary value.

When you run the utility, enter the value you want to convert on the command line after the program name. The program checks the first one or two characters of the number to determine the base of the data. If the first character is a nonzero digit, the number is assumed to be a decimal (base 10) integer. If the first character is a *0*, BASE checks the second character as well. A digit in the second position indicates an octal (base 8) value, and an *X* (or a lowercase *x*) indicates a hexadecimal (base 16) entry. A single quotation mark in the first position indicates that the subsequent character is an ASCII character value.

Consider the following example:

```
C>base 100

Dec: 100
Hex: 0x64
Oct: 0144
Chr: 'd'
```

The BASE utility converts decimal 100 to the hexadecimal equivalent 0x64, the octal equivalent 0144, and the corresponding ASCII character 'd'. In a similar way, the command *base 0x100* converts hexadecimal 100, and *base 0100* converts octal 100. To convert the binary byte value for a lowercase *a*, enter *base 'a*. In each case, the BASE utility displays the value in all four formats.

The BASE program demonstrates a simple use of a command line parameter, which is accessed in the *argv* variable. The program might also have checked the command line parameter count, passed to *main()* in *argc*, to verify that the command line contains both parameters (strictly speaking, the name of the program is counted as a parameter), but in this case the program simply prints some random value if no number is given. The other programs in this book that access command line parameters do check for the correct number of command line entries. You might try adding such a check to this program.

```
/* ------------------------------------------------------------------
    Name:           BASE.C
    Type:           Utility program
    Language:       Microsoft QuickC
    Video:          (no special video requirements)

    Program list:   (not required)

    Usage:          base number
                    Where number is expressed as one of the following:
                    base nnn      (decimal)
                    base 0xnnn    (hexadecimal)
                    base 0nnn     (octal)
                    base 'c'      (character)

    Description:    Converts number to four common number bases
    ------------------------------------------------------------------
*/

#include <stdio.h>
#include <stdlib.h>
#include <math.h>

main( int argc, char *argv[] )
{
    char *buf;
    char fmt[8];
    char c1, c2;
    int n = 0;

    /* Get the second command line parameter */
    buf = argv[1];
```

(continued)

```
    /* Grab the first two characters */
    c1 = *buf;
    c2 = *( buf + 1 );

    /* Is first character a single quotation mark? */
    if ( c1 == '\'' )
        {
        buf++;
        sscanf( buf, "%c", &n );
        }

    /* Is the number octal or hexadecimal? */
    else if ( c1 == '0' )
        {

        /* Is it hexadecimal? */
        if ( c2 == 'x' || c2 == 'X' )
            {
            buf += 2;
            sscanf(buf,"%x",&n);
            }

        /* Must be octal */
        else
            sscanf( buf, "%o", &n );
        }

    /* Must be decimal */
    else
        sscanf( buf,"%d",&n );

    /* Print number in all four formats */
    printf( "\nDec: %d",n );
    if ( n < 0 )
        printf( "     %u",n );
    printf( "\nHex: 0x%X",n );
    printf( "\nOct: 0%o",n );
    printf( "\nChr: '%c'\n",n );

    /* All done */
    return ( 0 );
}
```

BINTOHEX

SYNTAX

```
bintohex infile.ext outfile.ext
```

infile.ext is a binary file to be converted to hexadecimal characters.
outfile.ext is the filename for the hexadecimal output file.

The BINTOHEX program converts any file to a file of hexadecimal characters. The created file is a standard text file that contains no graphics or control characters. Such a file is suitable for editing, viewing, or printing and can be transmitted reliably over a modem using the normal ASCII transfer protocol.

A user who receives a printed copy of the created hexadecimal file can easily enter the series of numbers as a text file and then process that file with the companion program HEXTOBIN to re-create the original file. For example, an 11-byte program named NUMLOCK.COM is a useful addition to AUTOEXEC.BAT—it clears the Num Lock light during the bootup process. NUMLOCK.COM is a binary file, and you would therefore have difficulty sending a copy in a letter to a friend. By entering the command

```
C>bintohex numlock.com numlock.hex
```

you can create a file that contains one line of hexadecimal characters:

```
B8 40 00 8E D8 31 C0 A3 - 17 00 C3
```

Print a copy of this file and drop it in the mail. Using any text editor, your friend could enter this line of text into a new file and then use the HEXTOBIN program to re-create the original NUMLOCK.COM file.

See the HEXTOBIN utility on page 433 for more information about converting the hexadecimal files to their original binary form.

```
/* ----------------------------------------------------------------
    Name:           BINTOHEX.C
    Type:           Utility program
    Language:       Microsoft QuickC
    Video:          (no special video requirements)

    Program list:   (not required)

    Usage:          bintohex infile.ext outfile.ext

    Description:    Converts any file to an ASCII file of hexadecimal
                    characters.  Use HEXTOBIN to reverse the process.
   ----------------------------------------------------------------
*/

#include <stdio.h>
#include <stdlib.h>

main( int argc, char *argv[] )
{
    int c;
    int n = 0;
    FILE *fin, *fout;

    /* Verify command line parameters */
    if ( argc != 3 )
        {
        fprintf( stderr, "Usage: bintohex infile.ext outfile.ext\n" );
        exit( 1 );
        }

    /* Try to open the input file */
    if (( fin = fopen( argv[1], "rb" )) == NULL )
        {
        fprintf( stderr, "Can't open %s\n", argv[1] );
        exit( 1 );
        }

    /* Try to open the output file */
    if (( fout = fopen( argv[2], "wb" )) == NULL )
        {
        fprintf( stderr, "Can't open %s\n", argv[2] );
        exit( 1 );
        }
```

(continued)

BINTOHEX.C *continued*

```
    /* Process each byte of the file */
    while (( c = fgetc( fin )) != EOF )
        {
        fprintf( fout, "%2.2X ", c );

        /* Group eight bytes each side of "-" */
        if ( ++n == 8 )
            fprintf( fout,"- " );

        /* 16 bytes per output line */
        if ( n == 16 )
            {
            n = 0;
            fprintf( fout, "\r\n" );
            }
        }

    /* End the last line */
    fprintf( fout, "\n" );

    /* Close the files */
    fclose( fin );
    fclose( fout );

    /* All done */
    return ( 0 );
}
```

CALC

SYNTAX

calc *numbers* *operation*

numbers is one or more optional operands.
operator specifies the calculation to be performed.
CALC can handle a series of operations on a single command line.

The CALC utility provides convenient scientific calculator functions from the DOS command line. You can easily expand the program to include any new functions you might want to add. Use the existing CALC functions as templates for creating others.

This calculator uses RPN (reverse Polish notation) for keeping track of intermediate values. Each number entered is pushed onto a last-in-first-out stack. (Actually, this program simulates such a stack by keeping the values in an indexed array. The concept is the same, however.)

Begin by compiling and linking the CALC.C program to create CALC.EXE. To use the program, you need to be able to enter calculations using RPN. Consider the problem of adding 4 to 5 and then subtracting 2. To find the result using CALC, enter the following command at the DOS prompt:

C>calc 4 5 + 2 -

The CALC program receives the five subsequent parameters in the *argv* array and processes them in the order in which they appear. (Be sure to separate all numbers and operators with spaces.) The value 4 is "pushed onto the stack," followed by the value 5. The + parameter causes the two preceding values to be added, and the result (9) replaces the two values on the stack. The value 2 is then pushed onto the stack, and the − parameter causes the 2 to be subtracted from 9 and leaves the value 7 on the stack. After CALC processes all the command line parameters, it displays the contents of the stack.

The + and − parameters are examples of operations that use two stack values and return a single result to the stack. Other operations might use fewer values, and some functions replace the operands with two, rather than one, resulting values. For example, the SIN (sine) function uses one value and pushes one result onto the stack. To find the sine of 0.5, enter the following command:

```
C>calc .5 sin
```

The value 0.5 is used by the SIN operation, and the result, 0.479426, is then pushed onto the stack.

The SIN operation is among seven existing CALC operations that use one value and return one result:

SQR	Square root
SIN	Sine
COS	Cosine
TAN	Tangent
ASN	Arc sine
ACS	Arc cosine
ATN	Arc tangent

Six operations use two values and return one result:

+	Addition
−	Subtraction
*	Multiplication
/	Division
ANG	Angle from origin to point x,y
POW	Power operation, y raised to exponent x

Three operations demonstrate other combinations of operands and returned results:

RND	Generates a random number in the range 0 to 1. Uses no operands and pushes one result onto the stack.
DUP	Duplicates the last value entered. Uses one operand and pushes two results onto the stack.
SWP	Swaps the order of the last two values entered. Uses two operands and pushes two results onto the stack.

```
/* -------------------------------------------------------------------
   Name:          CALC.C
   Type:          Utility program
   Language:      Microsoft QuickC
   Video:         (no special video requirements)

   Program list: (not required)

   Usage:         calc [numbers] operation ...

   Description:   Command line calculator using reverse Polish
                  notation
   -------------------------------------------------------------------
*/

#include <stdio.h>
#include <stdlib.h>
#include <string.h>
#include <math.h>
#include <time.h>

#define MAXSTK  50
#define AOK      0
#define NOTENUF  1
#define UFLOW    2

/* Function prototypes */
void process( char * );
void error_return( int );

/* Global variables */
double stk[MAXSTK];
int ptr = -1;

main( int argc, char *argv[] )
{
    int i;

    /* Check for minimum number of command line parameters */
    if ( argc < 2 )
        error_return( NOTENUF );
```

(continued)

CALC.C *continued*

```
    /* Shuffle the random numbers */
    srand( (unsigned)time( NULL ));

    /* Process each command line parameter */
    for ( i = 1; i < argc; i++ )
        process( argv[i] );

    /* Display the results */
    printf( "\n" );
    if ( !ptr )
        printf( "Result:  %16G\n", stk[0] );
    else
        for ( i = 0; i <= ptr; i++ )
            printf( "Stack[%d]:\t%16G\n", ptr - i + 1, stk[i] );

    /* All done */
    return ( AOK );
}

/*
    Processes each command line parameter
*/
void process( char *cmd )
{
    double tmp;

    /* Addition */
    if ( !strcmp( cmd, "+" ))
        {
        if ( ptr > 0 )
            {
            ptr--;
            stk[ptr] += stk[ptr + 1];
            }
        else
            error_return( UFLOW );
        }

    /* Subtraction */
    else if ( !strcmp( cmd, "-" ))
        {
        if ( ptr > 0 )
```

(continued)

```
            {
            ptr--;
            stk[ptr] -= stk[ptr + 1];
            }
        else
            error_return( UFLOW );
        }

    /* Multiplication */
    else if ( !strcmp( cmd, "*" ))
        {
        if ( ptr > 0 )
            {
            ptr--;
            stk[ptr] *= stk[ptr + 1];
            }
        else
            error_return( UFLOW );
        }

    /* Division */
    else if ( !strcmp( cmd, "/" ))
        {
        if ( ptr > 0 )
            {
            ptr--;
            stk[ptr] /= stk[ptr + 1];
            }
        else
            error_return( UFLOW );
        }

    /* Square root */
    else if ( !strcmp( strupr( cmd ), "SQR" ))
        {
        if ( ptr >= 0 )
            stk[ptr] = sqrt( stk[ptr] );
        else
            error_return( UFLOW );
        }
```

(continued)

CALC.C *continued*

```
    /* Sine */
    else if ( !strcmp( strupr( cmd ), "SIN" ))
        {
        if ( ptr >= 0 )
            stk[ptr] = sin( stk[ptr] );
        else
            error_return( UFLOW );
        }

    /* Cosine */
    else if ( !strcmp( strupr( cmd ), "COS" ))
        {
        if ( ptr >= 0 )
            stk[ptr] = cos( stk[ptr] );
        else
            error_return( UFLOW );
        }

    /* Tangent */
    else if ( !strcmp( strupr( cmd ), "TAN" ))
        {
        if ( ptr >= 0 )
            stk[ptr] = tan( stk[ptr] );
        else
            error_return( UFLOW );
        }

    /* Arc sine */
    else if ( !strcmp( strupr( cmd ), "ASN" ))
        {
        if ( ptr >= 0 )
            stk[ptr] = asin( stk[ptr] );
        else
            error_return( UFLOW );
        }

    /* Arc cosine */
    else if ( !strcmp( strupr( cmd ), "ACS" ))
        {
        if ( ptr >= 0 )
            stk[ptr] = acos( stk[ptr] );
```

(continued)

CALC.C *continued*

```
        else
            error_return( UFLOW );
        }

    /* Arc tangent */
    else if ( !strcmp( strupr( cmd ), "ATN" ))
        {
        if ( ptr >= 0 )
            stk[ptr] = atan( stk[ptr] );
        else
            error_return( UFLOW );
        }

    /* Angle */
    else if ( !strcmp( strupr( cmd ), "ANG" ))
        {
        if ( ptr > 0 )
            {
            ptr--;
            stk[ptr] = atan2( stk[ptr], stk[ptr + 1] );
            }
        else
            error_return( UFLOW );
        }

    /* Raise y to x */
    else if ( !strcmp( strupr( cmd ), "POW" ))
        {
        if ( ptr > 0 )
            {
            ptr--;
            stk[ptr] = pow( stk[ptr], stk[ptr + 1] );
            }
        else
            error_return( UFLOW );
        }

    /* Random between 0 and 1 */
    else if ( !strcmp( strupr( cmd ), "RND" ))
        {
        ptr++;
        stk[ptr] = (double)rand() / 32768.0;
        }
```

(continued)

CALC.C *continued*

```
    /* Duplicate entry */
    else if ( !strcmp( strupr( cmd ), "DUP" ))
        {
        ptr++;
        stk[ptr] = stk[ptr - 1];
        }


    /* Swap */
    else if ( !strcmp( strupr( cmd ), "SWP" ))
        {
        if ( ptr > 0 )
            {
            tmp = stk[ptr];
            stk[ptr] = stk[ptr - 1];
            stk[ptr - 1] = tmp;
            }
        else
            error_return( UFLOW );
        }

    /* Assumed to be a number */
    else
        {
        ptr++;
        stk[ptr] = atof( cmd );
        }
}

/*
    Error messages displayed
*/
void error_return( int error )
{
    printf( "\nError - " );
    switch ( error )
        {
        case NOTENUF:
            printf( "Usage:\tcalc [numbers] [operation] ...\n\n" );
            printf( "Examp:\tcalc 2 3 +\t\t(sum of 2 and 3)\n" );
            printf( "\tcalc 1.23 sin\t\t(Sine of 1.23)\n" );
            printf( "\tcalc 1e1 1e2 1e3 + -\t(10-(100+1000))\n\n" );
            printf( "Functions:\n" );
```

(continued)

CALC.C *continued*

```
            printf( "\t+ - * /\n" );
            printf( "\tSQR SIN COS TAN\n" );
            printf( "\tASN ACS ATN ANG\n" );
            printf( "\tPOW RND DUP SWP\n\n" );
            break;
        case UFLOW:
            printf( "stack underflow\n" );
            break;
        default:
            printf( "undefined problem\n" );
            break;
        }
    exit( 1 );
}
```

CAT

SYNTAX

```
cat filename.ext
```

filename.ext identifies a filename or pathname that you want to list. File-names can contain wildcard characters. A series of *filename.ext* entries can appear on the command line.

The CAT utility is a stripped-down version of the familiar DIR command provided by DOS. (It also resembles the UNIX *cat* command.) CAT can process wildcard filenames to generate a list of matching files. For example, to list all files in the current directory, type

```
C>cat *.*
```

To list only C source code files in the current directory, type

```
C>cat *.c
```

The CAT and DIR commands differ in several ways. Unlike the DIR command, CAT displays filenames with no extra space between the basenames and their extensions. Also, CAT provides no other information about the files, such as size, time of creation, and so on.

The advantage of the streamlined output from CAT is that you can use the generated list of filenames as input to other utility programs. Also, if you redirect the output from CAT to a batch command file, you can edit the results into a list of DOS commands.

To generate a sorted list of the files in the current directory, for example, you can pipe the CAT output into the DOS SORT filter:

```
C>cat *.* : sort
```

The CAT program is instructive in that it shows how to expand wild-cards in filename arguments. The technique is simple and very useful for creating utility programs that can operate on more than one file. Several other programs in this book use wildcard expansion, but the CAT program is a particularly straightforward illustration.

QuickC provides an object file, SETARGV.OBJ, that does most of the work of wildcard expansion. To link your program to SETARGV.OBJ, simply add it to your program list. (Be sure to type the entire path to the location of the object file or copy SETARGV.OBJ into your current directory. For example, if you add the object file to the program list, specify it as *C:\QC2\BIN\SETARGV.OBJ*.)

To use wildcard expansion, you must also deactivate the Extended Dictionary. To do so, choose Make from the Options menu, and then choose Linker Flags. An *X* in the brackets beside Extended Dictionary indicates that the option is active. To change this status, tab to the option and press the Spacebar.

When you link with SETARGV.OBJ to provide wildcard expansion, the list of matching filenames is placed in the *argv* array passed to *main()*, exactly as though all the filenames had been typed on the command line. In your program, you simply loop through all the command line parameters, using *argc* to determine the number of filenames to process. The CAT program loops through the elements of the *argv* array and prints each parameter.

Unlike DIR, the CAT program can handle more than one filename parameter on the command line. The SETARGV.OBJ code expands all wildcards provided on the command line. For example, to generate a list of all .C and .H files in a directory named C:\WORKDIR, type

```
C>cat  c:\workdir\*.c  c:\workdir\*.h
```

```
/* -----------------------------------------------------------------
    Name:          CAT.C
    Type:          Utility program
    Language:      Microsoft QuickC
    Video:         (no special video requirements)

    Program list:  CAT.C
                   SETARGV.OBJ

    Note:          Extended Dictionary flag must be set off
                   (Options-Make-Linker Flags)

    Usage:         cat filename.ext ...
```

(continued)

CAT.C *continued*

```
    Description:    Generates a list of files matching filename.ext
    ---------------------------------------------------------------
*/

#include <stdio.h>
#include <string.h>

main( int argc, char *argv[] )
{
    int i;

    /* List all command line arguments (filenames) */
    for ( i = 1; i < argc; i++ )
        puts( strupr( argv[i] ));

    /* All done */
    return ( 0 );
}
```

CHKSUM

SYNTAX

chksum *filename.ext*

filename.ext identifies the file for which you want the utility to calculate a checksum.

The CHKSUM program lets you determine quickly whether a file has changed since you last used CHKSUM to check it, or whether two files have exactly the same contents.

    CHKSUM reads files in binary mode. You can use it to read any file, whether text or binary. The program uses each byte to calculate a running checksum value. The method creates a different checksum if any byte values change or if their order is altered. (Simply summing the values won't tell you whether the order of the bytes is different.)

    The checksum output is an unsigned integer value in the range 0 through 65,535. A slight chance does exist that two files can have different contents but the same checksum value. The probability of such a coincidence is only 1 in 65,536, however.

```
/* --------------------------------------------------------------

    Name:         CHKSUM.C
    Type:         Utility program
    Language:     Microsoft QuickC
    Video:        (no special video requirements)

    Program list: (not required)

    Usage:        chksum filename.ext

    Description:  Calculates a checksum for a file
    --------------------------------------------------------------
*/
```

(continued)

CHKSUM.C *continued*

```c
#include <stdio.h>
#include <stdlib.h>

main( int argc, char *argv[] )
{
    FILE *fp;
    unsigned c, sum = 0;
    /* Check for filename */
    if ( argc != 2 )
        {
        printf( "USAGE: chksum filename.ext\n" );
        exit( 0 );
        }

    /* Open the file */
    if (( fp = fopen( argv[1], "r+b" )) == NULL )
        {
        printf( "Input file error: %s\n", argv[1] );
        exit( 1 );
        }

    /* Process each byte in the file */
    while (( c = getc( fp )) != EOF )
        sum = ( sum ^ c ) * 317 + 21317;

    /* Close the file */
    fclose( fp );

    /* Report the checksum */
    printf( "chksum: %u\n", sum );

    /* All done */
    return ( 0 );
}
```

CIPHER

SYNTAX

cipher *filename.ext*
$\longrightarrow$

filename.ext identifies the file or files to be enciphered (or deciphered). The program can handle wildcards in *filename.ext* and multiple file-name arguments.

The CIPHER utility efficiently enciphers and deciphers any files. The program performs an exclusive OR operation between each byte of the file and a pseudorandom number generated by RANDOMS toolbox functions. You can restore the original file contents by running CIPHER on the enciphered file using the same key sequence.

To encipher one or more files, a key sequence, or cipher key, is required. The cipher key is the seed for the random number generator and is thus the key to the repeatability of the enciphering sequence. The CIPHER program expects an environment variable named KEYSTR containing a string that functions as the cipher key. If the program does not find the KEYSTR environment variable, it displays a message to remind you that a cipher key is required.

As a precaution, do not set the KEYSTR environment variable by placing a command in AUTOEXEC.BAT: The key string can be found by anyone who searches the file. A better approach is to create a batch file that enters the environment variable for you. The following file, KEY.BAT, lets you enter the cipher key environment variable with minimal trouble and a measure of security:

```
set KEYSTR=%1 %2 %3 %4 %5 %6 %7 %8 %9
cls
```

Suppose you want to set the cipher key to *ApplePI&MeOhMy*. (The stranger the key sequence the better, but you must not forget it! Also, case is significant. To restore a file, you must enter all characters precisely as you did when you enciphered the file.) Using the KEY.BAT file, type the following command:

```
C>key ApplePI&MeOhMy
```

To verify that the variable is set, type *SET* at the DOS prompt. A list of all environment variables will appear, among which you will find the entry *KEYSTR=ApplePI&MeOhMy*. To erase the cipher key from the environment, simply type *KEY* with no arguments at the DOS prompt.

The CIPHER program supports wildcard expansion. You can encipher one or many files with a single command. Don't forget to deactivate the Extended Dictionary flag before you build the program. For more information on using wildcard expansion, see the CAT utility on page 408.

To increase the file access speed, CIPHER opens the file in binary mode and creates a buffer so that it can read the file in large chunks. The program creates a temporary file to hold intermediate results only if the entire file won't fit in the memory buffer. As an additional security provision, the contents of the temporary file (or the contents of the memory buffer) overwrite the original file contents.

The CIPHER program demonstrates a number of useful techniques: It expands wildcards in command line arguments, uses functions from a toolbox module, accesses environment variables, and reads and writes large files rapidly in binary mode.

```
/* -----------------------------------------------------------------
    Name:          CIPHER.C
    Type:          Utility program
    Language:      Microsoft QuickC
    Video:         (no special video requirements)

    Program list:  CIPHER.C
                   RANDOMS.C
                   SETARGV.OBJ

    Note:          Extended Dictionary flag must be set off
                   (Options-Make-Linker Flags)
```

(continued)

```
    Usage:          cipher filename.ext
                    (wildcards allowed for filename.ext)

    Description:    Enciphers any file(s). Reusing the utility with
                    the same key string restores the file(s).
    ----------------------------------------------------------------
*/

#include <stdio.h>
#include <stdlib.h>
#include <string.h>
#include <fcntl.h>
#include <malloc.h>
#include <io.h>

#include "randoms.h"

#define BYTECOUNT 15000

union
    {
    unsigned long lbuf[BYTECOUNT / sizeof( long )];
    unsigned char cbuf[BYTECOUNT];
    } rnd;

main( int argc, char *argv[], char *envp[] )
{
    int use_tmp_file;
    int endx = 0;
    int rindex, fndx;
    size_t bytes, count, i;
    long fsize;
    char *buf;
    FILE *fp1, *fp2;

    /* Find the key string environment variable */
    while( envp[endx] != NULL )
        if ( strstr( envp[endx], "KEYSTR" ) == envp[endx] )
            break;
        else
            endx++;
```

(continued)

CIPHER.C *continued*

```
/* No KEYSTR environment variable? */
if ( envp[endx] == NULL )
    {
    printf( "\nYou must set an environment variable named\n" );
    printf( "KEYSTR to provide the key for enciphering or\n" );
    printf( "restoring files. \n\nFor example, type...\n" );
    printf( "\"SET KEYSTR=This is a sample key string\"\n" );
    exit( 1 );
    }

/* Check for at least one filename in the command line */
if ( argc < 2 )
    {
    printf( "Usage: cipher filename.ext\n" );
    printf( "(wildcards allowed for filename.ext)\n" );
    exit( 1 );
    }

/* Allocate a big buffer */
bytes = _memmax();
buf = (char *) malloc( bytes );

/* Process each filename */
for ( fndx = 1; fndx < argc; fndx++ )
    {

    /* Initialize random number sequence using the given key string */
    rand_shuffle( envp[endx] );
    rindex = 0;

    /* Open the file to be processed */
    if (( fp1 = fopen( argv[fndx], "r+b" )) == NULL )
        {
        printf( "Can't open %s\n", argv[fndx] );
        exit( 1 );
        }
    else
        printf( "Ciphering: %s\n", argv[fndx] );

    /* Get the file size */
    fsize = filelength( fileno( fp1 ));
```

(continued)

CIPHER.C *continued*

```
        /* Use a temporary file only if buffer can't hold entire file */
        use_tmp_file = ( (long)bytes < fsize );

        if ( use_tmp_file )
            {

            /* Change default file-translation mode (affects tmpfile()) */
            _fmode = O_BINARY;

            /* Open a temporary file */
            if (( fp2 = tmpfile() ) == NULL )
                {
                printf( "Can't open temporary file\n" );
                exit( 1 );
                }
            }

        /* Process all the file bytes */
        do
            {

            /* Read bytes (maximum-buffer size) */
            count = fread( buf, 1, bytes, fp1 );

            /* XOR each byte with pseudorandom byte */
            for ( i = 0; i < count; i++ )
                {

                /* Get BYTECOUNT random bytes at a time */
                if ( rindex == 0 )
                    {

                    /* Get a buffer full of pseudorandom bytes */
                    rand_long_buf( BYTECOUNT / sizeof( long ), rnd.lbuf );

                    /* Point to end of random bytes */
                    rindex = BYTECOUNT;
                    }

                /* Now do the actual XORing */
                buf[i] ^= rnd.cbuf[--rindex];
                }
```

(continued)

CIPHER.C *continued*

```
                /* Write the enciphered/restored bytes to temporary file */
                if ( use_tmp_file )
                    fwrite( buf, 1, count, fp2 );

                /* Repeat the processing until all of file is processed */
                }
        while ( count == bytes );

        /* Go back to the start of the file(s) */
        rewind( fp1 );
        if ( use_tmp_file )
            rewind( fp2 );

        /* Copy the temporary file (or buf) back into the original file */
        do
            {
            if ( use_tmp_file )
                count = fread( buf, 1, bytes, fp2 );
            fwrite( buf, 1, count, fp1 );
            }
        while ( count == bytes );

        /* Close all files, flushing the buffers */
        fclose( fp1 );
        fclose( fp2 );
        }

    /* Delete the allocated buffer */
    free( buf );

    /* All done */
    printf( "Finished\n" );
    return ( 0 );
    }
```

COLORS

SYNTAX

```
colors
```

The utility does not use command line parameters.

The COLORS utility lets you display any shade of color in the VGA color palette. The utility works interactively, enabling you to control the amount of red, green, or blue in the shade you are mixing.

This program uses several functions from toolbox modules presented earlier in this book. It calls MOUSEFUN functions to let you adjust the various color levels with the mouse. It also calls functions in the GETKEY module that let you control the color bars with the arrow keys.

The COLORS utility uses several QuickC graphics library functions to draw and update the color bars, borders, and displayed text. The _settextposition(), _settextcolor(), and _outtext() functions work together to display colorful text quickly and efficiently. The _setcolor(), _ellipse(), and _rectangle() functions draw and update the various graphics images. The color constants passed to _remappalette() are defined in GRAPH.H. Use of these standard color constants simplifies many graphics programming tasks.

When you run the program, it creates a large ellipse. You can experiment with the color of the ellipse. In the foreground, the program draws three color bars using red, green, and blue fill colors. The height of the color in each bar indicates the intensity of that color in the current shade of the ellipse. Use the arrow keys or move the mouse to choose a color bar and to change the color level. The effect of the change is immediately evident in the color of the ellipse.

Any change in the composite shade is reflected by a change in the unsigned long hexadecimal integer displayed in the bottom right part of the screen. You can use this number to reproduce the given color shade in any program that runs in a VGA graphics environment. To indicate the color, call _remappalette() with the long integer as the second parameter.

```
/* ----------------------------------------------------------------
    Name:           COLORS.C
    Type:           Utility program
    Language:       Microsoft QuickC version 2
    Video:          VGA required

    Program list:   COLORS.C
                    MOUSEFUN.C
                    GETKEY.C
                    GRAPHICS.LIB

    Usage:          colors

    Description:    Lets you select color shades interactively
                    for the 320-by-200, 256-color VGA mode
    ----------------------------------------------------------------
*/

#include <stdio.h>
#include <stdlib.h>
#include <conio.h>
#include <graph.h>

#include "mousefun.h"
#include "getkey.h"
#include "t_colors.h"

#define BACKGROUND 0
#define REDBAR 1
#define GREENBAR 2
#define BLUEBAR 3
#define TEXTBRIGHT 4
#define TEXTDIM 5
#define BARBLACK 6
#define NEWCOLOR 7
#define REDBORDER 8
#define GREENBORDER 9
#define BLUEBORDER 10
#define TEXTYELLOW 11

/* Macro for setting a VGA color, range 0 through 63 */
#define rgb( r, g, b )          \
    (((( (long)(b) ) << 16 )    \
    : ( (long)(g) ) << 8        \
    : ( (long)(r) )) & 0x3F3F3FL )
```

(continued)

```
main()
{
    int key;
    int red = 32, green = 32, blue = 32;
    int cptr = 1, oldcptr = 0;
    int edge;
    unsigned long cnum;
    char buf[80];

    /* Set the video mode */
    if ( _setvideomode( _MRES256COLOR ) == 0 )
        {
        printf( "Can't set the 256-color VGA mode\n" );
        exit( 1 );
        }

    /* Set the starting color palette entries */
    _remappalette( BACKGROUND, _BLACK );
    _remappalette( REDBAR, _RED );
    _remappalette( GREENBAR, _GREEN );
    _remappalette( BLUEBAR, _BLUE );
    _remappalette( TEXTBRIGHT, _BRIGHTWHITE );
    _remappalette( TEXTDIM, _CYAN );
    _remappalette( BARBLACK, _BLACK );
    _remappalette( NEWCOLOR, _BROWN );
    _remappalette( REDBORDER, _MAGENTA );
    _remappalette( GREENBORDER, _MAGENTA );
    _remappalette( BLUEBORDER, _MAGENTA );
    _remappalette( TEXTYELLOW, _LIGHTYELLOW );

    /* Display the title */
    _settextcolor( TEXTBRIGHT );
    _settextposition( 1, 9 );
    _outtext( "-COLORS-\n\n" );

    /* Display the instructions */
    _settextcolor( TEXTDIM );
    _outtext( "Colors:      Arrow keys or mouse\n" );
    _outtext( "Quit:        Esc key or right button" );

    /* Create the ellipse of color */
    _setcolor( NEWCOLOR );
    _ellipse( _GFILLINTERIOR, 5, 40, 315, 190 );
```

(continued)

COLORS.C *continued*

```
/* Create the red bar */
_setcolor( REDBORDER );
_rectangle( _GFILLINTERIOR, 18, 48, 42, 179 );
_setcolor( REDBAR );
_rectangle( _GFILLINTERIOR, 20, 114, 40, 177 );
_setcolor( BARBLACK );
_rectangle( _GFILLINTERIOR, 20, 50, 40, 113 );

/* Create the green bar */
_setcolor( GREENBORDER );
_rectangle( _GFILLINTERIOR, 68, 48, 92, 179 );
_setcolor( GREENBAR );
_rectangle( _GFILLINTERIOR, 70, 114, 90, 177 );
_setcolor( BARBLACK );
_rectangle( _GFILLINTERIOR, 70, 50, 90, 113 );

/* Create the blue bar */
_setcolor( BLUEBORDER );
_rectangle( _GFILLINTERIOR, 118, 48, 142, 179 );
_setcolor( BLUEBAR );
_rectangle( _GFILLINTERIOR, 120, 114, 140, 177 );
_setcolor( BARBLACK );
_rectangle( _GFILLINTERIOR, 120, 50, 140, 113 );

/* The main processing loop */
while ( 1 )
    {

    /* Set the new color */
    cnum = rgb( red, green, blue );
    _remappalette( NEWCOLOR, cnum );

    /* Display the new color number */
    _settextcolor( TEXTYELLOW );
    _settextposition( 25, 27 );
    sprintf( buf, "0x%06lX", cnum );
    _outtext( buf );

    /* Fill in the red color bar */
    if ( cptr == 1 )
        {
        edge = 177 - 2 * red;
```

(continued)

```
            _setcolor( REDBAR );
            _rectangle( _GFILLINTERIOR, 20, edge + 1, 40, edge );
            _setcolor( BARBLACK );
            _rectangle( _GFILLINTERIOR, 20, edge - 1, 40, edge - 2 );
            }

        /* Fill in the green color bar */
        if ( cptr == 2 )
            {
            edge = 177 - 2 * green;
            _setcolor( GREENBAR );
            _rectangle( _GFILLINTERIOR, 70, edge + 1, 90, edge );
            _setcolor( BARBLACK );
            _rectangle( _GFILLINTERIOR, 70, edge - 1, 90, edge - 2 );
            }

        /* Fill in the blue color bar */
        if ( cptr == 3 )
            {
            edge = 177 - 2 * blue;
            _setcolor( BLUEBAR );
            _rectangle( _GFILLINTERIOR, 120, edge + 1, 140, edge );
            _setcolor( BARBLACK );
            _rectangle( _GFILLINTERIOR, 120, edge - 1, 140, edge - 2 );
            }

        /* Set the red bar border color */
        if ( oldcptr != cptr )
            {
            oldcptr = cptr;

            if ( cptr == 1 )
                _remappalette( REDBORDER, _BRIGHTWHITE );
            else
                _remappalette( REDBORDER, _MAGENTA );

            /* Set the green bar border color */
            if ( cptr == 2 )
                _remappalette( GREENBORDER, _BRIGHTWHITE );
            else
                _remappalette( GREENBORDER, _MAGENTA );
```

(continued)

COLORS.C *continued*

```
                /* Set the blue bar border color */
                if ( cptr == 3 )
                    _remappalette( BLUEBORDER, _BRIGHTWHITE );
                else
                    _remappalette( BLUEBORDER, _MAGENTA );
                }

        /* Get a keypress */
        key = getkey_or_mouse();

        /* Left Arrow key? */
        if ( key == KEY_LEFT )
            if ( cptr > 1 )
                cptr--;

        /* Right Arrow key? */
        if ( key == KEY_RIGHT )
            if ( cptr < 3 )
                cptr++;

        /* Up Arrow key? */
        if ( key == KEY_UP )
            {
            if ( cptr == 1 && red < 63 )
                red++;
            if ( cptr == 2 && green < 63 )
                green++;
            if ( cptr == 3 && blue < 63 )
                blue++;
            }

        /* Down Arrow key? */
        if ( key == KEY_DOWN )
            {
            if ( cptr == 1 && red > 0 )
                red--;
            if ( cptr == 2 && green > 0 )
                green--;
            if ( cptr == 3 && blue > 0 )
                blue--;
            }
```

(continued)

COLORS.C *continued*

```
        /* Escape key pressed? */
        if ( key == KEY_ESCAPE )
            break;
        }

    /* All done */
    _setvideomode( _DEFAULTMODE );
    return ( 0 );
}
```

DETAB

SYNTAX

detab *columns* *filename.ext*

columns is the interval between tab stops.

filename.ext identifies the file or files in which you want tabs replaced with spaces. The program can handle wildcards in *filename.ext* and multiple filename arguments.

The DETAB utility replaces all tab characters in a file with an appropriate number of spaces. This program is particularly handy if you've changed the Tab Stops setting in the QuickC environment.

For example, a 4-column tab setting is convenient for indenting each brace level of a source file. When you print the file, however, the tabs are expanded to 8-column intervals, and the result is often a less readable printed copy. To prepare a file for printing, use the DETAB program:

```
C>detab 4 source.c
```

DETAB replaces each tab character with spaces so that the text aligns to match the QuickC screen (with Tab Stops set to 4).

This program can expand wildcards in the filename argument or arguments. See the explanation of the CAT.C program (on page 408) for more information about wildcard expansion.

```
/* ------------------------------------------------------------------
    Name:         DETAB.C
    Type:         Utility program
    Language:     Microsoft QuickC
    Video:        (no special video requirements)

 Program list:  (not required)
```

(continued)

DETAB.C *continued*

```
    Note:          Extended Dictionary flag must be set off
                   (Options-Make-Linker Flags)

    Usage:         detab columns filename.ext
                   (wildcards allowed for filename.ext)

    Description:   Removes tabs from a file or files.  Spaces are
                   added for proper alignment.
    ----------------------------------------------------------------
*/

#include <stdio.h>
#include <stdlib.h>
#include <string.h>

#define MAXLINE 255

main( int argc, char *argv[] )
{
    int i, col;
    int tabbing;
    char buf[256], *bufptr;
    char c, filnam[80];
    FILE *fp1, *fp2;

    /* Get tabbing parameter */
    if ( argc > 2 )
        tabbing = atoi( argv[1] );

    /* Check for filenames and positive tabbing amount */
    if ( argc < 3 !! tabbing < 1 )
        {
        printf( "\nUsage: detab columns filename.ext\n" );
        printf( "(wildcards allowed for filename.ext)\n" );
        exit( 1 );
        }

    /* Process each filename */
    for ( i = 2; i < argc; i++ )
        {
```

(continued)

DETAB.C *continued*

```
        /* Keep user informed of progress */
        strcpy( filnam, argv[i] );
        printf( "%s\n", filnam );

        /* Open the file to be processed */
        if (( fp1 = fopen( filnam, "r" )) == NULL )
            {
            printf( "Can't open %s\n", filnam );
            exit( 1 );
            }

        /* Open a new file */
        if (( fp2 = fopen( "DETABTMP.TMP", "w" )) == NULL )
            {
            printf( "Can't open temporary file\n" );
            exit( 1 );
            }

        /* Process each line from file */
        while ( fgets( buf, MAXLINE, fp1 ) != NULL )
            {

            /* Special case if first character in line is a tab */
            if ( *(bufptr = buf) == '\t' )
                {
                fputc( ' ', fp2 );
                col = 1;
                }
            else
                col = 0;

            /* Send out the line, watching for tab characters */
            do
                {
                if ( *bufptr == '\t' )
                    do
                        {
                        fputc( ' ', fp2 );
                        col++;
                        col %= tabbing;
                        }
                    while( col );
```

(continued)

DETAB.C *continued*

```
            else
                {
                fputc( *bufptr, fp2 );
                col++;
                }
            }
        while ( *(++bufptr) );
        }

    /* Close the files */
    fclose( fp1 );
    fclose( fp2 );

    /* Delete the original file */
    remove( argv[i] );

    /* Rename new file as original */
    rename( "DETABTMP.TMP", filnam );
    }

/* All done */
printf( "Finished\n" );
return ( 0 );
}
```

FREQ

SYNTAX

```
freq filename.ext
```

filename.ext identifies a file to be analyzed for byte frequency.

The FREQ utility tabulates the occurrences of bytes in a file. The output shows the count for each of the 256 possible byte values. Bytes that don't occur in the file are not reported.

You can use this program as a quick check for graphics characters, tabs, or other binary byte values in a file. Programs that employ file-packing and enciphering algorithms often depend on a character frequency table to improve their efficiency. The FREQ program can serve as a starting point for developing such programs.

The output generated by FREQ scrolls off the screen if more than 25 unique bytes occur in the specified file. Use the MORE filter provided by DOS to review the byte frequency data, or capture the data in a file by redirecting the program output. For example, use one of the following commands:

```
C>freq mobydick.txt | more
C>freq mobydick.txt > output.fil
```

```
/* ----------------------------------------------------------------
    Name:          FREQ.C
    Type:          Utility program
    Language:      Microsoft QuickC
    Video:         (no special video requirements)

    Program list:  (not required)

    Usage:         freq filename.ext

    Description:   Counts occurrences of characters in a file
    ----------------------------------------------------------------
*/
```

(continued)

FREQ.C *continued*

```c
#include <stdio.h>
#include <stdlib.h>

main( int argc, char *argv[] )
{
    int c;
    int i;
    long n[256], tot = 0L;
    FILE *fin;

    /* Check command line parameters */
    if ( argc != 2 )
        {
        printf( "USAGE: freq filename.ext\n" );
        exit( 1 );
        }

    /* Open the file */
    if (( fin = fopen( argv[1], "rb" )) == NULL )
        {
        printf( "Can't open %s\n", argv[1] );
        exit( 1 );
        }

    /* Initialize the counts */
    for ( i = 0; i < 256; i++ )
        n[i] = 0L;

    /* Tally the bytes */
    while (( c = fgetc( fin )) != EOF )
        {
        n[c]++;
        tot++;
        }

    /* Close the file */
    fclose( fin );

    /* Report the totals */
    for ( i = 0; i < 256; i++ )
        if ( n[i] )
            {
            printf( "ASCII: %d", i );
```

(continued)

FREQ.C *continued*

```
            if ( i > 13 )
                printf( "  %c", i );
            else
                printf( "    " );
            printf( "\tCount: %d\n", n[i] );
            }
    printf( "\nTotal: %ld\n", tot );

    /* All done */
    return ( 0 );
}
```

HEXTOBIN

SYNTAX

`hextobin` *infile.ext outfile.ext*

infile.ext identifies the hexadecimal file you want to convert to binary. *outfile.ext* is the file to which the utility writes the binary values.

The HEXTOBIN utility converts a file of hexadecimal characters to a binary file. The program re-creates binary files that were converted to hexadecimal by the BINTOHEX program. If the input file meets certain restrictions, however, HEXTOBIN can convert any file of hexadecimal character pairs to the binary bytes they represent.

The program uses the *strtok()* function provided by QuickC to extract each pair of hexadecimal characters in the input file. The hexadecimal characters A through F must be uppercase, and each pair must be separated from other pairs by one or more spaces, dashes, or newlines. The length of each line is not important, nor is the number of separation characters.

HEXTOBIN can be handy for rebuilding a .COM file published in a magazine article. Often, a BASIC program appears in print with a series of DATA statements that contain hexadecimal character pairs. Rather than entering the entire BASIC program, you can type only the hexadecimal characters into a file and process that file using HEXTOBIN.

The HEXTOBIN utility provides a good example of the *strtok()* function at work. See your QuickC documentation for more information about this useful function. Also see the BINTOHEX utility on page 396 for information about converting binary files to hexadecimal character format.

```
/* -----------------------------------------------------------------
   Name:          HEXTOBIN.C
   Type:          Utility program
   Language:      Microsoft QuickC
   Video:         (no special video requirements)

   Program list:  (not required)

   Usage:         hextobin infile.ext outfile.ext

   Description:   Converts a file of hexadecimal characters to a file
                  of bytes
   -----------------------------------------------------------------
*/

#include <string.h>
#include <stdio.h>
#include <stdlib.h>

main( int argc, char *argv[] )
{
    int c;
    int n = 0;
    FILE *fin, *fout;
    char string[80];
    char *token;
    char *endstr;

    /* Verify command line parameters */
    if ( argc != 3 )
        {
        fprintf( stderr, "Usage: hextobin infile.ext outfile.ext\n" );
        exit( 1 );
        }

    /* Try to open the input file */
    if (( fin = fopen( argv[1], "r" )) == NULL )
        {
        fprintf( stderr, "Can't open %s\n", argv[1] );
        exit(1);
        }
```

(continued)

```
    /* Try to open the output file */
    if (( fout = fopen( argv[2], "wb" )) == NULL )
        {
        fprintf( stderr, "Can't open %s\n", argv[2] );
        exit( 1 );
        }

    /* Process each line from the input file */
    while( fgets( string, 80, fin ) != NULL )
        {

        /* Get each pair of hexadecimal characters */
        token = strtok( string, " -\n" );
        while (( token != NULL ) && ( strlen( token ) == 2 ))
            {

            /* Convert character pairs to bytes and write them */
            fputc( (int)strtol( token, &endstr, 16 ), fout );

            /* Get the next pair of hexadecimal characters */
            token = strtok( NULL, " -\n" );
            }
        }

    /* Close the files */
    fcloseall();

    /* All done */
    return (0);
}
```

LOG

SYNTAX

log `message`

message is an optional message that the utility writes after the time and date entry in the log file.

The LOG utility appends a date, time, and optional message line to a log file. These entries can provide a useful record of time spent at various tasks. For example, to keep track of the amount of time you spend working with QuickC, you could create the following batch file, Q.BAT:

```
log Starting session with QuickC
c:\qc2\bin\qc %1
log Ending session with QuickC
```

If you execute the batch file to load QuickC, the LOG utility records the beginning and ending times of your session. After the first session, the log file will contain two entries similar to the following:

```
03/09/90 19:27:28 Starting session with QuickC
03/09/90 21:17:17 Ending session with QuickC
```

The LOG program uses the *_strdate()* and *_strtime()* functions provided by QuickC. These functions return the date and time in a convenient, condensed format. Examine the TIMEDATE utility to see how you can get a more detailed string of date and time information.

Notice that the utility opens the log file for appending by specifying the "a" parameter in the call to *fopen()*. New entries therefore appear at the end of the file.

The name of the log file is declared in the #*define* statement at the start of the program. Change this statement to put the log file in any directory you choose. Be sure to use two backslashes for each single backslash in the path, as shown in the listing. If you use a single backslash, the QuickC compiler interprets it as a special escape character, and the name of the log file will not be what you intended.

```
/* ----------------------------------------------------------------
   Name:          LOG.C
   Type:          Utility program
   Language:      Microsoft QuickC
   Video:         (no special video requirements)

   Program list: (not required)

   Usage:         log [message]

   Description:   Appends date, time, and message to a log file
   ----------------------------------------------------------------
*/

#include <stdio.h>
#include <stdlib.h>
#include <time.h>

#define LOGFILE "C:\\LOG"

main( int argc, char *argv[] )
{
    FILE *stream;
    int i;
    char d[9], t[9];

    /* Open the log file for appending */
    stream = fopen( LOGFILE, "a" );
    if ( stream == NULL )
        {
        printf( "\nCan't open log file\n" );
        exit( 1 );
        }

    /* Log the time and date information */
    fprintf( stream, "%s %s", _strdate( d ), _strtime( t ));

    /* Include the message */
    for ( i = 1; i < argc; i++ )
        fprintf( stream, " %s", argv[i] );
```

(continued)

LOG.C *continued*

```
    /* Terminate the line */
    fprintf( stream, "\n" );

    /* Close the log file */
    fclose( stream );

    /* All done */
    return ( 0 );
}
```

LOOK

SYNTAX

```
look filename.ext
```

filename.ext is the name of a file you want to display.

The LOOK utility displays any readable file for quick review. This program copies the functionality and, to a degree, the appearance of the SHOW.ASM program that is provided with the Microsoft Macro Assembler package.

The LOOK program provides a few features not found in SHOW. Whereas SHOW can display files no larger than 64 KB, LOOK lets you view files as large as the available memory. The LOOK program also lets you use a mouse to scroll through the file. To increase the scrolling speed, press and hold the left mouse button while you move the mouse. Clicking the right mouse button ends the program (as does pressing the Esc key).

The LOOK program also responds to a few keys that SHOW ignores. You can press the 1 key to jump to the line number that is about 10 percent of the way through the file. Pressing the 2 key displays the file at the 20 percent point, the 3 key displays the 30 percent point, and so on. Using the Home and End keys displays the beginning and end of the file.

To allocate string space, the program uses the *malloc()* function. It also creates an array of pointers to the strings. For each string, LOOK allocates exactly the number of bytes required for reading each line from the file. This technique lets you allocate all available memory, and it saves a substantial amount of space compared to creating a "rectangular" array, in which all strings are created the same length.

The string storage space is allocated in far memory, and each string could theoretically be as large as 65,536 (64 KB) characters. For these reasons, you should compile the LOOK program using one of the memory models that allows multiple data segments—compact, large, or huge. Because the program itself fits easily in one segment, the compact memory model works well.

```
/* --------------------------------------------------------------------
   Name:            LOOK.C
   Type:            Utility program
   Language:        Microsoft QuickC
   Video:           (no special video requirements)

   Program list:    LOOK.C
                    GETKEY.C
                    MOUSEFUN.C
                    GRAPHICS.LIB

   Usage:           look filename.ext

   Note:            Use COMPACT memory model

   Description:     Displays the contents of a file; similar to
                    SHOW.ASM except that it lets you display files
                    larger than 64 KB
   --------------------------------------------------------------------
*/

#include <stdio.h>
#include <stdlib.h>
#include <conio.h>
#include <string.h>
#include <graph.h>
#include <malloc.h>

#include "getkey.h"
#include "mousefun.h"
#include "t_colors.h"

#define PTRSPACE 65000
#define MAXLINES ( PTRSPACE / sizeof( char ** ))
#define MAXLINELEN 81
#define OKAY 1
#define QUIT 0
#define NOCURSOR 0x2000
```

(continued)

LOOK.C *continued*

```
main( int argc, char *argv[] )
{
    FILE *fptr;
    char buf[MAXLINELEN];
    int i, j = 0, k, len;
    int n = 0, status = OKAY;
    unsigned key;
    int l_btn, r_btn, h_pos, v_pos;
    char **ary;

    /* Check that a filename was given */
    if ( argc != 2 )
        {
        printf( "Usage:  look filename.ext\n" );
        exit( 1 );
        }

    /* Check for good filename */
    if (( fptr = fopen( argv[1], "r" )) == NULL )
        {
        printf( "Can't open file\n" );
        exit( 1 );
        }

    /* Allocate string pointer array */
    if (( ary = (char **)malloc( PTRSPACE )) == NULL )
        {
        printf( "Couldn't allocate string address list\n" );
        exit( 1 );
        }

    /* Remove the cursor */
    _settextcursor( NOCURSOR );

    /* Create the top prompt line */
    _setbkcolor( BK_CYAN );
    _settextcolor( T_BLACK );
    _settextposition( 1, 1 );
    strcpy( buf, " Line:        File:            Qu" );
    /*(alignment) 123456789012345678901234567890123456789012345678901234567890 */
    strcat( buf, "it: ESC    Move: u d PGUP PGDN HOME END " );
    /* Arrow characters go here... ^ ^ */
```

(continued)

LOOK.C *continued*

```
/* Insert the Up and Down Arrow characters */
buf[57] = '\030';
buf[59] = '\031';

/* Display the top prompt line */
_outtext( buf );

/* Label the name of the file */
_settextposition( 1, 23 );
_outtext( strupr( argv[1] ) );

/* Display the bottom information line */
_settextposition( 25, 1 );
_outtext( " LOOK.C   '1'...'9'= 10% to 90% of file,   " );
_outtext( " Left mouse button = fast, Right = ESC " );

/* Set the main colors */
_setbkcolor( BK_BLUE );
_settextcolor( T_WHITE );

/* Read the file */
do
    {

    /* Read each line */
    if ( fgets( buf, MAXLINELEN, fptr ) == NULL )
        status = QUIT;
    else
        {

        /* Make sure string isn't too long */
        buf[MAXLINELEN - 1] = '\0';

        /* Remove the newline */
        len = strlen( buf );
        if ( len )
            buf[len - 1] = '\0';

        /* Allocate string space for the line */
        len = strlen( buf );
        ary[n] = (char *)malloc( len + 1 );
```

(continued)

```
                /* Store the string away */
                if ( ary[n] == NULL )
                    status = QUIT;
                else if ( n == MAXLINES - 1 )
                    status = QUIT;
                else
                    strcpy( ary[n++], buf );


                }
            }
    while ( status == OKAY );

    /* Make the last string NULL */
    *ary[n] = NULL;

    /* Reset the status indicator */
    status = OKAY;

    /* Main display loop */
    do
        {

        /* Set the colors for the top line */
        _setbkcolor( BK_CYAN );
        _settextcolor( T_BLACK );

        /* Position for displaying the line number */
        _settextposition( 1, 8 );

        /* Create 9-byte string containing the line number */
        ultoa( (unsigned long)(j+1), buf, 10 );
        while ( strlen( buf ) < 9 )
            strcat( buf, " " );

        /* Display the line number */
        _outtext( buf );

        /* Set the main text colors */
        _setbkcolor( BK_BLUE );
        _settextcolor( T_WHITE );
```

(continued)

LOOK.C *continued*

```
        /* Display block of lines */
        for ( i = 0; i < 23; i++ )
            {

            /* Position for each line */
            _settextposition( i + 2, 1 );

            /* Get line of text or blank line past end */
            if ( i + j < n )
                strcpy( buf, ary[i+j] );
            else
                strcpy( buf, " " );

            /* Pad the string with spaces */
            len = strlen( buf );
            for ( k = len; k < MAXLINELEN - 1; k++ )
                buf[k] = ' ';

            /* Set the length of the string */
            buf[MAXLINELEN - 1] = '\0';

            /* Display the line */
            _outtext( buf );
            }

        /* Get the next keystroke or mouse movement */
        key = getkey_or_mouse();

        /* Check the left mouse button status */
        mouse_status( &l_btn, &r_btn, &h_pos, &v_pos );

        /* Process the keypress or mouse movement */
        switch ( key )
            {
            case KEY_UP:
                if ( l_btn )
                    j -= 24;
                else
                    j--;
                break;
```

(continued)

```
            case KEY_DOWN:
                if ( l_btn )
                    j += 24;
                else
                    j++;
                break;
            case KEY_PGUP:
                j -= 24;
                break;
            case KEY_PGDN:
                j += 24;
                break;
            case KEY_HOME:
                j = 0;
                break;
            case KEY_END:
                j = n;
                break;
            case '1':
            case '2':
            case '3':
            case '4':
            case '5':
            case '6':
            case '7':
            case '8':
            case '9':
                j = (unsigned)( (long)( key - '0' ) * n / 10L );
                break;
            case KEY_ESCAPE:
                status = QUIT;
                break;
            default:
                break;
            }

        /* Adjust the line pointer to be in range */
        if ( j > n - 12 )
            j = n - 12;
        if ( j < 0 )
            j = 0;
```

(continued)

LOOK.C *continued*

```
        }
    while ( status == OKAY );

    /* Free up the strings */
    for ( i = 0; i < n; i++ )
        free( ary[i] );

    /* Free up the string addresses */
    free( ary );

    /* Restore the cursor and original colors */
    _setvideomode( _DEFAULTMODE );

    /* All done */
    return ( 0 );
}
```

MOUSGCRS

SYNTAX

`mousgcrs` `filename.ext`

filename.ext identifies an optional file that you can edit.

The MOUSGCRS utility provides an interactive editor for the graphics mode mouse cursor. The program enables you to use a mouse to edit the screen mask bits, the cursor mask bits, and the location of the hot spot. Taken together, this information constitutes a data structure that defines a mouse cursor icon. MOUSGCRS produces QuickC source code that lets you use the new cursor in any program.

The utility interface displays instructions and options around the edges of the mask-editing rectangles. To make selections, click with the left mouse button on these areas. For example, to reset the cursor masks to those for a pointing hand, click on the *hand* label along the right side of the display. To view the new cursor at any time, move the mouse cursor to the left side of the screen into the area marked *New Cursor View Area.* When you want to save the results of your edit, click on *Save New Cursor.* Click on *Quit* to end the program.

The MOUSGCRS program demonstrates the use of several of the mouse functions defined in MOUSEFUN.C. See the MOUSEFUN toolbox module for more information about these functions.

You can use this utility to create graphics mode mouse cursors only, and you must have CGA, EGA, or VGA graphics capability to run the program. The screen and cursor mask bit patterns for all graphics modes are the same, which means that the cursor icons you create with MOUSGCRS can be used in any graphics mode. For an excellent explanation of all aspects of mouse programming see the *Microsoft Mouse Programmer's Reference,* published by Microsoft Press.

By default, the source code MOUSGCRS produces is written to a file named WORKGCRS. If you identify an alternative work file in the command line, the utility lets you edit the cursor defined by that file and saves the result to the named file instead of WORKGCRS. To use the cursor definition code in a program of your own, merge the output file into the program immediately before *main()* and add the following statement to your program:

```
#include "mousefun.h"
```

Finally, add MOUSEFUN.C to the program list. Your program should use *mouse_init()* to initialize the mouse, *mouse_setgcurs()* to set the new graphics cursor as defined by the data structure, and *mouse_show()* to make the new cursor appear. Use other mouse functions as required throughout your program. The following short program, GCRSTEST.C, demonstrates the use of an alternate mouse cursor. In this case, the data structure, *gcursor_work*, gives the cursor the appearance of a jet airplane.

```
/* GCRSTEST.C */

#include <stdio.h>
#include <graph.h>
#include "mousefun.h"

static struct graphics_cursor far gcursor_work =
    {

    /*  screen mask  */
    0xFFFF,     /* 1111111111111111 */
    0xFEFF,     /* 1111111011111111 */
    0xFC7F,     /* 1111110001111111 */
    0xF83F,     /* 1111100000111111 */
    0xF83F,     /* 1111100000111111 */
    0xF83F,     /* 1111100000111111 */
    0xF01F,     /* 1111000000011111 */
    0xE00F,     /* 1110000000001111 */
    0xC007,     /* 1100000000000111 */
    0x8003,     /* 1000000000000011 */
    0x8003,     /* 1000000000000011 */
    0xF83F,     /* 1111100000111111 */
    0xF83F,     /* 1111100000111111 */
    0xF01F,     /* 1111000000011111 */
    0xE00F,     /* 1110000000001111 */
    0xFFFF,     /* 1111111111111111 */
```

(continued)

GCRSTEST.C *continued*

```
    /*  cursor mask */
    0x0000,    /* 0000000000000000 */
    0x0000,    /* 0000000000000000 */
    0x0100,    /* 0000000100000000 */
    0x0380,    /* 0000001110000000 */
    0x0380,    /* 0000001110000000 */
    0x0380,    /* 0000001110000000 */
    0x07C0,    /* 0000011111000000 */
    0x0FE0,    /* 0000111111100000 */
    0x1FF0,    /* 0001111111110000 */
    0x3FF8,    /* 0011111111111000 */
    0x638C,    /* 0110001110001100 */
    0x0380,    /* 0000001110000000 */
    0x0380,    /* 0000001110000000 */
    0x07C0,    /* 0000011111000000 */
    0x0C60,    /* 0000110001100000 */
    0x0000,    /* 0000000000000000 */

    /* hot spot x,y */
    07, 01
    };

main()
{
    int status, buttons;

    _setvideomode( _HRESBW );
    mouse_reset( &status, &buttons );
    mouse_setgcurs( &gcursor_work );
    mouse_show();
    return ( 0 );
}
```

This program sets high-resolution CGA graphics mode, creates a jet-shaped mouse cursor, and displays the new cursor on the screen. The purpose of GCRSTEST is to demonstrate, using a minimum of coding, how to use one of the mouse cursors created by the MOUSGCRS program.

```
/* -------------------------------------------------------------------
    Name:          MOUSGCRS.C
    Type:          Utility program
    Language:      Microsoft QuickC version 2
    Video:         CGA capability required

    Program list:  MOUSGCRS.C
                   MOUSEFUN.C
                   GRAPHICS.LIB

    Note:          Use COMPACT model

    Usage:         mousgcrs [filename.ext]

    Description:   Interactive editor for mouse cursor icon
   -------------------------------------------------------------------
*/

#include <stdio.h>
#include <stdlib.h>
#include <graph.h>
#include <time.h>
#include <io.h>
#include <conio.h>
#include <string.h>

#include "mousefun.h"

/* Local function prototypes */
void strings_to_numbers( void );
void numbers_to_strings( void );
void draw_masks( void );

/* Data structures */
static struct graphics_cursor far gc;
char *tbuf[44] =
    {
    "\n",
    "static struct graphics_cursor far gcursor_work =\n",
    "    {\n",
    "\n",
    "    /*   screen mask  */\n",
    "    0xCFFF,    /* 1100111111111111 */\n",
    "    0xC7FF,    /* 1100011111111111 */\n",
    "    0xC3FF,    /* 1100001111111111 */\n",
    "    0xC1FF,    /* 1100000111111111 */\n",
```

(continued)

MOUSGCRS.C *continued*

```
    "      0xC0FF,   /* 1100000011111111 */\n",
    "      0xC07F,   /* 1100000001111111 */\n",
    "      0xC03F,   /* 1100000000111111 */\n",
    "      0xC01F,   /* 1100000000011111 */\n",
    "      0xC00F,   /* 1100000000001111 */\n",
    "      0xC007,   /* 1100000000000111 */\n",
    "      0xC07F,   /* 1100000001111111 */\n",
    "      0xC43F,   /* 1100010000111111 */\n",
    "      0xCC3F,   /* 1100110000111111 */\n",
    "      0xFE1F,   /* 1111111000011111 */\n",
    "      0xFE1F,   /* 1111111000011111 */\n",
    "      0xFF1F,   /* 1111111100011111 */\n",
    "\n",
    "      /*  cursor mask  */\n",
    "      0x0000,   /* 0000000000000000 */\n",
    "      0x1000,   /* 0001000000000000 */\n",
    "      0x1800,   /* 0001100000000000 */\n",
    "      0x1C00,   /* 0001110000000000 */\n",
    "      0x1E00,   /* 0001111000000000 */\n",
    "      0x1F00,   /* 0001111100000000 */\n",
    "      0x1F80,   /* 0001111110000000 */\n",
    "      0x1FC0,   /* 0001111111000000 */\n",
    "      0x1FE0,   /* 0001111111100000 */\n",
    "      0x1F00,   /* 0001111100000000 */\n",
    "      0x1B00,   /* 0001101100000000 */\n",
    "      0x1180,   /* 0001000110000000 */\n",
    "      0x0180,   /* 0000000110000000 */\n",
    "      0x00C0,   /* 0000000011000000 */\n",
    "      0x00C0,   /* 0000000011000000 */\n",
    "      0x0000,   /* 0000000000000000 */\n",
    "\n",
    "      /* hot spot x,y */\n",
    "      02, 00\n",
    "      };\n",
    "\n"
    };

main( int argc, char *argv[] )
{
    int i;
    int status, buttons, maskptr, x, y;
    int left, right, horz, vert;
    int view_status, old_view_status;
```

(continued)

MOUSGCRS.C *continued*

```
    int lpress, lhorz, lvert, rpress, rhorz, rvert;
    int xbox1, ybox1, xbox2, ybox2;
    int quit_flag = 0;
    long seconds, oldseconds;
    char workfile[80];
    FILE *fptr;
    char tmp[80];

    /* Set the work file name */
    if ( argc == 2 )
        strcpy( workfile, argv[1]);
    else
        strcpy( workfile, "WORKGCRS" );

    /* Create the work file if it doesn't exist */
    if ( access( workfile, 0 ))
        {
        fptr = fopen( workfile, "w+" );
        for ( i = 0; i < 44; i++ )
            fputs( tbuf[i], fptr );
        }

    /* Otherwise, read the work file into the text buffer */
    else
        {
        fptr = fopen( workfile, "r+" );
        for ( i = 0; i < 44; i++ )
            {
            fgets( tmp, 80, fptr );
            if ( strlen( tmp ) == strlen( tbuf[i] ))
                strcpy( tbuf[i], tmp );
            }
        }

    /* Be sure work file was opened without error */
    if ( fptr == NULL )
        {
        printf( "Failed to open the work file\n" );
        exit( 1 );
        }

    /* Rewind the file for later output */
    rewind( fptr );
```

(continued)

MOUSGCRS.C *continued*

```
/* Extract the numerical data from the strings */
strings_to_numbers();

/* Initialize the graphics screen */
if ( !_setvideomode( _HRESBW ))
    {
    printf( "This program requires at least CGA resolution\n" );
    exit( 1 );
    }
_clearscreen( _GCLEARSCREEN );

/* Draw the vertical pixel outline boxes */
for ( x = 119; x <= 311; x += 12 )
    {
    _moveto( x, 19 );
    _lineto( x, 163 );
    _moveto( x + 222, 19 );
    _lineto( x + 222, 163 );
    }

/* Draw the horizontal pixel outline boxes */
for ( y = 19; y <= 163; y += 9 )
    {
    _moveto( 119, y );
    _lineto( 311, y );
    _moveto( 341, y );
    _lineto( 533, y );
    }

/* Title at the top */
_settextposition( 1, 22 );
_outtext( "MOUSGCRS - Graphics Mouse Cursor Editor" );

/* Label the mask areas */
_settextposition( 2, 22 );
_outtext( "Screen Mask" );
_settextposition( 2, 50 );
_outtext( "Cursor Mask" );
```

(continued)

MOUSGCRS.C *continued*

```
    /* Instruction text at bottom of display */
    _settextposition( 23, 16 );
    _outtext( "Left button        Right button        Both buttons" );
    _settextposition( 24, 16 );
    _outtext( "to set pixel       to clear pixel      for hot spot" );

    /* Cursor list at right */
    _settextposition( 4, 70 );
    _outtext( "Reset" );
    _settextposition( 5, 70 );
    _outtext( "New Cursor" );
    _settextposition( 6, 70 );
    _outtext( "Masks" );
    _settextposition( 8, 71 );
    _outtext( "default" );

    _settextposition( 9, 71 );
    _outtext( "hand" );
    _settextposition( 10, 71 );
    _outtext( "check" );
    _settextposition( 11, 71 );
    _outtext( "hour" );
    _settextposition( 12, 71 );
    _outtext( "jet" );
    _settextposition( 13, 71 );
    _outtext( "left" );
    _settextposition( 14, 71 );
    _outtext( "plus" );
    _settextposition( 15, 71 );
    _outtext( "up" );
    _settextposition( 16, 71 );
    _outtext( "x" );

    /* Label the view area */
    _settextposition( 5, 3 );
    _outtext( "New Cursor" );
    _settextposition( 6, 3 );
    _outtext( "View Area" );

    /* Label the program control choices */
    _settextposition( 20, 3 );
    _outtext( "Save New" );
    _settextposition( 21, 3 );
    _outtext( "Cursor" );
```

(continued)

MOUSGCRS.C *continued*

```
    _settextposition( 24, 3 );
    _outtext( "Quit" );

    /* Create the viewing area backgrounds */
    _rectangle( _GBORDER, 16, 50, 90, 140 );
    _rectangle( _GFILLINTERIOR, 16, 50, 90, 95 );

    /* Fill the current mask pixels */
    draw_masks();

    /* Initialize the mouse */
    mouse_reset( &status, &buttons );
    mouse_show();

    /* Main processing loop starts here */
    while( !quit_flag )
        {

        /* Toggle the hot spot once per second */
        seconds = clock() / CLK_TCK;
        if ( seconds != oldseconds )
            {
            oldseconds = seconds;
            if ( seconds & 1 )
                _setcolor( 0xFFFF );
            else
                _setcolor( 0x0000 );

            _rectangle( _GFILLINTERIOR,
                        gc.hot_spot_x * 12 + 124, gc.hot_spot_y * 9 + 22,
                        gc.hot_spot_x * 12 + 126, gc.hot_spot_y * 9 + 25 );

            _rectangle( _GFILLINTERIOR,
                        gc.hot_spot_x * 12 + 346, gc.hot_spot_y * 9 + 22,
                        gc.hot_spot_x * 12 + 348, gc.hot_spot_y * 9 + 25 );
            }

        /* Get the press information for each button */
        mouse_press( LBUTTON, &left, &lpress, &lhorz, &lvert );
        mouse_press( RBUTTON, &right, &rpress, &rhorz, &rvert );

        /* Get the current status of the mouse */
        mouse_status( &left, &right, &horz, &vert );
```

(continued)

MOUSGCRS.C *continued*

```
            /* Check for both buttons pressed */
            if ( left && right )
                {
                if ( lhorz < 300 )
                    x = ( lhorz - 120 ) / 12;
                else
                    x = ( lhorz - 342 ) / 12;
                y = ( lvert - 20 ) / 9;
                if ( x >= 0 && x < 16 && y >= 0 && y < 16 )
                    {
                    gc.hot_spot_x = x;
                    gc.hot_spot_y = y;
                    draw_masks();
                    }
                }

            /* Show new test cursor if cursor moves into viewing area */
            old_view_status = view_status;
            view_status = ( horz < 90 && vert < 140 );
            if ( view_status != old_view_status )
                if ( view_status )
                    mouse_setgcurs( &gc );
                else
                    mouse_setgcurs( &gcursor_default );

            /* If left button was pressed, check location */
            if ( lpress )
                {

                /* Check for "Save New Cursor" */
                if ( lhorz < 91 && lvert > 149 && lvert < 171 )
                    {
                    numbers_to_strings();
                    for ( i = 0; i < 44; i++ )
                        fputs( tbuf[i], fptr );
                    rewind( fptr );
                    }

                /* Check for "Quit" */
                if ( lhorz < 56 && lvert > 179 && lvert < 196 )
                    quit_flag = 1;
```

(continued)

MOUSGCRS.C *continued*

```
            /* Check for a cursor reset */
            if ( lhorz > 549 && lhorz < 621 )
                {
                switch( ( lvert - 56 ) / 8 )
                    {
                    case 0:
                        gc = gcursor_default;
                        numbers_to_strings();
                        draw_masks();
                        break;
                    case 1:
                        gc = gcursor_hand;
                        numbers_to_strings();
                        draw_masks();
                        break;
                    case 2:
                        gc = gcursor_check;
                        numbers_to_strings();
                        draw_masks();
                        break;
                    case 3:
                        gc = gcursor_hour;
                        numbers_to_strings();
                        draw_masks();
                        break;
                    case 4:
                        gc = gcursor_jet;
                        numbers_to_strings();
                        draw_masks();
                        break;
                    case 5:
                        gc = gcursor_left;
                        numbers_to_strings();
                        draw_masks();
                        break;
                    case 6:
                        gc = gcursor_plus;
                        numbers_to_strings();
                        draw_masks();
                        break;
                    case 7:
                        gc = gcursor_up;
                        numbers_to_strings();
```

(continued)

MOUSGCRS.C *continued*

```
                        draw_masks();
                        break;
                case 8:
                        gc = gcursor_x;
                        numbers_to_strings();
                        draw_masks();
                        break;
                default:
                        break;
                }
        }

    /* Check if in mask region, vertically */
    if ( lvert > 19 && lvert < 164 )
        {
        /* Check for screen mask location */
        if ( lhorz > 119 && lhorz < 312 )
            {
            _setcolor( 0xFFFF );
            x = ( lhorz - 120 ) / 12;
            y = ( lvert - 20 ) / 9;
            mouse_hide();
            _rectangle( _GFILLINTERIOR,
                        x * 12 + 122, y * 9 + 21,
                        x * 12 + 128, y * 9 + 26 );
            mouse_show();
            gc.screen_mask[y] != ( 1 << ( 15 - x ));
            }

        /* Check for cursor mask location */
        if ( lhorz > 341 && lhorz < 534 )
            {
            _setcolor( 0xFFFF );
            x = ( lhorz - 342 ) / 12;
            y = ( lvert - 20 ) / 9;
            mouse_hide();
            _rectangle( _GFILLINTERIOR,
                        x * 12 + 344, y * 9 + 21,
                        x * 12 + 350, y * 9 + 26 );
            mouse_show();
            gc.cursor_mask[y] != ( 1 << ( 15 - x ));
            }
        }
    }
```

(continued)

MOUSGCRS.C *continued*

```
        /* If right button was pressed, check location */
        if ( rpress )
            {

            /* Check if in mask region, vertically */
            if ( rvert > 19 && rvert < 164 )
                {

                /* Check for screen mask location */
                if ( rhorz > 119 && rhorz < 312 )
                    {
                    _setcolor( 0x0000 );
                    x = ( rhorz - 120 ) / 12;
                    y = ( rvert - 20 ) / 9;
                    mouse_hide();
                    _rectangle( _GFILLINTERIOR,
                                x * 12 + 122, y * 9 + 21,
                                x * 12 + 128, y * 9 + 26 );
                    mouse_show();
                    gc.screen_mask[y] &= ~( 1 << ( 15 - x ));
                    }

                /* Check for cursor mask location */
                if ( rhorz > 341 && rhorz < 534 )
                    {
                    _setcolor( 0x0000 );
                    x = ( rhorz - 342 ) / 12;
                    y = ( rvert - 20 ) / 9;
                    mouse_hide();
                    _rectangle( _GFILLINTERIOR,
                                x * 12 + 344, y * 9 + 21,
                                x * 12 + 350, y * 9 + 26 );
                    mouse_show();
                    gc.cursor_mask[y] &= ~( 1 << ( 15 - x ));
                    }
                }
            }
        }

/* Close the new graphics cursor file */
fclose( fptr );
```

(continued)

MOUSGCRS.C *continued*

```c
    /* Restore the default video mode */
    _setvideomode( _DEFAULTMODE );
    _clearscreen( _GCLEARSCREEN );

    /* All done */
    return ( 0 );
}

/*
    Extract data structure numbers from mask strings
*/
void strings_to_numbers()
{
    int i;

    /* Extract from the screen mask strings */
    for ( i = 0; i < 16; i++ )
        sscanf( tbuf[i+5], " %i", &gc.screen_mask[i] );

    /* Extract from the cursor mask strings */
    for ( i = 0; i < 16; i++ )
        sscanf( tbuf[i+23], " %i", &gc.cursor_mask[i] );

    /* Extract from the hot spot string */
    sscanf( tbuf[41], " %i, %i", &gc.hot_spot_x, &gc.hot_spot_y );
}

/*
    Build mask strings from the data structures
*/
void numbers_to_strings()
{
    int i, j;

    /* Set the screen mask strings */
    for ( i = 0; i < 16; i++ )
        {
        sprintf( tbuf[i+5], "    0x%04X", gc.screen_mask[i] );
        tbuf[i+5][10] = ',';
        for ( j = 0; j < 16; j++ )
            if (( gc.screen_mask[i] >> j ) & 1 )
                tbuf[i+5][33-j] = '1';
```

(continued)

MOUSGCRS.C *continued*

```
            else
                tbuf[i+5][33-j] = '0';
        }

    /* Set the cursor mask strings */
    for ( i = 0; i < 16; i++ )
        {
        sprintf( tbuf[i+23], "    0x%04X", gc.cursor_mask[i] );
        tbuf[i+23][10] = ',';
        for ( j = 0; j < 16; j++ )
            if (( gc.cursor_mask[i] >> j ) & 1 )
                tbuf[i+23][33-j] = '1';
            else
                tbuf[i+23][33-j] = '0';
        }

    /* Set the hot spot string */
    sprintf( tbuf[41], "    %02d, %02d\n", gc.hot_spot_x, gc.hot_spot_y );
}


/*
    Update the display of mouse cursor mask pixels
*/
void draw_masks()
{
    int i, j;

    /* Hide the mouse cursor temporarily */
    mouse_hide();

    /* Set the screen mask pixels */
    for ( i = 0; i < 16; i++ )
        for ( j = 0; j < 16; j++ )
            {
            if (( gc.screen_mask[i] >> j ) & 1 )
                _setcolor( 0xFFFF );
            else
                _setcolor( 0x0000 );
            _rectangle( _GFILLINTERIOR,
                        (16 - j) * 12 + 110, (i + 1) * 9 + 12,
                        (16 - j) * 12 + 116, (i + 1) * 9 + 17 );
            }
```

(continued)

MOUSGCRS.C *continued*

```
    /* Set the cursor mask pixels */
    for ( i = 0; i < 16; i++ )
        for ( j = 0; j < 16; j++ )
            {
            if (( gc.cursor_mask[i] >> j ) & 1 )
                _setcolor( 0xFFFF );
            else
                _setcolor( 0x0000 );

            _rectangle( _GFILLINTERIOR,
                        (16 - j) * 12 + 332, (i + 1) * 9 + 12,
                        (16 - j) * 12 + 338, (i + 1) * 9 + 17 );
            }

    /* Show the mouse cursor again */
    mouse_show();
}
```

MOVE

SYNTAX

move *filename.ext newpath*

filename.ext is the name of the file you want to move. The filename can include wildcard characters.

newpath is the pathname of the destination directory, which must reside on the same drive as the file to be moved.

The MOVE utility moves files from one subdirectory to another. This program works faster than copying a file to another directory and then deleting it from its original location, because the file contents are not moved—only the directory entries are changed. Of course, this technique works only for moving files from directory to directory on a given drive, not to another disk or disk drive.

DOS function 0x56 performs the critical task in this program: It renames the specified file to accommodate the destination path. To use this DOS service, a calling program must pass far addresses for strings that contain the original path and the new path. The in-line assembler capability of QuickC provides an excellent mechanism for placing information in the appropriate registers and activating the interrupt.

The MOVE program lets you use wildcards in the filename to be processed. You can therefore move whole groups of files with a single invocation of the MOVE program. See the CAT utility, described on page 408, for more information about using wildcard expansion.

```
/* -------------------------------------------------------------------
    Name:           MOVE.C
    Type:           Utility program
    Language:       Microsoft QuickC version 2
    Video:          (no special video requirements)

    Program list:   MOVE.C
                    SETARGV.OBJ
```

(continued)

MOVE.C *continued*

```
    Note:           Build with Extended Dictionary flag turned off
                    (Options-Make-Linker Flags)

    Usage:          move filename.ext newpath
                    (wildcards allowed for filename.ext)

    Description:    Moves a file or a set of files to a new
                    directory on the same disk drive
    ----------------------------------------------------------------
/*

#include <stdio.h>
#include <stdlib.h>
#include <string.h>
#include <dos.h>

#define BELL 7

main( int argc, char *argv[] )
{
    int i;
    unsigned result;
    char newpath[255], source[255], destination[255];
    char *sname;
    void far *so = (void far *)source;
    void far *de = (void far *)destination;
    unsigned src_seg = FP_SEG( so );
    unsigned src_off = FP_OFF( so );
    unsigned des_seg = FP_SEG( de );
    unsigned des_off = FP_OFF( de );

    /* Check for minimum number of command line parameters */
    if ( argc < 3 )
        {
        printf( "Usage: move filename.ext newpath\n" );
        printf( "(wildcards allowed for filename.ext)\n" );
        exit( 1 );
        }

    /* Get the new path */
    strcpy( newpath, argv[--argc] );
    strcat( newpath, "\\" );
```

(continued)

MOVE.C *continued*

```
    /* Process each of the files */
    for ( i = 1; i < argc; i++ )
        {

        /* Get the name of the source file */
        strcpy( source, argv[i] );

        /* Build the full destination pathname */
        strcpy( destination, newpath );
        sname = strrchr( source, '\\' );
        if ( sname == NULL )
            strcat( destination, source );
        else
            strcat( destination, sname + 1 );

        /* DOS function 0x56 - Rename File */
        _asm
            {
            /* save ds and di registers */
            push ds
            push di

            /* Stack up the string addresses */
            mov ax, src_seg
            push ax
            mov ax, src_off
            push ax
            mov ax, des_seg
            push ax
            mov ax, des_off
            push ax

            /* Pop addresses into desired registers */
            pop di
            pop es
            pop dx
            pop ds

            /* DOS function 0x56 (interrupt 0x21) */
            mov ah, 0x56
            int 0x21

            /* Restore di and ds registers */
            pop di
            pop ds
```

(continued)

MOVE.C *continued*

```
            /* Carry flag indicates result */
            mov result, 0
            jnc done
            mov result, 1

            done:
            }

        /* Inform user of the results */
        printf( "Moving %s to %s\n", source, destination );
        if ( result )
            printf( "...FAILED%c\n", BELL );
        }

    /* All done */
    return ( 0 );
}
```

OBJECT

SYNTAX

object *filename.ext*

filename.ext identifies an optional file that you can edit.

The OBJECT utility lets you interactively create graphics objects, or icons, for programs that require animation. The program works like a simple "paint" program: You use the mouse to select colors, draw the image, and save the results.

The output from this program is a QuickC source code file named, by default, WORKOBJ.C. If you include a filename in the command line, the output is saved to the named file. The work file contains an array declaration that you can merge into any 16-color, medium-resolution graphics program to re-create the graphics object. The *_putimage()* function quickly "bit-pumps" the array contents onto the display. The function works fast enough to allow animation effects.

The OBJECT utility is perhaps the largest program in this book. The MOUSEFUN and GETKEY toolbox modules provide mouse and keyboard support, and several large arrays are defined for saving and restoring the graphics images. The structure *cross_hair* redefines the graphics mode mouse cursor. (The alternate cursor was created with the MOUSGCRS utility.) OBJECT.C contains ample comments; the resulting source code is quite long, but it is more easily understood.

The program first verifies that the hardware supports the 16-color, medium-resolution EGA graphics mode. (You might convert this program for other graphics modes as a way of learning more about the video parameters.) After drawing the background items, the program checks for a mouse. The program is designed for mouse use only, and it will screech to a halt if no mouse is available. (Again, as a good learning experience, try modifying the program for keyboard use only.)

If the necessary video mode and the mouse are both available, the program tries to load the current work file as a starting point for the current editing session. If it does not find the default work file or a specified alternative, the utility begins with a blank work area.

Use the mouse to select one of the 16 colors from the boxes along the bottom of the display. Click the left mouse button to select a color. The box around the current color selection will be highlighted.

Next, move the cursor into the drawing area and press the left button to fill the indicated pixel. For freehand drawing, press and hold the left button as you move the mouse. To erase pixels, simply choose black as the current color and draw over the unwanted pixels.

The OBJECT utility provides three menu choices along the left side of the display. Click on *Erase* to clear all pixels in the drawing area. Click on *Save* to create an output file that contains the pixel pattern for the object in the work area. When you're ready to quit, click on *Quit* to exit the program.

When you choose the *Save* option, a thin white line flickers across the drawing area. This line appears as the program searches for the far left, right, top, and bottom edges of the graphics image. By obtaining this information, OBJECT can dimension the rectangular array that defines the graphics object. Large objects therefore result in larger work files than do small objects.

The OBJECT program effectively demonstrates several QuickC graphics functions. In particular, it uses _getimage() and _putimage() in several places, along with the associated _imagesize() function. The program also uses the _floodfill() function to fill in the border around the drawing area.

Notice that OBJECT makes several calls to the *mouse_hide()* and *mouse_show()* functions. Whenever a program modifies graphics pixels, it should turn off the mouse cursor temporarily. This precaution prevents unwanted interaction between the cursor image and the modified pixels.

```
/* -----------------------------------------------------------------
    Name:          OBJECT.C
    Type:          Utility program
    Language:      Microsoft QuickC
    Video:         EGA or VGA required

    Notes:         Mouse required
                   Use LARGE memory model
```

(continued)

OBJECT.C *continued*

```
     Program list:    OBJECT.C
                      MOUSEFUN.C
                      GETKEY.C
                      GRAPHICS.LIB


     Usage:           object [filename.ext]


     Description:     Interactive source code builder for graphics icons
     ----------------------------------------------------------------
*/

#include <stdio.h>
#include <stdlib.h>
#include <io.h>
#include <graph.h>
#include <string.h>

#include "mousefun.h"
#include "getkey.h"
#include "t_colors.h"

/* Define labels for default color palette */
#define BLACK        0
#define BLUE         1
#define GREEN        2
#define CYAN         3
#define RED          4
#define MAGENTA      5
#define BROWN        6
#define WHITE        7
#define GRAY         8
#define LIGHTBLUE    9
#define LIGHTGREEN   10
#define LIGHTCYAN    11
#define LIGHTRED     12
#define LIGHTMAGENTA 13
#define LIGHTYELLOW  14
#define BRIGHTWHITE  15
```

(continued)

OBJECT.C *continued*

```
static struct graphics_cursor far cross_hair =
{

    /*  screen mask  */
    0xFFFF,     /* 1111111111111111 */
    0xFC7F,     /* 1111110001111111 */
    0xFC7F,     /* 1111110001111111 */
    0xFC7F,     /* 1111110001111111 */
    0xFC7F,     /* 1111110001111111 */
    0xFFFF,     /* 1111111111111111 */
    0x07C1,     /* 0000011111000001 */
    0x07C1,     /* 0000011111000001 */
    0x07C1,     /* 0000011111000001 */
    0xFFFF,     /* 1111111111111111 */
    0xFC7F,     /* 1111110001111111 */
    0xFC7F,     /* 1111110001111111 */
    0xFC7F,     /* 1111110001111111 */
    0xFC7F,     /* 1111110001111111 */
    0xFFFF,     /* 1111111111111111 */
    0xFFFF,     /* 1111111111111111 */

    /*  cursor mask  */
    0x0000,     /* 0000000000000000 */
    0x0000,     /* 0000000000000000 */
    0x0100,     /* 0000000100000000 */
    0x0100,     /* 0000000100000000 */
    0x0100,     /* 0000000100000000 */
    0x0000,     /* 0000000000000000 */
    0x0000,     /* 0000000000000000 */
    0x783C,     /* 0111100000111100 */
    0x0000,     /* 0000000000000000 */
    0x0000,     /* 0000000000000000 */
    0x0100,     /* 0000000100000000 */
    0x0100,     /* 0000000100000000 */
    0x0100,     /* 0000000100000000 */
    0x0000,     /* 0000000000000000 */
    0x0000,     /* 0000000000000000 */
    0x0000,     /* 0000000000000000 */

    /* hot spot x,y */
    14, 07
};
```

(continued)

```
/* Arrays for _getimage() and _putimage() manipulations */
char far vslice[624];
char far hslice[120];
char far object[17984];

main( int argc, char *argv[] )
{
    int i, j;
    int x1, y1, x2, y2;
    int x, y, x_old = 0, y_old = 0;
    int status, buttons;
    int lpress, lhorz, lvert;
    int left_btn, right_btn;
    int horz_now, vert_now;
    int quit_flag = 0;
    int color_old = 0, color_now = WHITE;
    long asize;
    FILE *wfile;
    char workfile[80];
    char buf[80];
    char **dmy;

    /* Set the video mode */
    if ( _setvideomode( _MRES16COLOR ) == 0 )
        {
        printf( "Can't set the _MRES16COLOR EGA mode\n" );
        exit( 1 );
        }

    /* Set name of work file */
    if ( argc == 2 )
        strcpy( workfile, argv[1] );
    else
        strcpy( workfile, "WORKOBJ.C" );

    /* Draw border around object drawing area */
    _clearscreen( _GCLEARSCREEN );
    _setcolor( BROWN );
    _rectangle( _GBORDER, 40, 10, 270, 170 );
    _rectangle( _GBORDER, 42, 12, 268, 168 );
    _floodfill( 41, 11, BROWN );
```

(continued)

OBJECT.C *continued*

```
/* Display the title */
_settextposition( 1, 15 );
_settextcolor( LIGHTYELLOW );
_outtext( "- OBJECT -" );

/* Draw the color selection boxes */
_setcolor( WHITE );
_rectangle( _GFILLINTERIOR, 0, 179, 319, 199 );
for ( i = 0; i < 16; i++ )
    {
    _setcolor( i );
    x1 = i * 20 + 2;
    y1 = 181;
    x2 = i * 20 + 17;
    y2 = 197;
    _rectangle( _GFILLINTERIOR, x1, y1, x2, y2 );
    }

/* Place the menu selections */
_settextcolor( BRIGHTWHITE );
_settextposition( 9, 1 );
_outtext( "Erase" );
_settextposition( 11, 1 );
_outtext( "Save" );
_settextposition( 17, 1 );
_outtext( "Quit" );

/* Place the short instructions */
_settextcolor( CYAN );
_settextposition( 6, 35 );
_outtext( "Use" );
_settextposition( 7, 35 );
_outtext( "mouse" );
_settextposition( 8, 35 );
_outtext( "to" );
_settextposition( 9, 35 );
_outtext( "set" );
_settextposition( 10, 35 );
_outtext( "pixels" );
_settextposition( 11, 35 );
_outtext( "and" );
_settextposition( 12, 35 );
_outtext( "to" );
```

(continued)

OBJECT.C *continued*

```
    _settextposition( 13, 35 );
    _outtext( "select" );
    _settextposition( 14, 35 );
    _outtext( "from" );
    _settextposition( 15, 35 );
    _outtext( "menu" );
    _settextposition( 16, 35 );
    _outtext( "items" );

    /* Start up the mouse */
    mouse_reset( &status, &buttons );
    if ( status == 0 )
        {
        printf( "Can't access the mouse\n" );
        exit( 1 );
        }

    /* Set the cross-hair cursor */
    mouse_setgcurs( &cross_hair );

    /* Try to open the work file to get the latest edit */
    if (( wfile = fopen( workfile, "r" )) != NULL )
        {

        /* First line contains no numbers */
        fgets( buf, 80, wfile );

        /* Second line tells size of array */
        fgets( buf, 80, wfile );
        asize = atol( &buf[16] );

        /* Third line contains no numbers */
        fgets( buf, 80, wfile );

        /* Get each of the bytes from the rest of the file */
        for ( i = 0; i < (int)asize; i++ )
            {

            /* Eight numbers per line, then read next line */
            if (( i % 8 ) == 0 )
                {
                fgets( buf, 80, wfile );
                j = 3;
                }
```

(continued)

OBJECT.C *continued*

```
              /* Extract each hexadecimal number from the line */
              object[i] = (char)strtol( &buf[j], dmy, 16 );

              /* Index to the next number in the line */
              j += 6;
              }

        /* Put the old image up for editing */
        _putimage( 155 - ( object[0] >> 1 ),
                   90 - ( object[2] >> 1 ), object, _GPSET );

        /* Close the file */
        fclose( wfile );
        }

/* Make the mouse cursor visible */
mouse_show();

/* Main loop starts here */
while ( !quit_flag )
    {

    /* Get button press information */
    mouse_press( LBUTTON, &status, &lpress, &lhorz, &lvert );

    /* Get current state of the mouse */
    mouse_status( &left_btn, &right_btn, &horz_now, &vert_now );

    /* Check if left mouse button is currently depressed */
    if ( left_btn )
        {

        /* Is the cursor in the drawing area? */
        if ( horz_now > 84 && horz_now < 536 &&
             vert_now > 12 && vert_now < 168 )
            {

            /* Determine the coordinates of the pixel */
            x = horz_now >> 1;
            y = vert_now;
```

(continued)

```
                /* Set the pixel only if cursor has moved */
                if ( x_old != x || y_old != y )
                    {

                    /* Hide the mouse cursor */
                    mouse_hide();

                    /* Color the pixel */
                    _setcolor( color_now );
                    _setpixel( x, y );

                    /* Show the mouse cursor */
                    mouse_show();

                    x_old = x;
                    y_old = y;
                    }
                }
            }

    /* Check for "Erase" selection */
    if ( lpress && lhorz < 77 && lvert > 61 && lvert < 73 )
        {

        /* Hide the mouse cursor */
        mouse_hide();

        /* Erase the drawing area */
        _setcolor( BLACK );
        _rectangle( _GFILLINTERIOR, 43, 13, 267, 167 );

        /* Show the mouse cursor */
        mouse_show();
        }

    /* Check for "Save" selection */
    if ( lpress && lhorz < 77 && lvert > 77 && lvert < 89 )
        {

        /* Hide the mouse cursor */
        mouse_hide();
```

(continued)

OBJECT.C *continued*

```
               /* Draw lines in bright white */
               _setcolor( BRIGHTWHITE );

               /* Find the left edge of the object */
               for ( x = 43; x < 268; x++ )
                   {

                   /* Set x1 same as x */
                   x1 = x;

                   /* Get a vertical slice of the image area */
                   _getimage( x, 13, x, 167, vslice );

                   /* Draw a line to show the progress */
                   _moveto( x, 13 );
                   _lineto( x, 167 );

                   /* Check for any nonzero pixels */
                   for ( i = 4; i < 624; i++ )
                       {
                       if ( vslice[i] )
                           x = 269;
                       }

                   /* Restore the slice */
                   _putimage( x1, 13, vslice, _GPSET );
                   }

               /* Find the right edge of the object */
               for ( x = 267; x > 42; x-- )
                   {

                   /* Set x2 same as x */
                   x2 = x;

                   /* Get a vertical slice of the image area */
                   _getimage( x, 13, x, 167, vslice );

                   /* Draw a line to show the progress */
                   _moveto( x, 13 );
                   _lineto( x, 167 );
```

(continued)

```
                    /* Check for any nonzero pixels */
                    for ( i = 4; i < 624; i++ )
                        {
                        if ( vslice[i] )
                            x = 41;
                        }

                    /* Restore the slice */
                    _putimage( x2, 13, vslice, _GPSET );
                    }

                /* Find the top edge of the object */
                for ( y = 13; y < 168; y++ )
                    {

                    /* Set y1 same as y */
                    y1 = y;

                    /* Get a horizontal slice of the image area */
                    _getimage( 43, y, 267, y, hslice );

                    /* Draw a line to show the progress */
                    _moveto( 43, y );
                    _lineto( 267, y );

                    /* Check for any nonzero pixels */
                    for ( i = 4; i < 120; i++ )
                        {
                        if ( hslice[i] )
                            y = 168;
                        }

                    /* Restore the slice */
                    _putimage( 43, y1, hslice, _GPSET );
                    }

                /* Find the bottom edge of the object */
                for ( y = 167; y > 12; y-- )
                    {

                    /* Set y2 same as y */
                    y2 = y;
```

(continued)

OBJECT.C *continued*

```
                /* Get a horizontal slice of the image area */
                _getimage( 43, y, 267, y, hslice );

                /* Draw a line to show the progress */
                _moveto( 43, y );
                _lineto( 267, y );

                /* Check for any nonzero pixels */
                for ( i = 4; i < 120; i++ )
                    {
                    if ( hslice[i] )
                        y = 12;
                    }

                /* Restore the slice */
                _putimage( 43, y2, hslice, _GPSET );
                }

        /* Determine size of array for image save */
        asize = _imagesize( x1, y1, x2, y2 );

        /* Get the object */
        _getimage( x1, y1, x2, y2, object );

        /* Open the output file */
        if (( wfile = fopen( workfile, "w" )) == NULL )
            {
            printf( "Can't open output file" );
            exit( 1 );
            }

        /* Write to the output file */
        fprintf( wfile, "\nchar far object[%ld] =\n{", asize );

        /* Write the lines of eight hexadecimal bytes each */
        for ( i = 0; i < (int)asize; i++ )
            {
```

(continued)

```
                /* Every eight bytes go to next line */
                if (( i % 8 ) == 0 )
                    {
                    if ( i )
                        fprintf( wfile, ",\n    " );
                    else
                        fprintf( wfile, "\n    " );
                    }
                else
                    fprintf( wfile, ", " );
                fprintf( wfile, "0x%2.2X", (unsigned char)object[i] );
                }

        /* Write last lines to file */
        fprintf( wfile, "\n};\n" );

        /* Close the output file */
        fclose( wfile );

        /* Show the mouse cursor */
        mouse_show();
        }

    /* Check for "Quit" selection */
    if ( lpress && lhorz < 77 && lvert > 125 && lvert < 137 )
        quit_flag = 1;

    /* Check for a color selection */
    if ( lpress && lvert > 180 )
        color_now = lhorz / 40;

    /* Check for a change in the selected color */
    if ( color_now != color_old )
        {

        /* Hide the mouse cursor */
        mouse_hide();

        /* Erase bright border on old color choice */
        _setcolor( WHITE );
        _rectangle( _GBORDER, color_old * 20 + 1, 180,
                    color_old * 20 + 18, 198 );
        _rectangle( _GBORDER, color_old * 20, 179,
                    color_old * 20 + 19, 199 );
```

(continued)

OBJECT.C *continued*

```
            /* Set new bright border */
            _setcolor( BRIGHTWHITE );
            _rectangle( _GBORDER, color_now * 20 + 1, 180,
                        color_now * 20 + 18, 198 );
            _rectangle( _GBORDER, color_now * 20, 179,
                        color_now * 20 + 19, 199 );

            /* Make the mouse cursor visible again */
            mouse_show();

            /* Update the old color */
            color_old = color_now;
            }

        }

    /* All done */
    mouse_hide();
    _setvideomode( _DEFAULTMODE );
    return ( 0 );
}
```

OUT

SYNTAX

out *value*

value is a byte value (or a series of byte values) to be sent to standard output.

The OUT utility sends byte values from the command line to standard output. Given the capability of DOS to redirect output, the utility provides a convenient way to send escape code sequences or other byte sequences to a printer, an ANSI.SYS display device driver, or any other output device.

You can specify byte values in a number of different formats. OUT interprets the command line parameters based on the first character in each value. If the first character is a nonzero digit, the utility assumes that the parameter is a decimal value. If the first character is *0*, OUT checks the second character as well: An uppercase or lowercase *X* indicates hexadecimal format; otherwise, OUT interprets the parameter as an octal value. If the first character is not a digit, OUT sends the parameter as a string of character bytes.

A few examples can help clarify these interpretation rules. Consider the following command lines and the displayed output that results from each:

```
C>out 65 66 67
ABC

C>out 0x43 0x41 0x44
CAD

C>out 0101 0103 0105
ACE

C>out This is a string
Thisisastring

C>out "This is a string"
This is a string
```

The last two OUT commands differ only in the use of double quotation marks around the string elements. With the quotation marks in place, the entire string is parsed as a single parameter; hence, the OUT utility sends all the characters to the output device, including the spaces. Without the quotation marks, the words are parsed as four separate parameters, and the output contains no intervening spaces.

This program has proved to be quite useful for some DOS tasks. For example, a batch file that contains the following OUT command sends the proper escape code sequence to set an EPSON MX-80 printer into "tiny print" (superscript) text mode:

```
out 0x8F 0x1B 0x53 0x01 0x1B 0x33 0x0F > prn
```

If you install ANSI.SYS at bootup time, you can use OUT to send escape code sequences within AUTOEXEC.BAT that set the screen colors. You can place other OUT commands in AUTOEXEC.BAT to initialize printers or other devices.

```
/* ------------------------------------------------------------------
    Name:           OUT.C
    Type:           Utility program
    Language:       Microsoft QuickC
    Video:          (no special video requirements)

    Program list:   (not required)

    Usage:          out value ...
                    where value is expressed as one of the following:
                    Oxnnn or OXnnn  Hexadecimal byte value
                    Onnn            Octal byte value
                    nnn             Decimal byte value
                    (anything else) Characters to be sent literally

    Description:    Send bytes or characters to stdout
    ------------------------------------------------------------------
*/

#include <stdio.h>
#include <string.h>
```

(continued)

```
main( int argc, char *argv[] )
{
    char *buf;
    char c1, c2;
    int i, n;

    /* Process each command line parameter */
    for ( i = 1; i < argc; i++ )
        {

        /* Get the next parameter */
        buf = argv[i];

        /* Grab the first and second characters */
        c1 = *buf;
        c2 = *(buf + 1);

        /* Determine the type of parameter */
        switch( c1 )
            {

            /* Hexadecimal or octal? */
            case '0':

                /* Hexadecimal? */
                if ( c2 == 'x' || c2 == 'X' )
                    {
                    buf += 2;
                    sscanf( buf, "%x", &n );
                    putchar( n );
                    }

                /* Must be octal */
                else
                    {
                    sscanf( buf, "%o", &n );
                    putchar( n );
                    }
                break;
```

(continued)

OUT.C *continued*

```
            /* Decimal digit? */
            case '1':
            case '2':
            case '3':
            case '4':
            case '5':
            case '6':
            case '7':
            case '8':
            case '9':
                sscanf( buf, "%d", &n );
                putchar( n );
                break;

            /* Must be some other ASCII characters */
            default:
                while ( *buf != '\n' && *buf != '\0' )
                    putchar( *(buf++) );
                break;
            }
        }

    /* All done */
    return ( 0 );
}
```

PI

pi *digits*

digits is the total number of digits to which you want to calculate pi.

The PI utility computes the value of pi to a given number of digits. Over the centuries, efforts to determine the precise digits of pi have fascinated many scientists and science enthusiasts. As recently as July, 1961, computers had been used to calculate pi to only 20,000 decimal places.

The PI program can calculate pi to over 65,000 digits, although the time required for such an extensive calculation could run to a few days, depending on the speed of your computer. The execution time is proportional to the square of the number of digits. In simpler terms, when you double the number of digits to be found, the program takes four times as long to run. On a 20-MHz 80386 computer, PI required only a few minutes to find pi to 2000 digits—a respectable calculation rate.

Several formulas have proven useful for the computer calculation of pi. This program uses the following equation:

```
pi = 4 * ( 4 * atan( 1/5 ) - atan( 1/239 ))
```

To calculate the arctangent, the program expands a series in which each of the diminishing terms is found and summed until a term of zero is reached. When expanded, the calculations take the following form:

```
pi = 4 * (( 4 * ( 1/(1*5¹) - 1/(3*5³) + 1/(5*5⁵) - ...)
              - ( 1/(1*239¹) - 1/(3*239³) + 1/(5*239⁵) - ...)))
```

The PI utility uses several functions for performing basic math operations on large arrays of digits. You might find these functions useful in other programs that involve extremely large numbers.

The program declares several large global character arrays just before the *main()* function. After you compile and link the source file, the resulting PI.EXE file is larger than 200 KB because memory images of these large arrays are placed in the file to be loaded at run time.

You can compress the executable file to less than 12 KB with the /E linker option. To use this option with QuickC, create a program list, PI.MAK, and add PI.C to the list. After you save the list, load PI.MAK into the editor, look for the first linker command that starts with LFLAGS_G, and add the /E option to the end of this line. Reload PI.C, set the program list to PI.MAK (to load the edited make file), and rebuild the program. The new PI.EXE file is much smaller than the original. The linker options are described in detail in *Microsoft QuickC Tool Kit* (which accompanies the software product).

```
/* ------------------------------------------------------------------

    Name:           PI.C
    Type:           Utility program
    Language:       Microsoft QuickC
    Video:          (no special video requirements)

    Program list:   PI.C

    Note:           Use COMPACT memory model

    Usage:          pi digits

    Description:    Calculates pi to the given number of digits

    Equation:       pi = 4 * ( 4 * atan( 1/5 ) - atan( 1/239 ))


    ------------------------------------------------------------------
*/

#include <stdio.h>
#include <stdlib.h>
#include <string.h>

#define MAXDIG 65535

/* Function prototypes */
void arraymult( unsigned mult );
void arraydivide( unsigned div );
```

(continued)

PI.C *continued*

```
void arrayadd( void );
void arraysub( void );
int bzero( void );
void arctangent( unsigned s );

/* Global variables */
char a[MAXDIG], b[MAXDIG], c[MAXDIG];
unsigned digits;

main( int argc, char *argv[] )
{
    unsigned i, j1 = 0, j2 = 0, j3 = 0;

    /* Check the input parameter for number of digits */
    if ( argc != 2 )
        {
        printf("You must specify number of digits... pi n\n");
        abort();
        }

    /* Get the number of digits */
    digits = atoi( argv[1] );

    /* Find the atan() of 1/239 */
    arctangent( 239 );

    /* Store result in c */
    memcpy( c, a, MAXDIG );

    /* Find the atan() of 1/5 */
    arctangent( 5 );

    /* Store result in b */
    memcpy( b, á, MAXDIG );

    /* Multiply b by 4 */
    arraymult( 4 );

    /* Store result in a */
    memcpy( a, b, MAXDIG );

    /* Get the atan() of 1/239 into b */
    memcpy( b, c, MAXDIG );
```

(continued)

PI.C *continued*

```
    /* Subtract b from a */
    arraysub();

    /* Store result in b */
    memcpy( b, a, MAXDIG );

    /* Multiply b by 4 to get final answer */
    arraymult( 4 );

    /* Output the first short line */
    printf( "PI = 3.+\n" );

    /* Output the digits */
    for ( i = 1; i < digits; i++ )
        {

        /* Output each digit as correct character */
        printf( "%c", b[i] + '0' );

        /* Space out each group of ten digits */
        if ( ++j1 == 10 )
            {
            j1 = 0;
            printf( " " );

            /* New line after five groups of digits */
            if ( ++j2 == 5 )
                {
                j2 = 0;
                printf( "\n" );

                /* Blank line after five lines of digits */
                if ( ++j3 == 5 )
                    {
                    j3 = 0;
                    printf( "\n" );
                    }
                }
            }
        }
    printf( "\n" );

    /* All done */
    return ( 0 );
}
```

(continued)

```
/* Multiply b array of digits by mult */
void arraymult( unsigned mult )
{
    unsigned i;
    unsigned carry = 0, temp;
    unsigned long lcarry = 0L, ltemp, lmult;
    char *bptr;

    bptr = b + digits + 1;
    lmult = (unsigned long)mult;

    if ( mult < 6552 )
        {
        for ( i = 0; i <= digits; i++ )
            {
            temp = *bptr * mult + carry;
            carry = temp / 10;
            *(bptr--) = (char)( temp % 10 );
            }
        }
    else
        {
        for ( i = 0; i <= digits; i++ )
            {
            ltemp = *bptr * lmult + lcarry;
            lcarry = ltemp / 10;
            *(bptr--) = (char)( ltemp % 10 );
            }
        }
}

/* Divide b array of digits by div */
void arraydivide( unsigned div )
{
    unsigned i;
    unsigned borrow = 0, temp;
    unsigned long lborrow = 0L, ltemp;
    char *bptr = b;
```

(continued)

PI.C *continued*

```
    if ( div < 6552 )
        {
        for ( i = 0; i <= digits; i++ )
            {
            temp = *bptr + borrow * 10;
            *(bptr++) = (char)( temp / div );
            borrow = temp % div;
            }
        }
    else
        {
        for ( i = 0; i <= digits; i++ )
            {
            ltemp = *bptr + lborrow * 10;
            *(bptr++) = (char)( ltemp / div );
            lborrow = ltemp % div;
            }
        }
}

/* Add b array into a array */
void arrayadd( void )
{
    unsigned carry = 0, temp, i;
    char *aptr, *bptr;

    aptr = a + digits + 1;
    bptr = b + digits + 1;

    for ( i = 0; i <= digits; i++ )
        {
        temp = *aptr + *(bptr--) + carry;
        carry = temp / 10;
        *(aptr--) = (char)( temp % 10 );
        }
}
```

(continued)

490

PI.C *continued*

```
/* Subtract b array from a array */
void arraysub( void )
{
    unsigned temp, i;
    char *aptr, *bptr;

    aptr = a + digits + 1;
    bptr = b + digits + 1;

    for ( i = 0; i <= digits; i++ )
        {
        temp = *aptr - *(bptr--) + 10;
        *(aptr--) = (char)( temp % 10 );
        if ( temp < 10 )
            *aptr -= 1;
        }
}

/* Check b array for being all zero */
int bzero( void )
{
    unsigned i;
    char *bptr = b;

    for ( i = 0; i <= digits; i++ )
        if ( *(bptr++) )
            return ( 0 );

    return ( 1 );
}

/* Find atan() of 1 / s, leaving result in the a array */
void arctangent( unsigned s )
{
    unsigned n = 1, z = 1, tog = 1;
    unsigned m, quot, rmdr;

    memset( a, 0, MAXDIG );
    memset( b, 0, MAXDIG );
    b[0] = 1;
    arraydivide( s );
    memcpy( a, b, MAXDIG );
```

(continued)

PI.C *continued*

```
    do
        {
        arraymult( n );
        arraydivide( s * s );
        n += 2;
        arraydivide( n );
        if (( tog = -tog ) == 1 )
            arrayadd();
        else
            arraysub();
        }
    while ( !bzero() );
}
```

PS

SYNTAX

ps *options* < *input* > *output*

options is a format setting (or a series of format settings) that controls the printed output. The input source would normally be a file, and output would be redirected to a printer.

The PS utility provides a simple method for sending ASCII files to a Post-Script printer. Expensive, cumbersome word-processing programs are usually equipped for printing PostScript files. The PS utility, however, provides a "minimalist" alternative—a filter that takes input redirected from a file and allows its output to be redirected to a PostScript printer.

This utility actually creates a PostScript program and sends it to the standard output. The program contains commands to set up the output formatting and to print the lines from the file. Assuming that you redirect the output to a printer that has a built-in PostScript interpreter, the printer then interprets the program and prints the file contents.

PS recognizes several command line parameters that control the format of the printed output. All these parameters have reasonable defaults, so you can safely omit them. (To change these defaults permanently, edit the corresponding *#define* directives.) These optional parameters and their default values are listed in the following table.

OPTION	DEFAULT	DESCRIPTION
?		Displays help information
LI*nn*	6.0	Sets the number of lines per inch
LM*nn*	0.5	Sets the left margin in inches
TM*nn*	1.0	Sets the top margin in inches
BM*nn*	1.0	Sets the bottom margin in inches
SF*nn*	1.0	Sets the scale font factor

The following command demonstrates the use of command line redirection with PS. The command sends a file named TEXT.TXT to a printer:

```
C>ps < text.txt > prn
```

If you redirect the output to a file rather than to the printer, you can study a copy of the PostScript program designed to control the printer. If you do not redirect the output, PS sends the PostScript program to your screen.

If you forget to redirect the input to have PS read from a file, the program will appear to hang. In this state, the program is actually waiting for input from the keyboard. Type Ctrl-Z and then press Enter to signal the end of input from the keyboard. PS then proceeds with the conversion to PostScript and ends normally.

```
/* --------------------------------------------------------------------
    Name:          PS.C
    Type:          Utility program
    Language:      Microsoft QuickC
    Video:         (no special video requirements)

    Program list:  (not required)

    Usage:         ps [ options ... ][ < input ][ > output ]
    Options:       ?    - Help
                   LInn - Lines per inch
                   LMnn - Left margin
                   TMnn - Top margin
                   BMnn - Bottom margin
                   SFnn - Scale font factor

    Description:   Filters files for output to a PostScript printer
    --------------------------------------------------------------------
*/

#include <stdio.h>
#include <stdlib.h>
#include <string.h>
```

(continued)

PS.C *continued*

```
/* Default format options */
#define LINESPERINCH   6.0
#define LEFTMARGIN     0.5
#define TOPMARGIN      1.0
#define BOTTOMMARGIN   1.0
#define SCALEFACTOR    1.0

main( int argc, char *argv[] )
{
    int i;
    int first_time = 1;
    double scale;
    double lines_per_inch = LINESPERINCH;
    double left_margin = LEFTMARGIN;
    double top_margin = TOPMARGIN;
    double bottom_margin = BOTTOMMARGIN;
    double scale_factor = SCALEFACTOR;
    double y_location = 0.0;
    double line_increment;
    char buf[256], c;

    /* Get parameters, use defaults if not given by user */
    for ( i = 1; i < argc; i++ )
        {

        /* Convert to uppercase */
        strupr( argv[i] );

        /* Check for "?", requesting help */
        if ( argv[i][0] == '?' )
            {
            printf( "\nUsage:  ps [options ...]\n" );
            printf( "Options:\n" );
            printf( "\tlinn - Lines per inch, default = 6.0\n" );
            printf( "\tlmnn - Left margin, default = 0.5 inches\n" );
            printf( "\ttmnn - Top margin, default = 1.0 inches\n" );
            printf( "\tbmnn - Bottom margin, default = 1.0 inches\n" );
            printf( "\tsfnn - Font scale factor, default = 1.0\n\n" );
            exit( 0 );
            }
```

(continued)

PS.C *continued*

```
        /* Check for "LI", number of lines per inch */
        if ( argv[i][0] == 'L' && argv[i][1] == 'I' )
            lines_per_inch = atof( &argv[i][2] );

        /* Check for "LM", left margin in inches */
        if ( argv[i][0] == 'L' && argv[i][1] == 'M' )
            left_margin = atof( &argv[i][2] );

        /* Check for "TM", top margin in inches */
        if ( argv[i][0] == 'T' && argv[i][1] == 'M' )
            top_margin = atof( &argv[i][2] );

        /* Check for "BM", bottom margin in inches */
        if ( argv[i][0] == 'B' && argv[i][1] == 'M' )
            bottom_margin = atof( &argv[i][2] );

        /* Check for "SF", character scale factor */
        if ( argv[i][0] == 'S' && argv[i][1] == 'F' )
            scale_factor = atof( &argv[i][2] );
        }

    /* Set line increment as function of number of lines per inch */
    line_increment = 1.0 / lines_per_inch;

    /* Set font scale as function of scale factor and lines per inch */
    scale = scale_factor / lines_per_inch;

    /* Main processing loop */
    while ( 1 )
        {

        /* Get each line from stdin */
        if ( gets( buf ) == NULL )
            break;

        /* Move down to the next line */
        y_location -= line_increment;

        /* Check for bottom of page */
        if ( y_location < bottom_margin )
            {
```

(continued)

```
            /* Finish page if not the first time here */
            if ( !first_time )
                printf( "showpage restore\n" );

            /* Start another page */
            y_location = 11.0 - top_margin - line_increment;
            printf( "save 72 72 scale\n" );
            printf( "/courier findfont %.4f scalefont setfont\n", scale );
            printf( "%.4g 0 translate .93 1 scale\n", left_margin );

            /* Signal that first time through is over */
            first_time = 0;
            }

        /* Send out the line header */
        printf( "0 %.4g moveto (", y_location );

        /* Send out the line, watching for special characters */
        for ( i = 0; buf[i]; i++ )
            {
            c = buf[i];
            if ( c == '(' || c == ')' || c == '\\' )
                putchar( '\\' );
            putchar( c );
            }

        /* Send out the line trailer */
        printf( ") show\n" );
        }

    /* Send out the final line */
    printf( "showpage restore\n" );

    /* All done */
    return ( 0 );
}
```

REFRESH

SYNTAX

`refresh filename.ext`

filename.ext is the file for which you want to revise the date and time stamp. The filename parameter can contain wildcard characters.

The REFRESH utility changes the date and time stamp for a given file to the current date and time. One use for the program is to force a development tool such as MAKE or NMAKE to recompile a source file that is otherwise unchanged.

This program lets you use wildcard characters in the filename to be processed. See the description of CAT.C on page 408 for more information about using wildcard expansion.

DOS updates the date and time stamp of a file only if data has been written to the file. To force an update, the REFRESH program opens the file in binary mode for reading and writing and then reads and writes the first byte of the file. The actual contents are unchanged.

```
/* ----------------------------------------------------------------
    Name:          REFRESH.C
    Type:          Utility program
    Language:      Microsoft QuickC
    Video:         (no special video requirements)

    Program list:  REFRESH.C
                   SETARGV.OBJ

    Note:          Extended Dictionary flag must be set off
                   (Options-Make-Linker Flags)

    Usage:         refresh filename.ext
                   (wildcards allowed for filename.ext)
```

(continued)

```
    Description:     Updates date and time stamp of a file
                     to the current date and time
    ----------------------------------------------------------------
*/

#include <stdio.h>
#include <stdlib.h>
#include <string.h>
#include <fcntl.h>
#include <io.h>
#include <sys\types.h>
#include <sys\stat.h>

main( int argc, char *argv[] )
{
    int i, fhandle;
    char c;

    /* Check for minimum number of command line parameters */
    if ( argc < 2 )
        {
        printf( "Usage: refresh filename.ext\n" );
        printf( "(wildcards allowed for filename.ext)\n" );
        exit( 1 );
        }

    /* Process each file */
    for ( i = 1; i < argc; i++ )
        {

        /* Convert each file name to uppercase */
        strupr( argv[i] );

        /* List each file refreshed */
        printf( "%s\n", argv[i] );

        /* Open the file for binary read and write */
        fhandle = open( argv[i], O_RDWR : O_BINARY );
        if ( fhandle == -1 )
            {
            printf( "Can't refresh %s\n", argv[i] );
            exit( 1 );
            }
```

(continued)

REFRESH.C *continued*

```
        /* Read and rewrite the first byte in the file */
        else
            {
            read( fhandle, &c, 1 );
            lseek( fhandle, -1L, SEEK_CUR );
            write( fhandle, &c, 1 );
            }

        /* Close file and let DOS update date and time stamp */
        close( fhandle );
        }

    /* All done */
    return ( 0 );
}
```

SEE

SYNTAX

see *filename.ext minimum_string_length*

filename.ext is a binary file in which you want to locate and display readable text.

minimum_string_length is the smallest group of consecutive printable characters you want the utility to display.

The SEE utility lets you peek into binary files; it opens and reads a specified file and then displays printable characters that occur in groups of a given size. The program skips nonprintable characters and any groupings of fewer than the given number of printable characters.

Sometimes the textual information that exists in a binary file can be quite useful. For example, to determine the version number of the MOUSE.COM driver, type the following command:

C>see mouse.com 30

SEE displays several lines of text, consisting mostly of error messages embedded in the driver file. Toward the end of the list, however, you will see a statement that reveals the version number of the mouse driver. If no message is displayed, try a smaller number for the *minimum_string_length* parameter. More messages are likely to appear when you set the minimum length smaller, so you'll have to wade through more extraneous text.

If SEE displays a large number of text lines, redirect the output to a file and then use an editor or the LOOK utility presented in this book to review the output.

```
/* ----------------------------------------------------------------- --
    Name:        SEE.C
    Type:        Utility program
    Language:    Microsoft QuickC
    Video:       (no special video requirements)
```

(continued)

SEE.C *continued*

```
   Program list:    (not required)

   Usage:           see filename.ext minimum_string_length

   Description:     Reads a file and displays strings of printable
                    characters that occur in groups of a given length
   -----------------------------------------------------------------
*/

#include <stdio.h>
#include <stdlib.h>
#include <ctype.h>

main( int argc, char *argv[] )
{
   int i;
   int count = 0;
   int min_str_len;
   unsigned char c;
   unsigned char cold[80];
   FILE *s1;

   /* Check for proper command syntax */
   if ( argc != 3 )
      {
      printf( "\nUsage:      see filename.ext minimum_string_length" );
      printf( "\nExample:   see command.com 7\n\n" );
      exit( 1 );
      }

   /* Get the minimum number of displayable characters per group */
   min_str_len = atoi( argv[2] );

   /* Open the input file */
   s1 = fopen( argv[1], "rb" );
   if ( s1 == NULL )
      {
      printf( "Can't open file: %s\n", argv[1] );
      exit( 1 );
      }
```

(continued)

```
   /* Process the file */
   while ( fread( &c, 1, 1, s1 ))
      {

      /* Is the character displayable? */
      if ( isprint( c ))
         {

         /* Accumulate displayable characters */
         if ( count++ <= min_str_len )
            cold[count - 1] = c;

         /* Found enough in this sequence? */
         if ( count == min_str_len )
            {
            for ( i = 0; i < min_str_len; i++ )
               putchar( cold[i] );
            }

         /* Still working on a long sequence? */
         if ( count > min_str_len )
            putchar( c );
         }

      /* Not displayable */
      else
         {

         /* Newline at the end of each displayable sequence */
         if ( count >= min_str_len )
            printf( "\n" );

         /* Reset the group count */
         count = 0;
         }
      }

   /* Tidy up a bit */
   printf( "\n" );
   fclose( s1 );

   /* All done */
   return ( 0 );
}
```

SETVIDEO

SYNTAX

`setvideo` *mode rows*

mode is the video mode you want to set.
rows is the number of text rows you want the screen to accommodate.

The SETVIDEO utility lets you set any video mode and number of text rows supported by the QuickC function _*setvideomoderows()*. The range of possible modes is greater than that available with the DOS MODE command.

One convenient way to use the SETVIDEO program is as a batch command to set a certain video mode. For example, to boot up in 43-line text mode, add the following command to your AUTOEXEC.BAT file:

`setvideo 3 43`

Video mode 3 corresponds to _TEXTC80, as defined in the QuickC header file graph.h. Refer to graph.h for the correct mode number to use for any video mode you want to set. Also, see the QuickC documentation and on-line help for more information about which combinations of modes and text rows are allowed.

If you boot up in 43-line mode and then load QuickC, the program is displayed in 43-line mode. (The QuickC environment maintains the current text mode setting.) The benefit of this approach is especially significant if you have VGA graphics. In that case, loading QuickC with the /H option causes the program to run in 50-line mode. (The /H option always sets the video mode to use the maximum number of text lines that the graphics hardware can support.)

If your display hardware supports 43-line mode, you might want to create a small batch file that you can use to run QuickC. The following series of commands sets the mode, runs QuickC, and then resets 25-line mode when you exit the QuickC environment.

```
setvideo 3 43
qc %1
setvideo 3 25
```

```
/* ----------------------------------------------------------------
    Name:           SETVIDEO.C
    Type:           Utility program
    Language:       Microsoft QuickC
    Video:          (Hardware must support mode and rows given)

    Program list:   SETVIDEO.C
                    GRAPHICS.LIB

    Usage:          setvideo mode rows

    Description:    Sets the indicated video mode and the number of
                    rows if possible
   ----------------------------------------------------------------
*/

#include <stdio.h>
#include <stdlib.h>
#include <graph.h>

main( int argc, char *argv[] )
{
    int mode, rows, result;

    if ( argc != 3 )
        {
        printf( "\nUsage: setvideo mode rows\n\n" );
        printf( "See _setvideomoderows() and graph.h\n" );
        printf( "for allowable mode and row values\n" );
        exit( 1 );
        };

    mode = atoi( argv[1] );
    rows = atoi( argv[2] );
```

(continued)

SETVIDEO.C *continued*

```
    result = _setvideomoderows( mode, rows );
    if ( result == 0 !! result != rows )
        {
        _setvideomode( _DEFAULTMODE );
        printf( "\nCan't set video mode = %d and rows = %d\n",
                mode, rows );
        exit( 1 );
        }

    /* All done */
    return ( 0 );
}
```

TIMEDATE

SYNTAX

```
timedate
```

The TIMEDATE utility uses no command line parameters.

The TIMEDATE utility displays the time and date. It uses the QuickC functions *time()* and *ctime()* to read the system clock and format a string that contains the time and date information, accurate to the nearest second. Compare the resulting format with that created by *_strdate()* and *_strtime()*, which are used by the LOG utility.

The TIMEDATE utility is useful when you need to display the system time quickly. You might also find it a handy command to insert in batch files for timing program execution.

```
/*   ---------------------------------------------------------------
     Name:          TIMEDATE.C
     Type:          Utility program
     Language:      Microsoft QuickC
     Video:         (no special video requirements)

     Program list:  (not required)

     Usage:         timedate

     Description:   Displays date and time
     ---------------------------------------------------------------
*/

#include <stdio.h>
#include <time.h>
```

(continued)

TIMEDATE.C *continued*

```
main()
{
    time_t ltime;

    /* Get the system time */
    time( &ltime );

    /* Format and display the date and time */
    puts( ctime( &ltime ) );

    /* All done */
    return ( 0 );
}
```

WORDS

SYNTAX

words `< input > output`

The WORDS utility requires no command line parameters, but input would normally be redirected to a file.

The WORDS utility counts the number of words read from standard input and reports the total to standard output. To display the number of words in a file, redirect the input to come from the file. For example, to count the words in AUTOEXEC.BAT, type the following command:

C>words < autoexec.bat

The program defines words as groups of non-white-space characters separated by one or more white-space characters. It uses the QuickC macro *isspace()* to determine whether a character is part of a word or part of the white space between words.

```
/* -----------------------------------------------------------------
    Name:           WORDS.C
    Type:           Utility program
    Language:       Microsoft QuickC
    Video:          (no special video requirements)

    Program list:   (not required)

    Usage:          words [ < input ][ > output ]

    Description:    Counts words from stdin and reports total to
                    stdout
    -----------------------------------------------------------------
*/

#include <stdio.h>
#include <ctype.h>
```

(continued)

WORDS.C *continued*

```
#define FALSE 0
#define TRUE !FALSE

main()
    {
    int c;
    int word = 0;
    int wordflag = 0;
    unsigned long cnt = 0L;

    /* Process all characters from stdin */
    while (( c = getchar() ) != EOF )
        {

        /* White-space character between words? */
        if ( isspace( c ))
            word = FALSE;

        /* Character is part of a word */
        else
            {
            word = TRUE;
            wordflag = TRUE;
            }

        /* Just finished reading a word? */
        if ( wordflag == TRUE && word == FALSE )
            {
            cnt++;
            wordflag = FALSE;
            }
        }

    /* Check for possible last word */
    if ( word == TRUE )
        cnt++;

    /* Report the total number of words */
    printf( "Word count is %lu\n", cnt );

    /* All done */
    return ( 0 );
    }
```

PART IV

APPENDIXES

APPENDIX A: Function-to-Module Cross-Reference

This appendix lists all the functions in the toolbox alphabetically. It provides a brief description of each function and identifies both the module in which each function is defined and the page number on which the function description begins.

FUNCTION	MODULE	PAGE	FUNCTION DESCRIPTION
angle_between()	GEOMETRY	192	Calculates the angle formed by three x,y points
angle_between_3d()	GEOMETRY	198	Calculates the angle formed by connecting three x,y,z points
area()	GEOMETRY	193	Calculates the area of a triangle defined by three x,y points
area_3d()	GEOMETRY	200	Calculates the area of a triangle defined by three x,y,z points
arithmetic_mean()	PROBSTAT	333	Returns the arithmetic mean of an array
array_fill()	GAME	171	Fills part or all of an integer array with sequential integers
array_shuffle()	GAME	172	Shuffles the contents of part or all of an integer array
bitclr()	BITS	45	Clears (sets to 0) one bit in a buffer
bitget()	BITS	46	Returns one bit from a buffer
bitset()	BITS	44	Sets one bit in a buffer
bittog()	BITS	46	Toggles (inverts) one bit in a buffer
box_charfill()	BOX	61	Fills a rectangular area of the screen with a character

FUNCTION	MODULE	PAGE	FUNCTION DESCRIPTION
box_color()	BOX	59	Sets the foreground and background colors for all characters in a screen box
box_draw()	BOX	62	Draws a single-line or double-line border around a box
box_erase()	BOX	65	Fills a box with spaces
box_get()	BOX	56	Saves contents of a rectangular area of the screen in a buffer
box_put()	BOX	58	Restores screen contents that were saved in a buffer by *box_get()*
bresenham()	GRAPHICS	227	Builds a table of line coordinates
cadd()	COMPLEX	113	Adds two complex numbers
card_name()	GAME	174	Returns the name of a playing card
case_map()	DOSCALL	135	Translates a character using the country-specific case map function
cdiv()	COMPLEX	115	Divides two complex numbers
cexp()	COMPLEX	118	Finds the exponential function of a complex number
clock_face_make()	CLOCK	100	Draws a graphics analog clock face
clock_face_update()	CLOCK	102	Updates the analog clock face
clog()	COMPLEX	118	Finds the complex natural logarithm of a complex number
cmul()	COMPLEX	114	Multiplies two complex numbers
collision()	GRAPHICS	226	Checks for collision of two graphics objects
combinations()	PROBSTAT	336	Returns the possible combinations for n things taken r at a time
complex_to_polar()	COMPLEX	121	Converts a complex number to its polar notation equivalent
country()	DOSCALL	132	Fills a structure with country-specific information

FUNCTION	MODULE	PAGE	FUNCTION DESCRIPTION
cpow()	COMPLEX	116	Raises complex number *a* to the power *b*
crec()	COMPLEX	119	Calculates the complex reciprocal of a complex number
croot()	COMPLEX	117	Finds the complex *b* root of *a*
csqr()	COMPLEX	120	Calculates the square root of a complex number
cstr()	COMPLEX	111	Formats a complex number into a string
csub()	COMPLEX	113	Subtracts two complex numbers
cyl_to_sph()	GEOMETRY	206	Converts a space point from cylindrical to spherical notation
cyl_to_xyz()	GEOMETRY	205	Converts a space point from cylindrical to Cartesian notation
date_get()	CALENDAR	74	Gets the current date from the system clock
date_set()	CALENDAR	75	Sets the system clock to a given date
datestr()	CALENDAR	76	Creates a formatted string for a given date
date_to_julian()	CALENDAR	77	Calculates the astronomical Julian day number for a given date
day_of_century()	CALENDAR	83	Calculates the day of the century for a given date
day_of_week()	CALENDAR	81	Calculates the day of the week for a given date
day_of_year()	CALENDAR	82	Calculates the day of the year for a given date
days_between_dates()	CALENDAR	84	Calculates number of days between two dates
delay()	CLOCK	98	Delays the program for a given number of seconds
delete_char()	EDIT	146	Deletes one character from the string
determine_video()	BOX	66	Determines the text mode video segment and the number of character columns currently set

FUNCTION	MODULE	PAGE	FUNCTION DESCRIPTION
dice()	GAME	176	Returns the sum of a roll of *n* dice
direction()	GEOMETRY	189	Calculates the direction in radians from one x,y point to another
distance()	GEOMETRY	188	Calculates the distance between two x,y points
distance_3d()	GEOMETRY	197	Calculates the straight line distance between two points in space
dollar()	MONEY	275	Formats a dollar amount into a string
dos_version()	DOSCALL	128	Returns the version number for DOS
editline()	EDIT	151	Allows user to edit a string with standard editing keys
equidistant()	GEOMETRY	194	Finds the point that is equidistant from three given x,y points
factorial()	PROBSTAT	339	Returns the factorial of *n*
fadd()	FRACTION	160	Adds two fractions
fdiv()	FRACTION	162	Divides two fractions
fmul()	FRACTION	161	Multiplies two fractions
frac_to_s()	FRACTION	165	Formats a fraction into a string representation
fsub()	FRACTION	160	Subtracts two fractions
gcd()	FRACTION	164	Returns the greatest common divisor of two long integers
geometric_mean()	PROBSTAT	333	Returns the geometric mean of an array
getkey()	GETKEY	215	Returns an unsigned integer that corresponds to a keypress
getkey_or_mouse()	GETKEY	215	Returns an unsigned integer that corresponds to a keypress; also detects mouse motion and converts it to equivalent keypresses
hardware_coprocessor()	BIOSCALL	24	Checks for the existence of a math coprocessor
hardware_floppies()	BIOSCALL	25	Returns the number of floppy disk drives

FUNCTION	MODULE	PAGE	FUNCTION DESCRIPTION
hardware_game_adapter()	BIOSCALL	27	Checks for the existence of a game adapter
hardware_printers()	BIOSCALL	28	Returns the number of attached printers
hardware_serial_ports()	BIOSCALL	26	Returns the number of serial ports
hardware_serial_printer()	BIOSCALL	27	Checks for the existence of a serial printer
hardware_start_videomode()	BIOSCALL	24	Determines the initial video mode set by the system when rebooted
harmonic_mean()	PROBSTAT	334	Returns the harmonic mean of an array
insert_char()	EDIT	147	Inserts a character into a string
insert_spaces()	EDIT	148	Inserts spaces into a string
julian_to_date()	CALENDAR	78	Calculates the month, day, and year numbers for a given Julian day number
lcm()	FRACTION	165	Returns the least common multiple of two long integers
menu_back_color()	MENU	251	Sets the background color for boxes
menu_bar()	MENU	256	Creates a pop-up menu bar
menu_box_lines()	MENU	249	Sets the single-line or double-line box border (or none)
menu_box_shadow()	MENU	250	Sets the menu box shadow control on or off
menu_drop()	MENU	261	Creates a pull-down menu
menu_erase()	MENU	269	Restores the background behind a menu bar, pull-down menu, or message box
menu_hilight_back()	MENU	255	Sets the background color for the highlighted line in the menu box
menu_hilight_letter()	MENU	254	Sets highlighted character color for menu options
menu_hilight_text()	MENU	255	Sets highlighted text color for menu options
menu_line_color()	MENU	251	Sets the box outline color

FUNCTION	MODULE	PAGE	FUNCTION DESCRIPTION
menu_message()	MENU	266	Creates a pop-up message box
menu_prompt_color()	MENU	253	Sets the text color for the menu-box prompt line
menu_text_color()	MENU	253	Sets the text for the menu box color
menu_title_color()	MENU	252	Sets the text color for the title
monthly_payment()	MONEY	277	Calculates a simple loan payment amount
month_name()	CALENDAR	85	Provides the name of the month that corresponds to a given month number
mouse_condoff()	MOUSEFUN	316	Sets a region for conditionally turning off the mouse cursor
mouse_getlang()	MOUSEFUN	327	Gets the language for mouse driver messages
mouse_getpage()	MOUSEFUN	325	Gets the video page in which the mouse cursor appears
mouse_getsensitivity()	MOUSEFUN	322	Gets the mouse sensitivity and double speed threshold
mouse_getversion()	MOUSEFUN	328	Gets the mouse driver version number, mouse type, and interrupt request type
mouse_hide()	MOUSEFUN	303	Makes the mouse cursor invisible
mouse_motion()	MOUSEFUN	314	Gets the accumulated mouse motion counts (mickeys) since the last call to this function
mouse_press()	MOUSEFUN	306	Gets button press information
mouse_release()	MOUSEFUN	308	Gets button release information
mouse_reset()	MOUSEFUN	301	Resets the mouse and verifies its existence
mouse_restore()	MOUSEFUN	320	Restores the current state of the mouse
mouse_save()	MOUSEFUN	319	Saves the current state of the mouse
mouse_setdouble()	MOUSEFUN	317	Sets the mouse double speed threshold
mouse_setgcurs()	MOUSEFUN	311	Creates a graphics mode mouse cursor

FUNCTION	MODULE	PAGE	FUNCTION DESCRIPTION
mouse_sethorz()	MOUSEFUN	309	Sets minimum and maximum horizontal mouse cursor position
mouse_setlang()	MOUSEFUN	326	Sets the language for mouse driver messages
mouse_setmaxrate()	MOUSEFUN	323	Sets the interrupt rate (InPort mouse only)
mouse_setpage()	MOUSEFUN	324	Sets the video page in which the mouse cursor appears
mouse_setpos()	MOUSEFUN	306	Sets the mouse cursor to the indicated position
mouse_setratios()	MOUSEFUN	315	Sets the mickey/pixel ratios for mouse motion
mouse_setsensitivity()	MOUSEFUN	321	Sets the mouse sensitivity and double speed threshold
mouse_settcurs()	MOUSEFUN	313	Sets the text mode hardware or software cursor
mouse_setvert()	MOUSEFUN	310	Sets minimum and maximum vertical mouse cursor positions
mouse_show()	MOUSEFUN	302	Makes the mouse cursor visible
mouse_status()	MOUSEFUN	304	Gets the current state of the mouse buttons and the mouse cursor position
mouse_storage()	MOUSEFUN	318	Determines the number of bytes required for saving the current state of the mouse
next_word()	EDIT	143	Finds the start of the next word in a string
note()	SOUND	369	Creates a tone given its frequency and duration
oem_number()	DOSCALL	129	Returns the optional original equipment manufacturer's serial number
one_month()	CALENDAR	86	Fills a string array with a one-month calendar suitable for display or printing
permutations()	PROBSTAT	338	Returns the possible permutations for n things taken r at a time

FUNCTION	MODULE	PAGE	FUNCTION DESCRIPTION
polar_to_complex()	COMPLEX	122	Converts a polar number to the equivalent complex number
polar_to_rect()	GEOMETRY	186	Converts point notation from polar to rectangular
polygon()	GRAPHICS	237	Draws a polygon, optionally filled in
prev_word()	EDIT	144	Finds start of the previous word in a string
prntscrn()	BIOSCALL	34	Causes the screen contents to be sent to the printer, exactly as if the PrtSc key were pressed
quadratic_mean()	PROBSTAT	335	Returns the quadratic mean of an array
rand_double()	RANDOMS	352	Returns a pseudorandom double in the specified range
rand_exponential()	RANDOMS	354	Returns a pseudorandom double with an exponential distribution defined by a given mean
rand_frac()	RANDOMS	350	Returns a pseudorandom, positive double in the range 0.0 through 1.0
rand_int_range()	RANDOMS	351	Returns a pseudorandom integer in the specified range
rand_long()	RANDOMS	348	Returns a pseudorandom, unsigned long integer
rand_long_buf()	RANDOMS	354	Fills a buffer with pseudorandom long integers
rand_normal()	RANDOMS	353	Returns a pseudorandom double with a normal distribution defined by a given mean and standard deviation
rand_short()	RANDOMS	350	Returns a pseudorandom, unsigned short integer
rand_shuffle()	RANDOMS	346	Shuffles the pseudorandom number sequence
reboot()	BIOSCALL	35	Causes the system to reboot
rect_to_polar()	GEOMETRY	187	Converts point notation from rectangular to polar

FUNCTION	MODULE	PAGE	FUNCTION DESCRIPTION
reduce()	FRACTION	163	Reduces a fraction to its lowest terms
replace()	EDIT	149	Replaces each occurrence of *substr1* in *str* with *substr2*
rotate()	GEOMETRY	191	Rotates an x,y point around the origin by a given angle
round()	MONEY	274	Rounds a double to the given power-of-ten place
s_center()	STRINGS	381	Centers a string by balancing the spaces on each end
scroll()	BIOSCALL	36	Scrolls a rectangular area of a text mode screen
serial_number()	DOSCALL	130	Returns the optional user serial number
s_fill()	STRINGS	386	Fills a string to the given length by using multiple copies of the fill string
shift_alt()	BIOSCALL	31	Returns the status of the Alt key
shift_caps_lock()	BIOSCALL	33	Returns the Caps Lock state
shift_ctrl()	BIOSCALL	30	Returns the status of the Ctrl key
shift_insert_state()	BIOSCALL	33	Returns the Insert state
shift_left()	BIOSCALL	29	Returns the status of the left Shift key
shift_num_lock()	BIOSCALL	32	Returns the Num Lock state
shift_right()	BIOSCALL	29	Returns the status of the right Shift key
shift_scroll_lock()	BIOSCALL	31	Returns the Scroll Lock state
shuffle_rand()	GAME	178	Uses the system clock to seed the sequence of pseudorandom numbers
shuffle_str()	GAME	176	Randomly shuffles the characters in a string
silence()	SOUND	363	Turns off the tone generator
siren()	SOUND	366	Creates a sound whose frequency rises and falls
s_ljust()	STRINGS	378	Justifies string to left

FUNCTION	MODULE	PAGE	FUNCTION DESCRIPTION
s_lrjust()	STRINGS	382	Justifies a string by adding and removing spaces so that the spacing is even and so that no spaces remain at either end
s_ltrm()	STRINGS	374	Trims spaces from left end of a string
sound()	SOUND	361	Sets a tone at a given frequency
speaker_toggle()	SOUND	360	Pulses the speaker in or out with each call
sph_to_cyl()	GEOMETRY	208	Converts a space point from spherical to cylindrical notation
sph_to_xyz()	GEOMETRY	207	Converts a space point from spherical to Cartesian notation
s_rjust()	STRINGS	379	Justifies string to right
s_rot()	STRINGS	377	Rotates characters in a string plus or minus n places
s_rtrm()	STRINGS	375	Trims spaces from right end of a string
s_shuffle()	STRINGS	385	Shuffles a string by randomizing the order of characters
s_split()	STRINGS	387	Splits a string between words
s_to_frac()	FRACTION	166	Scans a string to convert it to a fraction
strc()	COMPLEX	112	Converts a string designation of a complex number into a complex number structure
s_trm()	STRINGS	376	Trims spaces from both ends of a string
time_get()	CLOCK	96	Gets the current time from the system clock
time_set()	CLOCK	97	Sets the system clock to the given time
timestr()	CLOCK	99	Formats hour, minute, and second values into a string of the form "HH:MM:SS"
translate()	GEOMETRY	190	Translates an x,y point
translate_3d()	GEOMETRY	197	Shifts an x,y,z point in space by adding variables x, y, and z to the coordinates

FUNCTION	MODULE	PAGE	FUNCTION DESCRIPTION
triangle()	GRAPHICS	232	Draws a triangle, optionally filled in
validate()	CALENDAR	79	Verifies that a given date represents a date that actually existed or will exist
verify()	DOSCALL	131	Returns the state of the verify flag
volume_3d()	GEOMETRY	201	Calculates the volume defined by four points in space
wait_ticks()	SOUND	363	Delays for a given number of clock ticks
warble()	SOUND	364	Creates a three-tone warble
weekday_name()	CALENDAR	85	Returns the name of the day of the week that corresponds to a given weekday number
weird()	SOUND	365	Creates a modulated sound
white_noise()	SOUND	367	Creates white noise
xyz_to_cyl()	GEOMETRY	203	Converts a space point from Cartesian to cylindrical notation
xyz_to_sph()	GEOMETRY	204	Converts a space point from Cartesian to spherical notation

APPENDIX B:
Line-drawing Characters

To enter line-drawing characters into QuickC programs, press and hold the Alt key and then type the decimal value associated with the character you want to display. The QuickC on-line help system provides a chart of the extended character set arranged by value. In the illustration below, the line-drawing characters are arranged by type rather than by value. You might find these groupings convenient when you are trying to locate a particular character for a drawing project.

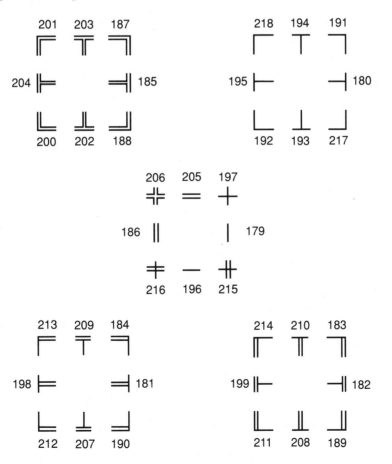

Invest in CD-ROM Technology!

Microsoft® Programmer's Library is the ultimate programmer's reference on a single CD-ROM disc. It contains full text of the OS/2 Software Development Kit (SDK) manuals, the Windows SDK manuals, most Microsoft Language manuals, and several Microsoft Press books written for the serious programmer, including THE MS-DOS ENCYCLOPEDIA. Plus 20 floppies' worth of "clip art" sample code. Navigate through this mass of programming knowledge with boolean searches and hypertextual links between related data. The price is $395 suggested retail— a fraction of the price for this material in print form.

For a limited time, Programmer's Library is available <u>System Complete</u> with the Denon DRD-253 CD-ROM drive for $949. That's a savings of $799!

And if you order now, you'll receive FREE Microsoft Audio Software ($99 value) that turns your CD-ROM drive into a programmable CD audio player. So you can *listen* to a keyboard for a change.

Call (800) 227-4679 for details.

For a Free Demo Disk* please
Print your name and address:

_____
NAME

_____
COMPANY NAME (if applicable)

_____
STREET ADDRESS

_____
CITY   STATE   ZIP

_____
DAYTIME TELEPHONE (in case we have questions about your order)

Check the appropriate box

☐ **1.2 MB floppy Demo Disk:** Contains the self-running demo as well as self-guided and interactive demos of the features of Programmer's Library. Also includes a portion of the actual Programmer's Library database.

☐ **1.44 MB floppy Demo Disk:** Same as above for 3.5 inch drives.

☐ **360K floppy Demo Disk:** The self-running demo showing the impressive features of Programmer's Library.

Send this coupon to:
Microsoft Corporation ▪ Attn: Special Promotions, Dept 127
One Microsoft Way ▪ Redmond, WA 98052-6399

*Offer Valid While Supplies Last

John Clark Craig has written several books on computer programming since 1980, including *True BASIC Programs and Subroutines* (TAB Books) and *Microsoft QuickBASIC Programmer's Toolbox* (Microsoft Press, 1988). He also made substantial contributions to the *Microsoft Mouse Programmer's Reference* (Microsoft Press, 1989). Craig lives with his family in Bozeman, Montana, where he is a software engineer for TMA Technologies, Inc.

The manuscript for this book was prepared and submitted to Microsoft Press in electronic form. Text files were processed and formatted using Microsoft Word.

Cover design by Ted Mader and Associates
Interior text design by Darcie S. Furlan
Principal typography by Lisa Iversen and Katherine Erickson

Text composition by Microsoft Press in Baskerville with display in Helvetica, using the Magna composition system and the Linotronic 300 laser imagesetter.